ART ISN'T EASY

Joanne Gordon

DA CAPO PRESS

ART ISN'T EASY

THE THEATER OF STEPHEN SONDHEIM

UPDATED EDITION

This Da Capo Press paperback edition of *Art Isn't Easy* is an unabridged republication of the edition published in Carbondale, Illinois in 1990, with the addition of a new chapter. It is reprinted by arrangement with Southern Illinois University Press.

5 6 7 8 9 10

Published by Da Capo Press, Inc.
A member of the Perseus Books Group

Manufactured in the United States of America

Library of Congress Cataloging in Publication Data

Gordon, Joanne Lesley, 1947- Art isn't easy: the theater of Stephen Sondheim / Joanne Gordon.—Updated ed.

p. cm. Reprint. Originally published: Carbondale: Southern Illinois University Press, c1990.

Includes bibliographical references and index.

ISBN 0-306-80468-9

1. Sondheim, Stephen—Criticism and interpretation. 2. Musicals—United States—History and criticism. I. Title. II. Title: Stephen Sondheim.

NL410.S6872G7 1992 91-46691
782.1 4 092—dc20 CIP
MN

CONTENTS

Illustrations vii
Acknowledgments viii

1 The Musical Comes of Age 1

2 Something Familiar?
A Funny Thing Happened on the Way to the Forum and *Anyone Can Whistle* 19

3 No One Is Alone?
Company 38

4 "Through the Unknown, Remembered Gate"
Follies 76

5 "We Are Such Stuff as Dreams Are Made On"
A Little Night Music 123

6 Is Beauty Truth, Truth Beauty?
Pacific Overtures 174

7 Grander Than Guignol
Sweeney Todd 207

8 A Bumpy Ride
Merrily We Roll Along 255

CONTENTS

9 The Musical Stops Singing and Finds Its Voice
Sunday in the Park with George 262

10 Sondheim Isn't Grim
Into the Woods 301

11 From Madonna and Muppets to Mayhem
Assassins 317

Notes 339
Bibliography 349
Index 355

ILLUSTRATIONS

Following p. 156

Zero Mostel and Jack Gilford in *A Funny Thing Happened on the Way to the Forum*
Angela Lansbury in *Anyone Can Whistle*
Dean Jones in *Company*
Dean Jones and Elaine Stritch in *Company*
John McMartin and Dorothy Collins in *Follies*
Florence Klotz's costumes for *Follies*
Glynis Johns, Judy Kahan, and Hermione Gingold in *A Little Night Music*
Glynis Johns and Len Cariou in *A Little Night Music*
Sab Shimono, Isao Sato, and Yuki Shimoda in *Pacific Overtures*
Boris Aronson's set for *Pacific Overtures*
Angela Lansbury and Len Cariou in *Sweeney Todd*
Eugene Lee's set for *Sweeney Todd*
Lonny Price, Ann Morrison, Jim Walton, and Sally Klein in *Merrily We Roll Along*
The final tableau of the first act of *Sunday in the Park with George*
Bernadette Peters and Mandy Patinkin in *Sunday in the Park with George*
Kim Crosby, Robert Westenberg, Philip Hoffman, and Merle Louise in *Into the Woods*
Pamela Winslow and Bernadette Peters in *Into the Woods*

ACKNOWLEDGMENTS

I would like to thank the following publishers for their permission to use extended quotations from copyrighted works:

> Warner/Chappell Music, Inc., for quotations from *Into the Woods*, music and lyrics by Stephen Sondheim, copyright © 1987 Rilting Music, Inc. (ASCAP), all rights administered by Geffen Music (ASCAP), all rights reserved, used by permission;
>
> Tommy Valando Publishing Group, Inc., for quotations from *Sunday in the Park with George*, music and lyrics by Stephen Sondheim, copyright © 1984 Revelation Music Publishing Corp. & Rilting Music, Inc., A Tommy Valando Publication; *Merrily We Roll Along*, music and lyrics by Stephen Sondheim, copyright © 1981 Revelation Music Publishing Corp. & Rilting Music, Inc., A Tommy Valando Publication; *Sweeney Todd*, music and lyrics by Stephen Sondheim, copyright © 1979 Revelation Music Publishing Corp. & Rilting Music, Inc., A Tommy Valando Publication; *Pacific Overtures*, music and lyrics by Stephen Sondheim, copyright © 1976 Revelation Music Publishing Corp. & Rilting Music, Inc., A Tommy Valando Publication; and *A Little Night Music*, music and lyrics by Stephen Sondheim, copyright © 1973 Revelation Music Publishing Corp. & Rilting Music, Inc., A Tommy Valando Publication;
>
> Herald Square Music, Inc., for quotations from *Follies*, by Stephen Sondheim, copyright © 1971 Range Road Music, Inc., Quartet Music, Inc., Rilting Music, Inc., and Burthen Music, Inc., all rights reserved, used by permission, and *Company*, by Stephen Sondheim, copyright © 1970 Range Road Music, Inc., Quartet Music, Inc., and Rilting Music, Inc., all rights reserved, used by permission; and

ACKNOWLEDGMENTS

Chappell and Co., Inc., for quotations from *Anyone Can Whistle*, copyright © 1964 Stephen Sondheim, all rights administered by Chappell and Co., international copyright secured, all rights reserved, used by permission, and *A Funny Thing Happened on the Way to the Forum*, copyright © 1962 Stephen Sondheim, all rights administered by Chappell and Co., international copyright secured, all rights reserved, used by permission.

I would also like to express my gratitude to Stephen Sondheim, Robert S. Phillips, Curtis L. Clark, and Antonia Turman.

ART ISN'T EASY

1

THE MUSICAL COMES OF AGE

America's greatest original contribution to the theater is the musical; yet the genre is too often dismissed as escapist entertainment. The reasons for the musical's disrepute are many. In its infancy, in the early years of this century, musical theater was unsophisticated. The plot line was thin. There was little attempt to integrate song and dance, and a basic formula of delight and diversion, beautiful girls, slapstick comics, and romantic ballads prevailed. The simplistic moralism, the naïve optimism, the noble hero and simpering heroine were adopted, unaltered, from nineteenth-century melodrama. The commercial success of these pieces encouraged their fossilization into a predictable pattern of sensational extravaganzas. Artistic merit was deemed less important than financial gain. The musical was viewed solely as a commercial commodity.

Not all musicals stuck rigidly to this pattern. Some tried to introduce thematic depth and social relevance. Particularly in the fervent political climate of the 1930s, musicals began to reflect social anxieties. Kurt Weill realized that Broadway was the heart of American theater and adapted his political commitment to its idiom. His major works of the thirties—*Johnny Johnson* (1936), a diatribe against war, written with Paul Green and produced by the Group Theatre; *The Eternal Road* (1937), a pageant of Jewish history written with Franz Werfel and directed by Max Reinhardt; and *Knickerbocker Holiday* (1938), in which, together with Maxwell Anderson, he attempted to expose the evils of fascism—present a sharp contrast to the work of Irving Berlin, Cole Porter, and Jerome Kern. Harold Rome wrote a pro-union *lehrstuck* in his revue *Pins and Needles* (1937), for the International Ladies' Garment Workers' Union, and Marc Blitzstein's *The Cradle Will*

Rock (1937), a project of the W.P.A. Federal Theater, achieved notoriety with its overtly anticapitalist stance. George Gershwin's *Porgy and Bess*, first produced in 1935, represented yet another radical new direction and form for the American musical theater. Unfortunately, it was not an immediate commercial success, closing after only 125 performances. E. Y. ("Yip") Harburg's song "Brother, Can You Spare a Dime?" was also a pertinent reflection of America in the thirties, but it was not until 1947, with *Finian's Rainbow*, that Harburg fleshed out his social commitment in a complete musical production. Indeed, all these works were essentially fringe elements, never really penetrating the mainstream of Broadway's musical consciousness.

From the twenties onward, however, disturbing elements did intrude more and more frequently onto the musical stage. Kern and Hammerstein's *Showboat* (1927), the epochal production in this regard, combined the glamor associated with its producer, Flo Ziegfeld, with the serious themes of miscegenation, racial prejudice, marital problems, and gambling. This erosion in the glistening surface of musical theater disturbed many critics. George Jean Nathan, for example, writing in 1947, laments: "Sense and intelligence are desiderata of drama. Musical Comedy is best when it abjures them and substitutes for them absurd fancy and all the wonderful illogic of a wonderful world that never was." He adds: "What we want, despite the academic critics, is a return of the oldtime enchanting absurdity, the oldtime refusal to reflect life and reality in any degree, the oldtime razzle and dazzle of the unreal and the incredible."[1] Too many contemporary critics echo these sentiments.[2]

The evolutionary progression of the musical from *Showboat* to Rodgers and Hammerstein's *Oklahoma!* is well documented in histories of the American musical.[3] The form changed and became increasingly complex. Integration became the key word as Rodgers and Hammerstein wove the texture of song, dance, and plot closely together. Yet despite the fact that such themes as racial prejudice (in *South Pacific* and *Finian's Rainbow*, for example), marital disharmony and infidelity (in *Carousel* and *The Most Happy Fella*), and capitalist venality (in *Allegro* and *How to Succeed in Business Without Really Trying*) were introduced, this kind of theater retained an essential naïvete. The musicals of the forties and fifties were escapist in that they transported their audience into a larger-than-life world where emotions were expressed in melody and the evening was capped with a reassuring reprise at the final curtain. It was a world of romance, in which love and happiness were guaranteed. These musicals did not mirror life as it was, but as it should be. The average gave way to the unique, emotion prevailed over reason, passion over decorum. The Rodgers and Hammerstein formula was based on the dictum "You feel, therefore you are."

The optimism of America after the Second World War is reflected in this body of work. Although it is a generalization, the America of the Eisenhower era was a country united by a complacent self-confidence. It found in the musical theater an image of itself that it chose and enjoyed. Audiences knew that they would be diverted and also that their bourgeois values would remain inviolate. As the popular theater of the period, musical theater reinforced prevalent attitudes.

Escapism is not, however, a necessary component of the musical. After the social and artistic upheavals of the sixties, Stephen Sondheim faced the sterile disillusion of the seventies by confronting the typical Broadway musical audience of tired businessmen and their wives with the very problems they had fled to the theater to escape. This was an audacious course to follow, for in so doing Sondheim flouted convention and flew in the face of audience expectation. Although his work is often condemned as sterile, cynical, over-intellectualized, and arid, it cannot be dismissed as glib theatricality, or superficial sentimentality.

Most of the significant artificers of the American musical theater have come from secure, middle-class environments, which may explain why their work reflects an enthusiasm for the material world. Sondheim, although he shares this affluent background, belongs to a different generation. The climate of progress and promise that prevailed during the creative period of Rodgers and Hammerstein's career no longer existed by the late 1960s. From that point on, for an artist in the commercial theater to comment on, or attempt to change, prevalent attitudes has been an invitation to financial disaster and obscurity.

Yet Sondheim and his collaborators have blazed a trail of creativity and commitment on Broadway. Rather than an esoteric style, they have chosen the popular form of American theater and invested it with a truth and vitality rarely associated with Broadway musicals. It may be true that "social comment is as unwelcome to most Broadway producers as syphilis is to a whore,"[4] but this has not deterred Sondheim. Inflationary economics, the rising crime rate in the inner city, and the deterioration of the theater district in New York may have all had a chilling effect on theatrical creativity. (As lyricist Sheldon Harnick rather ruefully comments: "I keep remembering that fine old definition of theater: 'Two planks and a passion!' I keep thinking that whatever happens that still holds true, and then I notice the price of lumber."[5]) But commercial success, though obviously important for survival, has never been the raison d'être for any of Sondheim's work.

One of the foremost influences on Sondheim's work, producer/director Harold Prince, repeatedly emphasizes his own commitment to serious musical theater:

> I am stuck with "why am I doing it." And in fact all the plays that I see suffer the same criticism. I did not enjoy *Mame*. Why did they bother? I see that it is amusing, and I appreciate the polish the talent provided. But the why anyone bothered, the why consistently gets in the way.
>
> That doesn't imply that all musicals need be trenchant. God knows, *A Funny Thing* wasn't, but it had classical antecedents and it was conceptualized. . . .
>
> There is a kind of deliciously unmotivated musical, a cherished memory of yesteryear, which some of our critics lament the loss of. Not I. I think that shows in which songs are utterly unmotivated, in which characters react inconsistently for laughs, mindless and pleasantly entertaining though they may be, through overpraise dangerously inhibit the future of the musical theater.[6]

Sondheim admits that he, like Prince, is committed to didactic theater, but they both recognize that didacticism must never become overpowering nor unentertaining. In discussing the development of *Sweeney Todd*, the two agree:

> Prince: . . . It amuses me the number of people who tell us that the set for *Sweeney* is large, as though we hadn't noticed! Then the people who point out that the show neglects the industrial revolution in its text. We discussed all of that and agreed that it should.
>
> Sondheim: In fact, . . . when Hal first started to shape the show in his head that way, and we started to talk about the whole aspect of the piece, I was most concerned that we not soap-box it. He was too, because we both like didactic theater but don't like soap boxing. I try to do it by just inserting here and there throughout the lyrics words like "engine," basic images, not just inserting the words but using them as little motivating forces to make a slightly wispy connection with the industrial revolution. I was afraid if we made too much of a connection it would put too heavy a weight on the image or on the metaphor. I don't think it did.[7]

Sondheim and his collaborators choose both complex subjects and consistently experimental techniques, and their musicals begin after the traditional happily-ever-after has run into trouble. In an interview with Hubert Saal of *Newsweek*, Harold Prince explains his and Sondheim's commitment to "truth" in the musical theater: "I work in the theater, not in the musical theater. . . . Who says to be entertained means to be tickled? . . . I think it's more stimulating to be upset. I try to be part of what I want to see. And I go to the theater to see a little blood drawn."[8]

The experience of catharsis is not generally associated with the American musical theater, although one happily applies the term to Wagnerian opera. Sondheim has shown, however, that a gut-wrenching theatrical experience of music and word does not always have to be presented in a language other than English. Though Sondheim also explores the unique joy, delight, and wonder of our time, his musicals, thus, are not as popular or readily accepted as those of Rodgers and Hammerstein, Lerner and Loewe, and Loesser. They disturb and challenge. Commercial and aesthetic criteria should not be confused, however. Sondheim explores new territory every time he writes a new musical. This does not lead to automatic acclaim and financial success; Sondheim's triumphs are of a different order.

It would be misleading, though, to suggest that the innovation of Sondheim's work is to be found exclusively in the seriousness of its themes and the disturbing quality of its content. Much of the significance of his work lies in his creative use of form.

A great deal has been written about the "integrated" structures of the Rodgers and Hammerstein type of musical. From 1943 (with the unprecedented success of *Oklahoma!*) until the death of Hammerstein in 1960, that team's musical creations dominated American musical theater. Their work provided a model, not only for audiences and for critics, but for other writers and composers as well. There were naturally experiments and deviations, but generally the Rodgers and Hammerstein formula set the standard for what the musical could and should be. In their work they fused the two primary streams of influence in American musical theater: the sentimental romance of European operetta and the jazzy colloquialism of revue. The form of their work was pioneered by Hammerstein and Kern in *Showboat* and consisted of a scene-song scenario in which plot action is climaxed with a song that delineates character. After a blackout, the scene changes, and the basic pattern repeats. This sounds simplistic when summarized, but prior to such work there was no intimate and necessary connection between the songs, dances, and book scenes. The music of the early musicals was essentially noncontextual. Songs could be fitted into any show and frequently were shifted about. With *Oklahoma!* integration of song, dance, and dialogue became mandatory, as the structure of Rodgers and Hammerstein was adopted without any real modification by such masters as Lerner and Loewe, Loesser, and Harnick and Bock.

Although the formula has proven successful and lucrative, it had become tired and predictable by the time *West Side Story* (1957) raised "integration" to a new height of excellence as song, dance, and dramatic action coalesced into a theatrical totality (Rodgers and Hammerstein themselves had tried, unsuccessfully, to modify the formula as early as 1947 with *Allegro*). The boundaries between the components of the musical were blurred. Consequently, *West Side Story* possesses a unity previously unknown in the musical theater.

It was from such antecedents as these that Sondheim's talents evolved. He developed from Oscar Hammerstein's young protégé, who had assisted Hammerstein on the experimental *Allegro*, into the lyricist for *West Side Story* and *Gypsy*. Of *Gypsy* and *Allegro* he asserts:

> I really believe that *Gypsy* is one of the two or three best shows ever. It was the last good one in the Rodgers and Hammerstein musical form—where you take a story and tell it with scene-song-scene-song, where peaks of emotion are carried forward in song. . . . *Allegro* was a development that used the Greek chorus—it started the type of musical that Hal Prince likes to do, like *Cabaret* and *Zorba*, where there is comment on the story at the same time the story is being told.[9]

The form of a Sondheim musical goes well beyond *Allegro*, *Gypsy*, and *West Side Story*, however. Although the songs and dances in a Rodgers and Hammerstein musical relate to character and text, they have an active life outside the theater. Many of their tunes are standards in the world of popular music. Sondheim's music and lyrics rarely possess this independent life. They are so intimately linked to text and so intricately woven into the fabric of the entire work that they cannot easily stand alone. Other than "Send in the Clowns," Sondheim has not written a "hit" tune.

Many detractors claim that this lack of popularity resides in the unmelodic quality of his music. Critics often complain that one does not leave a Sondheim show "humming," but as Sondheim points out, anything that can be sung can be hummed. The fact is, Sondheim's music overflows with haunting melodies, but his melodic line is intimately tied to the lyric, and the lyric, rhythm, and tone of each song belong specifically to the character who is singing the song at that particular stage of the action.

Moreover, Sondheim's music is more sophisticated and complex, more advanced in harmony, form, and melody than the work of previous theater composers. Sondheim modifies—and often spurns—the conventional structure of the theater song, with its AABA form. This structure assured the traditional composer that the listener was exposed to the theme at least three times. And songs were often reprised, sometimes several times, as the cover for a scenic change. If audiences do not hum after a Sondheim musical, it is both because they have not been exposed to the melodies as often and because Sondheim's music is not simple. The texture is denser and the content more complex. It is consequently more difficult to grasp in the fleeting immediacy of the theatrical moment. With each musical and lyrical nuance perfectly matched to the particular character in the particular situation, music, lyric, character, and plot are interwoven into a seamless whole, closer to Wagnerian opera than traditional musical comedy.

If, though, all Sondheim offered was a more intricate blend of the elements of the musical, then his work would be an extension rather than an innovation. *Concept*, the word coined to describe the form of the Sondheim musical, suggests that all elements of the musical, thematic and presentational, are integrated to suggest a central theatrical image or idea. This unity is certainly to be found in Sondheim's work, but no label can possibly encompass the broad range of Sondheim's innovations. Sondheim himself, with his loathing for glib generalizations, repudiates the designation:

> "Concept" is this decade's vogue word, just as "integrated" was the vogue theatrical word of the '40s, referring to an approach in which a story is told and characters are advanced through song. The watershed, the landmark musical was indisputably *Oklahoma!* Everything that followed can be seen as a development of it—either a rejection or a carrying on. Me, I'm carrying it on, making variations.[10]

Prior to Sondheim, the musical was built around its plot. The narrative structure focused primarily on a love relationship and provided a framework for all songs, dances, and dialogue. Sets were naturalistic, if extravagant, and a basic pattern of exposition, complication, and resolution pertained. The book structure of these musicals meant the story. The book structure for Sondheim, on the other hand, means the *idea*. Music, lyric, dance, dialogue, design, and direction fuse to support a focal thought. A central conceit controls and shapes an entire production, for every aspect of the production is blended and subordinated to a single vision. The thematic thrust of the work is conveyed to the audience through a primary image or metaphor that dictates not only the content of the piece but also its presentational form. Form and content cannot really be separated, for the one dictates and is dependent on the other.

It is for this reason that each of Sondheim's works is unique. The pattern in all of the Rodgers and Hammerstein type of musical is basically the same, but Sondheim develops a new lyric, musical, and theatrical language for each work. Sondheim's music and lyrics grow out of the dramatic idea inherent in the show's concept and themselves *become* part of the drama that previous theater songs would only reflect. Rodgers and Hammerstein may have set *The King and I* in Siam, but that work's Eastern locale is merely decorative. The music and sets may suggest the East, but the texture and impact of the work is little different from those of *Oklahoma!* The contrasting effect of Sondheim's *Pacific Overtures*, where all elements of the work are products of its central idea, could not be more marked.

Sondheim's contribution to the advancement of the genre can also be seen in his break with the traditional logical development of realistic theater. Sondheim's structures are closer to the freewheeling patterns of avant-garde nonmusical theater. Time and place are fragmented and distorted. Logical connections are associative rather than linear. Sondheim and director Harold Prince acknowledge that this presentational style is inspired by the work of Joan Littlewood, whose innovative directional approach resulted in such productions as *Oh, What a Lovely War!* and *The Hostage*. Littlewood rejected traditional narrative patterns and chose instead a revuelike format. This, combined with her ability to blend reality and fantasy and use song fragments to upbraid audiences, intrigued Sondheim and Prince. They acknowledge, for example, that the style of *Company* was consciously derived from Littlewood's work.[11]

Sondheim and his collaborators experiment with the notion of theater as a game that the audience actively plays. Many of the imaginative leaps necessary for comprehension are achieved only through audience collaboration. This does not mean that Sondheim's musicals resemble the "tribal rock" phenomena of environmental theater. In Sondheim's musicals, rather, the empathic bond is both established and examined. Audience activity is intellectual rather than physical.

As an extension of this gamelike quality, Sondheim has evolved a particular category of musical language. The heightening emotional impact of tonality; the stimulating effect of rhythm; the soothing quality of harmony; the expansion and compression of time and feeling—these emotive powers of music are well established, and Sondheim naturally exploits all the connotative resonances of musical form. His work is subtle and intricate, but no different in kind, in this regard, from that of his predecessors. One facet of his work, however, is unique. Sondheim uses the various forms and patterns of theater music as comments upon themselves. This point will be clarified in the actual analysis of his work, but Sondheim's technique can be likened to that of Bertrand Russell's second-order language. Music's ability to convey emotion is commonly recognized. That is its first-order dimension. But certain musical styles are definitely associated in an audience's mind with certain eras, certain emotions, and certain truths. Sondheim takes these well-known musical forms and places them in antithetical situations. Lyric and character are thus at odds with the musical suggestion. Such dislocation of style and content achieves a number of interesting and effective results, as the audience is forced into examining both the truth of the lyric and the contrasting emotional implications of the musical structure. The psychological gestalt of audience expectation is placed in ironic relief. The effect can be alienating in a Brechtian sense and unquestionably enhances the multileveled implications of the experience.

Sondheim mentions his use of this technique very briefly in two interviews given in the early seventies:

> I had begun to feel, way back during *Gypsy*, that the whole notion of Broadway musicals depending on "integrated" songs—numbers that spring from the dialogue and further the plot—ought to be re-examined, and perhaps changed. Though the tone of *Anyone Can Whistle* was off, the songs did break with tradition: they commented on the action instead of advancing it, and I think their relation to the book was excellent. In *Forum*, I'd already tried another break: songs that were respites from the action. In *Company* the songs were respites and comments.[12]

> *Anyone Can Whistle* is a cult show. . . . It was experimental and started a technique for me which I've used ever since and hope never to use again—the use of traditional musical comedy language to make points. All the numbers that Angela [Lansbury] sang in the show were pastiche. . . .
>
> Incidentally, the technique of using attitudes instead of emotions for Angela in *Whistle* I used in "Side by Side by Side" and "You Could Drive a Person Crazy" in *Company* and a great deal in *Follies* where it's really called for.[13]

But Sondheim's use of musical-comedy language is far more complex and effective than these remarks suggest. The "pastiche" results not only in a comment on character, but also in a comment on audiences and on society in general.

Martin Gottfried, the only critic to comment upon this stylistic device, has a negative response: "Musical satire is always around the corner in Sondheim's work. He indulges this taste too frequently and it grows tiresome. It might be the result of his retentive musical mind or a reflection of his disinclination to be emotionally expressive. Mockery, after all, is a form of self-disguise."[14] Gottfried is correct that the device is satiric, but Sondheim is not using it simply as a means to hide self. The juxtaposition of an earlier, more frivolous style, with a contemporary issue or character serves as a highlight and ironic comment both upon the two contrasting eras and the difference in audience expectation then and now. Gottfried rejects the technique because it results in a severing of the empathic bond. There is a vast distance, however, between the beliefs that produced the cheerful tunes of early musical comedy and the biting cynicism of today. Sondheim's musicals are not reassuring and complacent. One of his chief methods for making his audience uneasy is this technique of double exposure. Gottfried is an intelligent and sensitive critic, but his unstated premise is that musicals should be primarily escapist entertainment.

Careful examination of Sondheim's work shows that although satire may be characteristic, it is not confining. Sondheim's musicals are not sentimental, but this does not mean that they are sterile or heartless. An overwhelming emotional blast lies at the heart of Sondheim's theater, but for Sondheim it is a *referent* rather than an *ingredient*. The old forms, the well-loved styles, remind us of what the theater can do, and what society once was. The satiric lyrics inform us of what our lives now are. The conflict and contrast between the two set up a stimulating theatrical experience. Sondheim's theater is not simply "show" but is also "tell." Sondheim's use of theatrical language, furthermore, is not restricted to individual songs or even to musical-comedy antecedents. Each major work is also refracted through a contrasting or complementary theatrical, or related, form: *A Funny Thing Happened on the Way to the Forum* and Roman farce; *Company* and drawing-room drama; *Follies* and the Ziegfeld revue; *A Little Night Music* and operetta; *Pacific Overtures* and Kabuki; *Sweeney Todd* and Victorian melodrama; *Sunday in the Park with George* and pointillism; and *Into the Woods* and fairy tales.

Sondheim's departure from the traditional patterns of realist theater has affected the fundamental nature of his characters. Lehman Engel asserts, "One of the chief differences between most plays and most musicals . . . is that characters in plays are often not what they seem; in musicals they invariably must be."[15] This intrinsic simplicity and superficiality of character may have been true in the early years of the musical's development, but is not an essential quality of the genre. It is certainly not true of Sondheim's work. Sondheim repeatedly emphasizes the importance of multidimensional characters and admits a preference for "neurotic personalities." He acknowledges: "At least half of my songs deal with ambivalence, feeling two things at once. . . . I like neurotic people. I like troubled people. Not that I don't like squared-away people, but I *prefer* neurotic people. I like to hear rumblings beneath the surface."[16] These troubled, complex characters have little in common with the straightforward, ingenuous creations Engel suggests are endemic to the musical theater.

The songs Sondheim composes for his dramatis personae explore the depth and turmoil inherent in each character. Sondheim's characters are never secure in any complete self-knowledge, for, as he explains: "Not enough songwriters understand the function of a song in a play. . . . They write songs in which a character explains himself. This is self-defeating. A song should reveal the character to the audience but the character does not have enough self-knowledge to describe himself in these terms."[17] Sondheim's music and lyrics investigate the particular intricate maze of emotional sensibility of which the character is constituted. The audience is party to the character's confused search for self and stability. Consequently the characters are never one-dimensional cutouts.

Sondheim believes that drama is to be found in character, and one of his favorite maxims is Wilson Mizner's "People beat scenery." He writes songs that are not simply decorative or entertaining but are necessary to his characters. In his lyrics he attempts to direct all humor toward a fuller realization of the particular personality. He maintains that true theatrical wit results, not from an author's cleverness, but from the accuracy with which an observation matches the established temperament of a character: "that is what humor is all about: character, not cleverness."[18]

Whether or not Sondheim achieves this complexity of character delineation is an open question. The answer is certainly influenced by the particular book writer with whom he has collaborated. John Lahr, one of Sondheim's ardent castigators, vehemently denies the validity of Sondheim's character portrayals. He asserts:

> Sondheim speaks proudly of how his songs define and advance the characters in his musicals. But what distinguishes the characters in most of his later work is that they have no character. As he himself has pointed out, "In *Company* we were up against one of the oldest dramatic problems in the world: how do you write about a cipher without making him a cipher? In *Follies* we deliberately decided not to create characters with warts and all. Everyone would be, not a type, but an essence . . . *Pacific Overtures* was an attempt to tell a story that has no characters at all." Sondheim makes an asset out of a liability and calls it a breakthrough.[19]

Certainly Sondheim's characters do not possess the immediate appeal of Rodgers and Hammerstein's Anna Leonowens, the King of Siam, Nellie Forbush, or Ado Annie, but in exchange for that direct emotional simplicity, Sondheim's characters possess a complexity that is equally theatrically valid and exciting.

Although some have cast doubt on Sondheim's genius as a composer, no one has questioned his brilliance as a lyricist. In the American musical, word and sound are intimately related and much of the theatrical impact of any production is dependent upon the wit, insight, and perspicacity of the lyrics. It does matter what the characters are saying, for the score cannot be reduced to beautiful but meaningless melodic patterns. The words of a libretto are as essential as the notes to which they are set, for "beautiful sounds are not always beautifully theatrical, and no one goes to the theater to close his eyes."[20] One of the achievements of American musical theater is its exploration of the musical and theatrical possibilities of the American vernacular. Sondheim, in his scintillating lyrics and complex harmonies, has evolved a compelling synthesis of musical idiom and the American language and thought patterns. Word and sound blend, contrast and complement each other, and create an appropriate theatrical moment, a valid expression of a particular character's personality. Word and note are inseparable.

Sondheim makes it quite clear that the lyrics that interest him belong very specifically to the theater. They are "lyrics in a dramatic situation on a stage in terms of character."[21] As Arthur Laurents, who has worked with Sondheim on four shows, explains, "Steve is the only lyricist who almost always writes songs that can only be sung by the particular character they are written for."[22] Sondheim believes there are two basic principles that dictate what a lyric writer can and should do. The first is that lyrics exist in *time*. An audience cannot ask a performer to slow down or repeat, for "the music is a relentless engine and keeps the lyrics going."[23] This principle then leads to the next, which Sondheim explains thus:

> Lyrics go with music, and music is very rich, in my opinion the richest form of art. It's also abstract and does very strange things to your emotions. So not only do you have that going, but you also have lights, costumes, scenery, characters, performers. There's a great deal to hear and get. Lyrics therefore have to be underwritten. They have to be very simple in essence. That doesn't mean you can't do convoluted lyrics, but essentially the thought is what counts and you have to stretch the thought out enough so that the listener has a fair chance to get it. Many lyrics suffer from being much too packed.[24]

The lyricist's task is difficult because he or she has to charge each word with significance. Lyrics can possess all the complexity of poetry, exploring both the connotative and denotative resonances of each word. In addition, the music itself adds further depth and different levels of meaning. Yet because each lyric is ephemeral and has an extremely restricted exposure, each word must count. Consequently, lyric writing is an extraordinarily precise craft. Sondheim shows just how exact a lyricist should be in his sensitive analysis of the opening line of DuBose Heyward's "Summertime" from *Porgy and Bess*. Of the line, "Summertime and the livin' is easy," Sondheim writes:

> That "and" is worth a great deal of attention. I would write "Summertime when" but that "and" sets up a tone, a whole poetic tone, not to mention a whole kind of diction that is going to be used in the play; an informal, uneducated diction and a stream of consciousness, as in many of the songs like "My Man's Gone Now." It's the exact right word, and that word is worth its weight in gold. "Summertime when the livin' is easy" is a boring line compared to "Summertime and." The choices of "ands" [and] "buts" become almost traumatic as you are writing a lyric—or should, anyway—because each one weighs so much.[25]

Sondheim acknowledges three major influences on his work: Oscar Hammerstein, Burt Shevelove, and Arthur Laurents. Like Hammerstein, Sondheim is acutely aware of the needs of his singers. Technicalities like ending a song on an open sound, choosing consonants with care, building a number to an applause-pulling finale are all evident in the work of both men. More important, from Hammerstein Sondheim learned that "it's content that counts. It's what you say rather than how you say it, and clarity of thought, making the thought clear to the listener. . . . Oscar also said, 'Say what you feel, not what other song writers feel.' "[26] Sondheim heeded Hammerstein's advice, and for this reason his work is profoundly different from that of his mentor. Whereas Hammerstein believed in and could express a basic optimism and faith, Sondheim's work reflects a cynicism and distance.

The second major influence on Sondheim's writing was Burt Shevelove, who together with Larry Gelbart wrote the book for *A Funny Thing Happened on the Way to the Forum*. Shevelove stressed clarity, teaching Sondheim that

> clarity of language was important as well as clarity of thought. He believes that the best art always seems effortless—maybe not true of something like Guernica, but true of lyric writing, I think. Burt advised me, "Never sacrifice smoothness for cleverness. Better dull than clumsy." I agree. An awful lot of lyrics suffer from the lyric writer having a really clever, sharp idea which he can't quite fit into the music, so it sits there clumsily and the actor is stuck with singing it. The net result is always that it doesn't land with the audience. It has to be smooth if you are going to make the point.[27]

Sondheim worked with Authur Laurents, his third major influence, on *West Side Story*, *Gypsy*, *Anyone Can Whistle*, and *Do I Hear a Waltz?* From Laurents, Sondheim believes, he learned to appreciate the significance and importance of "subtext." By "subtext" Sondheim means "giving the actor something to act."[28] In all his lyrics Sondheim attempts to invest words with several levels of meaning. Often the meaning of the subtext will be in complete contrast to the overt content of the lyric, but this complexity is not accidental, or something added by a subtle actor. It is written by the lyricist. (Sondheim not only explores the subtext necessary to the full realization of character but also attempts to invent staging for each number as he writes. It is not important to him that the director or choreographer adhere rigidly to his staging suggestions, but by envisaging the theatrical possibilities Sondheim assures that his work will be viable on stage.)

Another axiom in Sondheim's system is "Content dictates form." The structure, rhythm, and complexity of the rhyme scheme and the melodic form and tone of each song are carefully matched to the dramatic needs of the characters. Sondheim stresses that the "grammatical structure" of music and the lyric must match exactly. Stressed meter in verse must be coupled with accented notes in music, for otherwise the clarity of expression will be seriously impaired. Sondheim advises:

> When a phrase of music comes to an end the lyric should come to an end, otherwise it sets up a conflict in the listener's ear. The lyric should match the music with a comma, a semi-colon, or just the completion of a phrase. . . .
>
> Words have to sit on music in order to become clear to the audience. I am talking about clarity, . . . and clarity has to do with that thing I talked about, time. You don't get a chance to hear the lyric twice or to read it, and if the lyric doesn't sit and bounce when the music bounces and rise when the music rises, it isn't just a question of mis-accents, which are bad enough, but if it is too crowded and doesn't rise and fall with the music, the audience becomes confused.[29]

Music and lyrics should complement each other. Music, Sondheim points out, is so rich a medium that the lyricist must be careful never to overwrite. He believes that if a very rich lyric is coupled with a passionate musical phrase, the audience will be overwhelmed. In order for a characterization to be completed with the addition of music, something must be left unsaid or implied. A lyric may often look banal on paper, for it only acquires its own poetic dimension when sung.

Sondheim has very definite attitudes about the use of rhymes, identities, and alliteration in lyric writing, but most of these practical details about the basics of the craft are more useful to the practitioner than to the critic. One area, however, is of interest: Sondheim emphasizes his conviction that rhyme suggests education. The quality of language must match the character, for in many ways a song functions like a soliloquy in which the internal motivation of a character can be conveyed. He admits to loathing one of his own lyrics from *West Side Story* for this reason:

> One of the most embarrassing moments of my life as a lyric writer was after a runthrough of *West Side Story* when some of my friends including Sheldon Harnick were out front. I asked Sheldon after the show, "What do you think?" knowing he was going to fall to his knees and lick the sidewalk. But he didn't, and I asked him to tell me what was wrong. "There's that lyric 'I Feel Pretty,' " he said. Now, I thought "I Feel Pretty" was just terrific, I had spent the previous year of my life rhyming "day" and "way" and "me" and "be," and with "I Feel Pretty" I wanted to show that I could do inner rhymes too. So I had this uneducated Puerto Rican girl singing, "It's alarming how charming I feel." You know, she would not have been unwel-

> come in Noel Coward's living room. Sheldon was very gentle, but oh! did it hurt. I immediately went back to the drawing board and wrote a simplified version of the lyric which nobody connected with the show would accept; so there it is, embarrassing me every time it's sung, because it's full of mistakes like that. Well, when rhyme goes against character, out it should go, and rhyme always implies education and mind working, and the more rhymes the sharper the mind.[30]

In contrast with Maria's simplicity, Sondheim has subsequently created many complex sophisticated characters who can display their creator's complex, sophisticated mind. Joanne' singing "The Ladies Who Lunch" (*Company*), Phyllis's vitriolic attack "Could I Leave You?" (*Follies*), Fredrik's witty use of literary allusion in his aborted seduction attempt "Now" (*A Little Night Music*); and the smart but vacuous chatter of the New Yorkers in "Putting It Together" (*Sunday in The Park with George*) are just a few of the examples that demonstrate how brilliantly Sondheim can combine a dextrous mind and intriguing rhyme schemes with the fabric of character.

Martin Gottfried writes of Sondheim's lyrics:

> If Sondheim's work has weaknesses, they are excess complexity and a lack of warmth. Yet he *is* without question, the most influential lyricist of his time, because his work deals not merely with words but with the entire structure of the musical. Sondheim is attempting to do more with lyrics than anyone has ever attempted. . . . Even his peers have been influenced by his theatrical approach to lyric writing. For he writes not mere songs but musical scenes, in a style peculiarly devised for the theater. While we may miss the simplicity and warmth of the plain song in his work, Sondheim is drawing music and lyrics toward a higher purpose than the free-standing song. It will be because of his work that a musical's lyrics will finally be recognized for being as important to a musical as the book and music.[31]

Despite the innovation of form, content, and style, despite the numerous Tony Awards, accolades, and a Pulitzer Prize, Sondheim's work remains controversial. The reasons for both his succès d'estime and lack of popular appeal are related. Sondheim's work is complex and much of America's theatergoing public does not want to be challenged. The prevailing attitudes of his detractors is articulately expressed by John Lahr:

> Traditional musicals dramatize the triumph of hope over experience. Characteristic of their flirtation with modernism, Sondheim's shows make a cult of blasted joys and jubilant despairs. He admits that joy escapes

> him. "If I consciously sat down and said I wanted to write something that would send people out of the theater *really* happy, I would not know how to do it." His mature musicals sing about a new American excellence: desolation. . . .
>
> Sondheim sat out the turmoil of the late '60s in his Manhattan townhouse, reemerging with *Company*, a musical in tune with the new, winded, post-protest times. Sondheim had come of age: his own diminished sense of life and guarded emotions were now shared by a nation obsessed with its despair. Sondheim's glib toughness echoed the mood of the unromantic era. He became a phenomenon new to the Broadway musical: a laureate of disillusion.
>
> A society that feels itself irredeemably lost requires a legend of defeat. And Sondheim's shows are at the vanguard of this atmosphere of collapse. He shares both the culture's sense of impotence and its new habit of wrenching vitality from madness. He is a connoisseur of chaos. . . .
>
> Sondheim's mature scores mythologize desolation.[32]

Lahr writes persuasively and with intelligence about the nihilism he finds in Sondheim's work. His criticism is fascinating, but ultimately old-fashioned in its premise. He displays his prejudice in the following brief sentence, "Before it was Art, the musical was fun."[33] Lahr is at heart little different from George Jean Nathan, nostalgically longing for the "mindless" musicals of the past. Lahr is intrigued, fascinated, but ultimately offended by Sondheim's ability to fuse the serious psychological, political, and social angst of contemporary America with a form that he believes should be ultimately frivolous. He takes issue with the fact that "Sondheim has set himself up as an avant gardist in an avowedly popular form,"[34] for Lahr is essentially contemptuous of the genre. He unequivocally states, "Musical comedy is to music what Ping-Pong is to tennis."[35] Even his use of the term "musical comedy" rather than "musical theater" displays his prejudice. Lahr concludes his condemnation of Sondheim thus:

> From My Lai to Guyana, the American public has become casual about absorbing catastrophe. And Sondheim has turned this numbed anguish into a mass product. Too chic to register disapproval, Sondheim is an entrepreneur of modern anxieties. His musicals claim victories for themselves as new departures, but they are the end of the musical's glorious tradition of trivialization. Sondheim's cold elegance matches the spiritual pall that has settled over American life. His musicals are chronicles in song of the society's growing decrepitude. They foreshadow the newest barbarism—a nation that has no faith in the peace it seeks or the pleasure it finds.[36]

Lahr's conclusions are unconvincing. The musical may have been "trivial" in the past, but its greatness did not lie in that triviality. Sondheim has shown that musical theater can be serious, poignant, and still exhilarating.

In his article "In Search of a New Consensus," Julius Novick confronts the kind of attitude exemplified by Lahr and argues that musicals have changed because the country, its culture, and people have changed.[37] The American musical theater cannot return to the carefree days of escapist entertainment because there no longer exists a real consensus among the majority of Americans. The American self-image has been shattered. A monumental disillusion prevails. The mythic pattern of good triumphing over evil has not been substantiated in recent history. As Alan J. Lerner so succinctly expressed it: "The point is, I wouldn't write *My Fair Lady* today. I don't feel *My Fair Lady* today."[38] In contrast with the biting cynicism and nostalgic longing of Lahr, Novick does not see this transition as a disaster:

> It is no longer assumed that a musical is or should be an escapist entertainment. Over the past couple of decades, American musicals have been reflecting with increasing vividness the changes in the society out of which they grew. These last two decades have not been carefree ones, and they have not given rise to carefree musicals. The Broadway musical, instead, has opened itself more and more to the real world: the fearful, divided, confused real world we live in every day. . . .
>
> . . . Broadway musicals have lost something in gaiety, charm, and exhilaration over the past 20 years, but they have gained something in variety, imaginative freedom, and truth to life.[39]

Sondheim is the preeminent exponent of this new musical form. His work has redefined the genre and as a result the gulf that separated "serious," "legitimate" theater from the musical theater has effectively been bridged.

2

SOMETHING FAMILIAR? *A Funny Thing Happened on the Way to the Forum* and *Anyone Can Whistle*

It is ironic that the man whose name has become synonymous with serious and provocative musical theater should present as his first work on Broadway both as composer and lyricist a ribald, rollicking, low farce. The first draft of *A Funny Thing Happened on the Way to the Forum*, a collaboration between Burt Shevelove, Larry Gelbart, and Sondheim, was completed in 1958, but the musical did not open in New York until May 1962, after eleven distinct revisions and numerous changes in both cast and director.

The book, which some argue is the best book associated with any subsequent Sondheim collaboration,[1] is an intricate synthesis of several plays by Plautus. Using a character from one text and a situation from another, Shevelove and Gelbart have created a unified farce, complete with its myriad of ingeniously combined subplots and complications. Although the resultant plot structure is original, the authors have managed to retain the spirit of the Roman comic theater and infuse the play with the zany humor of American burlesque, thus combining "Roman convention and American invention."[2] The classic slapstick situations common to the ancient texts and the "lazzi" of the comedians of early twentieth-century vaudeville have been incorporated into the convoluted comic scheme. One-liners, sexual innuendo, double takes and generous displays of female pulchritude are the staples of burlesque humor and are used liberally in the text, which Shevelove described as "a scenario for vaudevillians."[3] Even the title, based on the cliché introduction to stand-up comedy routines, sets the tone for the wedding of modern broad humor with its classical antecedents.

In creating a score and lyrics for *Forum*, Sondheim broke completely with the Rodgers and Hammerstein tradition. As a lyricist for *West Side Story* and *Gypsy*, he had employed his mentor's technique, in which a song is an inevitable, almost uncontrollable expression of a character's emotional state and is invariably utilized to advance the story. For a rapidly paced farce, the characters of which are drawn as prototypes with names like Domina, Hero, Pseudolus, and Vibrata, an integrated score in which each song leads the audience to a better understanding of the character's inner life would hardly be appropriate. Consequently Sondheim wrote the songs as respites from the frantic activity of the farce. They do not develop the characters but serve "to pinpoint moments of joy or delight or desire."[4]

It is for this reason that Sondheim maintains that the piece is truly "experimental." It is the complete antithesis of the Rodgers and Hammerstein structure, for the songs interrupt the action and prevent the frenetic comedy from becoming excessive and unrelieved. As Shevelove said: "Without the songs the show would become relentless. It would exhaust you and you wouldn't get any breathers, any savoring of certain moments. 'Everybody Ought to Have a Maid' is a chance to stop running in and out of doors and conniving."[5] Because the songs are not designed to advance the plot, nor to reveal the soul behind the characters' masks, Sondheim had to find an alternative way to sustain dramatic interest. He has achieved this by structuring an internal development within the boundaries of each particular number. Sondheim himself says: "What I wanted to do was give each song in *Forum* an inner movement. So in 'Pretty Little Picture' there's an actual physical journey. In 'Free' you have someone toying with different aspects of an idea, the idea of freedom."[6]

Yet despite this use of an almost revuelike format and the wit, intelligence, and charm of the lyrics and score, Sondheim's contribution to this musical is not entirely satisfactory. His intellectual wit, rich in puns, innuendo, and word play, is inconsistent with the bawdy, vulgar humor of the book and acting style. The tone of the score and lyrics is too refined, subtle, and delicate. Sondheim has acknowledged this disparity of tone:

> [Writing in a style at odds with the Rodgers and Hammerstein prototype was] very hard for me to do. It was like a series of night club numbers. It was precisely in doing it that I made the error, and the result was that the

> numbers didn't hold up on their own because they were written in a different style. There was a big difference between what was going on on the stage and what was going on in the songs. . . . "Pretty Little Picture" is a perfect example of what's wrong. . . . It's a very elegant, rather witty song, very verbal, and has nothing to do with the way the play is written.[7]

With the exception of "Everybody Ought to Have a Maid," and perhaps "Comedy Tonight," Sondheim did not infuse the overall structure of the piece into his compositional style or lyric structure. In his subsequent work, Sondheim has expanded stylistic boundaries without violating them. His work is designed both to encompass and expose the formal imperatives of different theatrical patterns. But in this first work this duality is missing. The classic farce structure is a given, and is not consistently questioned, reflected, or highlighted in the score.

Although *Forum* lacks the complexity and artistic innovation of Sondheim's later work, it nevertheless possesses a definite charm. The score and lyrics are witty and, despite the initial critical reaction, are highly melodic. The show is of primary interest, however, as an indicator of the trends and techniques Sondheim went on to perfect in works like *Company*, *Follies*, and *Sweeney Todd*.

One of the most significant lessons the composer/lyricist learned during out-of-town tryouts of his first show is the function of an opening number. Initially Sondheim composed an appropriately humorous song, "Invocation," but director George Abbott refused to accept it, arguing that it was not "hummable." (Sondheim's frustration at this inane criterion, which has plagued him throughout his career, is finally expressed in his very funny parody of the crass and fatuous producer in *Merrily We Roll Along*.) Sondheim acceded to Abbott's demands and composed a charming song, "Love Is in the Air." This number, based on the conceit that love is an infection and all are susceptible to it, possessed a simple, pleasing melodic line and delighted the director. Sondheim sensed that this delicate, winsome song in no way prepares the audience for the low comedy to follow, but Abbott remained adamant and refused to accept "Invocation." Only after Jerome Robbins was called in, when the show ran into deep audience resistance while still in Washington, were Sondheim's instincts vindicated and a third number, "Comedy Tonight," written. The function of an opening number, as Hammerstein had repeatedly emphasized, is to set the tone for the evening and let the audience know what to expect. Simply by changing the opening "it was cheers and laughter throughout the entire evening at the same lines the audience had received in silence four days earlier."[8] If one thinks of the clarity and specificity of tone and meaning in the opening numbers of *Company* and *Sweeney Todd*, it is plain that Sondheim learned the lesson well.

The quality that shines through the lyrics of *Forum* most clearly is the composer's wit. "Comedy Tonight," which Sondheim, while admitting his fondness for it, dismisses as a "list" number, contains many examples:

> Something that's gaudy,
> Something that's bawdy,
> Something for everybawdy—
> Comedy tonight![9]

The wit is emphasized by the inventive rhyming and wordplay in which antitheses are neatly juxtaposed:

> Pantaloons and tunics,
> Courtesans and eunuchs,
> Funerals and chases,
> Baritones and basses,
> Panderers,
> Philanderers,
> Cupidity,
> Timidity,
> Mistakes,
> Fakes,
> Rhymes,
> Mimes,
> Tumblers, grumblers, fumblers, bumblers ...
> (pp. 3–7)

The piling on of rhymes that reflect the rhythmic pattern of the song represents another of Sondheim's characteristic stylistic accomplishments. Word and sound are perfectly synchronized. The music supports the text, and the text defines the music.

The humor of the lyric is predominantly cerebral, relying mainly on an intellectual cleverness and subtlety that titillates the mind rather than provoking belly laughs. When Pseudolus the slave sings longingly of freedom, the jokes abound:

> *Pseudolus*
>
> Can you see me as a voter fighting graft and vice?

(Sing it soft and nice)

Hero

Free!

Pseudolus

Why I'll be so conscientious that I may vote twice! . . .
Now, not so fast ...
I didn't think ...
The way I am,
I have a roof,
Three meals a day ...
And I don't have to pay a thing ...
I'm a slave and everything's free.
If I were free,
Then nothing would be free.
(pp. 14–15)

The vaudeville structure of the climax of this song, which builds to a big finish, supplements the comic impact.

In all the songs the humor reflects the work's milieu but is not of it. To an exaggerated funeral march, for example, the mourners wail:

All Crete was at her feet,
All Thrace was in her thrall.
All Sparta loved her sweetness and Gaul . . .
(p. 69)

The military hero, Miles Gloriosus, is given one of Sondheim's favorite laugh lines, the only exact translation from the Latin original, when he sings, "I am a parade!"

Sondheim's ability to fuse lyric structure, musical form, and the conflicting internal stresses of personality is also apparent in this early example of his work, as can be seen in "Love I Hear," in which a stammering young lover's tensions, fears, hopes, and anxiety are conveyed in the broken musical and verse structure:

What's love, I hear,
I feel, I fear,
I know I am,
I'm sure ... I mean ...
I hope ... I trust ...
I pray ... I must ...

SOMETHING FAMILIAR?

Be in!

(p. 11)

Confusion and misunderstanding have become synonymous with the sound and style of Sondheim's characters. The attempts of an elderly father and his youthful son who, fearing that they both covet the same nubile courtesan, try to interpret each other's behavior, reveal these characteristic ambiguities:

Senex

She's a lovely, blooming flower,
He's just a sprout—impossible!

Hero

She's a lovely, blooming flower,
He's all worn out—impossible!
(p. 42)

The song's development is deftly inverted as each character's initial self-confidence gives way to doubt:

Hero

Women often want a father,
She may want mine—it's possible!

Senex

He's a handsome lad of twenty,
I'm thirty-nine—it's possible!

Hero

Older men know so much more ...

Senex

In a way, I'm forty-four ...

Hero

Next to him, I'll seem a bore ...

Senex

All right—fifty!
(pp. 42–43)

The reluctant expression of love sung by the matronly virago, Domina, to her lecherous husband also expresses ambivalence:

> Where is he?
> That dirty old man,
> Where can he be?
> Profaning our vows for all to see,
> Complaining how he's misunderstood,
> Abusing me (if he only would!)
> (p. 59)

The parenthetical phrase encapsulates both Domina's longing and the lyricist's comic sense.

The musical has traditionally been a genre in which sentimental excess is not only accepted but demanded. This trait is never characteristic of Sondheim's work. In Pseudolus's description of an escape plan for the two lovers, the inherent sentimentality of "The boat and the bed and the boy and the bride" is undercut not only by the playful alliterative structure and exaggerated repetition of the conjunction "and," but also by the acerbic social jibe from the slave who longs for his freedom:

> Feel the roll of the playful waves,
> See the sails as they swell.
> Hear the whips on the galley slaves—
> Pretty little picture?
> (p. 27)

Shevelove and Gelbart wrote an impeccable farce. Sondheim recognizes the flawless quality of their work:

> I think that the book is vastly underrated. It's brilliantly constructed. . . . The plotting is intricate, the dialogue is never anachronistic, and there are only two or three jokes—the rest is comic situation. It's almost like a senior thesis on two thousand years of comedy with an intricate Swiss watchlike farce plot.[10]

> I think that *Forum* is the best farce ever written. I think it makes Feydeau look like a piker. *Forum* is much more elegant than anything Feydeau ever wrote and much, much more tightly plotted. There's not a wasted moment in *Forum*, and the truth and the test of it is that the play is just as funny when performed by a group of high school students as it is when it is performed on Broadway. It is never *not* funny. The reason is, it is based on situations so solid that you cannot *not* laugh.[11]

SOMETHING FAMILIAR?

When Sondheim infuses that same comedic brilliance into his composition, the musical is at its most successful. In "Everybody Ought to Have a Maid" the burlesque technique of developing a humorous situation by repetition is employed. With each chorus a new character joins in the fun until a line of lechers prances across the stage singing with a vaudevillean strut of the joys of having a maid:

Senex

Everybody ought to have a menial,
Consistently congenial
And quieter than a mouse.
Oh! Oh! Wouldn't she be delicious,
Tidying up the dishes,
Neat as a pin?
Oh! Oh! Wouldn't she be delightful,
Sweeping out, sleeping in?
(p. 33)

The double entendres, the bawdy suggestions, and the actual structuring of the verses place the song firmly in the burlesque mode:

All

Oh! Oh!
Wouldn't she be delightful,

Hysterium

Living in ...

Senex

Giving out?
(p. 34)

The broad physical humor and sexual innuendo is extended with a series of triple rhymes to delight the ear:

Fluttering up the stairway,
Shuttering up the windows,
Cluttering up the bedroom,
Buttering up the master,
Puttering all around
The house!
(p. 33)

The final word, rhyming as it does with the heretofore unmatched "mouse" of the first stanza, indicates the elaborate structure underlying the comic turn. In this song Sondheim discovers the ideal lyric and musical structure to express the style of *Forum*.

One other number, although totally different from "Everybody Ought to Have a Maid," is an impeccable expression of the book's comedic intentions. This romantic ballad, sung by the beautiful but brainless Philia, whose only function in life is to be "lovely," is "a love song that makes us laugh at all other love songs."[12] Philia, who has been taught "beauty and grace and no more," sings:

> I'm lovely,
> All I am is lovely,
> Lovely is the one thing I can do.
> (p. 23)

The verb "do" inverts audience expectation and invariably provokes a chuckle. The narcissism and indulgence of most romantic ballads is gently satirized in Sondheim's lyric parody:

> Oh,
> Isn't it a shame?
> I can neither sew
> Nor cook nor read nor write my name.
> But I'm happy,
> Merely being lovely,
> For it's one thing I can give to you.
> (p. 23)

The comic potential of this number is not exhausted in its first rendering. It is reprised later in the show. The manipulative slave Pseudolus convinces the terrified Hysterium, disguised as a dead virgin, that he makes a beautiful corpse. The love duet, sung to reassure the quaking comic in drag, provides one of the funniest sequences in the Sondheim oeuvre.

The show's appeal, far from dating, has increased with time, and the revival ten years after the original production was universally praised. It is instructive to note the contrast between the critical opinions in the two sets of reviews. Although the piece had been generally well received in 1962, receiving six Tony Awards, including Best Musical, Sondheim's contribution was either totally ignored, deprecated or cursorily dismissed. "Unobtrusive . . . generally pleasant"; "pleasing"; "I don't think I'd give you much for the music, by Stephen Sondheim, but the lyrics, also by him, aren't bad"; "Stephen Sondheim's score is less than inspired"; and "Stephen Sondheim's music would have been second rate even in 1940" were typical responses.[13] Despite the fact that the musical was given the Tony Award as Best Musical in 1962, Sondheim was never mentioned. His contribution to the show's success was disregarded, discounted, and negated.

The revival, however, was treated as a Sondheim triumph: "brilliant music and lyrics by Sondheim"; "Stephen Sondheim's melodious score is one of the season's greatest joys. . . . This early score by the talented Mr. Sondheim is both humorous and charming"; Sondheim's "music is superb: technically fresh, filled with melody, accurate in satire and, most of all, theatrically conceived."[14] Sondheim's altered critical status can even be perceived in the reviewers' list of credits. In 1962 they had seen the musical as a piece by Shevelove, Gelbart, and Sondheim. In 1972 it had become Sondheim, Shevelove, and Gelbart. Sondheim's creative activity in the intervening years had established him as *the* creative musical talent in Broadway theater.

Sondheim's next exposure on the New York stage was brief. *Anyone Can Whistle* opened in April 1964 and closed after only nine performances. Yet despite its ephemeral existence, the musical refuses to die, retaining a cult following attested by the re-release of the original cast album eleven years after this show's closing. The show's book, by Arthur Laurents, who also directed, is a confused surrealistic satire whose primary thesis asserts the sanity of madness and the virtue of nonconformity. In addition, this moral parable attacks numerous social evils and contrasts the extremes of idealism, rationalism, and romanticism. In short, it tries far too hard to do far too much. Yet out of this potpourri, Sondheim's work emerges as experimental and provocative—a tantalizing foretaste of the talent that later work would reveal more strikingly.

The most fascinating facets of *Anyone Can Whistle* are those initial explorations of the different techniques and stylistic devices that Sondheim would go on to develop and perfect in his subsequent compositions. Chief among these is his use of the conventions of musical theater as a means of commenting on or revealing a character's inner nature. In portraying the venal character of the mayoress, Cora, played in the original production by Angela Lansbury, Sondheim wanted to project her lack of sincerity and her patronizing affectation. He achieved this by writing most of her material as readily recognizable pastiche. As Sondheim has noted, "The character always sang in musical comedy terms because she was a lady who dealt in attitudes instead of emotions."[15]

The mayoress is constantly escorted by four adoring, dancing chorus boys, and her duplicity and egocentric opportunism are defined as she belts out her leading-lady numbers backed by this sycophantic entourage. Her first number is, Sondheim has explained, a Hugh Martin–Kay Thompson pastiche.[16] These composers of the 1940s perfected the star turn, which backed a musical comedy prima donna with a lineup of singing, dancing males. The dazzling surface splendor of the star, whose performance was all style and no content, is utilized in Sondheim's work as an ironic comment on Cora's avaricious narcissism.

The song alternates between the throaty lament of the blues singer and a lively jazz exchange. Cora's lack of concern for her people's problems is conveyed in the exaggerated soulfulness of a torch song:

> Everyone hates me—yes, yes—
> Being the Mayoress—yes.
> All of the peasants
> Throw rocks in my presence,
> Which causes me nervous distress, yes.
> Oooooooooooh, Oooh-ooh Oooooooooooh ...
>
> Me and my town, battered about,
> Everyone in it would like to get out.
> Me and my town,
> We just wanna be loved![17]

The grammatical solecisms and the colloquialism of "wanna be loved" reflect the forties image that Cora projects, while the jazzy patter sections, which are sung almost a capella with only a rhythmic base in the background, convey her slick heartlessness:

> *Boys*
>
> Hi there, Cora. What's new?
>
> *Cora*
>
> The bank went bust and I'm feeling blue.
>
> *Boys*
>
> And who took over the bankruptcy?
>
> *Cora*

SOMETHING FAMILIAR?

Me, boys, me!
(pp. 7–8)

The satire does become a little heavy-handed but this excess is redeemed by Sondheim's light comic touch:

Cora and Boys

I see a terrible depression all over the town—. . .
What a terrible depression,
And I'm so depressed I can hardly talk on the phone.
I feel all alone.
(p. 10)

In a show-business finish, in which Cora sees to it that she takes the final bow by pushing her boys off the stage, her self-image and the editorial comment are clearly dramatized.

This theatricalization of attitudes and relationships is extended in a later number. Cora's plans are going awry. Her only hope is to turn the crowd against Hapgood. As she ruthlessly plans a mob riot and the lynching of the hero, she asserts her dependence on and need for her bureaucratic buddies in a typical musical-comedy "friendship" number. The hyperbole in both lyric content and musical structure dictates that the number be staged using the standard clichés of the form. The ironic conflict between the horror of the plan and the frivolity implicit in the form makes a riveting theatrical statement:

Cora

. . . When everything's hopelessly gray,
You'll notice I'm youthfully gay!
There isn't a sing—
Le great thing
I can't do,
Not with you to lean on,
Darling you! . . .

Boys

When everything's hollow and black,
You'll always have us at your back.
No matter how hollow,
We'll follow
Your lead—

And with us to lean on,
You'll succeed!
(pp. 142–47)

This use of the musical-theater idiom is uniquely Sondheim's. His parodies of various musical styles are not merely send-ups, although he includes a number of musical spoofs in his scores. His use of different, identifiable structures serves a definite thematic purpose. The styles function as a second-order language reflecting, intensifying and clarifying the characters' psyches. Sondheim echoes the sound patterns and recognizable styles and forms of other musical theater composers and their connotative associations as a dramatically effective device, but this does not mean that his work is unoriginal or plagiaristic:

> Sondheim works through parody in the old and respectable musical sense, where the word was used to describe the borrowing by a religious composer of a secular theme. . . . As with his lyrics, which are rooted in the received tradition, there is no element of derogation from a higher musical intention. . . . [T]he American musical . . . is the language he speaks.
>
> And while he borrows the styles and forms he loves according to the dramatic context which he is facing, and fashions his vocal line, in rhythm and in emotional intention, according to the expressive needs of his lyric, the intervals themselves—the actual thematic material from which he works—are his own. To the casual listener the antecedents of a Sondheim number may be more apparent than the originality, just as Mahler sounds romantic, Mozart classical, and Purcell baroque. But a Sondheim number is not like Jerome Kern, or Cole Porter, or Richard Rodgers, even when it is the type of number they might have produced.[18]

In *Anyone Can Whistle* Sondheim is experimenting with this technique, introducing a number of satiric parodies. In proclaiming a phony miracle, which they hope will restore their town's prosperity, Cora and her henchmen sing an evangelical gospel song. The close harmony and clearly defined rhythmic pattern identify the satiric target. The exploitation of the gullible populace's need for the miraculous is lampooned both in Sondheim's musical travesty and in the sacrilegious overtones of the lyric:

There's water that you part,
Water that you walk on,
Water that you turn to wine!
But water from a rock—Lord! What a miracle!
This is a miracle that's divine,

Truly divine! . . .
Water is a boon, we'll soon be in clover!

Cora

Better issue stock, my rock runneth over!
(p. 20)

The silly simplifications of an old B-grade French movie are caricatured in "Come Play Wiz Me." Not included arbitrarily to display Sondheim's mimicry or satiric skill, the song functions as a commentary on the character of the coolly rational Nurse Fay Apple, who dares to express emotion only when she assumes the disguise of a French seductress. Sondheim incorporates the circumlocutions of a phony French accent into the pattern of his melody:

You like my style, yes? My brand, yes?
Ze lay of my—how you say?—of my land, yes?
You wish to pray wiz me?
To stray wiz me?
Come out and play wiz me.
(p. 91)

Sondheim's most extended musical satire for a choreographed sequence was written for the "Cookie Chase," a stylized ballet sequence in which the town attempts to capture forty-nine mad people. The score, with its Delibes-like overtones, pokes fun at the syrupy excesses of nineteenth-century ballet waltzes. The musical suggestions are funny and, judging from reviews, the sequence was theatrically very effective, but like the other experiments with pastiche and musical satire in this score, "Cookie Chase" is not organically related to the rest of the musical. Sondheim's use of musical emblems is less than successful in *Anyone Can Whistle* because these satiric referents are not thoroughly integrated into the fabric of the work. The musical-comedy language Cora employs reveals a great deal about her personality but is not carried through as a unifying technique. In contrast with his later work, in which such musical and lyric commentary defines the shape and meaning of the entire musical, Sondheim's initial use of this technique is sporadic and lacks an organic relationship with the entire score and text. Consequently, although individual numbers are interesting and effective, there is no unity of vision, no integrating concept.

Sondheim's innovative exploration in *Anyone Can Whistle* was not confined to his experiments with commentary through musical-theater forms.

There are extended sequences of dialogue, song, and dance in which one mode of communication flows into the next, coalescing into a complex *sprechgesang* wherein the collaboration between Sondheim, Laurents, and Herbert Ross, the choreographer, results in a seamless whole in which it is impossible to tell where the book ends and the lyric begins. (Sondheim went on to develop this kind of complex extended musical sequence in *A Little Night Music* and *Sweeney Todd.*) An entire scene, "Simple" (an unprecedented thirteen minutes long), is an amalgam of spoken word, chant, and song that Sondheim and Laurents devised by sitting together at a piano and combining Sondheim's lyric syllogisms with Laurents's paradoxical sketches. Confused sexual identity, for example, is successfully achieved in Laurents's rapid repartee and summarized in Sondheim's

> A woman's place is in the home,
> A woman's place is on the shelf.
> And home is where he hangs her hat,
> And that is where she hangs himself.
> (p. 63)

The authors strove for a unified tone so that the piece would sound like the work of a single creator.

Anyone Can Whistle is a stylistically exciting show. In attempting to explore the distortions of accepted reality and the truth of madness, the creators use an obvious theatricality to highlight the artificiality both of commonplace reality and self-indulgent idealism. They create a make-believe world in which the major characters are emblematic prototypes, the townspeople have the painted faces and wigs of circus clowns, and the scenery responds to the whim and command of the players. For example, a scene change shudders to a halt and waits for the mayoress to put on her gloves, and the seduction in French between Nurse Apple and the hero Hapgood is supplemented by subtitles flashed onto a screen above the lovers' heads (Nurse Apple consults the screens when she cannot understand Hapgood's atrocious French). The theatricality of style is further augmented by the dance sequences. A substantial portion of the action is conveyed through the choreography, and this musical contains far more dance than any of Sondheim's subsequent work.

The concluding moments of act 1 are particularly provocative. The wild complexity of the interrogation sequence builds to a frenzied climax:

The light goes almost black except for a weird glow from the footlights. The two Groups (a haphazard division of mad and sane) run down to the footlights and, in a straight line right across the stage, chant fast and shrill, with mounting intensity:

Who is what? Which is who?
Who is what? Which is who?
Who is what? Which is WHO is WHO?

Silence and a blackout except for a light on Hapgood. He looks at the audience with a smile and says, quietly:

You are all mad.

There is a burst of gay, wild circus music. A row of lights resembling the balcony rail of a theater has been lowered and it now begins to burn brighter and brighter with pink, blue, yellow lights, flooding the theater audience. At the same time, the real balcony rail lights in the theater are coming on and lighting up the stage. And there we see the company sitting in theater seats and laughing and applauding louder and louder as
The Curtain Falls. (pp. 79–80)

We have come to think of this theatrical gesture as originating with Peter Brook's production of *Marat/Sade*, but Laurents devised it four months earlier than Brook's epoch-making production.

Sondheim's contribution to the work's stylistic innovation is clear from the opening when the traditional overture is replaced by a brief, lively prelude "shaped of intriguing, mild dissonances with scant pleasantly tantalizing fragments of theme stated in short, irregular phrases."[19] This prelude evokes the circus motif that will recur throughout the piece. Sondheim's experimentations with form and the connotative impact of musical-comedy idiom, the complexity of his musical patterns with their extended passages of intricate contrapuntal singing, and the sophisticated tonal arrangements he introduces still retain their avant-garde character today.

Yet *Anyone Can Whistle* is not all futuristic experimentation. This musical not only contains some of Sondheim's loveliest music but also provides a key to the emotional depth, complexity, and oblique sensitivity of his work. Cora the mayoress is egotistical and mercenary, but she is not all unmitigated evil. After all in the town have rejected her, Sondheim has written her a tender song that reveals her vulnerability. The brassy, optimistic opening, which evokes the excitement generated by popularity, gives way to self-doubt and loneliness:

> Did you hear? Did you see?
> Was a parade in town?
> Were there drums without me?
> Was a parade in town?
> 'Cause I'm dressed at last, at my best, and my
> banners are high.
> Tell me, while I was getting ready,
> Did a parade go by?
> (pp. 111–12)

It is, however, in the title song that the clearest exposition of Sondheim's emotional priorities are to be found. The heroine, Nurse Fay Apple, has to struggle to express any human commitment or passion. She is controlled, distant, and supremely rational, yet she longs for the intoxicating ecstasy of sensuous abandon. Her struggle to break out of her inhuman frigidity is expressed with a deceptive simplicity of both musical and lyric structure:

> What's hard is simple,
> What's natural comes hard.
> Maybe you could show me
> How to let go,
> Lower my guard,
> Learn to be free,
> Maybe if you whistle,
> Whistle for me.
> (p. 108)

This song provides the key to all Sondheim's subsequent emotional opacity. His characters cannot unashamedly belt out songs of unrestrained passion. They are filled with doubt and insecurity. Robert in *Company*, Phyllis and Ben in *Follies*, Desirée in *A Little Night Music*, Franklin Shepard in *Merrily We Roll Along*, and George in *Sunday in the Park with George* are all inhibited by intense emotions. Their inability to express their feelings unambiguously with standard romantic impetuosity does not signify a lack of emotional depth but is an indication of a profound angst and sensitivity. Sondheim's characters and their love songs are not cold or heartless; instead they express an intellectual and emotional complexity rarely equalled in the American musical theater. The subtlety, anxiety, and fundamental seriousness of feeling is clearly an attribute of the composer's, and *Anyone Can Whistle*'s title song is assumed to be his personal statement. The concluding moments of a gala benefit in March 1973, which was held as a tribute to Sondheim's theatrical contribution, are described in a *Newsweek* cover story:

> After a glittering succession of performers had sung and danced their way through more than 40 Sondheim songs, Broadway's reigning music man sat down at the piano and with tears streaming down his face, sang the title number from *Anyone Can Whistle*. . . . Whereupon he was suddenly surrounded by a stageful of stars singing, from *Company*: "What would we do without you? How would we ever get through?"[20]

Sondheim recalls the evening differently: "There were no tears streaming down my face when I sang the number. That was Charles Michener, the reporter, waxing sentimental, to give his story a finish. I cried when I was thanking Burt Shevelove and Hal Prince."[21] What is clear is that Sondheim's emotional reticence is expressed in the oblique tentativeness of his love songs, which gives them unique intensity and depth.

Anyone Can Whistle is a flawed work, yet it is significant. It not only enabled Sondheim to flex his creative talents but began the gradual process of genre redefinition. The show was instructive, not only to its creator but also to its audience. On its own it did not succeed, but it became what composer Al Carmines calls a "sacrificial lamb." It eroded musical preconceptions and inevitably facilitated the acceptance of Sondheim's subsequent experimentation. It functioned in much the same way as Samuel Beckett's *Waiting for Godot* worked in the nonmusical theater. It "changed the consciousness of the critic"[22] and consequently of the audience. A few critics understood this:

> If *Anyone Can Whistle* is a success, the American musical theater will have advanced itself and prepared the way for further breakdown of now old and worn techniques and points of view. If it is not a success, we sink back into the old formula method and must wait for the breakthrough. . . . The new musical is not a perfect musical commentary by several chalks, but it is a bright first step toward a more enlightened and cerebral musical theater, a musical theater in which that kind of show can say something about its times and the mores of those times. . . . Let no one

> concerned be discouraged. . . . The American musical theater is less ponderous today because of *Anyone Can Whistle*, no matter what its fate.[23]

Not until Sondheim's next work as composer/lyricist was his real value finally appreciated.

3

NO ONE IS ALONE? *Company*

The irritating buzz of the busy signal; the syncopated staccato sounds of frenetic city life; the teeming isolation of Manhattan—this amalgam is synthesized as *Company*. Exploring the ambivalences and the frustrating lack of connection that characterize modern marriage, Sondheim's third work captures the essence of contemporary American existence as it breaks emphatically with the established tradition of the musical theater.

While Sondheim was working with playwright James Goldman on a murder-mystery musical titled *The Girls Upstairs*, which they were having trouble getting produced, an actor friend, George Furth, showed Sondheim seven one-act plays he had written, each with a lead part intended for Kim Stanley. Sondheim showed the plays to Harold Prince, who realized that they would provide interesting material for a semi-autobiographical musical about contemporary marriage. Sondheim was stimulated by the notion. He recalls: "I said, 'They're so unmusical. They are so unsinging.' George writes non-singing people. And Hal said, 'That's what's so interesting about it.' And I said, 'You've got me hooked.' "[1] Thus *Company* was born. Sondheim hoped to get *The Girls Upstairs* staged first, but his problems with producers continued. Finally it was agreed that Prince would produce and direct *The Girls Upstairs* (subsequently titled *Follies*) after *Company* had opened.

Company is an episodic collage focusing on the relationships of a thirty-five-year-old bachelor, Robert, with his doting and devoted married friends. As seen through the skeptical eye of this bemused hero, marriage is an oppressive state in which one inadequate individual is yoked forever to another less-than-perfect individual. The predatory group, united in a conspiracy to absorb Robert into their company of wedded bliss, are Sarah and

Harry, settling their suppressed frustrations with karate chops on the living room carpet; Susan and Peter, living together amicably after their divorce; Jenny and David, tentatively experimenting with pot (she high, he down; "incompatible even when stoned"); Amy, the terrified Catholic bride-to-be, fleeing the impending wedding to her adoring, long-established Jewish boyfriend, Paul; and Joanne and Larry, she intelligent and brittle, he much married, cynical, and world weary. For all these couples, Robert is the safe, necessary third party who maintains an uneasy peace between the antagonistic partners.

In addition to his married friends, Robert has three female companions: April, a vacant but charming air hostess; Marta, who has come to New York like a pilgrim in search of the Mecca of chic sophistication; and Kathy, who leaves the city to settle for marriage in Vermont. In a mélange of encounters, the audience watches Robert's struggles for human warmth, which are never entirely successful nor ever complete failures.

But *Company* is not simply the depiction of one man's inability to find a suitable spouse. It investigates the malaise of an age, the incapacitating fears of a generation fleeing the painful choices of commitment. While some have claimed that the work has two distinct plots, one concerning Robert and his friends and the other focusing on the problems of contemporary marriage, it seems clear that *Company* is a particularized dramatization of the more general problem. Terse, cynical, and sardonic, Sondheim and his collaborators illustrate a social reality familiar to audiences but not frequently the subject matter of musical theater.

Sondheim, Prince, and Furth agree that Manhattan was the perfect metaphor for their work. As Sondheim recollects:

> In every show there should be a secret metaphor that nobody knows except the authors. . . . In *Company* we were making a comparison between a contemporary marriage and the island of Manhattan—in fact it was even spoken about at one point. We made a vaudeville joke about it in the middle of "Side by Side by Side," and then we took it out because we decided never to let anybody know that that was what we were about. But it justified my writing a song about Manhattan, "Another Hundred People," which is the *only* song that doesn't deal with one-to-one relationships. . . . If you asked Hal Prince to state what *Company* is about in one sentence, and then asked George Furth, and asked me, we would probably come up with different sentences. But we all know about this underlying metaphor of Manhattan, which is after all the handiest locale for the inhumanity of contemporary living and the difficulties in making relationships.[2]

The metaphor was not that hidden, however, for it was readily grasped by the critics. *Company*, declared Leonard Harris, "is an ode to New York—not Staten Island, or Riverdale, or Bayside—the high tension, hyperthyroid world of midtown Manhattan. And it catches all the nervousness."[3] This high-tension Manhattan is markedly different from the exciting fun-city of earlier musicals (*On the Town*; *Wonderful Town*), just as the troubled relationships depicted in the piece are in stark contrast to the happily-ever-after ideal of traditional musical young love, and one critic explored the resulting parallels:

> *Company* makes Manhattan a metaphor for marriage. Manhattan is an island of anguish and delight; so is marriage. Manhattan is an incessant roar of competitive egos; marriage is a subdued echo of the same. Manhattan is a meeting of strangers; marriage is a mating of strangers. Manhattan is a war of nerves; marriage is a ferocious pillow-fight battle of the sexes. The links do not stop there. The tempo of Manhattan is a kind of running fever; modern marriage runs a fever and the partners are always taking its temperature. It simply is not the placid old heaven-ordained, till-death-do-us-part, for-better-for-worse institution it used to be.[4]

Contemporary society has enclosed humanity in sealed compartments. People are encouraged to retreat into their isolated cocoons and avoid the hazards of personal vulnerability and commitment. Nowhere is this isolation more apparent than in the crowded loneliness of the swarming Manhattan streets with their forbidding high-rise apartment buildings. Sondheim explains the choice of this environment:

> You never want to make a statement, but *Company* did become controversial because it dealt with the increasing difficulty of making one-to-one relationships in an increasingly dehumanized society. And one of the reasons we had it take place in front of chrome and glass and steel was that it took place in an urban society in which individuality and individual feeling become more and more difficult to maintain. It's the lonely crowd syndrome.[5]

In Prince's production, the focal concept of the piece was initially conveyed to the audience by Boris Aronson's towering set, which is vividly described in Stanley Kauffmann's review:

> It is a skeletonized structure of [seeming] plexi-glass and steel with two open elevators in it [there actually was only one elevator] and a huge

> cyclorama behind it on which rear projections flow past to supplement or specify the action. Yet this is no mere stack of boxes. . . . Aronson's set *dramatizes* the cellular, scarily clean feeling of a modern Manhattan apartment house, including a touch of wit and a lot of good varied playing spaces. . . . The mode is Constructivist and suggests the influence of two Russians, the sculptor Tatlin and the director-designer Meyerhold.[6]

The sleek set, sterile and cold, reflected the detachment of a society whose goals are fixed on upward mobility, both spatial and social: crowds struggling upward to nowhere. These elevated empty spaces expressed the essence of the city, all bustling efficiency, glittering surfaces, and emotional sterility. The labyrinth of stairs, platforms, and elevators also served as a visual metaphor for the barren maze of Robert's emotional turmoil.

Prince and Aronson complemented the stark structure with a constantly changing pattern of projections. These images served to highlight the overtones and undercurrents of the subtext:

> Most of the front projections . . . were abstractions designed to support the emotions of the scenes. Occasionally they contradicted the apparent mood, illuminating instead the undercurrents. . . . [For] the scenes we used black and white photographs in some details of locations in New York City; for the songs we used reverse negatives of the photographs, painted in color. There were six hundred slides in all, and most people weren't aware of them, which is as it should be.[7]

Company opens on a surprise birthday party given for Robert by his married friends. This scene recurs as a tableau concluding act 1, at the beginning of act 2, and in the final moments of the piece. The party is an apt choice as it dramatizes the protagonist's need to grow up. (The musical was described by Aaron Frankel as a "rite of passage," in the course of which the audience should perceive the gradual maturation of Robert.) Whether there are four different parties, or they are all one, is not clear. Prince has noted this ambiguity:

> We constructed a framework of gatherings for Robert's thirty-fifth birthday, each appearing to be the same, but dynamically different from the others. Pinteresque in feeling, the first was giddy, somewhat hysterical; the second . . . an abbreviated version of the first; the third hostile and staccato; and the final one at the end of the show, warm, loving, mature. Since Robert never arrives for the final celebration, there was some question whether they represented one birthday or a succession of them. I am

> certain they were one. I wouldn't be surprised if George Furth believes there were four. It doesn't matter.[8]

The time sequence of *Company* is fractured. We are presented with fragments of Robert's life: a theatrical montage of various encounters with his married companions and single female friends. These meetings have no particular sequential order or logic. They are all aspects of Robert's comfortable, empty existence. While this fragmentation of time and abandonment of logical causality are dramatically interesting, they militate against progressive development of the central character. Unlike the traditional hero, Robert does not journey forward. The audience can perceive the cumulative effect of his experiences but never has the sense of inevitable progression and growth that would suggest the gradual enlightenment of a hero.

Sondheim acknowledges the problem. He generally dislikes reprises because characters should not repeat themselves emotionally. This piece is different, however, as he contends: "*Company* was a show where we could have used reprises, because it is about a fellow who stays exactly the same; but I didn't want him to be an essentially singing character, so I decided not to."[9] Sondheim was challenged rather than dismayed by the lack of a traditional linear plot:

> A lot of the controversy about *Company* was that up until *Company* most musicals, if not all musicals, had plots. In fact, up until *Company*, I thought that musicals had to have very strong plots. One of the things that fascinated me about the challenge of the show was to see if a musical could be done without one. Many of the people who disliked the show disliked it for that reason. They wanted a strong story line and they didn't get one and were disappointed.[10]

Prince, too, is aware of their break with tradition:

> *Company* was the first musical I had done without conventional plot or subplot structure. The first without hero and heroine, without the comic relief couple. There are, of course, plots, but they are subtextual and grow out of subconscious behavior, psychological stresses, inadvertent revelations: the nature of the lie people accept to preserve their relationship.[11]

The structure of repeated encounters could have become monotonous, yet the show is integrated into a seamless unity of word, sound, and movement.

The opening party sequence is a restless exchange of bitchy sniping and treacly sentimentality. Robert's friends vie with one another, competing for his attention, but all seem to agree on one thing: Robert needs a wife. The atmosphere in this brief scene of supposed celebration crackles with acerbic asides and hostilities. Robert gamely, but unsuccessfully, attempts to blow out the candles on his birthday cake. The wives hurriedly extinguish the remaining candles, insisting that he make the obligatory wish. As the music sounds softly under the dialogue, Robert confesses he cannot wish for anything, thus providing the first clue to his emotional immaturity. He cannot make himself vulnerable, will not expose himself to the risk of possible failure inherent in wishing too hard for anything. Sealed into untouchable insularity and apparent completeness, he does not want to need anything or anyone.

As the couples slowly retreat to their individual apartments high in the set above Robert's head, he is left alone with the sound of a telephone busy signal reverberating in his head. This disheartening click-buzz characterizes the tone of *Company*. It succinctly dramatizes our failure to communicate in a depersonalized society.

Robert stands center stage, in a pool of light, as the busy signal throbs and the disembodied voices of his friends begin to echo down from their spaces above him. Sondheim observes: "The opening number of *Company* is about the set. I wrote it to present the cast and the set to the audience and also to tell them what the evening's about. I could never have written it without actually seeing the set and knowing there were five distinct playing areas where the couples could be."[12] Aronson's arrangement of space enables the couples to be simultaneously visible but oblivious to one another's presence. Thus Sondheim is able to create interesting contrapuntal combinations of voices, revealing both each couple's individuality and their unanimity of feeling concerning Robert. Moreover, the couples can comment on the center stage actions while remaining secluded in the privacy of their own apartments.

The rhythm of the friendly calls duplicates the impatient repetition of the telephone signal. The various names used in seeking Robert's attention are all diminutives, for his friends need to keep him in infantile dependence. Through the calls emerge the first clear sentences. All concern the attempts to communicate with, to "get in touch with," the elusive bachelor:

> Bobby, we've been trying to reach you all day. . . .
> Bobby, there was something we wanted to say.[13]

NO ONE IS ALONE?

The attempts to ensnare Robert become an insistent ostinato as he is flooded with a deluge of invitations. Sondheim itemizes all the feverish activity of the middle class. All their socializing, all the "company" is a frantic attempt to ignore the isolation of life in a big city. Michael Bennett, who choreographed the musical, noted that the style of this opening number is one of heightened reality: the demands, the transactions, the engagements are all recognizable but are hyperbolized into an exaggerated theatrical form.

The title of the piece, as with most of Sondheim's titles, has several levels of meaning, all of which are suggested in the opening number. "Company" is the opposite of being alone. "Company" is friends coming to call. Moreover, the close ensemble style of the show is accomplished by a small theatrical "company," in contrast to the large star-studded casts of earlier musicals.

As the voices overlap in their demands for his time and attention, Robert stands immobile. This is the pattern of his existence. His life is filled with animated social gatherings, warm, unthreatening, and definitely uncommitted. Finally the couples combine and demand:

> Bobby, come on over for dinner!
> Just be the three of us,
> Only the three of us,
> We loooooove you!
> (p. 13)

The threesome, safe for all its participants, is Robert's chosen life-style. An empty "love," which echoes hollowly, is his perennial emotional state.

The long sustained note with which Sondheim emphasizes the word *love* is effective in several different ways. Originally, Sondheim incorporated the note for a specifically technical reason. He wanted to highlight the moment when the elevator first worked and structured the song around this moment, writing a fifteen-second-long sustained note on the word *love*. The audience's attention was consequently focused on the moving set and Michael Bennett had sufficient time to get the actors from the top levels down to center stage. But the effectiveness of the sustained note is not simply the result of a technical necessity. The note is held on the key word epitomizing the glib hollowness of Robert's companions. As a result the theme of the song and the show is theatricalized.

Picking up the syncopated, frantic rhythm, Robert discloses the pattern of his life:

Phone rings, door chimes, in comes company!
No strings, good times, room hums, company!
Late nights, quick bites, party games,
Deep talks, long walks, telephone calls,
Thoughts shared, souls bared, private names,
All those photos up on the walls
"With love." . . .

(pp. 13–14)

The feverish social whirl, the brief encounters, the lack of involvement are enumerated in the short phrases, the tight internal rhymes, and the lively jazz rhythm. Sondheim uses mainly monosyllables, which intensify the staccato quality of hurried, harried city life. The short sharp sounds are matched to brief, rapid notes.

The idea for both style and content of this number occurred to Sondheim early in his work on the show:

> Looking back at the first page of notes I ever made about *Company*, I see that we sat around and talked about how to turn these one-act plays into a musical. We talked about the central character, and Hal Prince said it would be nice to have a number called "Company." . . . Then Hal said, "And also I would like it to introduce the various styles of the show, the way we are going to cut back and forth; also I would like it to introduce the main character and include all the other characters; also I would like it to use the set. . . ." So I replied in my usual grudging way, "Well, I'm not sure if I can, well, let me see if I can do it and maybe I can write the score, I don't know."
>
> I have my sketch sheets here. Let me read you some of the notes I put down: "Everybody loves Robert (Bob, Bobby) . . ." the idea of nicknames had already occurred to me. Then I had Robert say, "I've got the best friends in the world," and then the line occurred to me, "You I love and you I love and you and you I love," and then, talking about marriage, "A country I've never been to," and "Who wants vine-covered cottages, marriage is for children." It's all Bob's attitude: "Companion for life, who wants that?" And then he says, "I've got company, love is company, three is company, friends are company," and I started a list of what's company. . . . I started to spin free associations, and . . . the whole notion of short phrases, staccato phrases, occurred to me. By the time I got through just listing general thoughts, I had a smell of the rhythm of the vocal line, so that when I was able to turn to the next page and start expanding it I got into whole lists of things. . . . [W]hat came out of it eventually was the form of that song. . . .[14]

NO ONE IS ALONE?

Robert, echoing the declamations of his friends, repeatedly asserts that his life is filled with love. The quality of this emotion, however, is made suspect by its frequent statement and by the flippant tone of the number. These city dwellers fill their lives with social activities in order to hide from the emptiness that threatens to engulf them. For Robert, the safety of loving and being loved by married couples, whose primary commitment is to each other, is conveyed by his declaration "You I love and you I love and you and you I love" (p. 18), while his company of married friends insistently sing out "That's what it's really about, isn't it? / That's what it's really about, really about!" (p. 18). Sondheim establishes an ironic tone from the start, for as the number builds to its emphatic climax, the wives intone the much overused word *love* while the husbands querulously and insistently counterpoint their sustained note with the staccato "Isn't it? Isn't it? Isn't it? Isn't it?" (p. 18). The safety of their habitual routine is reasserted in the final lines:

> Company! Company! Company, lots of company!
> Years of company! Love is company!
> Company!
> (p. 18)

Robert and his married friends constantly stay in touch—but never connect.

With the conclusion of the title number, the stage fragments into a kaleidoscope of sounds and activities (horns, doorbells, and snatches of conversation) before the chaos coalesces into the first of Robert's encounters. This brief scene takes place in the comfort of a chic living room, where Harry and Sarah are entertaining their favorite guest, Robert, who is polite but bemused by their marital double-talk and game-playing. Sarah is on a diet but surreptitiously munches brownies, while Harry takes secret swigs from the forbidden bourbon bottle. The tensions of their relationship are expressed in an energetic karate tussle, as a baffled Robert tries to comprehend marital felicity.

As mentioned earlier, in many of his compositions Sondheim juxtaposes his work with other identifiable theatrical structures. *Company* is no exception. Many of the individual numbers are set in an incongruous musical style that contrasts with the lyrics and makes an ironic point about the character and the situation. But *Company* differs from Sondheim's later work in that the concept or metaphoric structure of the overall piece is not based on a clearly discernible theatrical genre. Although *Company* uses the organizational patterns of drawing-room comedy and is a contemporary comedy of manners, the structures of thought and action discernible in it are social rather than theatrical. The elaborate rituals, the games people play, these form the generic pattern upon which Sondheim builds his creation. The notion of social game-playing, with its assigned roles, its rules, its winner, and its losers, is suggested in the opening number and then developed throughout the piece. Robert feels obliged to play the married game. It is, after all, the accepted mode of behavior for contemporary man. But he sees only the empty rituals and fails to understand any of the human warmth that must underlie the gestures.

The marriages depicted in each scene are, in fact, deliberately distorted. They are seen through Robert's eyes. A lack of clarity on this issue, however, led some early critics to condemn the piece as misanthropic, misogynistic, and antimarriage. Walter Kerr, for example, remarks that "the mood is misanthropic, the view from the peephole jaundiced, the attitude middle-aged mean," while Clive Barnes laments that "these people are just the kind of people you expend hours each day trying to escape from . . . trivial, shallow, worthless and horrid."[15]

Sondheim and Prince were disturbed by this negative response. *Company*, Sondheim insists, is

> the most pro-marriage show in the world. It says very clearly that to be emotionally committed to somebody is very difficult, but to be alone is impossible; to commit is to live, and not to commit is to be dead. Every marriage on that stage has its problems, but every one is a good marriage. It's the central character, Robert, who is cold, who chooses to see his married friends at their worst moments. He's a type one sees more and more these days, a product of a depersonalized society, unable to commit himself.[16]

In a conversation with Craig Zadan, Sondheim adds: "People were mistaking our saying that relationships are difficult for relationships are impossible. What we clearly said over and over again was two is difficult but one is impossible. We said it over and over again and yet a lot of people missed it."[17] And Prince agrees:

> There are those admirers of *Company* who refuse to believe we intended the show to be pro marriage. I assure them not only was that our avowed

> purpose, but to this day we regard it as a fervent plea for interpersonal relationships.
>
> For those who still consider it an indictment, I can only drag out the old defense that some people are simply afraid to acknowledge the manifest difficulties of living together.[18]

One must acknowledge that the presentation of a multiplicity of flawed marriages makes it easy for an audience to see only a negative portrayal of relationships. Nonetheless, against these imperfect marriages *Company* balances the empty loneliness of Robert's life. In attempting to avoid a glib happily-ever-after triteness, *Company* may be faulted for swinging too far in the opposite direction. The determinedly unsentimental appraisal of marriage is harsh, but what *Company* tries to show is that marriage as an institution is not to be faulted. That the couples share a love that Robert adamantly refuses to see may not be adequately articulated in the dialogue, but is clearly expressed in the emotional connotations of the score.

One of Sondheim's most interesting accomplishments in this score is his ability to contrast the lies and superficiality Robert wants to believe with the genuine emotion that lurks beneath the surface in all the characters. This is the difference between Sondheim's creative achievement and that of Furth. Furth has written a clever script, filled with acerbic witticisms, but his characters are essentially one-dimensional. In Sondheim's score, however, the contradiction between what Robert thinks people are and what they really are is explored as the music lifts the audience out of the confines of what Robert thinks he thinks, into his subconscious. Moreover, it is only in song that Robert can finally break the bonds of fear and acknowledge his need for love.

By focusing on the complex evolving musical pattern, Sondheim and Prince could abandon linear causality and explore the inner world of memory, desire, and speculation. Robert's emotional development is traced in music rather than text, for the nondenotative quality of sound conveys more to the audience about the character's unacknowledged feelings than dialogue alone could convey. Robert's emotional progress can be charted as he outgrows the lyric fantasy of "Someone Is Waiting" and accepts his need in "Being Alive." This evolution is suggested not only in the lyric but in the contrasting melodic connotations. Through Sondheim's music the audience learns more about Robert and his company than Robert is aware of himself. Moreover, the recurring "*Company*" theme serves as cement, linking the fragments and emphasizing the predominant concerns of the protagonist. The music unifies the disparate elements and provides a cohesive structure for Furth's episodic script.

The critical response evinced some resistance to the characters in *Company*. John Simon, for example, writes:

> Sondheim . . . could have gone in two directions. He could have opted for expressionism and made the five couples and the three bachelor girls in Robert's life prototypes: figures that symbolize a cross section of our society. Or he could have gone deeper into characterization and discovered the person behind the wisecrack, the being behind the attitude. Instead, he lands on the floor between the two; a very smooth, polished, danceable-on floor, to be sure, but cold and empty.
>
> These semi-anonymous people are not only undeveloped, they are not even truly representative of our society.[19]

Simon, here, is surely too simple. These people are not intended to be fully rounded, naturalistic portrayals. Nor are they simply one-dimensional symbols. They are aspects of Robert's personal world view. There is obviously more to Sarah and Harry's marriage, for example, than bickering over the surreptitious snitching of a brownie or a bourbon and the energetic grappling of living-room karate. But this is all Robert chooses to see. He looks for restrictions and frustrations, and they are not difficult to find. Indeed we learn a great deal about him by observing which aspects of his friends' marriages he understands.

The role of Robert is difficult to play. As Sondheim points out, "In *Company* we were up against one of the oldest dramatic problems in the world: how do you write about a cipher without making him a cipher?"[20] And Anthony Perkins, the actor originally selected to play Robert, observes:

> I think it was inappropriate to have someone starring in that role. The character is there to make the other scenes possible and the show is really a musical with a cast of fourteen—all of whom have equal responsibilities. It's brilliant ensemble playing, but it's not a show that features a performer. For some reason, I was the first person to turn up backstage after the opening night performance, and Dean [Jones] was standing there and he said, "Man, I really tried. I tried to make this part mine but I couldn't." I sympathized with him. He was good in that role, but the person who plays that part is always unappreciated.[21]

Where one can excuse a certain one-dimensionality in the other characters as projections of Robert's mind, the character of Robert demands greater depth and complexity. Although this is not achieved through dialogue, it is unquestionably present in music and lyrics. It is through Sondheim's creative contribution that the character establishes a definite "voice." Robert may be passive and reactive in dialogue, but he is forceful and complex in song. Moreover, it must be emphasized that he is the sum total of all that occurs on stage, since everything is seen through his eyes.

As Harry and Sarah battle for marital supremacy on the rug in front of a bemused Robert, Joanne, the dry cynic, appears high above them and sings her commentary. The technique of using a singer outside of the scene to observe and comment on the action, while not unique to *Company*, is certainly different from the presentational mode of the American musical theater, based as it is on the Rodgers and Hammerstein formula. Sondheim recollects:

> We realized early on that the kind of song that would not work in the show was the Rodgers and Hammerstein kind of song in which the characters reach a certain point and then sing their emotions, because George writes the kind of people who do not sing. To spend time exploring the characters was wrong because they were primarily presented in vignettes, and as soon as you'd try to expand them with song it would be a mistake. All the songs had to be used . . . in a Brechtian way as comment and counterpoint.[22]

In another interview, he elaborates:

> In *Company* the songs are really outside the scenes rather than part of them. You can't guess so well in advance when the dialogue is building to a musical cue. . . . [Rodgers and Hammerstein] took stories that appealed to them, generally sentimental stories, and the very sentimentality of the content dictated the form they chose. But *Company* . . . is not sentimental. It needed a form to suit its cooler, drier attitude.[23]

Most of the numbers in *Company* function as this kind of detached intervention. They interrupt the action. They intrude into the fourth-wall illusion of the vignettes and clarify the focal issues. The songs inform and define Robert's world.

Joanne, sitting far above the action, singing her scathing assessment of marital foibles in "The Little Things You Do Together," epitomizes the style and tone of *Company*. This role, written for and originally played with consummate skill by Elaine Stritch, is the closest the show comes to having a *raisonneur*. She serves both as commentator and narrator. Unlike Robert's other friends, Joanne, a pragmatic realist, has no pretensions or illusions. Much married, she still advocates commitment. Although she is part of the company, her level-headed objectivity permits her to stand outside the action and comment on the folly of her friends—and from time to time of her own. To a jaunty bossa-nova beat, Sondheim, through Joanne, defines the quality of contemporary relationships, the empty mores and rituals of modern marriage. He points out that in an age confronted with the real possibility of nuclear annihilation, the things that give significance and meaning to our lives are the things we can control. It is the petty details, he contends, that fill our lives and provide a sense of order and meaning. Sondheim's frequent use of the term *little* confirms that he sees these apparently trivial details as the most significant clues to the meaning of existence.

In a wry, brief number, Joanne enumerates the "little" things that constitute marital bliss:

> The hobbies you pursue together,
> Savings you accrue together,
> Looks you misconstrue together . . .
> (p. 29)

By rhyming the penultimate word and repeating "together" Sondheim emphasizes the inescapable claustrophobia of marriage. The togetherness is pervasive as the routine rituals of life are played out:

> The concerts you enjoy together,
> Neighbors you annoy together,
> Children you destroy together . . .
> (p. 31)

The tone becomes progressively more ironic as the "perfect" relationships are exposed in a series of satiric verses.

Between each verse the truth of Joanne's commentary is demonstrated in the living room below her, as Harry and Sarah attack each other in a series of violent, aggressive but vastly enjoyable karate confrontations. Robert tries valiantly to separate them, but this results in his being hit in the front by Harry and the rear by Sarah. Obviously Robert is innocent of the delightful dynamics of marriage.

NO ONE IS ALONE?

Joanne is joined by the company and together they sing of the inconsequentialities that make up intimate conversation:

> It's not talk of God and the decade ahead that
> Allow you to get through the worst.
> It's "I do" and "You don't" and "Nobody said that"
> And "Who brought the subject up first?"
> (p. 32)

With a fine ear for the nuances of contemporary vernacular and keen insight into the middle-class psyche, Sondheim suggests the reality of modern relationships in a few carefully selected phrases. Although the notion of "perfect" is used with increasing irony, the positive intimacy of marriage is not demeaned. Joanne is given a series of comic one-line put-downs, but through her cynicism emerges a humorous acknowledgment of the need for relationship. The song ends with the ultimate devalued social gesture, "kiss, kiss." Modern marriages, Sondheim shows, are not the merging of twin souls. Robert's friends do not live happily-ever after lives, but in their "little" games there is affection and fun.

As Sarah steals one last brownie and Harry surreptitiously licks a drop off the bottle top, Robert watches their amorous provocation with bewilderment. It is the intimacy that underlies their conflicts that he subconsciously hungers for, and when Sarah exits he is compelled to ask Harry whether he ever regretted his marriage. In a gentle ballad, Harry tries to explain the contradictory qualities of marriage. The haunting melody, one of the loveliest in the work, refutes the accusations that Sondheim's music is "unhummable."

"Sorry-Grateful" is written with a basic two-line structure in which the positive and negative forces in a relationship are balanced and sustained in a carefully maintained equilibrium:

> You're always sorry
> You're always grateful,
> You're always wondering what might have been.
> Then she walks in.
>
> And still you're sorry,
> And still you're grateful,
> And still you wonder and still you doubt,
> And she goes out.
> (p. 35)

Harry possesses a maturity Robert lacks. He acknowledges that marital partners always have misgivings, and as his wife wanders in and out of his life his ambivalence is dramatized in deft parallelism. The interminable quality of married life is suggested by the repeated use of the words *always* and *still*. The irreconcilable ambiguities of relationships are revealed in enigmatic epigrams:

> Everything's different,
> Nothing's changed,
> Only maybe slightly
> Rearranged.
> (pp. 35-36)

Harry struggles to convey the elusive, relative quality of matrimony, but Robert cannot understand. He wants absolutes. He is seeking the ideal mate who exists only in the world of myth and fairy tale—or in the never-never-land of traditional American musical theater. The refrain, repeated by all the husbands, conveys the independence/dependence contradictions of marriage:

> You always are what you always were,
> Which has nothing to do with,
> All to do with her.
> (p. 36)

As Michael Adams points out, "The use of 'always' not only suggests perpetuity, but also an existence in the present, emphasized as well by the present tense. The impersonal pronoun 'you' permits the lyric a universality that transcends the lives of these characters alone. The song aims at truths that affect all personal relationships that encompass an emotional involvement."[24]

The interaction of isolation and companionship, claustrophobia and agoraphobia, are implied in the antinomies in the verse sung by David, one of the other husbands. Larry, another bemused spouse, adds a further little paradox:

> Good things get better,
> Bad gets worse,
> Wait—I think I meant that in reverse.
> (p. 36)

NO ONE IS ALONE?

The husbands try to convince Robert that there are no absolutes, no answers, that marriage is an acceptance of uncertainty and instability and yet is the only means of penetrating the isolation of the ego. The balance of opposites, the beauty of antitheses, is captured in both lyric and musical structure. As the two distinct individuals who make up a marital couple are counterpoised, so each musical phrase and each lyric idea is held in careful symmetry, thus supporting not only the central theme of the song but the ideological thrust of the overall production.

After a brief interlude in which he admires the apparent sentimental bliss of his friends Peter and Susan only to be told that they have decided to divorce, Robert descends into the children's playroom in Jenny and David's home and introduces his staid friends to the excitement of pot. As Jenny sheds her inhibitions, giggles, shouts, and curses, Robert looks on enviously and sighs, "Jenny, you're terrific. You're the girl I should have married" (p. 44), a rueful grumble that occurs in each of the episodes. Robert fearlessly covets his friends' wives for they are safely unattainable.

Jenny and David badger Robert about his single state, and he indignantly denies avoiding commitment. He boasts that he is surrounded by women and is currently seeing three. As he describes April, Kathy, and Marta, they appear and in close harmony begin to sing "You Could Drive a Person Crazy," a bravura performance. By writing this song in the style of the Andrews Sisters, Sondheim experiments with a technique he utilized for Cora and Boys in *Anyone Can Whistle* and which he will perfect in *Follies*. While the musical style suggests to the audience a period of innocence and naïvete, the lyrics are contemporary and cynical. Thus, style conflicts with content, and this tension serves as a pithy comment on changing societal norms and patterns of behavior.

The women are competing for Robert's attention but are united in their desire to comprehend and overcome his perversity. This unity of purpose is suggested by the tight harmonic structure of the number and their confusion in a complex series of puns and word games. The parody of the old-fashioned "sister number" in which all is sweetness and harmony both asserts and denies those romantic ideals. To emphasize Robert's lack of human warmth, Sondheim patterns the song around permutations of the word *person*. Robert is not given a name in the song. He is merely a "person," undefined by sex or distinct individuality. This "person's personality is personable" (p. 47) but he "impersonates" a person "better than a zombie should" (p. 48). The women too are unsexed and denied individuality, each referring to herself as "a person." Using all the catch words of contemporary vernacular (and inventing a few when it suits him), Sondheim investigates Robert's problem.

In an explosion of syncopated rhythms and rapid patter, Sondheim challenges both actors and audience to keep up with this dynamic number. The song is punctuated with a humorous series of scat sounds, which suggest the frivolous silliness of the earlier style and also function as punctuation and exclamation marks. They provide a maniacal sense of harmony that both disguises and paradoxically highlights the hurt and disillusion lurking beneath the frantic surface, as the women acknowledge that Robert's disinterest and inability to commit himself is tantalizing:

> . . . First you make a person hazy
> So a person could be had.
> Doo-doo doo-doo doo—
> Then you leave a person dangling sadly
> Outside your door,
> Which it only makes a person gladly
> Want you even more.
> (p. 46)

They have no doubt about his sexual identity, however: "I could understand a person / If a person was a fag" (p. 46).

The critics, on the other hand, were not quite so certain. Despite Robert's subsequent bedroom scene, Martin Gottfried, for example, writes in his review that Dean Jones as Robert "can seem sexless and must watch it or the show's theme (and honesty) will be confused by hints of homosexuality," and in his book on the musical theater he complains: "It is such pessimism toward marriage and the hero's inability to love that makes his heterosexuality suspect. Depending on one's sensitivity toward this, a subtle element of homosexuality might be considered a distracting aspect of *Company*."[25]

But there is no suggestion in text or score that Robert is homosexual. The emphasis of the work is to persuade Robert to make a commitment, "to want some*thing*," "to want some*body*," not simply to conform with societal norms. Critics who dwell on Robert's possible homosexuality are clearly uncomfortable with the show's antiromantic, unsentimental depiction of marriage.

In a coda between verses, Kathy, the one girl who leaves New York—and Robert—to marry in Vermont, analyzes his problem. With tongue-twisting virtuosity, she suggests that according to the codes of contemporary courtship, Robert should be playing the marrying game. In a line that echoes the busy signal that insistently recurs throughout the score, the women inquire, "Knock, knock, is anybody there?" (p. 47). They are bewildered, for Robert is not "dead"; he is no "zombie," and is, they reassure him, "good in bed." Yet he remains "elusive" and "exclusive" (p. 48). Before exiting, the women conclude:

> You're a moving, deeply maladjusted,
> Never to be trusted
> Crazy person
> Yourself.
> (p. 48)

The style of the song, music, lyric, and presentation, is highly theatrical. The women are in fact phantoms of Robert's psyche, who appear and disappear. The show is thus composed of fragments of Robert's actual experience and figments of his imagination, with the latter presented in a more stylized, theatrical form.

The female trio serves as a comment. It does not arise directly from the dramatic situation but intrudes and shatters any naturalistic illusion. As Sondheim observed, this technique is Brechtian, but *Company* has none of the obvious didacticism of Brecht. The women clarify Robert's character for the audience, and indirectly make a mordant comment about the unenviable lot of the single woman in contemporary society. They expose Robert's lies, but do not preach. The comic flair, the wit, and the jazz style entertain, but the censure implicit in the lyrics is not neglected.

After the pot scene with Jenny and David resumes as if there had been no interruption, the couple reject the experience, each claiming to have experimented only to please the other. Robert is once more confused by the marital double-talk and game-playing. This pattern, with Robert unable to penetrate the secret codes of a couple's discourse, recurs in each scene. At the end of each encounter, he is left alone, only to be inundated again with overlapping invitations from his concerned companions.

Now, however, the suggested social arrangements are subtly altered. The cozy threesome is no longer advocated, for each couple has an available female to offer the ostensibly willing and eligible Robert. The list of these women, "this girl from the office" (p. 51), "my niece from Ohio" (p. 52), introduces a prurient, envious song, sung with lascivious leers by the husbands. The rhythm of "Have I Got a Girl for You" pants and throbs, and one can almost hear the men salivating over their fantasies. With bawdy insinuation the male chorus makes its offers:

Have I got a girl for you? Wait till you meet her!
Have I got a girl for you, boy? Hoo, boy!
Dumb!—and with a weakness for Sazerac slings—
You give her even the fruit and she swings.
The kind of girl you can't send through the mails—
Call me tomorrow, I want the details.
(p. 52)

All hope to have their middle-aged daydreams satisfied through a vicarious enjoyment of Robert's exploits. Sondheim sustains the pattern of balanced opposites in this number, as the men offer Robert an all-inclusive selection of women. For Larry, the perfect female is "dumb"; for Peter, she is "smart." Their point of agreement is emphasized, however, as these amateur bawds sing in a lusty canon of their offerings and conclude unanimously: "Marriage may be where it's been, but it's not where it's at!" (p. 52).

The rhythmic pattern then modifies as the men bemoan the limitations and frustrations of conjugal bliss. Although their observations are cynical, the relaxed quality of the melody and musical style remove the sting from the words. Indeed, music and lyrics are constantly at odds with each other in this musical whose predominant tone is ironic. The conviction behind the husbands' antimarriage sentiments fades as they repeat less and less strenuously "Whaddaya wanna get married for?" (p. 53) and gradually drift back to their wives.

Robert, alone again, sings dreamily of his perfect woman, an amalgam of all his friends' wives. As he mentions each wife by name, she appears in her apartment embracing her husband. Robert only wants what clearly belongs to another. The rich melody of "Someone Is Waiting," which might seem inappropriate for this score, accurately reflects Robert's longing for the impossible. Robert thinks he wants someone, but he really desires a nonexistent perfection, a synthesis of all the endearing qualities of his friends:

Someone is waiting,
Cool as Sarah,
Easy and loving as Susan—
Jenny. . . .
Someone will hold me,
Soft as Jenny,

Skinny and blue-eyed as Amy—
Susan.
(p. 53)

The repeated soft "s" and "j" sounds emphasize the predominantly romantic tone of the piece. The final lines summarize the contradictory balance of Robert's emotional state, with the antithetical forces of longing and hesitation echoed in the tension between the musical line. The song concludes with Robert left alone in his insular pool of light, a recurrent pattern that theatricalizes Robert's solitary state.

Without any intervening dialogue, the lights come up on Marta, sitting on a park bench, with Robert gingerly perched on its opposite end. The fragmentation of space and time, more fully developed and explored in Sondheim's subsequent works, is an intriguing component of *Company*. Prince's indebtedness to the techniques of Joan Littlewood has been acknowledged, and it is interesting to note how completely he and Sondheim have incorporated her style into the traditional patterns of the Broadway musical. *Company* in fact has been described as a "cubist" musical. This is a useful analogy, for the audience sees Robert from all angles and in all moods. The different perspectives are not haphazardly ordered, but they do not conform with the linear structure of causal space-time relations.

"Another Hundred People," Marta's indictment of Manhattan, is, as Sondheim has pointed out, the only song in the score that doesn't deal directly with marital relationships. It does clarify, however, the parallels between Robert's dogged isolation and the loneliness of the city. To an agitated, rhythmic accompaniment, which evokes the teeming, bustling crowds of New York and suggests the insistence of clicking train wheels, the song begins with a phrase that describes the ever-increasing chaos of the metropolis: "Another hundred people just got off the train" (p. 55). With faceless hordes crowding up through the ground from trains, horizontally from buses, and out of the skies from planes, Sondheim populates his impersonal city with anonymous thousands. The sense of arrival with no destination permeates the song:

Another hundred people just got off the train
And came up through the ground
While another hundred people just got off the bus
And are looking around
At another hundred people who got off of the plane

And are looking at us
Who got off of the train
And the plane and the bus
Maybe yesterday.
(p. 55)

The forbidding insularity of the "city of strangers," the blasted wasteland of urban decay, is revealed in a series of vivid images. Sondheim conveys the ugly decrepitude and incipient violence of the rotting metropolitan center. The streets are "crowded," the parks "guarded," the fountains "rusty," and the trees "dusty with battered barks." In a travesty of the lovers strolling down a shady lane, the strangers of Manhattan "walk together past the postered walls with the crude remarks" (p. 55). Graffiti, the blight on the urban landscape, are pervasive. Yet it is important to note that, just as marriage in *Company* is revealed in all its inadequacy as the only way to survive, so Manhattan is displayed in spite of its harsh ugliness and impersonality as the center of the universe. The disdain that the inhabitants of this isle feel for anywhere other than New York is constantly reiterated.

When Sondheim turns to describing the pathos of loneliness, the scene becomes bleaker. The attitude is not unlike T. S. Eliot's preoccupation with the meaningless gestures of a bourgeois society that has no roots, no convictions, no goals. Eliot's trite conversations and lack of communication between people who do not know each other (or themselves) are evident in Sondheim's lyric:

And they meet at parties through the friends of friends who they never know,
Will you pick me up or do I meet you there or shall we let it go?
Did you get my message? 'Cause I looked in vain.
Can we see each other Tuesday if it doesn't rain?
Look, I'll call you in the morning or my service will explain.
(p. 59)

"Another Hundred People" is performed in three segments, and between each Robert conducts a cursory conversation with one of his three girlfriends. Each of these encounters illustrates the truth of the song, for it shows Robert's inability to understand the needs of these women. April dismisses herself as "dumb" and "boring" and is reduced to muttering "I don't have anything more to say" (p. 57). Kathy, the most mature of Robert's friends, has decided to leave New York and get married. The distinction between her acceptance of reality and his romantic yearnings is encapsulated in their parting exchange:

> *Kathy*
>
> . . . I'm getting married.
>
> *Robert*
>
> What?
>
> *Kathy*
>
> Some people still get married, you know.
>
> *Robert*
>
> Do you love him?
>
> *Kathy*
>
> I'll be a good wife. I just don't want to run around this city any more like I'm having a life. As I said before, some people have to know when to come to New York and some people have to know when to leave. (p. 58)

Marta's scene is one of the most humorous in the play. Her enthusiasm and naïvete, which she attempts to disguise beneath a veneer of phony sophistication, contrast with Robert's controlled nonchalance:

> *Marta*
>
> . . . You know what this city is? Where a person can feel it? It's in a person's ass. If you're really part of this city, relaxed, cool, and in the whole flow of it, your ass is like this. *(She makes a large round circle with her forefinger and thumb)* If you're just living here, running around uptight, not really part of this city, your ass is like this. *(She tightens the circle to nothing)*
>
> *Robert*
>
> I ... hesitate to ask. *(She holds up the "tight" sign high)* ... (p. 61)

The audience is jolted from this crude but accurate description of Robert's psyche by the pious strains of devotional music. A young woman in a white choir robe appears on an upper level, while Amy, the bride-to-be, nervously polishes a pair of men's black shoes. In a soaring soprano that exaggerates each sentimental excess, the choir woman sings:

> Bless this day, pinnacle of life,
> Husband joined to wife,

The heart leaps up to behold
This golden day.
(p. 62)

Paul, the prospective groom, hurries onto the stage frantically searching for his shoes. On seeing the apparently cozy scene of domesticity, he sings adoringly to her.

The lyrics Paul sings are overburdened with clichés of marital bliss and fidelity, and his florid baritone re-creates the mood of sentimental operetta, but this fairy-tale quality is immediately shattered as a paranoid Amy bursts into an explosive, panicked denial. With wit, speed, and a dazzling series of breath-defying run-on lines, "Getting Married Today" delineates Amy's terrified rejection, as looking at the audience she sings:

Pardon me, is everybody there? Because if everybody's
There I want to thank you all for coming to the wedding. I'd ap-
Preciate your going even more, I mean, you must have lots of
Better things to do. And not a word of it to Paul. Remember
Paul? You know, the man I'm gonna marry, but I'm not because I
Wouldn't ruin anyone as wonderful as he is . . .
(p. 63)

Although she is detached from the chaos in the kitchen below, the young woman in the robe, accompanied by the other members of the company, now also dressed in robes, reflects Amy's rapidly deteriorating state of mind as she sings solemnly:

Bless this day, tragedy of life,
Husband joined to wife.
The heart sinks down and feels dead
This dreadful day.
(p. 63)

Sondheim contrasts this stanza with the opening, matching "tragedy of life" with "pinnacle of life"; "sinks down" with "leaps up"; and "dreadful day" with "golden day" (p. 63). The deadpan delivery of this prognostication of gloom is sung with the same sweetness and to the same inspiring melody as the earlier paean of joy. Moreover, the measured solemnity of the liturgical sounds clash with the frantic pace of Amy's pleas.

Amy's terror becomes progressively more intense as she continues her implacable protest. In a neat antithesis to all the socializing sentiments expressed by the other members of the company in trying to woo Robert, Amy's song is filled with denial and rejection. Repeating "I'm not getting married" an emphatic sixteen times, she tries to rid herself of the claustrophobic peer-group pressure of the rest of the married company. Structured, rhymed verses alternate with unrhymed semihysterical portions as Amy's struggle for sanity is dramatized. The rapid delivery reminiscent of Gilbert and Sullivan, the witty rhymes and humor, the manic energy, do not obscure the undertone of anguish. Sondheim here manages to fuse the comic style with a subtextual quality of real pain. Then, in a synthesis of harmonizing and conflicting voices, Paul and Amy sing together. While Paul blissfully sings his heartfelt declaration of love, and the choir intones "Amen," Amy makes one last frenzied attempt to cancel the dreaded event.

The scene that follows is probably the most effectively written in the work. A petrified Amy almost succeeds in convincing Paul that she doesn't love him enough to marry him. Robert, trying to fathom the intense undercurrents, offers to marry Amy instead. As the company enticingly croons "Bobby, baby," Amy realizes: "I'm afraid to get married, and you're afraid not to. . . . It's just that you have to want to marry *some*body, not just some*body*" (p. 73). She rushes out into the rain after her husband-to-be. The kitchen slides away. Robert finds himself in his apartment surrounded by his birthday guests as Amy enters with the birthday cake, and the curtain falls.

Act 2 opens with Robert once more about to blow out the candles on his ubiquitous cake. Following their usual teasing preoccupation with Robert's lack of desire and the need to have him married, the company mouths platitudinous concern and exits, leaving Robert alone. To a relaxed swing rhythm he sings:

> Isn't it warm,
> Isn't it rosy,
> Side by side ...
> ... By side?
> (p. 79)

By modifying the traditional pattern, Sondheim dramatizes Robert's social and emotional position: Robert is the unexpected addition, the third "by side."

As Robert sings this song of camaraderie, the company peers down from its living spaces and makes fond but condescending remarks. Robert climbs upstairs and wanders through their rooms, but they ignore him, distance him, and behave as if he were still center stage. The emptiness of his life is emphasized repeatedly as he sings lines like "One is lonely and two is boring, / Think what you can keep ignoring" (p. 81). The structure of the song is based on the vaudeville routine, a series of two-liners, with the sung portions constantly being interrupted by spoken observation. Many of the contradictions of Robert's condition are emphasized in these interpolations: "A person like Bob doesn't have the good things and he doesn't have the bad things. But he doesn't have the good things" (p. 82). Again and again, Sondheim characterizes Robert's life: "One's impossible, two is dreary, / Three is company, safe and cheery" (p. 82).

Suddenly there is a complete change in mood and tone as the couples burst onto the stage. The relaxed rhythm of "Side by Side" is replaced by a boisterous comic vamp. The couples don straw hats and with plastic canes thump out their friendship. The chorus-line presentational form, however, makes a travesty of what it ostensibly presents. The glib bonhomie, the extroverted friendship, are revealed to be a protective mask for the loneliness of Robert's existence.

The insularity of Robert's life was dramatized in the original production by Michael Bennett's choreography for, as the couples separate into a tap routine, with each husband and wife tapping out an exchange to each other, it is clear that there is no one to tap back to Robert. This portion of the number "What Would We Do Without You?" was composed at Bennett's request. As he explained:

> I remember when Steve first played me "Side by Side by Side," and I told him that it was a good start but I had an idea for something which utilized the partners. . . . I told him to give me something that I could do in many different styles and that I could do over and over and over so that it becomes grating. . . . I'm not saying that these married couples aren't sincere about caring for Bobby in the show, but you need more than friendships or it becomes the old song and dance routine.[26]

The use of hats and canes, the short tap routines, the tug-of-war, all of which Bennett introduced into his choreography, highlight Sondheim's musical invention. Functioning as Brechtian comment in a similar way to "You Could Drive a Person Crazy" and many of the numbers in *Follies*, the number's musical style is clearly distanced from the period of the piece and the social mores of the contemporary characters. The serious subtext that underlies the frivolity conflicts with the exuberant vaudeville atmosphere. Robert and company are not singing out the "truth" of their relationships, but rather Sondheim and Bennett are theatricalizing and satirizing the fun-loving attitude these people find it necessary to assume. This chic, witty group can lie in dialogue to each other, themselves, and the audience, but in the musical form the intrinsic truth is laid bare. The number reveals that Robert and company share a life of fun and games. When the social mask is discarded, however, when the hats are doffed and the canes thrown down, Robert is expendable. Robert is a useful addition, but he can never be a part of the basic twosome of the married relationship.

The comic vamp builds to a climax in a series of rhetorical questions:

Who changes subjects on cue?
Who cheers us up when we're blue?
Who is a flirt but never a threat,
Reminds us of our birthdays, which we always forget?
How would we ever get through?
What would we do without you?
(p. 84)

Robert's unavoidable and inevitable answer is: "Just what you usually do!" (p. 84). He subconsciously knows he is redundant.

In his apartment, Robert expertly leads a timid but willing April, dressed in her stewardess's uniform, toward the bedroom. As the couple begins to "touch, embrace and then kiss, all in very slow motion" (p. 87), Robert's friends appear in their apartments and, in a piece of stage irony, the wives sing a mournful dirge, expressing their concern for the loneliness of Robert's life. The title, "Poor Baby," indicates the attitude that these woman adopt; Robert is their extra child, requiring all their maternal affection.

As Robert and April continue their elaborate mating ritual, rapidly disrobing and falling into bed, the married women, like harpies, hover above them. Their voices insistently call out for Robert's attention, and their need for Robert is revealed. They are reluctant to give up their unthreatening, always available, admirer. Their sabotage of Robert's admittedly tentative gestures toward marriage emerges. Initially declaring their desire for his happiness, they eventually explode into a paroxysm of criticism and condemnation:

Amy and Joanne

You know, no one

Wants you to be happy
More than I do. No one, but ...

All

Isn't she a little bit, well ...

Sarah

Dumb? Where is she from?

Amy

Tacky? Neurotic? She seems so dead.

Susan

Vulgar? Aggressive? Peculiar?

Jenny

Old? And cheap and

Joanne

Tall? She's tall enough to be your mother.
(pp. 93–94)

The comedic possibilities in staging terms alone are infinite, but Sondheim emphasizes that the real comedy of the scene depends on the comments being accurate reflections of character:

> In *Company*, the funniest lyric line isn't even rhymed, it is just shoved in there during the scene where Bobby is in bed with the stewardess. All the wives are singing "Poor Baby," knocking the girl he's in bed with, and Elaine Stritch comments, "She's tall enough to be your mother." It doesn't rhyme, it's not rhythmically like anything else, but it is again a character observation and that's what makes it funny; it consistently gets a laugh.[27]

Finding humor in personality and situation, Sondheim does not depend on dazzling his audience with his own wit and brilliance at the expense of character. His attitude is summed up in the aphorism "Humor is about character, not cleverness."[28]

The women's dirge ends on a sanctimonious note as they try to reassure themselves that they are the only source of tenderness in the lonely bachelor's life. Oblivious, Robert and April bounce about in the bed below as a dance sequence dramatizes the passion—or lack of it—in Robert's bed. From *Lady in the Dark* through *Oklahoma!* the American musical has used the nonliteral language of dance to explore sex and love. Kathy's solo in *Company* is the only real dance sequence in the show and functions in much the same way as the other overt theatrical devices, as a stylized exemplification and comment, in this case a comment meant to distinguish between mechanical sex and a more profound sensual commitment. As Furth writes in the stage directions, "Kathy's dance expresses the difference between having sex and making love" (p. 94).

The dance accompaniment, based on "Someone Is Waiting" set in various arrangements, fades in and out as Robert's and April's voices are heard over the orchestra. This dialogue, rather than Kathy's dance, reveals Robert's inability to love and contrasts that inability with the relationships of his friends. Robert enjoys sex, but cannot remember his bed companion's name. As the number draws to a close, April, accompanied by sentimental strings, mutters, "I love you." Robert, to the harsh twang of a guitar, can only stutter, "I... I..." as the music swells into the theme tune and the voices of the couples above Robert's head sing out their love for each other. Sarah loves Harry, and Harry loves Sarah. Jenny loves David, and David loves Jenny. The entire company chants "I love you, I love you, I love you" (p. 96), but Robert cannot join them. The couples love each other in a way that Robert cannot understand or share.

The rhythmic tick present throughout Kathy's dance sequence—with music appropriately titled "Tick-Tock"—provides a subtle lead into the next number for, as Kathy exits, the lights come up on a weary April and Robert and a shrilly ringing alarm clock. April's reluctant departure and Robert's sleepy attempts to detain her are conveyed in one of Sondheim's funniest songs. With a minimum of words but with a series of inanities, banalities, pauses, and grunts, Sondheim conveys the conflicting desires and intentions of the bed partners. In a seesaw lyric, the bleary-eyed, weary host goes through the motions of detaining his polite guest. He advances; she retreats. She advances; he collapses. The humor lies both in the accuracy of Sondheim's ear for dialogue and the incongruity of April's very literal answers:

Robert
Where you going?
April
Barcelona.
Robert
... Oh ...
(pp. 96–97)

Robert finally awakens sufficiently to sing with rather overzealous ardor:

> Look,
> You're a very special girl,
> Not just overnight.
> No, you're a very special girl,
> And not because you're bright—
> Not *just* because you're bright.
> *(Yawning)*
> You're just a very special girl,
> June!
>
> (p. 98)

Robert repeats his lines because he is drowsily groping to remember her name. He finally sings out in triumph, "June," but he has chosen the incorrect month and she gently corrects him. After an embarrassed pause, he dutifully asks, "Whatcha thinking?" Again April's ingenuous reply, "Barcelona" (p. 99), is both honest and funny. With almost Pinteresque economy, Sondheim extends Robert's halfhearted attempts to keep her in his bed and her reluctant commitment to duty. The lyric has the spare, natural simplicity of dialogue but is compact and rich, for the innocuous small talk is laden with unspoken emotions. In the final lines of the song, April capitulates. As she snuggles back into his arms, Robert concludes the number with a dismayed "Oh, God!" The validity of the three women's assessment of Robert as selfish, exploitative, and charming, in "You Could Drive a Person Crazy," is confirmed.

Following a brief, amusing scene in which Marta and Robert exchange pleasantries with a blissfully happy, now-divorced Susan and Peter, the stage is transformed into a lively nightclub. Joanne and Robert sit at a table getting progressively more drunk while her husband performs on the dance floor. Joanne, indelibly characterized by the dry, laconic delivery of Elaine Stritch, is a bitchy stereotype. The epitome of what an audience expects from the wealthy, spoiled, sophisticated New Yorker, she protests that she could not survive outside of Manhattan, a fact that precipitated her first divorce. With her cynicism, wit, and mature perspicacity she in many ways typifies the Sondheim generation. As she observes: "Do you know that we are suddenly at an age where we find ourselves too young for the old people and too old for the young ones? We're nowhere. I think we better drink to us. To us—the generation gap. WE ARE THE GENERATION GAP!" (p. 105).

NO ONE IS ALONE?

Aggressive, loud, and irresistible, Joanne smokes and drinks too much and in a devastating attack assaults the stereotype she has become. "The Ladies Who Lunch" doesn't reveal much about Robert, but it does lay bare the wasted lives of married middle-class matrons and serves to shatter any illusions he may still cling to. In a rigidly tight structure, which controls and heightens the fury of the character, Joanne spits out her contempt for herself and her class:

> Here's to the ladies who lunch—
> Everybody laugh.
> Lounging in their caftans and planning a brunch
> On their own behalf.
> Off to the gym,
> Then to a fitting,
> Claiming they're fat,
> And looking grim
> 'Cause they've been sitting
> Choosing a hat—
> Does anyone still wear a hat?
> I'll drink to that.
> (p. 106)

From the soft "l" sounds which suggest the loose-tongued effects of her liquid diet, to the additional inner rhymes ("laugh" / "caftans" / "behalf" [p. 106]), Sondheim builds a biting portrait of self-loathing. With each sardonic description of her friends, Joanne exposes a facet of her own empty existence.

The decadence of a life filled with indulgence, the affectation of the dilettante, and the loneliness of domesticity are ruthlessly catalogued. Each lifestyle has its defining characteristic. The "ladies who lunch" are obsessed with appearance. The "girls who stay smart" (Joanne reveals her contempt by denying them adult status) know what is culturally fashionable, but are bored by the complexity of modern art. They pursue art appreciation in order to avoid the emptiness of their existence. Joanne sings:

> Here's to the girls who stay smart—
> Aren't they a gas?
> Rushing to their classes in optical art,
> Wishing it would pass.
> (p. 106)

The viciously accurate dismissal of the "girls who play wife" is Sondheim's finest stanza. With a terseness emphasized by the internal rhymes, he evokes the sadness of a life lived at one remove, of culture and experience both frantically gleaned from the pages of a magazine:

> Here's to the girls who play wife—
> Aren't they too much?
> Keeping house but clutching a copy of *Life*
> Just to keep in touch.
> (p. 106)

As Joanne's description becomes self-revelation her bitterness intensifies. She and the "girls who just watch" are described as the living dead. Anesthetized from feeling anything at all by the effects of alcohol, somehow they survive. The optimism of "Another Hundred People" becomes a numbing excess as the same word, *another*, is repeated in this song:

> Another chance to disapprove,
> Another brilliant zinger,
> Another reason not to move,
> Another vodka stinger. . . .
> (p. 107)

Joanne concludes with:

> A toast to that invincible bunch—
> The dinosaurs surviving the crunch—
> Let's hear it for the ladies who lunch—
> Everybody rise! Rise!
> Rise! Rise! Rise! Rise! Rise! Rise!
> (p. 107)

The final, harshly repeated "Rise" celebrates the toast that Joanne is proposing and, echoing Eliot's *Waste Land*, suggests a multitude of nameless, faceless, chic zombies rising to consume society.

Michael Adams suggests that Joanne's strident condemnation of herself and her society is the spur that prods Robert into disentangling himself from the clutches of his friends. Adams argues that "The Ladies Who Lunch"

> is a damning indictment of their wasted lives, but even more so of Joanne's. . . . [H]er evaluation of her peers, which in its own way is self analysis, is bitter to the point of cruelty. However accurate her insults, she is merciless; Sondheim has created a character of bitter insight, but sadly unhappy. She represents the quintessence of his friends' flaws and the

> primary reason he must free himself from them. Its placement late in the second act acts as a summation of much that has preceded it—the jaded, jaundiced viewpoint, the vicious superiority, the emptiness of metropolitan chic.[29]

But if Joanne is cruel, she is also perceptive. Like all of the marriages portrayed, Joanne's is far from perfect, yet it is more rewarding and rich than Robert's life of cool detachment. She is a realist. She disabuses Robert of his romantic longings and propels him into the painful but fulfilling life of human involvement. Robert need not totally spurn his friends in order to find someone to love, but he must break his dependence on the safety of the threesome. Joanne's taunting words wake him from the dream of self-satisfied remoteness:

> *Robert*
>
> I never smoked.
>
> *Joanne*
>
> Why?
>
> *Robert*
>
> I don't know. I meant to. Does that count?
>
> *Joanne*
>
> Meant to! Meant to! Story of your life. Meant to! Jesus, you are lifted right out of a Krafft-Ebbing case history. You were always outside looking in the window while everybody was inside dancing at the party. (p. 108)

And later:

> *Joanne*
>
> Don't ever get married, Robby. Never. Why should you?
>
> *Robert*
>
> For company. I don't know. Like everybody else.
>
> *Joanne*
>
> Who else?
>
> *Robert*
>
> Everybody that ever fell in love and got married.

Joanne

I know both couples and they're both divorced. (p. 109)

It is fitting that hard-boiled, perceptive Joanne is the one who finally cracks Robert's carapace of control. With conscious vulgarity she propositions him:

Joanne

(Slowly, directly, sultrily, quietly and evenly) There's my place. It's free tomorrow at two. Larry goes to his gym then. Don't talk. Don't do your folksy Harold Teen with me. You're a terribly attractive man. The kind of man most women want and never seem to get. I'll—take care of you.

Robert

(A pause. He's been looking down; he looks up) But who will I take care of?

Joanne

(A big smile) Well, did you hear yourself? Did you hear what you just said, kiddo? (p. 110)

Robert's final realization that as an adult he doesn't need to be taken care of, but needs to care, is expected by the audience, if not entirely convincing. As the insistent calls from his friends bombard him again, Robert is still struggling with the inevitable. But ultimately, however uncomfortable marriage may be, he recognizes the necessity for some kind of commitment.

There was some friction between Sondheim and Prince over this unambiguously positive conclusion. Initially it was decided that Amy would not marry at the end of act 1 and Robert would propose to Amy in a song entitled "Marry Me a Little." Robert wants a limited commitment, an uneasy balance between intimacy and privacy:

We won't have to give up a thing,
We'll stay who we are,
Right?

It was felt, however, that this was too "knowing" a number and the audience might not comprehend that Robert is deceiving himself.

By the time *Company* opened in Boston, Robert was not to marry or love Amy, and a second concluding song was written. But Prince and Sondheim disagreed about its effectiveness. "Happily Ever After" was, Sondheim acknowledges, a "scream of pain":

> Someone to need you too much,
> Someone to read you too well,
> Someone to bleed you of all
> The things you don't want to tell—
> That's happily ever after.
> Ever, ever, ever after—
> In hell.[30]

Prince, supported by adverse audience reaction, insisted that the number was too "negative." Sondheim consequently wrote a third song, but he and Prince still disagree about its effectiveness:

> Sondheim: In Boston I wrote "Being Alive" and although I love the song I feel that the ending of the show was a cop-out. When Bobby suddenly realizes that he shouldn't be alone at the end of the scene, it's too small a moment and you don't believe it.
>
> Prince: I don't agree. The last ten minutes are not a cop-out. They're just not as skillfully done as the rest of the show. We worked hard but we never got it quite right. The marriages in the show are not bad marriages—they're just marriages that are holding together because people either live little lies or look the other way. It's called human. What happens to Robert in the end is what we wanted to have happen to him. We didn't ease into it properly and that's what's wrong with the show. . . . [T]here'll always be something.[31]

Although Robert's growing acceptance of his need for someone to love may appear a trifle facile, there is sufficient ambivalence in Sondheim's lyrics for "Being Alive" to maintain the character's consistency at least to some degree. Beginning with an impersonal "someone" (recalling the someone of "Someone Is Waiting") Robert reviews all the negative restrictions of the married state:

> Stop! What do you get?
>
> Someone to hold you too close,
> Someone to hurt you too deep,
> Someone to sit in your chair,
> To ruin your sleep ...
>
> (pp. 113–14)

With the shouted encouragement of his friends, he gradually moves closer to acknowledging his need. These prose interruptions reveal his friends' insights into the compromise that is marriage as they encourage Robert to abandon his unrealistic ideals and embrace imperfect reality; Peter, for example, counsels, "Hey, buddy, don't be afraid it won't be perfect. . . . The only thing to be afraid of really is that it won't *be*!" (p. 114). The recurring demand at the birthday party, that Robert accept dependence and grow up, is reinforced when Amy commands, "Blow out the candles, Robert, and make a wish. *Want* something! Want *something*! (p. 115).

Finally Robert breaks free of his inhibitions and overprotective friends. The impersonal "someone" and "you" become the particularized "somebody" and "me" as he accepts his need and sings out for somebody to help fulfill his life. He can now accept the restrictions, for he has learned "alone is alone, not alive" (p. 116). His decision is never easy, and right to the end Sondheim shows his internal struggles:

> Somebody crowd me with love,
> Somebody force me to care,
> Somebody let me come through.
> I'll always be there, as frightened as you,
> To help us survive
> Being alive, being alive, being alive.
> (p. 116)

The verbs Sondheim chooses are vigorous ("crowd" and "force"), for Robert cannot slide easily into love. He will have to be coerced. Frightened, he can now acknowledge that fear and still act.

Sondheim makes a minor word change from first to final chorus. The "who'll always be there" becomes "I'll always be there" as Robert recognizes his own vulnerability but is prepared to risk involvement. In this final stanza Robert uses the word *love* for the first time without any ironic connotation. He no longer needs the glib, fashionable gestures of the smart set but is prepared for the painful commitment to one individual.

In a brief coda, the company is once again in Robert's apartment awaiting his arrival for his "surprise" birthday. As they anxiously wonder why he has not come, a silent Robert stands center stage. He is aware of their concern but has finally broken free.

Company was enthusiastically received by the majority of New York critics.

NO ONE IS ALONE?

The show was described as: "simply in a league by itself," "the best musical of the year," "the season's best and most refreshingly original musical," "a sensationally attractive show."[32] Even the acerbic John Lahr admits: "Of all Sondheim's shows, *Company* is the most substantial. The limitations in Sondheim's music—its cold technique, its nervousness about emotion, its stylish defensiveness—match the brittle world *Company* describes."[33]

But there were several powerful critics who demurred. Clive Barnes was "antagonized by the slickness, the obviousness of *Company*," and Walter Kerr, in an extended piece for the *New York Sunday Times*, after complimenting Sondheim, Prince, Bennett, Aronson, and many of the actors, expresses serious reservations:

> Now ask me if I liked the show. I didn't like the show. I admired it, or admired vast portions of it, but that is another matter. Admiration stirs in the head; liking sends out its signals somewhere lower in the anatomy, the pit of the stomach maybe, and gradually lets you know that you are happy to have been born, or to have been lucky enough to have come tonight. I left *Company* feeling rather cool and queasy, whatever splendors my head may have been reminding me of, and there is the plain reason for that. At root, I didn't take to Mr. Jones's married friends any more than he did. I agreed with him.[34]

Why did *Company* antagonize not only some of the critics but many of its audience members? Sondheim maintains that the main reason for the antipathy was the lack of plot. As I mentioned in chapter 1, *Company* consciously opposed many of the traditions and conventions of the Broadway musical. Complex and challenging, it did not offer the escapist entertainment expected of the genre. Its characters were not romantic stereotypes but were uncomfortably close to the audience in both class and type. Jack Kroll, in describing the dramatis personae of *Company*, could with equal accuracy have been characterizing many of the individuals on the other side of the footlights:

> The despised, the disinherited class of our time, as far as the arts go, is that great swarm of Impossibles perched in our metropolises at high-rise level, those center-vented upper-middles who earn five figures but whose souls yaw along on some spiritual skid row. Increasingly the glamorous filthiness of the big cities belongs to them—to them and to the grimly milling under-class who peer balefully at them from across a terrain of dog droppings, police badges and inertia.[35]

Audiences presumably went to the musical expecting to be soothed and stroked; *Company* jolted, discomforted, and disturbed. Audiences were far from sure that they wanted to pay for this kind of assault, as Sondheim acknowledges: "We wanted to achieve a lot of surprise in *Company*. We wanted a show where the audience would sit for two hours screaming their heads off with laughter and then go home and not be able to sleep."[36] He and his collaborators had not compromised or condescended, creating instead a vital and unsettling evening of theater within a form that had traditionally striven for frivolity.

"THROUGH THE UNKNOWN, REMEMBERED GATE": *Follies*

Follies is about time and memory, illusion and reality, dreams and desires, fantasy and truth, theater and life—themes explored through one all-encompassing metaphor: the American musical theater. Steeped in all the traditions of the genre, *Follies* is *of* the musical theater and *about* the musical theater; yet it transcends the musical theater. Larger than life, it synthesizes the dreams of its audience, the illusions of its actors, the distorted memory of a youthful America of the past, and a harsh perception of the contemporary disillusion. As Martin Gottfried puts it: "The concept behind *Follies* is theater nostalgia, representing the rose colored glasses through which we face the fact of age. In exploring this idea—the fancied past and the painful reality—Harold Prince and Stephen Sondheim have carried the musical theater into size, into grandeur. *Follies* is awesome, it looms out of the Winter Garden's shadows like a giant ghost ship." *Follies*, Gottfried goes on to state in a different review, is "about age and an age, the glory of the past and the follies in letting nostalgia make the past seem more glorious (memory's compromise with reality), the truth of growing old and the acceptance of that truth."[1]

Follies, initially titled *The Girls Upstairs*, "deals with the loss of innocence in the United States, using the Ziegfeld *Follies* (a pretty girl is *no longer* like a melody) as its metaphor."[2] Directed by Harold Prince and Michael Bennett, this work, by Sondheim and playwright James Goldman, opened on Broadway on 4 April 1971.

Follies: the title alone suggests a series of meanings. The most obvious connotation is that of Ziegfeld, the glamorous world of the 1920s: gorgeous girls, splendid sets and costumes, fun, laughs, and frivolity. The Ziegfeld world is present in *Follies*, but the showgirls are huge black and white ghosts stalking about the stage, contrasting cruelly with their living contemporary selves. *Follies* also suggests foolishness; the foolishness of clinging to the past. The selective memory of nostalgia, which recalls only the good, never the real, is a central theme of the work. "I remember everything," claims Sondheim in an interview taped for the theater collection at Lincoln Center, adding with an ironic shrug, "falsely . . . which is what *Follies* is all about."[3] Finally, as Hal Prince points out, *folie* is the French word for madness, and the drama traces a Walpurgisnacht of mad confrontations in which cosy illusions are peeled away and the harsh reality of life without self-deception is revealed.

In all his work Sondheim manifests a fascination with structural patterns and their implications. Unlike a Lévi-Strauss or a Noam Chomsky, though, his aim is not to penetrate to the deepest organizational principles of the human mind, but rather to examine, employ, and exploit the connotative values of the structures underlying the American musical theater and to reveal their relationships to predominant social attitudes and presuppositions. Realizing that each age has its own particular style, its own unique structures that reflect its beliefs, truths, and assumptions, Sondheim uses these patterns both to suggest and to comment upon different social and aesthetic milieux. No style is "innocent," for a choice of a style is a choice of a particular reality and system of values. This interest in style and structure finds its ultimate expression in *Follies*.

In both the music and lyrics of *Follies*, Sondheim lays bare the contrasting and conflicting Weltanschauung of American society from the end of World War I to the present. These divergent mindsets are suggested through the interconnection and reflexive juxtaposition of different musical and lyric styles. The structural principles exposed and utilized in *Follies* are: (1) theatrical presentation now and then (the Ziegfeld era); (2) audience expectation now and then; (3) social (in contrast with theatrical) mores now and then; and (4) musical meaning, form, and connotation now and then. The intention of the work is to present in a surrealist-expressionist mode the confrontation of past and present. Reality and memory are so interwoven and deliberately ambiguous that absolute truth and judgment are emphatically repudiated.

The work is a voyage into the collective unconscious of America's theatrical imagination. Nostalgia is not merely the mood, it is the subject matter. The show is never "camp," however. It does not scoff at the past, nor does it glamorize it. Jack Kroll of *Newsweek* predicted that many people, both critics and public, would misinterpret *Follies*, seeing it as another example of nostalgic foolishness. But, he pointed out, it is in its many-leveled uses of theatricality as a profession, a state of mind, and a cultural milieu that *Follies* reveals a more profound truth about the American psyche.[4]

The insidious effect of basing one's life and choices on an illusory past is something both characters and audience experience through *Follies*. Memory suppresses the ugliness, the cruelty, and the boredom, for "nostalgia selects only what is agreeable, and even that it distorts or turns into myth. . . . The past is an illusion just as much as the future; it is utopia in reverse."[5] Utopianism, whether it looks backward or forward, robs the present of its impact and significance.

Some critics of the original Broadway production, refusing to recognize the play's critical intentions, did indeed judge *Follies* merely as a frivolous example of nostalgic excess, while others chastised it for being a self-absorbed indulgence for wealthy dilettantes,[6] an orgy of nostalgia,[7] and a callous betrayal of the precepts of musical comedy. But the carping of influential critics like Walter Kerr, who dogmatically claims that all musicals must be "mindless," infuriated Sondheim: "To live in the past is foolish. That's what's so annoying about Walter Kerr—he's living in the past and because he's in the position of power he can push it. *Follies* is about Walter Kerr. But dreams do tarnish and you can't live in the past forever, and that's why he dislikes it."[8] Hal Prince was equally indignant: "*Follies* isn't about will the guy get the girl? or will the boat arrive in the harbor in time? It's about this country, marriage, affluence, the loss of spiritual standards."[9]

The unshakable belief that musicals must possess an ultimately optimistic tone and reassuring theme lies, however, at the heart of even the most intelligent criticism. John Lahr argues that our loss of faith in the American Dream has left the musical with "nothing to sing about." He admires *Follies* but condemns it. Offended by the comparison of past ideals with the actuality of the aging performers, he contends:

> This crude juxtaposition trades on nostalgia to make a point about it, and them. But *Follies*' appetite for carrion is at once breathtaking and sinister. . . . In making death the subject of story and song, *Follies* also makes it spectacular. The audience is asked not only to watch decay, but to *love* it. . . . *Follies*' disenchantment isn't convincing because it hungers

> for traditional success. . . . The show's numbers take their energy not from what they ironically reveal about their characters but from their vision of the old mythic forms dusted off and lovingly put before an audience.[10]

Lahr seems doggedly determined never to relinquish his preconceptions. The dramatic action of *Follies* is centered on the gradual acceptance of life not death. The existence the characters must grow to love is not an escapist fantasy but the complex truths of modern society. The audience is not asked to "love decay" but maturely to accept the reality of age.

From its eerie opening sequence, *Follies* leads its audience into a world contrary to expectation. There is no rollicking overture. To the sound of soft tympani, "like thunder from a long time ago," the lights dim to an old asbestos fire curtain. After the curtain slowly rises, lights flash here and there, exposing the shell of an old theater surrounded by darkness. A tall, slim showgirl wearing a black and white dress comes to life and begins to move slowly to "soft, slow romantic, strange" music. After she is joined by a second showgirl, a majordomo followed by a line of waiters and waitresses strides past them. Finally a group of six ghostly chorus girls enters, each dressed in black and white, all dancing in slow motion as they silently open and close their mouths.[11]

The stage itself is a mysterious cavern. Fragments of the ornate past are suggested in the tarnished remains of old sets and the broken proscenium arch. Early audiences expecting the glamorous excitement of a Broadway musical, whose title has evoked memories of the glorious days of Ziegfeld, must have been bewildered. But in this gap, between the remembered glamor and the empty vast blackness of the present, *Follies* reveals its focus and its meaning.

Hal Prince recalls telling designer Boris Aronson that he wanted to create a mood of ambiguity in which anything was possible, nothing was absolute:

> It was to be surrealistic, inspired by [Fellini's film] *8½*, and rubble became the key word. Metaphoric rubble became visual rubble. A theater is being torn down. On its stage a party in celebration of that. The celebrants for whom the theater represents youth, dreams lost, a golden time, are to be orphaned. . . . Is the theater torn down? Will it be torn down tomorrow? Or was it torn down yesterday? Keep it ambiguous, a setting for the sort of introspection that reunions precipitate, a mood in which to lose sight of the present, to look back on the past.[12]

"THROUGH THE UNKNOWN, REMEMBERED GATE"

For Prince, the image of the piece is best conveyed by a photograph of Gloria Swanson taken in 1960, posing with her arms triumphantly uplifted amidst the rubble of the partially demolished Roxy Theater, a house that had opened in the late twenties with *The Loves of Sunya*, starring Swanson.

That *Follies* is a play about such aging yet ageless grandeur among the ruins is also clear to Sondheim:

> The reason that Jim [Goldman] chose that place for the reunion was that the *Follies* was a state of mind which represented America between the two world wars; up until 1945, America was the good guy and everything was hopeful and idealistic. Now the country is a riot of national guilt. The dream has collapsed. Everything has turned to rubble and that's what *Follies* is about—the collapse of the dream. How all your hopes tarnish, but if you live in despair you might as well pack up.[13]

Sondheim juxtaposes the complacency and optimism of a remembered past with the tired cynicism of the present by contrasting the connotative value of varying musical and lyric styles and modes of presentation. Through *Follies* Sondheim acknowledges the appeal of the frivolity, naïvete, and excitement of an age gone forever, but his work is never simply a wistful tribute. It compels both characters and audience to see the stultifying effects of living in the past and leads Americans on both sides of the footlights towards a new awareness, a new beginning, a new birth.

The original Hal Prince production opened at the Winter Garden theater. This theater, which under the Shubert management had been a stronghold of revue from approximately 1912 to 1924, served as a concrete exemplification, an objective correlative, of a certain period of American history, with all its associated hopes, despairs, and aspirations. It provided the perfect milieu for this piece about the death and resurrection of the American musical and all its concomitant illusions and disillusions.

The mysterious, partially demolished stage, the ghostly figures in black and white, and the scurrying waiters are drawn into an effective composition by the sonorous, eerie opening notes of Sondheim's score. The drums and trumpets, however, are not the sounds of triumph and joy that traditionally welcome one to a Broadway theater. Instead, the introduction is unsettling and vaguely depressing, its regular, unremitting beat suggesting the inexorable march of time. The music itself is filled with repeated, echoing phrases, conveying the theme of the piece; to quote from T. S. Eliot:

> Time present and time past
> Are both perhaps present in time future,
> And time future contained in time past.
> If all time is eternally present
> All time is unredeemable.[14]

It is interesting to note how many of the critics, in attempting to explain the meaning of *Follies*, have compared it with great literary masterpieces. Doris Hering, the reviewer for *Dance Magazine*, quotes extensively from Eliot's *Four Quartets* in her critique of *Follies*; Brendan Gill of the *New Yorker* makes reference to Yeats's *A Dialogue of Self and Soul*; Jack Kroll of *Newsweek* finds "Fitzgeraldian overtones"; and T. E. Kalem of *Time* sees the work as "Proustian." But Hering's choice of Eliot's *Four Quartets* seems most apposite. Both pieces deal with the unremitting quality of historic time, yet point to a significance beyond the temporal order. In both *Four Quartets* and *Follies* there is an attempt to stir an echo in the audience's mind, poetically and musically to create a construct so compelling that it will lead perceivers through the restrictive barriers of "time present" into the infinite possibilities of "what might have been and what has been."[15]

On one level, the story of *Follies* is simple. When Sondheim first approached James Goldman about collaborating on a musical, they had a vague idea about a reunion. The piece, Sondheim recalls:

> was a murder mystery musical originally. It was a "who'll-do-it" rather than a "whodunnit." By the end of the first act all four principals had reason to kill each other and the second act was who'll do it to whom. The whole show took on a Chekhovian quality—the less that happened the better. So gradually it grew into this incidentless show.[16]

In the final version, a theater that once had housed the spectacular Follies, after passing though various stages of decomposition, is finally about to be demolished to make way for a parking lot. Before this last indignity takes place, the producer of the Follies, a Ziegfeld-like figure, Dimitri Weismann, decides to hold a "first and last reunion" (p. 7) of all his former Follies performers. (Every critic sees Weismann as a thinly disguised Ziegfeld, but George White [real name Weitz], for whose *Scandals* Gershwin and DeSylva, Brown, and Henderson wrote some of their best music, could easily have been the Weismann model.)

The major focus of the complex plot is on two couples, former friends, Sally and Buddy Plummer and Phyllis and Ben Stone. When they were young, the women shared an apartment and danced in the Follies together, while the men were "college buddies." Sally, a vapid, sentimental type, was rejected by Ben and married Buddy on the rebound, retaining her unrealistic longing for the romantic hero of her dreams. Her husband, Buddy, has become an oil-rig salesman. Unsure of his wife's affections, he is a brash, insecure womanizer plagued with self-doubt. Smooth, sophisticated, and obviously wealthy, Ben and Phyllis are ostensibly more successful, but through the cracks of their brittle veneer desperation and despair are visible. In the ghostly environment of the theater, with its false frivolity of a wake, the four meet. The place, the encounter, reawaken and resurrect their awareness of the past, enacted by four young actors playing their ghostly younger selves. The clash of past and present in this atmosphere of heightened emotion forces each of the characters to recognize his or her own particular psychological malaise. This confrontation is finally achieved through a minifollies, an expressionistic extravaganza in which each of the leads confronts reality in song. Barely surviving this traumatic self-examination, each couple departs as the sun begins to penetrate the gloom of the once-more dilapidated stage. The audience is left with the hope that this catharsis has led the four to heightened self-understanding and a chance of happiness.

The empty, decaying stage of the opening is an effective theatrical metaphor for the present. The theater and society are in a state of degeneration and decline. The gloss and artificial glamor, the false values and insincerities are peeling away; ugly crevices have appeared in the shiny surface of the American dream. Downstage center stands a ghost of that glamorous past. She is "slim," "beautiful," and "elegant," but she is not real. She is black and white, drained of any living color. For the Broadway production, Michael Bennett chose exceptionally tall women and dressed them in very high-heeled shoes and enormous headdresses. Thus, through their towering appearance on stage, the evocation of the past was immediately shown to be distorted, the glamor exaggerated. Bennett describes his concept: "The show girls were on six-inch platforms and the headdresses they wore were huge and the girls were six feet two to begin with. I wanted it all to look bigger than life. I wanted those girls to be bigger than the Ziegfeld girls could ever have been. It was like looking into a mirror and seeing the past—not the *reality* of the past, but the glorification of it."[17] The play's indebtedness to certain theatrical techniques of German expressionism cannot be denied, although Goldman apparently prefers to categorize his work simply as "non-naturalistic."

As the majordomo and waiters hurry onto the scene, past and present are woven together by Sondheim's ghostly score. In fact, throughout the piece this synchronization is achieved musically. Sondheim creates music of the past and of the present and blends them into a sound that transcends time. In contrast to Jule Styne's score for *Gypsy* (another backstage musical for which Sondheim wrote the lyrics), Sondheim's score counterpoints the lush romanticism of the past with a dry cynicism of the present.

From the outset, in order to visually depict past and present concurrently, Prince staged the musical in an abstract, cinematic mode. Characters enter and exit on different levels. In midsentence a scene dissolves and a light cue refocuses the audience's attention. Simultaneous conversations are orchestrated in which it is clear that the different couples are unaware of each other's existence. The four major characters are combined into many different patterns, and their confrontations are further complicated by the presence of their younger ghostly selves. Time and space are fluid and malleable, as past and present relationships contrast and comment on each other with ever-deepening ramifications.

Throughout the piece the audience's attention is constantly being shifted. It was Prince's intention to create an effect similar to that of a film, in which one brief scene cuts to the next without any intervening fade to black. As Prince and Bennett explained:

> Prince: I purposely requested that the rehearsal scripts of *Follies* and *Company* read like screenplays. I had a sense that you could do close-ups and dissolves and wipes on the stage which had really been left to the cinema prior to both those shows.
>
> Bennett: One of the most boring holdovers from the traditional musical is the use of rideouts or blackouts. In *Company* and *Follies* we discovered ways of using dissolves . . . of never stopping the action. In *Follies* there was a place for your eye to go every minute.[18]

When Sally first enters, "flushed, terribly excited" (p. 4), she is oblivious of her ghostly younger self, who breaks from a spectral formation of dancers to examine her. Sally's opening speech is softly underscored by the opening music, but as she joins the party a band on stage bursts into lively sound. The music played *at* the party is true pastiche. Much has been written about Sondheim's uncanny musical mimicry and ability to re-create the sounds of the past. The difference between his ability to resurrect a past era through music and gently to satirize it is clearly discernible in the opening moments of *Follies*. The band at the party plays many of the numbers that will later be sung. These are ostensibly tunes of the twenties, thirties, and forties, which the contemporary musicians play with smiling condescension. The background party music reminds us of the past without literally re-creating it. The beat is modern, and Jonathan Tunick's orchestrations effectively highlight the distinctions. The sound of the stage band generates the party atmosphere, blending a nostalgic tribute with a somewhat sardonic, affectionate satirization.

Into this noisy theatrical gathering stride Phyllis and Ben. In contrast to Sally, who thinks and looks "remarkably like the girl she was thirty years ago" (p. 4), Phyllis is "probably more beautiful now" (p. 5). She has grown from a frivolous, innocently happy chorus girl into a mature woman who is stylish, intelligent, and extremely cynical. Her husband is described as "tall, trim, distinguished, a successful and authoritative man" (p. 5). (Hal Prince, who regards Ben as the cornerstone of the entire musical, writes, "Ben Stone is the perfect 1970s monolith approaching menopause on the cusp of a nervous breakdown."[19]) As the two stand back and wryly comment on the forced gaiety and decay all around them, they are silently observed by the ghosts of their younger selves.

With the arrival of the anxious-to-please Buddy, the orchestra blares forth the traditional vamp of the comic. The music immediately provides the clue to the internal insecurity and bravado of this character who, on cue, breaks into a "routine." He is nervous and is able to communicate only in a flow of stereotypical bad jokes. The tempo alters and once again the audience's attention is refocused as Dimitri Weismann welcomes his guests to his "first and last reunion," an opportunity to "glamorize the old days, stumble through a song or two and lie about ourselves a little." Then, with a flourish and "Maestro, if you please" (p. 7), Weismann introduces the first big number of the score. The archetypal image of the Follies is always one of stunning female beauty, opulence, a grand stairway, and the haunting strains of Irving Berlin's "A Pretty Girl Is Like a Melody." And this is exactly the image Sondheim and his collaborators exploit, for "an elderly tenor in top hat and tails moves downstage center, strikes a majestic pose, opens his mouth and, in an absolutely gorgeous voice, begins to sing, accompanied by the fourpiece onstage band" (p. 7). The man, the costume, the posture, all belong to a former age. Sondheim's music and lyrics are an homage but also manage to place in stark relief the remorseless passage of time. The melody and thematic thrust, so similar to Berlin's famous song, serve both to remind and disturb the audience. Berlin's work is essentially one-dimensional (it is simply what it purports to be), but Sondheim's work is double-edged. The melodic line is as rich, the lyric as effusive, but in contrast to the simplistic joy and adoration of the earlier song, Sondheim's number is sung by an aging tenor and the "girls" who totter down the crumbling stairway are concrete examples of the ravages of time.

In the original production, Prince gathered together an interesting collection of artists, including Alexis Smith, Dorothy Collins, Yvonne De Carlo, Ethel Barrymore Colt, Gene Nelson, Mary McCarty, Fifi D'Orsay, Justine Johnston, and even an original Ziegfeld girl, Ethel Shutta. Exemplifications of the decay of all things human, the mere presence of such stars embodied a set of values that was no longer relevant. This presentation of beauty in various stages of degeneration (or careful preservation) was not merely exploitative but essential to the meaning of the piece. As Martin Gottfried argues: The cast "have not been hired just for the sake of camp. They are to embody the point of *Follies* in their very presence. The audience knows these people from its own past, remembers their faces from a performing youth. Now they are aging and we see them aged, and *Follies* is about aging and age."[20]

One can imagine the mixture of excitement, surprise, and shock as the half-remembered, sometimes unrecognizable performers made their way carefully down the old stairway. As Ethan Mordden remembers, "the audience clapped for the familiar faces of past decades—. . . not realizing the trap it was falling into, reconfirming the old glamorous images only to see them shattered."[21] Yet the optimistic exuberance inherent in the musical genre was not destroyed. The audience may have been shocked by the reality of its past fantasies, yet talent does not decay and this cast could still lead its audience into paroxysms of ecstatic applause. The expectation of excitement and joy was both achieved and ironically denied in the production.

Thus, as the aging tenor Roscoe launches into "Beautiful Girls," the swelling score and opening lines possess an ironic thrust:

> Hats off,
> Here they come, those
> Beautiful girls.
> That's what
> You've been waiting for.
> (p. 8)

Sondheim's music captures the rich sounds of the twenties and thirties, and the lyrics overflow with hyperboles and lush metaphors:

Nature never fashioned
A flower so fair.
No rose can compare—
Nothing respectable
Half so delectable.
(p. 8)

Though often obvious, the simplicity of the rhymes is deceptive, and in the conjunction of words like *Loreleis* and *moralize* (p. 9) one can discern the Sondheim touch. Moreover, Sondheim never loses the cynical undertone. Thus the double implication of lines like

Beauty
Can't be hindered
From taking its toll
(p. 9)

temper the excess and sentimentality. Suggesting that "reason is undone" in this home of "beautiful girls" hints at what is to follow yet simultaneously alludes to the blithe innocence of a bygone age.

Past and present, beautiful illusion (the women are shadowed by their ghostly younger selves) and harsh reality are presented for the audience's inspection, if not its delight. One of the exciting elements of this scene is that the audience cannot really withdraw and disassociate itself. The reality of aging and disillusion encompasses the house.

Roscoe concludes his number with the traditional flamboyant flourish, and once again the theatrical focus fragments. The dialogue is disjointed as various Follies performers discuss their past and present lives. These jump-cuts are woven together as the subtle underscoring ebbs and swells. Sally, nervous, excited, and confused, dashes about, greeting Weismann (who has forgotten her) and recognizing former stars, and finally bursts into a feverish "Ta da!" The portion of the song she sings reveals her mental state. Its rhythm is restless and agitated, highlighting her insecurity and bluster. The tone of the words belongs to the glittering, glamorous world of show business, but the character's vulnerability blazes through. She sings:

Ta da!
Now, folks, we bring you,
Di-rect from Phoenix,
Live and in person,
Sally Durant!
(pp. 12–13)

Her embarrassment at her small-town, bourgeois existence and her determinedly cheerful bravado are captured in these few lines. But the song, the glimpse into the character's emotions, is interrupted by the arrival of Phyllis, whose call of "Sally" does not simply shatter Sally's reverie—it also conjures up the past. Young Phyllis and Young Sally rush down the stairs together, flushed and excited, and hug each other. Their warmth and joy contrast vividly with the two estranged, isolated women they have become. The rippling, agitated notes that accompany Sally's outburst continue under the dialogue as the youngsters reenact the past, but as the mature women greet each other, the sound of the stage band swells. Then and now, internal emotion and external facade are differentiated by musical underscoring. The brief interchange between the two women discloses the extent to which Sally has locked herself in the past and the contrast between what she regards as her dull and limited life in suburbia and the chic life of Phyllis and Ben.

As the party progresses, the audience encounters various members of the *Follies* cast, each of whom is given a specialty number that evokes the past and explains the present. The narrative line of the plot is repeatedly interrupted by these memory pieces, which are apparently unrelated to the main characters' problems but which in fact serve to exemplify and explore the thematic thrust of the musical. Each fragment of conversation, each fraction of a song, introduces a clearly recognizable type.

There are Vincent and Vanessa, the supple dance team who sweep into an extravagant tango, only to confess that they now run an Arthur Murray franchise. Their dance is choreographed for two couples, the elder pair at the party and their ghostly younger selves. The sequences are similar, but each move is modified by the older couple to reveal the accommodations necessitated by age. The lifts are limited and the kicks contained. There is also Heidi Schiller, the essential European soprano, who is delighted when she hears the band playing "her waltz" and reminisces: "Franz Lehar wrote it for me in Vienna. I was having coffee in my drawing room—in ran Franz and straight to the piano. 'Liebchen, it's for you.' Or was it Oscar Straus? Facts never interest me. What matters is the song." (pp. 16–17). (Her final sentiment can be seen as one of the work's guiding principles: "facts" are irrelevant; it is through the songs that the truth emerges.) There is Carlotta Campion (played by Yvonne De Carlo in Prince's production). The sometime movie star, who "not only has been everything but has liked the look of it" (p. 18), has a dazzling number that is both a tribute to the awesome staying power of the theatrical personality and a pithy résumé of recent American history. There are also Hattie Walker, "an appealing, tough, no-nonsense lady in her mid-seventies" (p. 11), and the obligatory figure of the very chic and very French Solange La Fitte. (From Anna Held onward each *Follies* had to have its own piquant Parisian coquette.) Each of these characters is only briefly introduced, but each will be more fully realized in a subsequent specialty number.

Though Sondheim sees the supporting characters not so much as representatives of distinct personality types as essential depictions, he nonetheless stresses the conscious decision to avoid naturalism:

> In *Follies* we deliberately decided *not* to create characters with warts and all. Everybody would be, not a type, but an essence of whatever they were about, which is why James Goldman's book got so heavily criticized. People didn't understand what he was trying to do. I kept hearing people say, "Those people seem so bloodless." Yes. That's the idea of the piece. Now that may be a wrong notion, but it was a very conscious choice, to create poetic essences, and by poetic I mean the reduction of a human character in a situation to its most succinct form. They never spoke a normal English sentence. Everything was written. Jim was drawing essences. That's his style of writing.[22]

In order to suggest the essence of each character musically, Sondheim's intention was

> to imitate the styles of great songwriters of the times, and affectionately comment on them as well: "One More Kiss" (written in the tradition of Friml-Romberg), "The Story of Lucy and Jessie" (Cole Porter), the verses of "You're Gonna Love Tomorrow" and "Love Will See Us Through" (Jerome Kern with an Ira Gershwin-E. Y. Harburg lyric), "Beautiful Girls" (Irving Berlin), "Broadway Baby" (DeSylva, Brown and Henderson), "Loveland" (Jerome Kern) and "Losing My Mind" (George Gershwin with a Dorothy Field lyric).[23]

For characters Emily and Theodore Whitman, Sondheim wrote a frivolous number evoking the silly nonsense of the twenties. The jaunty rhythm, simple melodic line, and winsome lyrics capture perfectly an era in which a youthful, naïve America was secure and silly. The "pit-pitty-pat" and "plunk-planka-plink" (p. 32) are puerile yet endearing. The tempo is upbeat; the optimism unquestioned. Yet, as in all these representational numbers, there is a significant double perspective, for this ridiculous little song is not sung by the scatty youngsters of the past but by two elderly actors valiantly striving to rekindle the simplistic gaiety of their youth.

The Whitmans are joined by Solange La Fitte, whose French number possesses the right touch of salacious innuendo. Punctuated with the appropriate "ooh-la-la" and "ah. . . ah," Sondheim's lyrics convey both the sensuality and disdain characteristic of the French. Listening to the recording of the original production, it is difficult to tell whether the effectiveness of this number should be attributed to the actress or the lyricist, but it certainly appears that Sondheim selected the most characteristic French sounds. Fifi D'Orsay's savoring of "ruins of Rome" (p. 34) and carefully dropped "h" in "hello" add the appropriate spice to this deliciously Gallic number.

The third song in this evocative medley is sung by Hattie Walker, originally played by Ethel Shutta, the only member of the cast who had actually appeared in Ziegfeld's Follies. As this dumpy, elderly lady comes center stage and belts out "I'm just a / Broadway Baby" (p. 34), the incongruity of the line and the singer provides a guaranteed laugh. Yet the humor of the number is not offensive. The fact that this song of yearning for the legendary fame and fortune of Broadway is sung, not by a naïve young innocent but by a "tough old broad" is funny but telling. The longing for immortality, for one's name in lights, does not fade. Sondheim's lyrics do suggest the hopeful girl the actress once was:

> Gee,
> I'd like to be
> On some marquee.
> (p. 35)

But the desperation and self-deprecating humor of the unemployed elderly actress is not ignored: "Hell, I'd even play the maid / To be in a show" (p. 35). Sondheim includes every theatrical cliché in Hattie's song but revitalizes them all: "Pounding Forty-second Street"; "Waiting for that one big chance"; "Someday, maybe, / All my dreams will be repaid"; "Making rounds all afternoon, / Eating at a greasy spoon / To save all my dough" (pp. 34—35). The dreams and illusions, the myths of "show business" are succinctly encapsulated, and the audience understands that "Broadway babies" may grow old without their determination and faith ever waivering.

As Hattie is joined by the Whitmans and Solange, their songs are performed simultaneously and build to a "shameless climax." This synchronization suggests that the music and words have been buzzing around in the characters' heads. They have not actually been performing at the party, but rather the place has thrust them back into the past. Their recollections have been externalized.

The progression of the major plot line is punctuated by three other memory numbers. One of the most exciting dance sequences in *Follies* is "Who's That Woman?" (often referred to as "the mirror number"). Sally, Phyllis, and some of the other women supposedly sang and danced to this song when they performed in the chorus together. Superficially exhilarating, the song is filled with the irony of hindsight. Sung by the flighty young women of the past, the cynicism and despondency of the number could easily be overlooked, but as it is performed in *Follies* the pertinence of its theme is poignantly evident. Despite its jaunty rhythms, this number conveys the primary thesis of the play, insisting that the false, cheery facades of social intercourse must be stripped away and the loneliness within each individual confronted.

This theme is both stated in the lyric and theatricalized as the women line up across the stage for their tap routine. They are joined by their younger selves. The focal image of the piece is a mirror. Youth mirrors age. Moreover, the young dancers are dressed in costumes made up of bits of mirror which "flash and sparkle as they move" (p. 51). Thus the event is fractured into sparkling units. Past and present, appearance and reality, are reflected and distorted. James Goldman describes the effect of Michael Bennett's choreography:

> One of the best numbers I've ever seen was "Who's That Woman?" The physical impression you got from that was anguishing. To see the decay of the flesh—all those bright, young, beautiful girls and their lovely bodies with all the sense of youth and promise of what's to come contrasted against what *actually* became of it. That's devastating. . . very disturbing and very movielike. The theater rarely utilizes visuals to make important statements, but films do. It's putting the picture in front of you and there was a lot of that in *Follies*.[24]

When the number reaches its climax and the chorus of women, young and old, sing in counterpoint "Mirror, mirror!" soloist Stella Deems accepts the painful truth: she is the foolish woman in the mirror who has tried to hide her pain and loneliness in a meaningless giddy social whirl. This number repeats in microcosm the action of the play. The distorted, sparkling but fragmented reflection of the past, the "cheery, weary" life of the social "carousel" (pp. 48–52), the "dressing for yet one more spree" (p. 48), the grinning clown with the breaking heart, all have to be acknowledged in order that a more complete and honest existence can commence.

"I'm Still Here," a song written in the frantic period of on-the-road tryouts, must surely be one of the wittiest and insightful numbers in the musical theater canon. Sung by Carlotta Campion, it brilliantly and economically evokes the demands, rewards, and necessary tenacity of a life on the stage. It also gives a kaleidoscopic synopsis of America and its theater between the wars. One of the most difficult tasks in analyzing the effect of Sondheim's work is dealing with comedy. There is nothing more distasteful than explaining a joke. The humor in "I'm Still Here" does not require explication. It is a pithy, pertinent tribute to those who survive in the theater:

> I've slept in shanties,
> Guest of the W.P.A.,
> But I'm here.
> Danced in my scanties,
> Three bucks a night was the pay,
> But I'm here.
> I've stood on bread lines
> With the best,
> Watched while the headlines
> Did the rest.
> In the Depression was I depressed?
> Nowhere near.
> I met a big financier
> And I'm here. . . .
>
> I've been through Reno,
> I've been through Beverly Hills,
> And I'm here.
> Reefers and vino,
> Rest cures, religion and pills,
> But I'm here.
> Been called a pinko
> Commie tool,
> Got through it stinko
> By my pool.
> I should have gone to an acting school,
> That seems clear.
> Still, someone said, "She's sincere,"
> So I'm here. . . .

> I've gotten through "Hey, lady, aren't you whoozis?
> Wow, what a looker you were."
> Or, better yet, "Sorry, I thought you were whoozis,
> Whatever happened to her?"
> (pp. 57–60)

The connotations of the representative items Sondheim selects to take his audience through America's recent history are both broadly comprehensive and particularly specific. He recalls distinctive decades and periods with a minimum of well-chosen words. His cynical wit is relentless. McCarthyism, Hollywood, method-acting jargon, nothing seems to be omitted. In this funny, sad, and satiric song Sondheim makes clear that in the world of theater fame fades with the deterioration of the flesh. One's very identity is in doubt, for without recognition you are no one. The "Whatever happened to her?" syndrome is all too familiar to the actual cast of *Follies* as well as the dramatis personae.

The final song in the memory category is sung by Heidi Schiller, the European soprano. The waltz Sondheim has composed for her conveys the lush romance of turn-of-the-century operetta. It possesses a tone of bittersweet heartache, for she sings of sad parting and the awakening from love's young dream. Heidi is joined by her younger self and the song acquires an extra poignancy as a duet for youth and age. As in all the memory numbers, the content illuminates the overall meaning of the play. The melancholy diva longs for "one more glimpse of the past" (p. 72), and it is this line that summons up the ghost of her younger self. But as the two women sing together they assert, "Dreams are a sweet mistake / All dreamers must awake" (p. 72). This is the lesson that the two unhappily married couples have to accept. Another line harmonized by youth and age, as the song reaches its final climactic high notes, stresses that "all things beautiful must die" (p. 73), a fact with which the audience and characters have become increasingly familiar. Yet the song is not merely sad. Its tone of rueful regret and the gentle admonition to "never look back" contrast with the cynicism and sexual profligacy of the party world of the seventies, for Heidi's song is bracketed between a short scene in which Ben propositions Carlotta and, as the lights come up after the waltz, the audience is aware of Phyllis embracing a young waiter.

As stated previously, the narrative line of *Follies* deals with the relationships of Ben, Phyllis, Buddy, and Sally. In analyzing their confrontations and self-examinations, I will be simplifying the structure of the play, the logical development of which is not linear. The meetings, the clashes, and the disintegrations of individuals and relationships are more a collage than a sequential presentation. Drawing the fragments together inevitably will create some distortions and oversimplifications, but this is the clearest way to demonstrate how Sondheim's songs function within the text.

From the moment she enters, Sally is determined to find Ben and resurrect the love she has never allowed to die. Consequently, when she finally sees him, her cry of "Ben!" causes her younger, passionately distressed self to materialize. The agitated, restless rhythm that underscores her initial fragmentary outburst continues as the two former lovers see each other and young Sally pours out her pain and frustration.

As the memory fades, mature Sally is able to express her nervous distress. She struggles to maintain her self-possessed facade. The "Ta-da" of the earlier presentation is missing, but her attempts to camouflage her vulnerability are clear. Sally, on seeing Ben, presents herself as "Sally Durant" (p. 19), her maiden name. The married side of her existence is rapidly cast off. With suppressed excitement, she greets Ben, but, before he can respond, her insecurity and confusion explode:

> No, don't look at me—
> Please, not just yet.
> Why am I here? This is crazy!
> No, don't look at me—
> I know that face,
> You're trying to place
> The name ...
> Say something, Ben, anything.
> (p. 19)

Her ambivalence is captured in the repeated "No, don't look at me," and her longing in the slow, simple plea, "Say something, Ben, anything" (p. 19). The short phrases and syncopated rhythm convey her agitation as none of her words are sustained notes until she asks "Why?" On this word and on the word *crazy* the held note emphasizes Sally's major preoccupation.

Sally tries to be suave and blasé, but with infectious enthusiasm and naïvete she concludes her internal monologue with a definite "I'm so glad I came!" (p. 20). The two old friends affectionately greet, and their former warmth is reestablished as they sing together. The empathic sharing of emotion, so difficult to convey within the confines of a rigidly naturalistic text, is immediately captured in the harmonious blending of voices.

"THROUGH THE UNKNOWN, REMEMBERED GATE"

As the two drift off in search of a drink, the band plays a lively tune and several couples materialize, dancing vigorously. The audience's attention is constantly shifted as the action flows and alters in brief scenes between Ben and Sally, Buddy and Phyllis. The four former friends rekindle their memories of the past until finally the memories become so powerful and vivid that, accompanied by ghostly music, their younger selves appear, and the young men call up the old stairway to their dates. As the scene progresses it becomes increasingly clear that Sally and Buddy live in the past, while Phyllis and Ben resolutely refuse to remember. Both reactions are extreme and have led to personality problems.

The sense of the past is so compelling that Buddy sings again, as he did long ago:

> Hey, up there!
> Way up there!
> Whaddaya say, up there?
> (p. 24)

and confesses:

> I see it all.
> It's like a movie in my head that plays and plays.
> It isn't just the bad things I remember. It's the whole show.
> (p. 26)

The movie image, dominant in the staging technique, is repeated again and again in the text. Buddy begins to recall in a bright, lively number, which lacks any of the bitter disillusion of the present, the many hours that he and Ben spent "waiting for the girls upstairs" (p. 31). The song is filled with the excitement of the two youths who listened with such expectation and ardor to the "clicking heels" and "giggles" of the girls above them "dressing to go on the town" (p. 24). The refrain, which emphasizes the pleasures of "waiting," embodies the positive mood of eagerness that characterized their lives. This hope and confidence contrast with the bleak pessimism of their current existence. As the memories become increasingly intense, Ben casts off his supercilious air and joins in Buddy's reminiscing.

Phyllis too sheds her arrogant manner as the frivolous teasing of the past is recalled. It is with warm humor that she remembers the poverty of their early days and re-creates in song a life that contrasts vividly with the meaningless opulence of her present:

> Waiting around for the boys downstairs,
> Stalling as long as we dare.
> Which dress from my wardrobe of two?
> (One of them was borrowed and the other was blue.)
> (p. 26)

The fun and silliness is suggested in the neatly rhymed lyrics "Giggling, wriggling out of our tights, / Chattering and clattering down all of those flights" (p. 26). The actual meaning of each word is blurred as the men and women badger each other in a tumult of confused voices, but the charged atmosphere is conveyed in the organized chaos of sound.

Then, "suddenly, as if the force of their collective memories" summoned them (p. 27), the two younger women race across a platform and down the stairs as the younger men appear. The pace accelerates as the two couples argue about where they are to spend the evening, the women pressing for dancing at "Tony's," the men attempting to persuade them to try an obviously less expensive "little joint" (p. 29). The argument flies back and forth as the voices blend and clash with both couples resolving into "All right, then, we'll go!" (p. 30). But this exuberance cannot last. As the younger characters fade, their older counterparts express their bitterness and regret in a final verse synthesizing the rejection, denial, and longing of the saddened adults. As the final refrain of "Waiting for the Girls" is repeated, the audience senses that the four soured, mature individuals need something to wait for.

When Sally and Ben reappear together, his amused condescension has become even more pronounced, but her unabashed admiration stirs something in him. He attempts to explain and justify his existence, as much to himself as to her. The song communicates the ambivalences and evasions that underlie so much self-examination. One of the interesting phenomena of a Sondheim musical, in fact, is the readiness with which an audience accepts the convention of confession in song. The flow of believability, the "willing suspension of disbelief," is not disturbed by this device. Phyllis has a lengthy monologue in Goldman's text. Though poignant and well-written, functioning in much the same way as the songs, it is not nearly as effective. As each of the major characters has several opportunities to reminisce and reflect on his or her past and present in song, it seems superfluous to repeat the process in the spoken text. It disturbs the established code of the musical.

Moreover, although Goldman's monologue is effective, it is not as revealing as Sondheim's music and lyrics.

As Ben begins to sing, the same agitated figure that accompanied Sally's interior monologue underscores his opening wry observations:

> You're either a poet
> Or you're a lover
> Or you're the famous
> Benjamin Stone.
> (p. 39)

His lack of respect for his own success is evident in the flat, dry declamation of the lines, as he attempts to convince both Sally and himself that one's choices in life are inevitable and unavoidable. Ben can only extricate himself from the consequences of his past mistakes by clearly understanding the reasons for those choices and by discarding the insincere, distorting facade he has assumed.

His life up to now, Ben acknowledges, has consisted of accommodation. His existence seems interminable (the first sustained note is "as the years go *on*" [p. 37]). Despite his attempts to ignore his regrets and mistakes, Sally's trusting admiration causes them to intrude. Sondheim suggests this awakening awareness in a series of rhetorical questions that become progressively more emphatic as the song develops. The song, like Ben's personality, is cynical. But as the past forces itself into his conscious mind, his attempts to repress it become more emotionally insistent, and the climactic notes of

> I don't remember,
> I don't remember
> At all
> (p. 38)

are poignantly sustained.

Ben's revelatory song is a good example of how well Sondheim absorbed Arthur Laurents's lessons with regard to subtext. Sondheim understands the actor's needs. In discussing the necessity for a clearly defined subtext, he uses this song to explain the levels of meaning that must be evident in a lyric as well as in the spoken dialogue:

> There is a song in *Follies* called "The Road You Didn't Take" which on the surface is a man saying, "Oh, I never look back on the past, I mean, my goodness, it just wouldn't be worth it." He's doing it to con himself as well as the lady he is with; in point of fact, he is ripped to shreds internally. Now, the actor has the ripped-to-shreds he can play. There is also a stabbing dissonance in the music, a note in the music that tells you, the audience, that something is not quite kosher about what this guy is saying. But more important, it gives the actor something to play.[25]

Try as he might to suppress the painful choices and struggles of his past, Ben's youthful self forces itself into his consciousness and onto the stage, and the audience learns one of the sources of his present moroseness. As a law student he had struggled financially. This deprivation and the resultant loss of pride haunt him still. Despite his attempts to convince himself that his decisions were irreversible, that nothing matters anyway, his doubts assert themselves and his questions proliferate:

> The lives I'll never lead
> Couldn't make me sing,
> Could they? Could they? Could they?
> (p. 39)

The tension increases, the tempo grows more urgent, and Ben becomes more determined to repress these unwelcome uncertainties. The particularized conclusion of the first verse, "I don't remember" (p. 38), is modified to the more universal "You won't remember" (p. 39). But he cannot subdue his memories, and his humiliation at being poor is recalled. The audience and the character understand why he chose what he chose, but question the validity of his choice:

> You take your road,
> The decades fly,
> The yearnings fade, the longings die.
> You learn to bid them all goodbye.
> (p. 40)

He tries to convince himself and Sally that he has reached a plateau, a state beyond desire ("And oh, the peace, / The blessed peace ..." [p. 40]), but despite the soothing tones of the words and music his self-deception is evident. In the final series of rhetorical questions, Ben attempts to justify and accept his chosen life-style, but his yearning for the naïve idealism of youth finally surfaces in his last question: "The Ben I'll never be / Who remembers him?" (p. 40).

And, of course, romantic, adoring Sally comes in on cue with "I remember him. I even think I loved him once" (p. 40). Sally has to learn, however, that the Ben of her dreams never existed. Loath to allow her mask of gaiety to slip and permit Ben to see the desperation it hides, she tries heroically to convince herself and Ben of the contentment of her life with Buddy. Yet in the song she sings, the audience is aware that her life is not what she claims it to be. She emphatically declares that Buddy's love makes her life worthwhile. But the assertion rings false. Sondheim explains:

> *Follies* contains a lesson in sub-text, a song called "In Buddy's Eyes." It's a woman's lie to her former lover in which she says that everything is just wonderful and she's having a terrific time at home, she's so happily married. Nothing in the lyric, not a single word tells you that maybe it isn't true. Nothing in the music tells you, although there is something in the orchestration. The actress has to tell you, and if you watch her deliver that song with intense anger because she feels that she has been had, because she was jilted by Ben (the former lover) 30 years before, the whole song takes on a very peculiar quality. . . . Jonathan Tunick, the orchestrator, also understands something about sub-text because every phrase in that song which refers to Buddy, her husband, is dry, it's all woodwinds. Whenever she refers to herself it's all strings again. Not one person in a thousand would get this but . . . it's there and it helps in forming the song.[26]

Sally's reiteration that it is Buddy who lifts her life above the mundane sounds a trifle hollow as Sondheim economically evokes the monotony of the middle-class domesticity of which Sally is so obviously ashamed in a series of trivia ("gourmet cooking," "letter writing," and "tending flowers" [p. 44]) that fill her days. Her embarrassment at the insignificant nature of her existence is suggested in her apologetic asides, "Don't faint" and "Can you believe it" (p. 44). She tries valiantly to affirm the value of a life she feels is meaningless, but her discomfort and envy surface:

> . . . yes, I miss a lot
> Living like a shut-in.
> No, I haven't got
> Cooks and cars and diamonds.
> Yes, my clothes are not
> Paris fashions ...
>
> (p. 44)

The carefully placed "yes" and "no" suggest her rising resentment and defensiveness as she anticipates his questions. She frantically tries to reestablish her self-worth. The music swells and she proclaims her value:

> . . . but in
> Buddy's eyes,
> I'm young, I'm beautiful.
> In Buddy's eyes
> I don't get older.
> (p. 44)

Confronted with the reality of her infatuation, however, her lie begins to disintegrate. She desperately attempts to sustain a flippant tone, but her yearning becomes too powerful and her song collapses as Young Ben and Young Sally break through her protective shell of self-deception.

In the same way that Ben's self-examination leads him back to his past anger and hurt, Sally is forced to relive the painful reenactment of her humiliation at Ben's hands. Yet, just as Sally was unable to accept the truth in the past, she is not ready to accept it in the present and she blindly reaffirms:

> And all I ever dreamed I'd be,
> The best I ever thought of me,
> Is every minute there to see
> In Buddy's eyes.
> (p. 46)

It is clear by the end of the song that she is attempting to convince herself as much as she is trying to persuade Ben. And as the song reaches its poignant climax, the audience knows that she must once more retreat into her self-created, comforting cocoon, sustained by the belief that Buddy's love is sufficient. He believes the lie she has evolved; therefore life is tolerable.

Ben sees through the pretense. He tenderly takes her in his arms and the two begin to dance. This intimate flirtation is abruptly halted when Phyllis cuts in and leads Sally away:

> *Phyllis*
>
> Let's dish. I can't wait, tell me everything.
> You ever miss New York?

Sally

It's changed so much.

Phyllis

It grows on you: you get to like hostility and filth and rotten manners. Tell me more. . . . How do you like my husband?

Sally

Ben? I've always liked him: you know that.

Phyllis

How was his conversation? Did he sparkle for you?

Sally

We just talked about old times and little things.

Phyllis

You find him changed?

Sally

Not really, not down deep.

Phyllis

I rarely dip beneath the surface.

(pp. 46–47)

This is Goldman at his best: funny, cruel, and unexpected. It is precisely this tone that Sondheim employs in all Phyllis's songs.

The layers of lies are beginning to peel away, but the couples cannot lower all their defenses. Ben and Sally try to unravel and understand the past. This delving soon causes their younger selves to reappear. Young Sally and her mature counterpart both turn to Ben in hopeless adoration. The audience perceives that the woman has not grown, that she is as enamored with romance at fifty as she was at twenty. In his frustration and anger at his own shortcomings Ben conflates past and present. He opens his arms and it is Young Sally who slips into them. It is to this youthful memory, this specter, that he sings his romantic ballad, "Too Many Mornings." But older Sally's arms are also filled with dreams, for although she stands alone, she moves precisely as Young Sally does. The theatricalization of two people in love with love, lost in a world of memory, desire, and illusion is realized.

Through Ben's ballad, audience and characters are intensely aware of the passing of time. Ben sings of a life filled with longing that can never be assuaged. The infinite quality of this ache is suggested by Sondheim's repeated use of the words *time* and *morning*. Years of waste stretch out interminably. Mornings become days; days become nights, which lengthen once more into dreary days. This pattern is woven intricately into the texture of the song. It is the same progression of endless, meaningless days and nights elaborated by Sally in her song "Losing My Mind."

As Ben reaches the climax of his declaration of unfulfilled longing, he proclaims that contentment could be found in the time left to him if he could

> . . . look up to see
> Sally standing at the door,
> Sally moving to the bed,
> Sally resting in my arms,
> With her head against my head.
> (p. 63)

But the audience suspects that his emotional outpouring is a trifle glib and self-serving. The Sally of whom he sings is a phantom. He longs for the past, unaware of the cruelty of manipulating the emotions of the abject middle-aged woman in front of him.

Sally is easily seduced. This dream has been her only reality for so many years. Her poignant, impatient "If you don't kiss me, Ben, I think I'm going to die" (p. 63) indicates that the song has been the fulfillment of all her fantasies. The fact that her words are spoken rather than sung emphasizes her urgency. Sally, Sondheim reveals, has been anticipating this passionate reunion for some time:

> How I planned:
> What I'd wear tonight and
> When I should get here,
> How I should find you,
> Where I'd stand,
> What I'd say in case you
> Didn't remember,
> How I'd remind you—
> You remembered,
> And my fears were wrong!
> (pp. 63–64)

Sally's insecurity and self-doubt are built into all her songs. Her life and songs are overloaded with how, what, when, and where formations. Consequently, the triumph underscoring "And my fears were wrong!" (p. 64) conveys just how full her heart is, just how ready she is to believe him. Yet she finds it difficult to accept the reality of this romantic fervor:

> Was it ever real?
> Did I ever love you this much?
> Did we ever feel
> So happy, then?
> (p. 64)

The two lovers' thoughts are parallel and overlap. Ben allows himself to sink into her sentimental reverie, while she continues to be plagued by insecurity and self-doubt:

> *Ben*
>
> It was always real ...
>
> *Sally*
>
> I should have worn green ...
>
> *Ben*
>
> And I've always loved you this much ...
>
> *Sally*
>
> I wore green the last time ...
>
> *Ben*
>
> We can always feel this happy ...
>
> *Sally*
>
> The time I was happy ...
> (p. 64)

In the following joyous duet the mornings and nights of Ben's solo extend:

> Too many mornings
> Wasted in pretending I reach for you.
> How many mornings
> Are there still to come?
>
> How much time can we hope that there will be?
> Not much time, but it's time enough for me,
> If there's time to look up and see

Sally standing at the door ...
(pp. 64–65)

Sondheim never allows his audience to stray too far from the central preoccupation of the work. Even in this love song the theme of time, the interconnection yet irreconcilable separation of past, present, and future is paramount. The two lovers believe that they can escape the plodding inevitability of time through the power of their love. The audience, however, is given an indication of the deception. The different directions of Ben's and Sally's desires is indicated in the subsequent dialogue, for Ben ardently declares "I want you, Sally," while she demurs, "We are getting married, aren't we?" (p. 65). The scene is a reenactment of the past. Nothing has changed. The suffering, the misunderstandings, the recriminations, and the desires of past and present undercut in a frenetic exchange between Ben and Sally, Young Ben and Young Sally. Neither understands the other's needs any more clearly now than thirty years before.

Throughout the scene the audience is aware of Buddy on a platform above the lovers' heads. He is in another part of the theater, not actually perceiving the seduction of his wife but sensing it. His frustration, restless anger, and occasional outbursts give a further emotional dimension to the encounter. After a distraught and apparently repentant Ben stumbles from the stage, Sally and her ghostly youth, still blindly refusing to accept rejection, exit. Buddy then explodes into a song filled with irrepressible fury and pain.

He knows that his marriage is flawed, yet his loathing is not directed primarily at Sally. In brief, angry phrases he expresses his need for "the right girl," one who's

. . . with you, no matter how you feel,
You're not the good guy, you're not the heel.
You're not the dreamboat that sank—you're real.
(p. 68)

He recognizes that Sally has never loved him for what he is. She has always been in love with an illusion. Yet part of him senses it is not entirely Sally's fault. He doesn't come out directly and blame her, and his diatribe breaks off abruptly as he declares "And I got—" (p. 68).

What has he got? A wife, a mistress, two sons, a job, and yet his life is empty. He cannot face this truth and cannot articulate his angry confusion. He therefore breaks into a violent dance. He expresses with his body what he cannot say or sing. In the frantic fury of the dance his passions cool, and as he sings of his young mistress, Margie, the quality of the mood and music alters. With a gentle softness he sings to her:

Hey, Margie, I'm back, babe.
Come help me unpack, babe.
Hey Margie, hey, bright girl,
I'm home.
(pp. 68–69)

Sondheim's gift for characterization in song is exemplified here. Buddy is a "simple guy," unpretentious and not very smart. There are no intricate and clever rhymes for Buddy (Sondheim had learned his lesson from "I Feel Pretty"). The unaffected charm and warmth of the character are conveyed in the straightforward simplicity of the melody and the frequent colloquialisms in the lyric. Most of the lines conclude with the word *babe*, which establishes his dependence, lack of sophistication, and immaturity. The plaint of the salesman, "Des Moines was rotten and the deal fell through," the obliging, endearing quality of trying to please,

Hey, Margie,
You wanna go dancing?
You wanna go driving? or something?

and his unaffected and incredulous delight when she expresses the desire simply to stay home with him,

Okay, babe,
Whatever you say, babe—
You wanna stay home!
You wanna stay home!
(p. 69)

are all suggested in his song (p.69).

Buddy is so filled with self-doubt that he cannot believe that Margie is happy "to stay home," and his joy at this sign of her love is conveyed in his crescendo. The tender dance he then performs with his imagined Margie is the antithesis of the angry, frenzied stomping of his earlier routine and serves as a temporal bridge taking Buddy through an imagined night with Margie to his morning departure. Vaguely reminiscent of the "Barcelona" scene in *Company*, the sleepy parting of the two lovers is far more poignant.

We know, she knows, and he knows that he has left her before and he will leave her again.

As the song continues, the word *home* accumulates meaning and significance through repetition and modification. Buddy first greets Margie with "I'm home"; is delighted when she wants to "stay home"; doesn't want to add to her suffering at his departure and advises her to "stay home," for after all he is married to another woman and they both accept that he has got to "go home." The painful realization of his hurt and hurtfulness causes his anger to flare up again, and his frustrated and confused search for the "right girl" who "sees you're nothing and thinks you're king" (p. 69) climaxes in another furious dance. Buddy knows that he has Margie, who should be the "right girl," but it is Sally he wants. His self-esteem is so low that he cannot love someone who admires him, only someone who shares his own self-contempt.

The emotional tension builds as Phyllis and Ben confront each other. Angry, hurt, and frustrated, they hurl insults at one another, each intent on articulating his or her own pain while oblivious of the other's fury. Ben insists he wants a divorce in order to find someone to love him and not remind him of his hollow core. Unaware of his debilitating insecurity, Phyllis bitterly insists that he cannot understand love for he has failed to appreciate all the love she has felt for him all these years. Phyllis's anger, however, has none of the pent-up incoherence of Buddy's outburst. Even in her torment at Ben's selfish lack of understanding, she is witty and articulate. The swirling rhythms of "Could I Leave You?" a vigorous waltz in the style of Ravel, sustain and contain her anger. Like "The Ladies Who Lunch," this piece possesses a biting, cynical wit that is devastatingly effective.

Much of the humor in this number lies in Phyllis's unexpected response when Ben angrily inquires how she could leave him and "give up the joys" (p. 75) she has known. Phyllis begins to enumerate the "joys":

> Not to fetch your pills again
> Every day at five,
> Not to give those dinners for ten
> Elderly men
> From the U.N.—
> How could I survive?
> (p. 76)

As her bitterness at the shallow values of their empty life of social climbing begins to emerge, the tempo increases and the rhymes proliferate. She details their life of specious values in which "shelves of the World's Best Books" (p. 76) are purchased for show, in which communication is reduced to

> . . . evenings of martyred looks,
> Cryptic sighs,
> Sullen glares from those injured eyes.
> . . . quips with a sting, jokes with a sneer,
> Passionless love-making once a year.
> (p. 76)

As the pain becomes unbearable, Phyllis copes, as one suspects she has coped for many years, with flippancy and vulgarity:

> Could I bury my rage
> With a boy half your age
> In the grass? Bet your ass.
> But I've done that already—or didn't you know, love?
> Tell me, how could I leave when I left long ago, love?
> (p. 76)

Phyllis taunts Ben with her infidelities and sustains her cool, tough facade, illustrating once again Sondheim's ability to capture the nuances of a person in pain. She retains her appearance of dignified restraint, but the audience perceives the anguish that underlies her contemptuous demeanor. The song explores her confusion, doubts, anomalies, and contradictions while the character heroically attempts to sustain her veneer of control.

As Phyllis's indignation intensifies, she becomes vindictive and "leave" acquires a new meaning. She demands possessions, and a flawlessly detailed world of materialistic acquisitiveness is satirized in her demands:

> No, the point is could you leave me?
> Well, I guess you could leave me the house,
> Leave me the flat,
> Leave me the Braques and Chagalls and all that.
> You could leave me the stocks for sentiment's sake
> And ninety percent of the money you make.
> (p. 77)

As the list grows, her temper mounts and unbridled emotion runs riot in the racing fury of the rhythms. Phyllis concludes her diatribe with the one all-significant question: "Will I leave you?" Neither she, her bemused spouse, nor the audience knows the answer as she explodes with a final "Guess!" (p. 77).

Again it is a vehement self-examination in song that causes the past to manifest itself. The lack of communication and misunderstandings between the young couple is relived. The two young people then turn on their alienated older selves. Past and present become further entangled as Buddy and his young counterpart attack Ben for seducing Sally, while Sally, who has completely regressed and become one with her younger self, waits in willing anticipation for her lover. All the lines, all the anguish, all the doubts and fears erupt, as all eight attack each other—and themselves. This emotional purgation climaxes as each of the characters turns on his or her past self in almost uncontrollable rage. Then:

> As the madness of the confrontation hits its peak—just as there seems no possible way out—drums start to roll, trumpeters in Medieval costumes emerge from the shadows, heavenly music is heard, drop after drop comes flying down, all valentines and lace, and as the lights rise to bright gold, dancers, young and beautiful, all dressed like Dresden Dolls and Cavaliers, appear. Ben, Phyllis, Buddy and Sally, eyes wild, and half-demented, stand in the midst of it all, taking their first look at "Loveland." (p. 83)

The wild passion of recrimination, the nervous antagonism and heightened fear push the characters over the edge of sanity and reality. Their pain is so intense that the characters and their world shatter and, accompanied by the opening bars of "Beautiful Girls," they enter the surreal world of the Follies.

Prince, Sondheim, Goldman, and Bennett wanted to re-create the musical extravaganza of the past but drastically alter the content. The "Loveland" sequence of the finale possesses all the "razzle and dazzle of the unreal and incredible" that George Jean Nathan had demanded of the genre, but its intention and meanings are radically different. The larger-than-life world of romance, the mythic quality of the musical prescribed by critics from Brooks Atkinson to John Lahr is re-created, but the emotional impact of this magnified passion is channeled into new areas of audience and character awareness. In "Loveland" the characters face the "falsehood they want to believe" and consequently grow toward an acceptance of reality.

Harold Prince explains the intention of this final section of the piece:

"THROUGH THE UNKNOWN, REMEMBERED GATE"

> The show arced to a mini *Ziegfeld Follies*, giving the audience in the final twenty minutes what it had expected all along. The only difference was that the stars of our Follies would confront in lavish production numbers the lies that had led them relentlessly to the brink of madness. Defenseless, they would lay waste the past, leave the rubble to the theater behind them, and start to live.[27]

The real world and the escapist world of the past and their different musical traditions are counterbalanced and function as correlative antitheses.

In an early edition of the script, Goldman concluded with these words: "What follows is a capsule Follies—costume parades, comedy routines, specialty acts—traditional and accurate in all ways but one. Sets, costumes, music, movement, all this is faithful to the past. What's different and unusual about it is the content, what it's all about."[28] Some measure of the successful embodiment of Goldman's vision can be gauged from the responses of two critics of this final sequence:

> Now the carousel runs amok. Mr. Aronson (the designer) drops down the tinsel and mirrors. Florence Klotz costumes the memories in crimson and satin, the chorus line comes up in top hats and tap shoes. The rememberers in the present dance with their memories. Bewildered, they watch their younger selves sing innocently of romance, the lyrics simultaneously mimicking the past and mocking the present. The whole machine cracks—like the theater in which it is set, like the kind of theater that is being buried, like the recalled bodies, like the optimism, cheerfulness and trust celebrated by the old show business. . . . The follies within the Follies within *Follies* turn grotesque and horrific.[29]

And:

> When suddenly and startlingly the stage flares into light, a lot of candy-box Valentine scenery descends and a troupe of pseudo-Fragonard boys and girls come prancing out and get into place, and sings: "In love land, where everybody loves!" In the middle of this blinding explosion of insanity stand the two couples, four haggard middle-aged wrecks—stunned and gaping—while the chorus boys and girls trill and pose relentlessly around them.
>
> It's a moment of such complicated brilliance, such triumphant soaring wryness that I can't honestly think of a parallel to it—except in other parts of *Follies* itself. For this is only an introduction to a "real" Follies sequence, an elaborate and brilliant show-within-a-show. In which finally each of the four main figures "stars" in a "number" of his own, which takes the nagging personal hang-ups we're by now familiar with and translates

> them without the slightest distortion—without losing any of the grubby essentials or any of the inevitable ironies—into the strong, liberated, full-bodied sounds of popular song-and-dance: the burlesque routine, the torch song, the "honky-tonk" production number out of a forties movie, the top-hat-and-tails style of Astaire in the thirties. And this transformation, you realize, is what *Follies* has been moving toward all along, with its growing impression of smallness and banality in the characters. Since it's exactly this inevitable side of ourselves—the petty and grudging, the self-concerned and self-pitying—that the American song-and-dance tradition—with its style and rue and humor—redeems and transforms at its best into something large and elegant and free. And *Follies* is not only a virtuoso of that tradition, but a rich, moving and complex comment on it.[30]

It should be noted that much of the success of this final sequence can be attributed to the work of Boris Aronson, the set designer; Florence Klotz, the costumer; and lighting designer Tharon Musser. *Follies* must surely be seen as a splendid example of a Wagnerian *Gesamtkuntswerk*: each artist's particular talent and insight contributing to the complex realization of the central concept.

The world the four ravaged adults enter is a world of illusion. It exists only in their tortured psyches, and through it they will confront the reality of their own failures, as "in a series of antinostalgic metaphors, each of the stars takes off the public mask and appears in his own Folly. It is a vaudevillification of their own benighted circumstances, in which the truth shines like a spotlight."[31] Yet the implications of the satire extend beyond the lives of the four protagonists: "*Follies* is at once a rousing piece of American show business and an acute criticism of the psychic, emotional and cultural implications of show business as an American phenomenon."[32] The controlling metaphor of the piece, its concept, is completed. In this escapist form, the characters—and by extension, the America of the seventies—confront their inner pain and come to terms with the limitations of "ordinary" life. Sondheim's work here exemplifies that unique quality only found in great musicals. The piece does not aim at a realistic depiction of life; it is unabashedly show. But through this "show" the audience gains a deeper understanding of "life."

The "Loveland" in which the four half-crazed characters stand is a perfect image of young, idealistic sentiment. It is a domain that has never existed, but in some form or other has always been part of the world of escapist musical theater—with its most extravagant depiction being the ornate creations of Ziegfeld—and an integral ingredient of the American dream. Certainly many people still come to the musical theater hoping to be led into this glossy realm.

For Sally, Buddy, Ben, and Phyllis this is the idealized world of their remembered past. Their lives have been shaped, their images of the past formulated, their concepts of love and beauty and desire patterned on the clichés of the theater that dominated their early experience. They enter this timeless realm in which nothing is ever amiss and

> Time stops, hearts are young,
> Only serenades are sung
> In Loveland,
> Where everybody lives to love.
> (p. 83)

This world in which "time stops," this Camelot-like existence in which sweetness and joy prevail, is a world in diametric opposition to the demented screams of pain that preceded it. But it is clearly illusory. Even the choreography has a precise symmetry absent from the earlier sequences. The Dresden dolls and cavaliers of the chorus, the gorgeous costumes and sets, and the naïve little tune with its banal lyrics exemplify escapist nostalgia. The audience laughs affectionately with Sondheim, who crams every cliché of romance into such lines as "See that sunny sun and honeymoon, / There where seven hundred days hath June" (p. 83). Yet the reason for the exaggeration is clear. This is a world of idealized love, a world that the American musical theater encouraged its audience to believe could be found, yet one that the disillusionment of maturity has proved to be a pipe dream.

As each extravagant and gorgeously clad embodiment of love descends, Sondheim, in a manner reminiscent of a Ziegfeld routine, describes her in purple prose. In its exaggeration this pastiche laughs at the past, but it also strikes a poignant note, simply because the dazzling world of the past differs so fundamentally from the disillusioned pain of the present. The opulence is essentially fraudulent: such a mythic world of romance can exist only in the imagination or on the stage. Yet, *Follies* suggests, it is precisely on this kind of hyperbolic illusion that the characters (and their society) have built their lives, their expectations, and their standards. The world of musical comedy, the optimistic arrogance of America in the twenties, was a distorting lie and needed to be shattered in order that a mature musical theater and a sane society could emerge.

The word *love* peals out as the opening number of the minifollies reaches its dramatic crescendo and "Young Ben and Young Phyllis come dancing on downstage. Memories no more, they sport bright colors and pink cheeks. They flash adoring smiles at one another and begin to sing" (p. 87). Sondheim re-creates in both music and lyrics the frivolity and naïve optimism of idealized young love. Choosing phrases that clearly belong to a different era, he establishes a sentimental, cheerful world of romance. In an interview with *Time* magazine, Sondheim comments: "I truly love the body of musical comedy of that period. The minute you hear the first line of the 'Loveland' sequence song, 'You're Gonna Love Tomorrow'—'What will tomorrow bring, / The pundits query'—it evokes an entire period. That's the kind of language they used. It could be parody, but obviously it's done with such affection and also it's really dealing with something."[33]

Young Phyllis and Young Ben belong to this halcyon world. They believe in the dream: they try to live the illusion. The audience must share with the impotent mature couple the awful pain of knowing that the dream will become a nightmare. Here the time theme is reversed. Rather than having a disillusioned adult regretting past decisions, we are presented with happy young people certain in their love for each other and in their consequent belief that the future must be rosy. There is a painful irony in the buoyant and carefree assertion of their continuing happiness:

> Today was perfectly perfect,
> You say.
> Well, don't go away,
> 'Cause if you think you liked today,
>
> You're gonna love tomorrow. . . .
> And if you love tomorrow,
> Then think of how it's gonna be:
> Tomorrow's what you're gonna have a lifetime of
> With me!
>
> (p. 89)

The knowledge of what that lifetime of tomorrows will become undermines the gaiety. The ebullient mood, the irrepressible optimism of the lyrics, and the jaunty liveliness of the melody are in stark contrast to the four bitter adults who silently observe the routine.

As Young Ben and Young Phyllis dance off, they are replaced by an equally animated Young Buddy and Young Sally. In an introductory verse that so perfectly captures the idiom of the twenties that one finds it hard to believe it wasn't written then, Sondheim creates two engaging, playful lovers. With consummate skill Sondheim evokes a period in which rhyme was used for rhyme's sake and deftly matches "soul-stirring" and "bolstering"; "warn you" and "cornu- / copia" (p. 90). With a cheery vitality that duplicates that of Young Ben and Young Phyllis, the two sing

> But no matter what goes wrong,
> Love will see us through
> Till something better comes along.
> (p. 91)

Having established the mood of naïve optimism, innocent love, and blind faith in the future that characterized the four protagonists and their country during the twenties, Sondheim then introduces the older personalities, and as they take turns performing, each clarifies his or her own crippling character flaw. This section of the musical belongs entirely to Sondheim, for there is no spoken dialogue at all. In it he proves how exquisitely and powerfully the unique quality of music can function as a key to the inner truths of passion. As Leonard Bernstein says, music can pinpoint and magnify basic human emotions "beyond life size so that you can't miss them."[34] Sondheim exploits music's ability to select and isolate the primary emotions; thus, the audience is granted a unique and immediate insight into each character's motivating passion through the musical style and language. As each number recalls a different composer and style, Sondheim pays tribute to the past, yet his aim is not to allow the characters or the audience to luxuriate in nostalgia.

Sondheim's ability to juxtapose ironically well-known and easily recognizable musical forms, which audiences immediately associate with certain periods and moods of American history, with probing antithetical lyrics has never been more brilliantly employed. He often writes lyric and character at odds with musical suggestion and connotation, provoking a unique audience response and involvement. In *Follies* the audience not only contrasts musical association and lyric implication in the characters' lives; the ironic comment also extends into the sociopolitical realm. The gap between a secure, remembered American past and the vulnerabilities and terrors of the present are exposed in this synthesis of musical comedy escapism and serious dramatic theater. The contemporary climate of disillusioned pessimism and pain is expressed in Sondheim's lyrics, the optimism of the past in his music. The two comment and reflect on each other in a dynamic antithesis as the work functions on three levels, Sondheim's insights applying to the death of hope in the individual, in society, and in the musical genre.

Buddy is the first character to perform in the minifollies. (I choose the word *perform* with care, for in the latter section of the piece there is no attempt at naturalistic acting and verisimilitude. The characters act out their problems. They do not "live" them, or attempt to conceal and disguise them, as they did in the first section of the work.) Buddy's anxious attempts to win love by being the fall guy, the comic telling jokes of which he is always the butt, is now given full theatrical expression. He is dressed in the traditional costume of the funny man, "plaid baggy pants, bright blue jacket and a shiny derby hat" (p. 95), his identity as traveling salesman suggested by the large plywood model car he wears suspended from his waist.

With a comic vamp, a strained laugh, and a spectacular slide down the curtain, Buddy launches into his routine. In his opening line, "Hello, folks, we're into the Follies" (p. 95), the notions of the Follies as foolish madness and as a type of theatrical diversion are drawn together. It is a show that will show, an entertainment that will reveal and relieve pain.

Buddy's problem, which he shares with the audience, is: "The things that I want, I don't seem to get. / The things that I get—You know what I mean?" (p. 95). Without losing the sense of period or the tone of the put-upon little chap delivering his rapid patter song, Sondheim manages to reveal the source of Buddy's discontent. The mortifying lack of self-confidence, so humorously and succinctly expressed in Groucho Marx's well-known aphorism "I would never belong to a club that would have me as a member," lies at the core of Buddy's personality. At a breakneck pace he explains his problem:

> I've got those
> "God-why-don't-you-love-me-oh-you-do-I'll-see-you later"
> Blues,
> That
> "Long-as-you-ignore-me-you're-the-only-thing-that matters"
> Feeling. . . .

Buddy is joined by a member of the chorus who "comes flouncing on as a caricature of his beloved Margie" (p. 96). In the world of the *Follies* nothing is real, each personality is exaggerated and distorted. In a modification of a technique he used in the "Echo Song" from *A Funny Thing Happened On The Way To The Forum*, Sondheim shows that Margie is merely a puppet parroting back what Buddy thinks he wants to hear. This causes him to become progressively more agitated, and on hearing her declare that she is his "forever," he responds with "I gotta get outta here quick!" (p. 97).

The number's carefully balanced humor and pathos, reminiscent of Chaplin, are sustained as the song builds to its climax. The audience realizes that Buddy can never come to terms with Sally until he learns to accept himself. This idea is clarified as Buddy is joined by a cartoon version of his wife. Unlike "Margie," she does not glibly repeat what he thinks he wants to hear, but subtly alters her responses to indicate her contempt. This humiliation he naturally finds irresistible. His life is then grotesquely caricatured as he frantically dashes about in his cardboard car, chasing "Sally" and colliding with "Margie." (Prince and Bennett staged this sequence under a strobe light so that the chase resembled the madcap pursuits of a Mack Sennett film.) The number concludes in a synthesis of all the contradictory desires ripping Buddy apart:

> Those
> "If-you-will-then-I-can't,"
> "If-you-don't-then-I-gotta,"
> "Give-it-to-me-I-don't-want-it-if-you-won't-I-gotta have it"
> "High-low-right-wrong-yes-no-black-white,"
> "God-why-don't-you-love-me-oh-you-do-I'll-see-you later"
> Blues.
> (pp. 99–100)

As Buddy and his two loves dash off, their place is taken by Sally, "costumed in a clinging, beaded silver gown, as if she were a screen seductress from the 1930s" (p. 100). Sally has imprisoned herself in this Helen–Morgan–like image of the glamorous, passionate siren dwelling in a romantic world of unrequited love. Her torch song, with its Gershwin overtones, expresses her preoccupation with Ben, her idealized lover. She clings to this obsession for without her love for Ben her life would be reduced to a series of empty gestures and meaningless activities. With infinite attention to detail, Sondheim leads Sally from sunrise to sleepless night, revealing that every second of her existence is defined by her longing:

The sun comes up,
I think about you. . . .
The morning ends,
I think about you. . . .
All afternoon
Doing every little chore,
The thought of you stays bright. . . .
I dim the lights
And think about you,
Spend sleepless nights
To think about you.
(p. 100)

Sally is tentatively aware that she may have built her life on a lie:

You said you loved me,
Or were you just being kind?
Or am I losing my mind?
(p. 101)

But she is unwilling and unable to rid herself of her infatuation. The fact that Sally enjoys and indulges in this state of hopeless rapture is conveyed in the lush, swelling quality of the melody. This type of song belongs clearly to the escapist world of the 1930s stage and screen. The genre denied, or at least ignored, the miseries of the depression as it created an alternate reality, a sphere in which all women were beautiful and romantic love was the only significant value. This highly artificial world offered Sally an escape route from the mundanity of her life. It also enabled her to ignore the cruelty of Ben's exploitative nature. It is interesting, and perhaps revealing, to note that the majority of critics select this song as the finest in the show.

The number ostensibly does not reveal the pain of the character but explores the extent to which she has lost herself in this make-believe world of undying desire. Muted horns, rippling harps, these are the instruments of Sally's love, but her passion has no basis in reality. It exists only in her mind. The lights dim and Sally's face is pinpointed by a spotlight as the curtains close. The traditional theatrical presentation for the blues singer is sustained.

As the last note of Sally's music fades, Phyllis is introduced by a "jazzy blare of trumpets" (p. 101). Her number, which suggests the wit and style of Cole Porter, is a racy, dazzling revelation of her personality problem. Two antithetical forces are warring within her, and her inability to reconcile them is destroying her. Phyllis calls the naïve person she once was "Lucy X." Lucy has

> . . . the purity,
> Along with the unsurety
> That comes with being only twenty-one.
> (p. 102)

The sophisticated cynic she has become, Phyllis calls "Jessie Y." Jessie

> . . . has maturity
> And plenty of security.
> Whatever you can do with them she's done.
> (p. 102)

In a superb display of wit in rhyme and content Sondheim explores this opposition:

> Lucy is juicy
> But terribly drab.
> Jessie is dressy
> But cold as a slab.
> Lucy wants to be dressy,
> Jessie wants to be juicy.
> Lucy wants to be Jessie,
> And Jessie Lucy. . .
> If Lucy and Jessie could only combine,
> I could tell you someone
> Who would finally feel just fine.
> (pp. 102–3)

I have avoided analyzing Sondheim's lyrics in terms of his use of formal poetic devices such as onomatopoeia, assonance, alliteration, and intricate rhyme schemes. His consummate skill with words is self-evident, particularly in patter numbers like the one above. In an interview Sondheim's mother once revealed that her son wanted to be America's Noel Coward, and indeed Coward would have been proud of these lyrics. Yet even in this intricate pattern of words, Sondheim does not allow his understanding of character to be subservient to a witty phrase. The evocative humor complements the character, for Sondheim's lyrics are far more character revealing than Coward's. The schizoid quality of Phyllis's personality is something the audience has been aware of even before the character's acknowledgment of the condition. Moreover, the theme of time, the dislocation of past and present that is so significant throughout the play, is carefully incorporated into the lyrics.

As she exits Phyllis casts one last look over her shoulder and sees Ben, a debonair Astaire in dazzling white top hat and tails, carrying a clear plastic cane. His attempt to project the image of the smooth, sophisticated man-about-town is now expressed in its ultimate theatrical form. The Astaire persona typifies all that is controlled and elegant. In a deft execution of song and dance, this character-type could gently but firmly control his women and his environment (no one is really surprised when Astaire lithely dances along walls and over the ceiling). Ben has assiduously cultivated such an urbane, aristocratic appearance. Moreover, although Ben knows his sophisticated veneer and caustic wit are a fragile facade, the other people in his life willingly accept and believe in his aura of confidence. He feels they have based their love and admiration on a character who does not really exist. A phantom of his own creation, he is terrified lest his disguise be penetrated and his essential weakness revealed.

Ben is given a big buildup as the chorus introduces him as "Mister Whiz," "raconteur," and "bon vivant" and humbly asks his advice. His personality still firmly intact, he joins the chorus and proceeds to come up with all the answers. The relaxed, easy rhythm and unobtrusive melodic line coincide precisely with the suave image Ben seeks to project. His "modus operandi," he proudly proclaims, is to accept all the vicissitudes of life with the minimum of distress:

> Learn how to laugh,
> Learn how to love,
> Learn how to live,
> That's my style.
> (pp. 104–5)

As Ben repeats this advice Sondheim modifies the verbs. These minor changes are not merely decorative, designed simply to avoid monotony, for each alteration gives a slightly different insight into Ben's character. He begins by advising "Learn how to laugh," admits later "I'd rather laugh," continues "I like to laugh" and concludes "I have to laugh" (pp. 104–7).

As he warms to his theme, Ben denies that he has ever had to struggle for anything:

Some fellows sweat
To get to be millionaires,
Some have a sport
They're devotees of.
Some like to be the champs
At saving postage stamps.
Me, I like to live,
Me, I like to laugh,
Me, I like to love.
(p. 105)

This devil-may-care attitude, the audience knows, has never been truly characteristic of the intense poor boy who clawed his way to the top, only to find his success meaningless.

In a recapitulation of the pattern of his life, Ben seems to be in perfect control, but as the subject matter of his advice becomes more personal and pertinent, his command begins to slip. In keeping with the theatrical metaphor in which he is working, Sondheim reveals Ben's disintegration in terms of a performer forgetting his lines. Ben has played the debonair song-and-dance man for many years, but within the heightened reality of the expressionist Follies the role becomes uncomfortable. He can't remember what he should say, or how he should behave. The realization that his life is a performance, a show played for effect rather than satisfaction, is clarified as Ben angrily sings:

Some break their asses
Passing their bar exams,
Lay out their lives
Like lines on a graph ...
One day they're diplomats—
Well, bully and congrats!
Me, I like to love,
Me, I ...
(p. 107)

It's the discovery that all that he has striven for is meaningless that causes Ben to forget his lines. As the orchestra continues an inexorable, relentless vamp in the background, Ben suddenly forgets his routine. As he desperately stutters out a phrase, the chorus dances on behind him. The world of illusion endures; the perfect chorus continues moving with precision, but Ben is forced to confront the awful reality of his own self-preoccupation with ultimate self-loathing. In anguish he cries out, "Me, I like—me, I love—me" (p. 107), but he is only halfway inside his nightmare Follies. The need for internal confession clashes with his habitually controlled appearance. Forced to step out of his assumed role, he "lunges forward out of the dance and shouts, 'I don't love me!' " (p. 108). In a paroxysm of guilt, rage, and agony he moves to the unheeding chorus line to confess his selfishness in a frantic attempt to find absolution:

> *(The chorus line goes on dancing, as if he didn't exist. He turns to the girl nearest him and shouts)*
> Her zipper stuck and you, you kept on
> saying how you loved her.
> *(To the next girl)*
> He was lying!
> *(And the next)*
> I just wanted her, that's all. I only
> wanted her until I had her.
> (p. 108)

The final cathartic moments of Ben's agony, as he is torn between a need for forgiveness and self-justification, are almost impossible to convey on paper. The total breakdown in Ben's psyche is represented by a complete disintegration of the real and theatrical world. A chaotic synthesis of past and present, illusion and reality, the internal world of romantic longing and the external world of disillusioned despair are suggested in an overwhelming theatrical spectacle. The entire cast simultaneously reenacts fragments of their performances; Goldman conveys something of Prince's staging in his description of Ben's collapse:

> The Follies drops begin to rise, and bit by bit we're back on the stage of the Weismann theater. Not literally, however. We're inside Ben's mind, and through his eyes we see a kind of madness.
>
> Everything we've seen and heard all evening is going on at once, as if the night's experience were being vomited. Ghosts, memories and party guests—all there. They stand on platforms which are moving insanely back and forth, they mill about the stage, and all of them are doing bits and pieces of their scenes and songs. And through it all, downstage, Ben's chorus line continues dancing.
>
> The cacophony is terrible, and we can barely hear Ben as he races from one group of people to another screaming. (p. 108)

"THROUGH THE UNKNOWN, REMEMBERED GATE"

Ben's hysterical self-flagellation increases in volume and intensity until the audience feels it can take no more. Then there is a moment of utter silence into which Ben passionately cries his wife's name. The madness resumes and finally fades as, once more and with an acknowledged sense of need and dependence, Ben calls "Phyllis."

As the gray light of dawn "seeps into the ruined theater" (p. 110), the two couples slowly come together and accept their reality. Sally sadly admits, "I left the dishes in the sink, I left them there, I was in such a hurry and there is no Ben for me, not ever, any place" (p. 109). She is deeply depressed and confesses that she wishes her first attempt at suicide, after Ben's initial rejection, had succeeded. But with Buddy's support there is a glimmer of hope, and the time theme reaches its culmination as Sally takes her first steps into the future:

> *Buddy*
>
> We're gonna go and get some
> rest ... And then we're gonna
> make plans for tomorrow.
>
> *Sally*
>
> For tomorrow ... Oh dear God,
> it *is* tomorrow.
> (p. 110)

Ben, who in the paroxysms of self-reproach had desperately called out for his wife, finally confesses to her, "I've always been afraid of you. You see straight through me and I've always thought, 'It isn't possible, it can't be me she loves' " (p. 110). As the two weary couples slowly exit, ghostly music plays softly. Their younger selves drift silently down stage. Past and present are momentarily reconciled, as they call once more up the stairwell, wistfully, "Hey, up there!" (p. 111).

This harmonious conclusion to the gut-wrenching evening is not totally convincing. Goldman admits he was not satisfied:

> The final scene of the show had always bothered me, I must admit. . . . I was pleased with the ending that Buddy and Sally had. I think it was honest and on target and about all you could do. I'm not so sure that if I had to write it over again that I would have had Ben and Phyllis together at the end. Marriage is a very difficult situation, but I don't think it's a bad one and I didn't want to write a show that was down on marriage. I wanted

> one of them, at least, to have hope in it, or at least the hope of something better. I'm not sure that's honest. I very much wanted them to get together at the end and I feel now that that was imposed on them. I can believe it of Phyllis, I just don't believe it of Ben. I think his game is over. I don't think there is any kind of life left in him. . . . [T]he man is finished . . . and I didn't want him to be. I wanted to leave the characters with a feeling that not everything is hopeless because, indeed, not everything *is* hopeless.[35]

The optimism, muted as it is, is a little too pat. It is undoubtedly comforting for an audience to accept that by confronting the past and all one's illusions and delusions one can cure all ills. I doubt whether this is convincing, however. It is consequently interesting that when *Follies* finally opened in London, sixteen years after its Broadway debut, Goldman chose to go against his instincts. He completely rewrote the book but rather than stay true to the intrinsic pain of the protagonists, he attempted a more rosy optimism. Sondheim's four new songs for the show, however, retained the tone of the original, his most effective addition being a cynical, sad duet for Phyllis and Ben, "A Country House," in which the two try to deny their alienation by contemplating the escapes offered by acquisitions. Wealth is shown to be no substitute for warmth. For devotees of the original, Sondheim's decision to replace Phyllis's and Ben's final songs is a violation.

But, both in the original and the revised London version, *Follies* dramatizes the unglamorous reality of aging and suggests that choices are essentially irrevocable. It reveals that significant values can only be discovered after the gauzy curtains of nostalgia have been stripped away. This musical's insistence that we accept the present, even if that present appears to be "a crumbling monument to the past, a decaying body painted over with flaky primary colors" is extremely provocative. These significant themes and issues cannot be satisfactorily resolved in the optimistic tradition of the genre. *Follies* poses searching and uncomfortable questions; it cannot then conclude on a note of mindless good humor. It may be a result of the modified, more optismistic ending that the revised *Follies* is a hit in London, but it is more likely that audiences are finally catching up with Sondheim. His work has reeducated theatergoers who no longer question the musical's ability to explore complex issues and painful truths.

Follies presents audiences with things many do not want to accept: youth denies age, and age glamorizes youth; the American faith that material wealth brings emotional maturity is inherently deceptive. The musical poses questions, not only about its characters and social milieu but about the validity of the musical form itself. Frank Rich, as a young critic for the *Harvard Crimson*, understood this:

> It is easy to avoid *Follies* on the grounds that it is, after all, a Broadway musical—and, given what Broadway musicals have come to mean, such a bias is understandable. But that is precisely why you should see it, for *Follies* is a musical about the death of the musical and everything musicals represented for the people who saw and enjoyed them when such entertainment flourished in this country. If nothing else, *Follies* will make it clear to you exactly why such a strange kind of theater was such an important part of the American consciousness for so long. In the playbill for this show, the setting is described as "a party on the stage of this theater tonight." They are not kidding, and there is no getting around the fact that a large part of the chilling fascination of *Follies* is that its creators are in essence presenting their own funeral.[36]

It is true, there is a death—the death of the old forms, old ideas, old conventions. The American musical should never have been the same again (unfortunately, for many it was). But there is also a birth. There were attempts prior to *Follies*, but with this work a serious and challenging art form firmly established itself in the domain of escapist fantasy.

5

"WE ARE SUCH STUFF AS DREAMS ARE MADE ON": *A Little Night Music*

Sondheim's next two works extend his experiments in form and craft. Lacking the raw emotional power that characterizes *Company* and *Follies*, they are more restricted in scope. Nevertheless, within their prescribed parameters they broaden the artistic horizons of the musical.

For many years Sondheim and Prince wanted to do an unabashedly romantic musical. As early as 1957, they attempted to acquire the rights to Jean Anouilh's *Ring 'Round the Moon*. When in 1971 their request was turned down a second time, Sondheim suggested adapting Ingmar Bergman's 1956 film *Smiles of a Summer Night*, a film containing precisely the elements of intricate romance, of "love and foolishness," for which they had been looking. The rights were readily obtained, and Hugh Wheeler was chosen to do the adaptation.

A Little Night Music's plot revolves around the complex amorous entanglements of Desirée Armfeldt, a mature, sensual actress who is in the process of discarding one admirer while attempting to entice a former lover into marriage. Both men are, naturally, married: Carl-Magnus, the pompous dragoon, whose fortunes are on the wane, to refined, devoted Charlotte; Fredrik Egerman, the stifled lawyer, to a naïve and still virginal Anne. The relationships are further complicated by Fredrik's son, Henrik, a devout Lutheran seminarian (whose real devotion is to his stepmother), and Desirée's daughter, Fredrika, the result of Desirée and Fredrik's previous dalliance. Desirée's patrician mother, an aging courtesan who longs only for the stylish intrigues of the past, presides over the festivities, while an elemental, healthy lustiness is added by the unrestrained passion of the servants, Petra and Frid.

As originally conceived, both the content and style of the piece were extremely complex. Sondheim recalls:

> Our original concept was that of a fantasy-ridden musical. It was to take place over a weekend, during which, in almost game-like fashion, Desirée would be the prime mover and would work the characters into different situations. The first time, everybody would get mixed up and through farcical situations, would end up with the wrong partner. Then magically, the weekend would start again. The next time, everything worked out, but Henrik committed suicide. The third time, Desirée arranged everything right but this time when she was left alone with Fredrik, he put on his gloves and started to walk off the stage because she hadn't done anything to make him want her.
>
> The way all this worked was that Madame Armfeldt, who was like a witch figure, would reshuffle the pack of cards and time would revert and we'd be back at the beginning of the weekend again. The characters would then re-form, waltz again, and start over. It was all to be presented like a court masque with a music box quality. But Hugh Wheeler finally gave up on it. He just couldn't make it work to his satisfaction.[1]

There are remnants of these original ideas evident in the final version: a surreal dance sequence; a *Liebeslieder* group; a masquelike quality in the dinner scene; magical overtones in Madame Armfeldt's cards and wine; and the mystical dusk of the Swedish white night. These elements provide tantalizing glimpses of what the musical might have been. As presented, however, the piece is less experimental and adventurous. Although it never conforms to the limited dictates of operetta, its predominant quality is that genre's rarefied delicacy. The intention is to skate on the surface of emotion, focusing on the social masks and theatrical disguises in the twilit world of late-nineteenth-century Sweden.

The structures of thought and theatrical form within which Sondheim worked and against which *A Little Night Music* is defined are the romantic rubrics of turn-of-the-century operetta. The entire score is set to variations of triple time. This technical feat is attempted not simply as a display of the composer's virtuosity, for as Sondheim explains, "In *Night Music* I put everything in some form of triple time so that the whole score would feel vaguely like a long waltz with scherzi in between so that no song would seem to have come from another texture."[2] The effect of this device is to give the score a sense of unity. Each song relates to the total mood and tone of the piece like varying shades of the same color. In addition, to enhance the sense of fin-de-siècle unease, Sondheim's score is filled with sudden key shifts and haunting dissonances reminiscent of the musical flavor of the turn of the century. The emotional tensions of Ravel and Richard Strauss rather than the blandness of Friml and Lehár color the music.

There is, however, an elegant precision in lyric and sound that relates the score to its apparently presumptuous Mozartian reference. The "little" in Sondheim's title is different in implication from the "little" used so extensively in *Company*. In this piece it suggests a light, rueful glimpse into the shadowy, illusory world of romance. In discussing the orchestrations with Jonathan Tunick, Sondheim suggested, "I want the whole show to have a perfumed quality, not just to bubble like champagne. It is about sex, and I'll take care of the bubble but I want some sense of musk on the stage all the time."[3] "Champagne," "bubble," "perfume," and "musk" are the affect tones Sondheim hoped to achieve in this delicate exploration of romantic human folly.

Just as in *Company* and *Follies*, Sondheim explores the theatrical implications of his chosen form. He is, however, never confined by the form. Traditionally, the world of romantic operetta is an exotic never-never land of sentimental escapism. Springing from the Viennese school of Johann Strauss and Franz Lehár and advanced in America by Rudolph Friml, Victor Herbert, and Sigmund Romberg, this genre evolved a definite set of characteristics. Although many are written in English for American audiences, the traditional operetta is remote from the vernacular. Overly elegant and stilted, characters in these fantasies communicate in a stylized speech unique to their make-believe milieu. Handsome decor, gorgeous costumes, beautiful people living in a realm removed from the humdrum banality of the daily grind, lovers' misunderstandings, jealousies, duels, numerous disguises, and the obligatory happy ending—these are the hallmarks of operetta. Blending these disparate elements into one romantic entity is a richly melodic score.

It is within this gestalt or mind-set that Sondheim works in *Night Music*, which conforms with many of the criteria of the operatic genre, but is significantly different. The twilight world of turn-of-the-century Sweden is certainly remote, both from the contemporary Broadway audience, and from the social and artistic milieu of the composer. This exotic locale was embodied in Boris Aronson's original sets. Hal Prince suggested to Aronson that the design should possess something of the quality of a Magritte painting. As Prince recalls: "Boris Aronson was reluctant to design *Night Music*. He kept reminding me that he is a Russian. I said I didn't know the difference between the landscape in Leningrad and the landscape in Helsinki: It's all birch trees as far as I am concerned. So he painted a forest of birch trees on clear plastic to look like Fabergé enamel on crystal. He carpeted the stage in a gently rolling lawn."[4] Aronson's sets were elegant rather than lush, with the quality of a Magritte painting suggested by the odd piece of antique furniture isolated among the trees. The characters are all figures out of context with their landscape, arbitrary and yet right.

The place, time, set, style (the costumes by Florence Klotz, who had been so wildly extravagant in *Follies*, epitomized stylish restraint), the convoluted love intrigues, and the denouement in which misunderstandings are resolved and couples are happily united, all conform with the rubrics of operetta; yet *Night Music* is not simply a contemporary reversion to a passé form. There is a dry cynicism in Sondheim's lyrics, a musical sophistication in his score. Most significantly there is a self-conscious awareness of the myths of romance in *Night Music*, which distinguishes it from traditional operetta. Both in musical and lyric suggestion, Sondheim explores the notions of illusion and disguise. The dramatis personae are all "acting out parts" and are intermittently made aware of their performances.

Night Music lacks the secure hero and heroine of the earlier genre, for all the individuals in this piece are ambivalent about themselves and their objectives. Indeed, Arthur Jackson finds the difference between *Night Music* and operetta in a "hard core of reality" that, he maintains, contrasts with the "vapid romanticism" of its precursors.[5] But this distinction is not borne out by the facts. The intricate maneuvers on a summer's night at a Swedish château have no basis in reality. The cynicism and sexual tension that permeate the show differentiate it from the simplistic naïvete of the earlier form. Sondheim creates a fantasy world, but simultaneously emphasizes its unreality.

Beginning with the vocal overture, the audience is presented with a meticulously organized theatrical construct. The *Liebeslieder* group that commences the action comments, advises, and acts as interior voices expressing the suppressed emotions of the protagonists. This chorus functions in a unique way. Its presence, whether outside the proscenium arch, crowded around a piano, or weaving in and out of the trees observing and interpreting, emphasizes the presentational nature of the production. Before the house-lights dim, Mr. Lindquist (each of the singers is distinguished by a name in the text, although they lack any specific individuality in performance) removes his gloves, strikes a note on the piano placed in a corner of the forestage and, accompanied by the other four singers, begins to vocalize. They are performers readying themselves for performance. The ground rules for the presentational mode of the piece are established.

This group of singers was introduced by Sondheim early on in the evolution of the musical, though at first Prince did not know how to integrate them:

> Early on, Steve asked me to substitute a *Liebeslieder Group* for a conventional chorus. I asked him how they were to function. He replied that was my problem. He needed them musically. As far as he was concerned, we could put a piano to the side of the stage and they could stand around it as in Balanchine's *Liebeslieder Walzer*. I was in trouble for three months.
>
> Then I got the idea that they might represent the positive spirits in a negative household. Everyone in *Night Music* is frustrated, humiliated by sexual role-playing. The five *Liebeslieder* people are secure. Perhaps they are operetta singers, optimistic, extroverted observers. Each is a personality, each has a response to the events of the evening. No two are alike. They make the piece accessible because they lead the audience into it.[6]

Whether Prince's intention is fully appreciated by an audience is doubtful (the positive individuality of the singers is difficult to determine), but certainly the device does lead an audience into the artificial world of the work. The group, detached from the fantastic realm of the action, mediates between the reality of the audience and the illusion of the stage. Many critics refer to this group as a "Greek Chorus," but, unlike the commentators of the classic theater, the *Liebeslieder* group is unaffected by events. Its members are not emotionally involved. Their cool disinterest serves to emphasize the floundering attempts of the characters to find sexual and emotional satisfaction.

The apparently random warm-ups of the singers modulate into a lilting waltz and the quality of *Night Music* is more firmly established. And the action begins—but not quite. The authors decided to preface the action with a surreal waltz in which the complex couplings of the text are dramatized in a choreographed exchange of dance partners. Although the waltz is introduced by the dry tones of the oboe, there is none of the ominous, ghostly quality present in the spectral opening sequence of *Follies*. The waltzing figures are insubstantial, but the musical and theatrical images suggest a world of beauty and luxury untouched by the depths of pain. This sequence, with its suitably mysterious music, seems to be a remnant of the creator's more elaborate earlier conception. It is certainly reminiscent of an Elizabethan dumbshow in which the action is portrayed in movement. But, as James Goldman complained:

> I never thought their beginning worked. I never thought that the *Lieder* singers singing the opening was an overture. . . . I thought it was the start of the show. Then there was that dance. It always seemed to me that the show had two opening numbers, two opening scenes, and I really wanted to get into the story. Also, unless you knew the show, you wouldn't have a clue that those people who were dancing were characters in the show. The things they did in the dance had application to what came later but you didn't know that in the beginning.[7]

The waltz takes places at twilight. The dancers are in perpetual motion, exchanging partners at will, with no profound alteration of pattern or mood. They are joined by the quintet of *Lieder* singers, who hum a lush accompaniment, and are observed, with self-contained composure, by Desirée's thirteen-year-old daughter, Fredrika. As the waltz ends, the dancers drift away into the trees and Madame Armfeldt is brought onto the stage in her wheelchair.

In the brief scene between grandmother (Madame Armfeldt) and granddaughter (Fredrika), the conventions of the evening are established. Wheeler recreates from the Bergman original a world in which the only thing one does not cheat at is a game of solitaire, and the mystical influence of the night's smile hovers over all. The action of the piece is delineated in the three smiles of the summer night that Madame Armfeldt tells Fredrika to watch for: "the smiles at the young who know nothing"; "at the fools who know too little"; and "at the old who know too much."[8]

As young Fredrika is dismissed to practice her scales on the piano, the scene shifts to the home of the lawyer Egerman, where his son, Henrik, is practicing the cello. The musical skills of the two youngsters, woven in and out of the text, serve to connect the two households. Though not startlingly innovative, this device is indicative of the meticulous concern with detail characteristic of the work. Fredrika's fingers flit lightly up and down the scales while Henrik elicits only the most somber and lugubrious tones from his instrument.

The glum, intense Henrik is teased and provoked by his stepmother, the nubile Anne, until his father returns and with blustering bonhomie announces that he has purchased tickets for the theater to see "the One and Only" Desirée Armfeldt. The sexual tensions shimmering under the dialogue are finally released in a formidable three-part soliloquy. The characters explore their confused longings in parallel form. Unaware of each other's desire, their conflicting urges are laid bare. No solutions are reached, no problems are solved. Each character is troubled and unable to disentangle his or her complex emotions and needs. They all want essentially the same thing, sexual release, but their timetables are radically different, as is suggested in the "Now / Later / Soon" structure of the song.

Sondheim uses this form of inner monologue in *Company* and *Follies*, but perfects it in *Night Music*. Conveying struggle and confusion, these songs show characters wrestling with their unexpressed and misunderstood desires, singing of their deepest thoughts, but seldom to each other. The characters do not understand themselves, and this lack of personal insight is conveyed to the audience. The effect of these emotional revelations is not to make an audience feel superior, however. Rather Sondheim is able to incorporate his audience, inviting its sympathy but compelling its identification with the helpless folly of human desire. This exploration into self does not rely solely on the denotative power of the word. Sondheim suggests all the conflicting contradictions of his characters through musical implication, connotative resonance, and well-placed silence.

Fredrik, whose sexual advances are spurned yet again by his wife, is the first to ruminate. His suppressed libidinous longings, his logical legal mind, and his disquieting awareness of the disparity between his and his wife's ages are incorporated into his music. With its impeccable combination of form and content, style and character, Fredrik's song is logically developed to the point of absurdity. Much is left unstated, yet the character's needs are clearly apparent. The vocabulary is erudite and sprinkled with ponderous legal locutions. The puns, the witty rhymes, and the verbal virtuosity reveal both Fredrik's education and his lack of insight.

As Anne burbles incessantly in the background, Fredrik contemplates his seduction tactics. From the opening line Fredrik reveals his awareness of his wife's foolish charm:

> Now, as the sweet imbecilities
> Tumble so lavishly
> Onto her lap ...
> (p. 23)

The oxymoron indicates the contradiction implicit in his ambiguous feeling. The key preoccupation, however, in each of the three soliloquies (Fredrik's, Henrik's, and Anne's) is time. Fredrik here feels his age. Having awaited consummation so long, he wants fulfillment "now." This word with all its urgency initiates his meandering thoughts and is repeated throughout the song. (Each of the three key words, *now*, *later*, and *soon*, has been incorporated into the preceding scene so that the soliloquies are expressions of existing preoccupations.) Sondheim inverts audience expectation, though, for rather than growing more insistent, Fredrik's demand for satisfaction "now" becomes progressively less assertive. During the entire monologue—structured into a series of syllogistic arguments—the lawyer's mind controls his emotions. But as he so carefully works out his lecherous tactics, he grows weary and is finally content to drift into a peaceful doze.

The incongruity of the dry, logical development of the argument and its lascivious content is amusing:

> *Fredrik*
>
> Now, as the sweet imbecilities
> Tumble so lavishly
> Onto her lap ...
>
> Now, there are two possibilities:
> A, I could ravish her,
> B, I could nap.
>
> Say it's the ravishment, then we see
> The option
> That follows, of course:
>
> A, the deployment of charm, or B,
> The adoption
> Of physical force ...
> (pp. 23–24)

Supplementing this witty structure is the character's own vanity and uncomfortable awareness of age. Eventually his middle-aged lack of youthful passion is confirmed in his acceptance of further delay and his welcome to the midafternoon sleep. His two original alternatives were ravishment or rest and having exhausted the logical possibilities of the former, he is content to settle for the latter.

Further humor is added by the character's apposite and clever exploitation of literary references as he contemplates reading "suggestively" to his young wife:

> In view of her penchant
> For something romantic,
> De Sade is too trenchant
> And Dickens too frantic,
> And Stendhal would ruin
> The plan of attack,
> As there isn't much blue in
> "The Red and the Black" ...
> (p. 27)

As his thoughts draw to a relaxed conclusion, the rhyme scheme builds to an anticipation of his wife's name, but the final declaration is affectionate rather than fervent.

A brief interchange between Henrik and the lusty maid, Petra, follows. Henrik's clumsy advances are laughingly dismissed with the tantalizing promise of "later." This provokes his gloomy, frustrated plea for release. To the melancholy sounds of his cello, he dejectedly contemplates his life. By constructing a character who sees himself almost exclusively in terms of other people's cavalier dismissals, Sondheim conveys Henrik's incapacitating insecurity:

> "Shush, Henrik—
> Goodness, how you gush, Henrik—
> Hush, Henrik!"
> You murmur,
> "I only ...
> It's just that ...
> For God's sake!"
> "Later, Henrik ..."
> (p. 30)

Henrik's cautious attempts to express himself are all aborted until he sings out in a cellistic cadenza the high, painful "for God's sake" (p. 30); but he sinks back, anticipating another delay.

The meandering of Henrik's mind, the barely suppressed frustration, and the veneer of sanctimoniousness are conveyed in the intricate lyric structure. Against the painful mumbling of the young man, the cello's mellow voice acts both as a restraint and as an expression of his romantic longings.

Sondheim achieves sympathy for the character by conluding his monologue with a gentle line expressing Henrik's yearning: "Doesn't anything begin?" (p. 31).

Focus shifts without intervening dialogue to Anne, a proximity emphasizing the affinity of the two young people. Where her husband demands immediate satisfaction and her stepson rails against undesired delay, Anne seeks only to procrastinate. In keeping with her personality, the most melodic of the extracts is hers. As her husband soundly sleeps, she expresses her insecurity. Light, lovely, and frivolous, Anne enjoys romantic titillation, but lyric and melody halt suddenly when the unpleasant realization of her husband's age intrudes into her thoughts:

> Soon, I promise.
> Soon I won't shy away,
> Dear old—
> *(She bites her lip)*
> Soon. I want to.
> Soon, whatever you say.
> (p. 31)

As Anne's sentimental musing regains its momentum the melodic line is strong. It never builds to a climax, however. The most enthusiastic sexual response Anne can muster is "I don't mind it too much" (p. 31). Then just as she goes skittering away from her husband's clasp, the rhythm, melody, and lyric become rapid and break the former tranquil pattern. Although she is a coquette, Anne is no fool. She acknowledges that her own insecurity may be the source of her frigidity:

> If I were perfect for you,
> Wouldn't you tire of me
> Soon?
> (p. 31)

Disturbed by the sound of Henrik's cello, Anne scolds him and further aggravates his frustration as she stands provocatively in a negligee. She returns to the bedroom and their two voices combine and express their discordant yet harmonious fears and longing. They are joined by Fredrik and in an intricate polyphony the three again articulate their desires, each song revealing more than the lyric broadly states. Although Fredrik demands satisfaction "now," the subtext of his argument reveals his lack of urgency.

Henrik's life of procrastination disguises his passionate intensity, and Anne's promised submission cannot hide her lack of sexual enthusiasm. The trio's conflicting desires suggest the central dynamic of the plot; with great psychological and emotional complexity this musical and lyric montage reveals to the audience the predominate concerns of each, without the characters themselves participating in this awareness.

The lyrics and melody blend, yet through the careful composition of sound Sondheim highlights key words and allows them to be expressed clearly. The pivotal notions are exchanged as Henrik demands "Come to me / Now" while his father counterpoints with a less assertive "Come to me / Soon" (p. 34). In the concluding phrases each character reverts to his original plea, but it is Fredrik who dominates the finale:

Anne	*Henrik*	*Fredrik*
Soon.	Later?	Now—
		I still want and/or
	Later ...	Love
		You,
Soon.		Now, as
	Later ...	Always,
Soon.		Now. . . .

(p. 35)

The final word, which sounds clearly without any harmonic distortion, is Fredrik's aching cry, not for his wife, but for "Desirée." Sondheim's theatrical acumen is obvious. This one word forces the action forward and adds a further dimension to the complexity of the preceding sequence. The audience realizes that Anne's insecurities are not baseless and that her husband's real fervor is directed towards someone else. Moreover, Henrik's incestuous longings need not be entirely hopeless.

The muffled repetition of Fredrika's scales returns the focus to Madame Armfeldt's château. Time and space are connected by sound. Prince's use of cinematic techniques in this piece may be less flamboyant than his directorial approach in *Follies*, but they are equally apparent. Montage, jump-cuts, fade-ins, overlaps, and musical underscoring, while mundane techniques on the screen, are stylistically innovative in the theater.

Having provided the audience with some insight into the conflicting emotions rampant in the Egerman household, Sondheim now reveals the tensions and dynamics of the Armfeldt ménage. Fredrika's light young voice explains the difference between "ordinary mothers" and her own:

> Ordinary mothers, like ordinary wives,
> Fry the eggs and dry the sheets and
> Try to deal with facts.
> Mine acts.
> (p. 35)

She is interrupted by a hurriedly sung dispatch from her mother. Desirée's interjection is composed of brief disjointed phrases that re-create the sketchy, incomplete communication existing between mother and daugher. Short, snatched phrases, hastily scribbled notes, and brief encounters epitomize the pattern of their lives.

The members of the quintet, as impartial observers, then encapsulate the pleasures and pains of an actress's life on the road:

> *Mrs. Segstrom*
>
> Ice in the basin, La La La
>
> *Mr. Erlansen*
>
> Cracks in the plaster, La La La
>
> *Mrs. Anderssen*
>
> Mice in the hallway, La La La
>
> *The Quintet*
>
> Hi-ho, the glamorous life!
> (p. 36)

Just as he used the "doo doo doo doo" in *Company*, Sondheim uses the "La La La" and "Hi-ho" for punctuation and emphasis. These nonwords suggest the frivolous inconsequential aspects of Desirée's life but also convey the fun. In addition, there is a sense of period in these exclamations. They distance the audience, re-create a past world, and highlight the ironic use of the word *glamorous*.

After Madame Armfeldt expresses her displeasure at Desirée's life-style (using the same melody used by her granddaughter, with whom she shares a level-headed sagacity), Desirée sings another brief note, this one to her mother. In it, she indicates her dissatisfaction with her "glamorous life." This discomfort is explored in the closing stanzas of the chorus, where

Sondheim exposes all the sham, contradiction, and vacuity of Desirée's theatrical posturing and apparently festive beau monde:

> *Mrs. Nordstrom*
>
> Cultural lunches, La La La
>
> *Mrs. Anderssen*
>
> Dead floral tributes, La La La
>
> *Mr. Lindquist*
>
> Ancient admirers, La La La
>
> *Quintet*
>
> Hi-ho, the glamorous life!
>
> (p. 38)

It should be noted that almost the entire first scene of *Night Music* is set to music. The short prose interludes are brief, and Sondheim, therefore, is responsible for the bulk of the work. This proportion is not sustained, however. The piece becomes increasingly burdened with dialogue. One can comprehend this design in terms of the show's operetta-like structure, but whereas Sondheim used his theatrical mode as a springboard to invention in *Follies*, the theatrical mode in *Night Music* confines his creative impetus. The liability for this, I suspect, is to be found in Wheeler's adaptation. The fantastic masquelike creation originally envisaged becomes progressively less apparent and a dialogue-heavy script takes precedence. It is not, therefore, necessary to provide a step-by-step synopsis of the convoluted twists and turns of the plot. To appreciate Sondheim's contribution, one need only analyze his work as it affects character and situation and advances the action.

At the theater where Fredrik has taken his young wife to see his sometime mistress in a light French farce (the choice of the play is not arbitrary), the two former lovers' eyes meet across the footlights. A chord is struck and this minor epiphany is expressed in song. As the memories surge forward they are articulated, not by the two characters themselves, but by the quintet. This technique of using other voices to express the characters' inner turmoil, is used with great effect in this work.

Unlike the formidable gap that exists between past and present in *Follies*, the romantic delusions of the past are part of the immediate present in *Night Music*. There is no demanding imperative that the harsh realities of time be accepted. The illusions and confusions of the characters in the latter musical are gentle and call for only minor readjustment rather than radical change. The tender, romantic longing for the past expressed by the *Liebeslieder* group is something the lovers can attain in the make-believe world of this play. The device of having this yearning expressed by a chorus serves both to sustain a fourth-wall believability for the characters and at the same time emphasizes the presentational style of the musical.

While Fredrik's and Desirée's interior worlds are given expression by the quintet, all on stage are immobilized by the powers of the two lovers' attraction and memories. The light refrain, with its quizzical "remember?" recurs as a leitmotif throughout the piece and sustains the tone of the evening. It is a commentary filled with sentimental memories and regrets. The recollections Sondheim evokes in a series of brief images ("The old deserted beach that we walked," "The café in the park where we talked" [p. 42], "The tenor on the boat that we chartered" [p. 43]) suggest a quick glance through an aging photograph album.

The contradictions of Fredrik and Desirée's romance, its ambivalences and tensions, are not omitted. It is a world of romance that the lovers know and recall, but it takes an evening of elaborate maneuvering to enable them to recapture it. Yet their reunion in this world of fantasy is inevitable. As the first segment of the song ends with an ambiguous "I think you were there" (p. 43), Anne, suspecting the attraction between her husband and the glamorous actress, rushes from the theater. But once Fredrik has put her safely to bed, the reminiscences expressed by the quintet become more compelling. His longing for the mature and very sensual Desirée grows more and more urgent. The focus of Fredrik's desire is clear, and Sondheim makes the recollected scenes more overtly sexual:

> *Mr. Lindquist*
>
> What we did with your perfume—
>
> *Mr. Erlansen*
>
> Remember, darling?
>
> *Mrs. Segstrom*
>
> The condition of the room
> When we were through ...
>
> *Mrs. Nordstrom*

Our inventions were unique—
Remember, darling?

Mr. Lindquist

I was limping for a week,
You caught the flu ...
(pp. 51—52)

One of the achievements of Sondheim's lyrics in this work is his combination of wit and eroticism. His lyrics are suggestive but never crude. All the characters are preoccupied with sex, but the musical is sensual in a healthy rather than in a salacious manner. The laughter and smiles he elicits from the characters and audience are genuine and sympathetic. "Remember?" concludes with a definite "I'm *sure* it was you" (p. 52), and Fredrik finds himself propelled unresistingly to Desirée's dressing room.

In an atmosphere electric with sexual tension, Desirée and Fredrick meet for the first time in fourteen years. Although his suppressed passion is obvious to them both, he tries to justify his existence and explain the reasons for his marriage. In a song directed as much at his own confusion as it is at Desirée's edification, Fredrik tells of his attraction for Anne. There is a poignant, regretful quality in the melody anticipating the pain and remorse he must acknowledge. Coming from a middle-aged man desperately clinging to youth while admitting the foolishness of his desires, Fredrik's confession is predominantly rueful.

Sondheim uses modulations in this song to assist the audience in feeling the character's inner turmoil. Fredrik changes key every few lines by descending half steps, which suggests his sinking morale but builds up energy for a false but hearty conclusion. Fredrik anticipates the alienating effect on Desirée, yet he feels impelled to convey the poignant sweetness of his young bride. Like so much of Sondheim's work, Fredrik's paean is filled with contradiction and confusion, with none of the unambiguous excitement and joy traditionally associated with a love song. While Anne disturbs and upsets the comfortable pattern of his life, he is irresistibly drawn to her:

She lightens my sadness,
She livens my days,
She bursts with a kind of madness
My well-ordered ways.
My happiest mistake,
The ache of my life:

You must meet my wife.
(p. 59)

The irony of the song, though, is that it is sung, not to his wife, but to his former mistress whom he is longing to bed. Fredrik's indulgent infatuation is suggested in the soft harmonies of his song. His exaggerated praise is rapidly deflated, however, by Desirée's acerbic interjections. Her wit penetrates Fredrik's self-deception and reveals the real status quo:

Fredrik

She makes me feel I'm—what?—

Desirée

A very old man?

Fredrik

Yes–no!
(p. 61)

Ultimately Fredrik confesses that his young wife is still a virgin. Desirée's response wins her audience approval. As the rhythm accelerates and her anger surfaces, she does not deride her vaguely ridiculous lover but defends him. Her passionate attack on the unfeeling heartlessness of the virgin bride reveals the intensity of her concern for Fredrik. He shamefacedly acknowledges that his need to see Desirée was prompted by the frightful tension of his eleven-month-old unconsummated marriage, and, with generosity and style, Desirée acquiesces with "Of course. What are old friends for?"

In direct contrast to her daughter's spontaneous but impractical ardor, Madame Armfeldt immediately regales the audience with a long and meandering recollection of her own amours. Desirée has leapt thoughtlessly into bed with a bourgeois lawyer who is infatuated with his own childbride. Her mother, however, has spent a long and fruitful career cultivating aristocratic paramours, calculating their yield in very concrete terms. As the elderly chatelaine's mind twists and turns, recollecting a past filled with intrigue and luxury, so the musical line wanders. Just as the lawyer's thought patterns were strictly logical and pragmatic, so the old lady's mental condition is conveyed in the tortuous convolutions of melody and lyric.

Madame Armfeldt's code of morality is far from conventional, her standards unabashedly material. Yet she represents a period of high style that she maintains is gone forever:

Liaisons! What's happened to them,
Liaisons today?
Disgraceful! What's become of them?
Some of them
Hardly pay their shoddy way.
What once was a rare champagne
Is now just an amiable hock;
What once was a villa, at least,
Is "digs" ...

What was once a gown with train
Is now just a simple little frock;
What once was a sumptuous feast
Is figs.
No, not even figs—raisins.
Ah, liaisons!
(p. 66)

The elegant vocabulary, the exotic locales and the vaguely Byzantine flavor of the accompaniment evoke a world of dissipation and luxury, in contrast to which the impetuous flings of her theatrical daughter appear gauche and inept.

Just as the world of *Night Music*, the world of operetta, elegant and stylish, is distant from the contemporary world of its audience, so Madame Armfeldt's world of carefully calculated seduction is remote from the world of Desirée and Fredrik. In part, the difference is to be found in the degree of style and calculated, imposed order. Madame Armfeldt demands:

Where is style? Where is skill?
Where is forethought?
Where's discretion of the heart,
Where's passion in the art,
Where's craft?
(p. 67)

But Madame Armfeldt is above all a cynical pragmatist. She advocates the shrewd manipulation of sex as a means to material gain, and she wants no part in the foolishness of love. For her, sex is merely a "pleasurable means / To a measurable end" (p. 68).

In a final recognition of the devaluation of her contemporary society, and by extension of that of the audience, Madame Armfeldt acknowledges the plebeian commonness of current social life and accepts that only in the past could an elevated style be retained. Style, order, elegance, and romantic fantasy can exist only in recollection. The present is made chaotic and complicated by the distracting confusion of sex and love.

Illustrative of the truth of Madame Armfeldt's sentiments, Desirée is abruptly revealed, trapped in the classic situation of low farce: one lover is caught in her bedroom while the other hammers imperiously at her door. Even though confronted with his disheveled mistress and a man dressed in his robe, Carl-Magnus refuses to accept the concrete evidence before him. He sings a spluttering song of denial with appropriate military flourish. He cannot contemplate the possibility of Desirée's infidelity and consequently the entire piece consists of incomplete queries:

> She wouldn't ...
> Therefore they didn't ...
> So then it wasn't ...
> Not unless it ...
> Would she?
> She doesn't ...
> God knows she needn't ...
> Therefore it's not.
> (p. 74)

The humor and pathos of the character's pompous rationalization is conveyed in the broken phrases. Under all the half-expressed thoughts, the militaristic rhythm marches forward. The troubled man cannot discard his soldier's mien. Sondheim concludes with an amusing revelation of the dragoon's unselfconscious male chauvinism. His dual standards, expressed with souring sentimental fervor, are displayed in all their tarnished glory:

> Fidelity is more than mere display,
> It's what a man expects from life.
> Fidelity, like mine to Desirée
> And Charlotte, my devoted wife.
> (p. 74)

On returning to his wife, Carl-Magnus cannot quite relinquish his doubts. The questions he could never articulate to another are expressed through a theatrical convention similar to the aside, as he sings out his fears in the middle of a conversation with his wife and then resumes talking as if there had been no interruption. Like the majority of songs in *Night Music*, his is an articulation of inner anxiety rather than an attempt to communicate. His song is directed inward, and Sondheim gives a different voice to each unique personality and problem. In the second fragment of Carl-Magnus's sung soliloquy, his self-deception is ironically highlighted in the concluding lines. In pompous and self-righteous tones, and to a richly melodic accompaniment, Carl-Magnus declares:

> Besides, no matter what one might infer,
> One must have faith to some degree.
> The least that I can do is trust in her
> The way that Charlotte trusts in me.
> (p. 76)

Having persuaded his pliable, devoted wife to go and tell young Anne Egerman of Fredrik's escapade in Desirée's dressing room, he then sings contentedly in praise of women. The qualities Carl-Magnus thinks he admires in his women reveal a great deal about the man:

> Durable, sensible ...
> Women, women ...
> Very nearly indispensable
> Creatures of grace.
> God knows the foolishness about them,
> But if one had to live without them,
> The world would surely be a poorer,
> If purer, place.
> (p. 78)

Despite his complacency about his wife's compliance, Carl-Magnus is still plagued with doubt. Sondheim reveals his confused mental state by breaking the gentle tribute and reintroducing the fractured series of unanswered questions. The contrast between the soothing melody of the praise and the troubled, broken phrases of Carl-Magnus's doubt reflect his ambiguous emotional condition. His obsession is suggested in repeated words and an onomatopoeic rhythmic scheme ("skip," "trip," "hip"), but Carl-Magnus, being a pragmatic soldier, concludes with a definite statement and unambiguous assertion of his possession. He cannot and will not contemplate that he may be the cuckold:

> She wouldn't ...
> Therefore they didn't ...

The woman's mine!
(p. 78)

Charlotte goes to Anne and, despite the fact that the revelation humiliates her, obliges her husband, telling Anne of Fredrik's infidelity. The two women, crushed by the perfidy of their husbands, sit in mutual commiseration. Charlotte then describes her life in song. More an interior monologue than a confession, the song concludes with a duet showing a common emotional condition rather than communication between the two women. In Charlotte's revelation, three of Sondheim's favorite words are brought together: *perfect*, *little*, and *death*. The piece is far from morbid but possesses a quality of melancholy that underscores many of the melodies and lyrics in *Night Music*. The play combines the predominate codes of operetta with many of the accepted elements of farce, yet in Sondheim's work one can detect an additional dimension of regret and loss. This quality is clearest in the dejected admissions of the exploited wife.

The pervasive despondency and the anesthetizing acceptance of the pain of marriage is clearly articulated by Charlotte:

Every day a little death
In the parlor, in the bed,
In the curtains, in the silver,
In the buttons, in the bread.
Every day a little sting
In the heart and in the head.
Every move and every breath,
And you hardly feel a thing,
Brings a perfect little death.
(p. 85)

But Sondheim does not set this song to a lugubrious melody or somber rhythm. These he reserves for the ridiculous excesses of Henrik's frustration. These "deaths" Charlotte experiences are after all "little" and Sondheim's light touch in melody, rhythm, and lyric pattern reveals the delicate agony of the pinpricks of humiliation that characterizes her life. Her views on men are not that different from her husband's attitude to women, but Charlotte possesses the painful insight of her own dependency:

I'm before him on my knees
And he kisses me.
He assumes I'll lose my reason,

And I do.
(pp. 85–86)

The "perfect little death" that epitomizes their existence dramatizes the subliminal pain latent in all the relationships. The quality of exquisite, ornamental suffering, which does not obviously intrude but gives a depth to the frivolous lives of the characters, is expressed by the dutiful and helpless wife.

In order to entrap Fredrik, Desirée persuades her mother to invite the Egermans for a weekend at her château in the country. Anne's reaction to the invitation, her maid's excitement, Fredrik's counterreaction, Charlotte's discovery of the social engagement, her husband's decision to gate-crash the party, her scheme to recapture her husband's love, and the sanctimonious observations of the pious Henrik are all conveyed in an intricate musical sequence. How the sequence evolved is described by Prince in his autobiography:

> The final scene in Act I was a sequence for the entire company, to be musicalized, a miniopera. I got tired of waiting, and one day with some ad libs from Hugh I began to move the actors around: "You go here and you hand this person an invitation and you say, 'Look what happened. We've been invited to a weekend at the Armfeldts' in the country,' and you say, 'Well, I don't want to go,' and you say, 'Oh, please,' and you say, 'Well, I'll reconsider,' and so on."
>
> I took the company through these little scenes, perhaps six of them. Each time I came to the end of one, I would say, "Now you sing" or "You two sing" or "All four of you sing." And catching the spirit, with vocalizing and appropriate gestures, they make a mock opera of it. Simultaneously I choreographed the birch trees to go with the scene changes and dialogue.
>
> I invited Steve to see what we'd done and he went home that night and wrote a fifteen-minute sequence so specifically that Pat Birch was able to choreograph the company without altering the blocking.[9]

Although this recollection is a trifle exaggerated and Sondheim had to alter a great deal of the scenario that Prince, Birch, and Wheeler had developed, nevertheless, the close collaborative nature of the endeavor is evident.

Sondheim's dramatic perspicacity is confirmed in this complex series of vignettes. Economically he condenses numerous decisions and actions essential to the plot, but of minimal dramatic interest, into a fast-paced rollicking first act finale. Six of the major characters express their reaction to the proposed weekend and join in the hearty refrain. Yet they retain their individual personalities. Meanwhile, the traditional theatrical structure of the operetta, in which a rousing finale prior to intermission is obligatory, is satisfied. All the dangers, traps, intrigues, and complications possible in the proposed weekend are suggested as the characters contemplate their contradictory strategies. The music possesses the quality of a roisterous hunting song. Certainly all of the participants are on the prowl, but each has a different prey. The only character who sings to a different melody is Henrik. In contrast with the galloping rhythms and clearly sounded hunting horns of the number, his segment is ponderous and measured by the solemn tolling of church bells. But Henrik fools no one but himself. All the members of the two households, including the Egermans' lusty maid, Petra, are quivering with anticipation at the erotic adventure before them.

Act 2 opens with a musical entr'acte, another remnant, one suspects, from the masquelike structure of the original conception. The quintet then sets the scene. Picking up the lilting waltz of the entr'acte, they describe the mysterious twilight existence of the Swedish white night. By setting his action in this magical nether world where the sun never sets—even though it is based on geographic reality—Sondheim creates a realm outside of the mundane sphere of normal time and place. The action at Madame Armfeldt's château is placed in this twilight zone between reality and illusion, a magical theatrical space in which anything is possible. The hands of the clock may move but nothing really changes.

The sylvan scene, complete with popping champagne corks, a picnic on the grass, and Desirée languidly playing croquet, is disturbed by the arrival of the rival lovers and their respective families in their spluttering motor vehicles. The antagonism is barely suppressed as Desirée tries valiantly to juggle the contending suitors. Their violence is bracketed by the quintet, who sing of the confused time in the uncertain, unstable light. The bluster, the anger, and the sexual tensions of the dialogue are distorted and reflected in the otherworldly quality of the quintet's musical observations. The short series of farcelike intrigues concludes with a wry, sung observation that emphasizes the lack of profound change. Even as the sun sets, "It instantly rises again" (p. 127). There is no night and consequently no one can steal away in the dark. All of the night waltzes are jokes about perpetual anticipation. There can be no release in the world of *Night Music*.

Initially oblivious of each other's presence, the two would-be swains contemplate their entanglement with Desirée in twin soliloquies. Set in a series of "needling triplets,"[10] the piece emphasizes the frustrated regrets of the two men. As they pace and ponder, they meet and dismiss each other with a curt acknowledgment. Both men, trying to extricate themselves from Desirée's charm, fantasize about what would be necessary to negate her appeal. In his naïvely logical fashion, Fredrik argues:

> I should never have gone
> To the theater.
> Then I'd never have come
> To the country.
> If I never had come
> To the country,
> Matters might have stayed
> As they were.
> (p. 128)

Although his deductions are clear, his argument is false because it is based on an untrue hypothesis. It is he who volunteers the theater tickets that precipitate all subsequent events. Fredrik refuses to recognize his readiness for Desirée, but Sondheim makes it clear to the audience.

Then to the measured rhythm of the men's pacing, Fredrik lists a series of arguments. Sondheim has observed that list songs are not intrinsically funny, but that the form can aid the comic potential. The humor in this number is sustained because Desirée is none of the things that the men catalog, nor would they want her to be. Contradiction is at the heart of the song, and, just as he balanced ambiguous opposites in musical and lyric idea in "Sorry—Grateful," so Sondheim sustains the tension in this composition. The negative qualities the suitors profess to yearn for implicitly suggest the positive attributes they obviously admire:

> If she'd only been faded,
> If she'd only been fat,
> If she'd only been jaded
> And bursting with chat,
> If she'd only been perfectly awful,
> It would have been wonderful.
> If ... if ...
> (pp. 128–29)

This ambivalence is accentuated in the lush, romantic assertion of the refrain. The glorification of the imperfections of human love is evoked in word and sound.

The two married men can barely acknowledge each other's existence, but their shared concerns are clarified as they alternate the lines of the song and ultimately join in a passionately sung refrain:

Carl-Magnus

If she had only been fearful ...

Fredrik

Or married ...

Carl-Magnus

Or tearful ...

Fredrik

Or dead ...

Both

It would have been wonderful.
But the woman was perfection,
And the prospects are grim,
That lovely perfection
That nothing can dim.
Yes, the woman was perfection,
So I'm here with him ...
(pp. 131–32)

The barely suppressed antagonism and rivalry between the two men intensify as they sail into the dining room with Desirée between them.

The dinner scene is another indication of the masque form that had been originally envisaged. The quintet sings a brief, almost Elizabethan, round generating a tense atmosphere at odds with the sumptuous meal and elaborate table setting that are moved on stage. This brief scene highlights the exotic elegance of the life-style, but simultaneously reveals the repressed sexual tensions that seethe beneath the genteel facade. It is this ferment that Sondheim highlights in his lyrics and in the intricate interweaving of the round. The only words sung clearly in unison indicate the fragility of the ostensible order:

Keeping control
While falling
Apart.
(p. 137)

Much of the dinner scene is taken up with the jostling tactics of the various intriguers. But again it is the score that provides the scene with its most electrifying moment. To the haunting theme of the "Twilight" song, Madame Armfeldt declares:

> Ladies and gentlemen, tonight I am serving you a very special desert wine. . . . The secret of its unique quality is unknown, but it is said to possess the power to open the eyes—even of the blindest among us ...
>
> To Life! ...
>
> And to the only other reality—Death!
> (pp. 142–43)

The mystical quality of the sound, and the otherworldly sentiments of the speaker, lift the scene out of the confines of elegant costume romance. Madame Armfeldt assumes a Prospero-like power as she evokes the magic of the traditional masque. The chilly silence that follows the toast emphasizes the solemn undercurrent, the awareness of death-in-life that recurs in the work.

It is Henrik who eventually can no longer tolerate the frivolous game-playing. He storms from the table intent on destroying himself. He is followed by young Fredrika, who reveals to Anne the real reason for Henrik's passionate outburst. The convoluted titillations of the wealthy are momentarily interrupted by the fresh passion of the two servants, Frid and Petra. They provide a touchstone of unaffected sensuality against which the artificiality of their employers' lives appears faintly ridiculous.

Desirée herself is beginning to realize the ludicrous quality of the sham, and in the subsequent bedroom scene with Fredrik she acknowledges the inanity of their respective life-styles: "What in God's name are we laughing about? Your son was right at dinner. We don't fool that boy, not for a moment. The One and Only Desirée Armfeldt, dragging around the country in shoddy tours, carrying on with someone else's dim-witted husband. And the Great Lawyer Egerman, busy renewing his unrenewable youth" (p. 152). She discards all the artifice and briefly gives voice to her genuine longing. But Fredrik turns his back on the reality of her love and chooses the make-believe fantasy of his life with Anne.

Desirée's poignant response, "Send in the Clowns," is Sondheim's only popular hit, but the fact that this song has had a life outside of the play does not imply that it does not come directly out of the emotional response of a particular character at that moment. Sondheim wrote the number only a few days before the company left for Boston, after seeing Glynis Johns play the scene. He admits:

> It was a song that I wrote under protest for a scene . . . I thought belonged to the man. Hal Prince felt that it was the woman's scene, and that she should have a song. While I was writing it, I figured it would be the man's song because the impulse for the scene, the impulse for singing was the man's as far as I was concerned. But Hal directed the scene in such a way that the impulse became the woman's. When I read the scene I still think it's his, but somehow on the stage it was hers.[11]

There were critics who found in the song's melodic beauty and emotional tenderness an indication that Sondheim was finally freeing himself from the confines of his rigid intellectuality.[12] But this response is a clear indication of a confusion between art object and artist. The sentiments are Desirée's, not Sondheim's. Moreover, despite its melodic richness, the song has little of the traditional affirmation of the love song. Sondheim describes the score of *Night Music* as "dry, unsentimental and soulful,"[13] and these qualities are all characteristic of "Send in the Clowns."

In a number filled with rueful melancholy, the hopeless incapacity of human beings honestly to confront each other is acknowledged and the necessity for play-acting and masks is accepted. The theatrical illusion, the pretense, the escapism inherent in the operetta form is suddenly placed in stark relief. The musical's structure becomes directly and strikingly revelatory of its thematic content. Desirée is resigned. She has stepped outside of her game, has tried to introduce mature commitment, and failed. She therefore recognizes her prescribed role:

> Don't you love farce?
> My fault, I fear.
> I thought that you'd want what I want—
> Sorry, my dear.
> But where are the clowns?
> Quick, send in the clowns.
> Don't bother, they're here.
> (p. 154)

The song is rich in theatrical imagery. Desirée is an actress who has bungled her most important role:

Making my entrance again
With my usual flair,
Sure of my lines,
No one is there.
(p. 154)

The song synthesizes the twin muses of pathos and farce. Her pain is hidden beneath the veneer of self-deprecating humor, but the wit and style of her performance do not disguise the emotional depth of her longing.

The farcical elements of the evening are reemphasized as Anne and Fredrika search out a desperate Henrik. His attempts at suicide are aborted, and Anne at last accepts her love for him. As Anne and Henrik "drop down onto the ground and start to make passionate love," Frid and Petra reappear. The satiated Frid is still asleep as Petra glorifies a life of easy and immediate gratification in song. In contrast to the complex, inhibited, troubled, moneyed women, Petra knows exactly what she wants. Like Madame Armfeldt she prizes financial security: "I shall marry the miller's son, / Pin my hat on a nice piece of property" (p. 158). But stodgy materialism alone is not her predominant creed. She accepts the inevitable necessity of domesticity but is intent on first actively pursuing a life of sensual abandon.

Sondheim conveys Petra's chosen life-style in a rapid electric fusion of lyric and rhythmic pace. The words, rhyme, and tempo combine to create an impression of fun-loving exhilaration. The poetic density of "The Miller's Son" is striking in many of its lines:

It's a very short road
From the pinch and the punch
To the paunch and the pouch and the pension.
It's a very short road
To the ten thousandth lunch
And the belch and the grouch and the sigh.
(p. 158)

The alliteration and the plosive "p" gives Sondheim's lines an added boost of energy as the lively girl contemplates the decline from sexual excess to domestic torpor. She has her priorities chosen and Sondheim reveals them in the ordering of his lines: "There are mouths to be kissed / Before mouths to be fed" (p. 158).

The parallel structure of each stanza reinforces the character's definite choices. The inevitable life of sober security, the inescapable decline from frivolity to fusty age and the grasping at the joys of the present are reiterated in various ways in each verse. The tight structure and the connotative reverberation of the images lift the lyric out of the ephemeral realm of song. Like the complex lines of "Another Hundred People," this lyric possesses the intricate economy of legitimate poetry. Sondheim's original syllabic pairing results in explosively funny rhymes and his metric control is unmatched. The rhyme scheme is complex, with an elaborate internal design:

> It's a push and a fumble
> And a tumble in the sheets
> And I'll foot the highland fancy,
> A dip in the butter
> And a flutter with what meets my eye.
> (pp. 158–59)

And Sondheim's depiction of the toll of time reveals the tightly ordered inevitability of poetry:

> It's a very short fetch
> From the push and the whoop
> To the squint and the stoop
> And the mumble.
> It's not much of a stretch
> To the cribs and the croup
> And the bosoms that droop
> And go dry.
> (p. 159)

Perhaps the accusation that the density and complexity of the poetic imagery and rhyme scheme are inappropriate to the lusty servant Petra is valid. However, the images Sondheim employs, and certainly the sentiments expressed, are perfectly in keeping with her character. The song, for example, concludes on a note of appetitive triumph:

> There are mouths to be kissed
> Before mouths to be fed,
> And there's many a tryst
> And there's many a bed,
> There's a lot I'll have missed
> But I'll not have been dead
> When I die!

This note is slightly modified in the final rueful acquiescence: "And I shall marry the miller's son" (p. 160). Petra sees through all the hypocritical proprieties and grabs life with both hands. Her vibrant impetuosity is a yardstick against which the lassitude of the more privileged class is measured.

The concluding sequences of the play are filled with action. The young lovers flee together. Carl-Magnus, mistakenly believing Fredrik is seducing his wife, challenges the lawyer to a game of Russian Roulette. Fredrik, as incompetent with a gun as he is with women, grazes his ear. Consequently Carl-Magnus and a delighted Charlotte are able to leave the château with Carl-Magnus's honor intact and their marital fervor renewed. As each person finds happiness, the *Liebeslieder* group sings a brief segment of its particular song as a lietmotif emphasizing the internal serenity of each character. Finally the stage is left to the two foolish but romantic lovers. As "Send in the Clowns" underscores the dialogue, Desirée and Fredrik tentatively reach for each other, and a happily-ever-after quality, so rare in a Sondheim-Prince musical, is given full expression. Desirée's solo becomes a duet as the two lovers share their love and accept their absurdity in harmony.

This resolution is what the audience wants to happen, for in traditional operetta lovers always begin apart, and their need to be together is the active ingredient of the evening. *Night Music* has, in fact, a proliferation of mismatched couples whose lives need to be more satisfactorily organized. The musical is set in the fantastic realm where what we will can be achieved and where lovers must be reunited.[14] Certainly the audience applauds as Desirée and Fredrik kiss and sing:

> *Fredrik*
>
> Make way for the clowns.
>
> *Desirée*
>
> Applause for the clowns.
>
> *Both*
>
> They're finally here.
>
> (p. 172)

The audience hopes the curtain will descend and all its illusions and romantic longings will be satisfied. But a Sondheim show could not conclude there. Sondheim always works within a form, but he also always simultaneously reveals its theatrical premises. In the case of *Night Music*, the play makes a full circle and concludes with Madame Armfeldt and her granddaughter:

> *Fredrika*
>
> I've watched and watched, but I haven't noticed the night smiling.
>
> *Madame Armfeldt*
>
> Young eyes are not ideal for watching. They stray too much. It has already smiled. Twice.
>
> *Fredrika*
>
> It has? Twice? For the young—and the fools?
>
> *Madame Armfeldt*
>
> The smile for the fools was particularly broad tonight.
>
> *Fredrika*
>
> So there's only the last to come.
>
> *Madame Armfeldt*
>
> Only the last.
> *(Madame Armfeldt dies)* (p. 173)

A dramatic neatness, an artificial order, is consequently imposed on the events. To further emphasize the structured theatricality of the evening, the opening waltz plays once more. The characters, now suitably partnered, waltz together, and then Mr. Lindquist returns to the piano and strikes a note "just as he did at the opening" (p. 174).

It is the quality of artifice, the sense that we're watching a play-within-a-play and that happily-ever-after romances can occur only in the unreal environ of operetta, that identifies the piece as a contemporary Sondheim work. It is an ephemeral magic fantasy, "insubstantial as a dream." And this is *Night Music*'s strength and its weakness. Certainly it was a commercial success, far more popular than either *Company* or *Follies*. Broadway audiences are comfortable with an unthreatening fantasy where wishes come true and lovers live happily ever after. The critics, too, favored *Night Music*, and the many allusions to its rarefied quality ("exquisite," "fragile," "refined," "tasteful," and "stylish") suggest that it was the delicacy, the unreal, illusory charm of the piece that appealed.

Yet one can detect a certain note of disappointment in the reviews,[15] the reluctant reservation that *Night Music* lacked the ground-breaking innovation of the previous works. Harold Prince admits that *Night Music*'s greatest appeal for him was its commercial success:

> I do not see the natural progression from *Company* to *Follies* to *Night Music* that some critics pointed out in their reviews, and I take perverse pleasure in the fact that *Night Music* has enough plot for two musicals and followed *Follies*, which had encouraged the critics to predict that we were moving inexorably in the direction of the plotless musical.
>
> I didn't enjoy doing *A Little Night Music*. I suffered no sleepless nights. I wasn't digging deep into myself. Of course, there are things I learned: the dinner-table scene, of which I'm very proud, and the final scene, on the lawn, are extensions of techniques begun with *Cabaret* and better realized with the birthday parties in *Company*.
>
> But mostly *Night Music* was about having a hit.[16]

James Goldman recalls that Prince kept wondering why he was doing *Night Music* and humorously referred to the piece as his "Gentile Musical." Furthermore, Goldman argues:

> I think Steve's score to *Night Music* is glorious . . . but I found the show too polite. I thought Hugh Wheeler's book was tastefully written and a fine piece of craftsmanship, but it lacks feeling and that's a pity. The abrasiveness that is part of Steve is what stimulates him most. On the other hand, he's dealing with musical styles that are very dear to him. . . . To have reference to all those styles was very rewarding to him.[17]

In terms of the innovative use of theatrical form, *Night Music* is as artistically successful as *Company* and *Follies*. The permutations of triple-time that unify the waltz score and the dry lyrics that contradict the romantic impulse of the music give a subtlety and depth to the musical. Moreover, the exposure of the dark undercurrents which are implicit in the make-believe realm of fantasy, the awareness of the artificiality of romance, and the sexual tensions smoldering beneath the refined facade, all contribute to the contemporary relevance of the piece.

Yet the work lacks the profound emotional depths that characterize Sondheim's two previous pieces. Audiences can be delighted, charmed, and moved, but the cathartic impact is missing. *Night Music* is lovely to listen to and gorgeous to see. It has wit and style but little inner tension. In an interview, Sondheim once confessed that he did not particularly care for Mozart: "I know it's my loss, but Mozart's whole body of music doesn't get to me gut-wise."[18] It is the cool, delicate purity of Mozart, however, that *Night*

Music emulates. The musical is elegant and refined but not revolutionary or profound. The characters are troubled but not enigmatic, and the audience's expectation that all will be resolved in the end is rewarded. The tortured ambiguity of personality that Sondheim admits fascinates him is absent in this world of romance.

Certainly if the creators' intentions were merely to re-create the lovely world of romantic illusion, to play an unrealistic game of sexual intrigue, then they succeeded. But the original intention was more complex. The fact that the *Liebeslieder* group, the dance prologue, the epilogue, and the other more overtly theatrical devices are not fully integrated suggests that the more adventurous exploration of the meaning of romantic fantasy and illusion was abandoned. Much of the resulting artistic failure can be attributed to Hugh Wheeler's book.

If one compares the musical with its Bergman inspiration one can see the extent to which Sondheim succeeds but Wheeler fails to capture the original's ephemeral charm. Bergman's response on seeing *Night Music* is indicative of the problem: "I was surprised that it was possible to eliminate the shadows of desperation, eroticism, and caprice without the whole story collapsing. At the moment I forgot that this entertaining and witty musical had anything to do with my picture. . . ."[19] I do not agree that these darker elements are eliminated from the score and lyrics, but they are largely absent in Wheeler's dialogue. The initial encounter between Desirée and Fredrik in the Bergman film is more passionate and angry, Anne is more flirtatious and cruel in her confused dealings with her stepson, and Carl-Magnus and Henrik are portrayed not as buffoon and fool but as vulnerable, troubled individuals. Sondheim explores these fervent inexpressible emotions in sound and word but Wheeler tends to gloss them over in dialogue. If, for example, Carl-Magnus is judged by his songs alone, he is pompous and chauvinistic but also insecure and charming. Only in dialogue is he reduced to a posturing idiot. He is a personality, no matter how good looking, who could never convincingly appeal to the sophisticated Desirée. Minor alterations in detail, such as the count and his wife who are legitimately invited to Madame Armfeldt's château in the film but who impose themselves in the musical, seem calculated to reduce the roles to a one-dimensional caricature. This flattening of character and pandering to cheap laughs rob Wheeler's scenes of any depth or real tension.

Sondheim, in contrast, is sensitive to the nuances of the Bergman screenplay. Although the characters of *Night Music* are not as complex and emotionally distressed as those of *Company* and *Follies*, Sondheim's music and lyrics do suggest levels of anxiety not evident in the dialogue. Sondheim has often acknowledged his indebtedness to his original source, and one can detect liberal borrowings from Bergman's screenplay. The encounter between Anne and Charlotte in Bergman's *Smiles of a Summer Night* clearly provides the inspiration for "Everyday a Little Death." Bergman's Charlotte says of Carl-Magnus, "He smiles to me, he kisses me, he comes to me at night, he makes me lose my reason, he caresses me, talks kindly to me, gives me flowers, always yellow roses, talks about his horses, his women, his duels, his soldiers, his hunting—talks, talks, talks." Though she knows that "love is a disgusting business!" she concludes: "In spite of everything, I love him. I would do anything for him. Do you understand that? Anything. Just so that he'll pat me and say: That's a good little dog."[20] And Sondheim's Charlotte sings:

> He smiles sweetly, strokes my hair,
> Says he misses me.
> I would murder him right there
> But first I die ...
>
> Men are stupid, men are vain,
> Love's disgusting, love's insane,
> A humiliating business!
> (pp. 85–86)

Sondheim is clearly stimulated by the Bergman original rather than the Wheeler work. He admits that he was more attracted to the former than to the more obviously commercial adaptation but believes that Prince was able to convince him to lighten his darker conception:

> I saw it as a darker Chekhovian musical. Hal didn't and admittedly it was a wilful lack of communication on my part. I had already written six songs that were much bleaker, more reflective, almost out of Strindberg, and Hal finally persuaded me that instead of it being as dark as Bergman, we should go entirely in reverse. And of course he was right. I usually love to write in dark colors about basic gut feelings, but Hal has a sense of audience that I sometimes lose when I'm writing. He wanted the darkness to peep through a whipped-cream surface. And, quite simply, I was writing for Bergman's film, not Hugh Wheeler's play.[21]

Although *Night Music*'s score is not gloomy or remote, Sondheim retains a penetrating insight into the reality behind the frivolous mask that Bergman suggests and Wheeler ignores. Yet Sondheim achieved this without alienating his Broadway audiences or losing the winsome appeal of romantic operetta. In his score he defines the action, embodies the drama, and reveals the complex person behind each player's mask. It is in his music and words that the various aspects of the lovers and love find full expression. The score elevates the script, lifting it out of the vapid realm of bedroom farce. The audience is disarmed by the enchanting waltz score, and its spontaneous resistance to the darker thematic implications of the lyrics is undermined by the apparent lighthearted frivolity of the musical design. This fusion of contemporary unease and traditional sentimentality is facilitated by a score that both reinforces and reveals the unreality of the fantasy world. This delicate balance between the audience's dreams and its social reality gives *Night Music* its distinction and guarantees it a continuing position of prominence in the musical theater repertoire.

Prologus (Zero Mostel) serenades a quaking Hysterium (Jack Gilford) in "Lovely" from *A Funny Thing Happened on the Way to the Forum* (1962). Photo: Fred Fehl.

Mayoress Cora Hoover (Angela Lansbury) struts her stuff in *Anyone Can Whistle* (1964). Photo: Fred Fehl.

Robert (Dean Jones) is serenaded by his company of married friends in *Company* (1970).

Robert (Dean Jones) absorbs Joanne's (Elaine Stritch) acerbic wisdom in "The Ladies Who Lunch" from *Company* (1970). © 1987 Martha Swope.

Ben (John McMartin) rekindles the flame of Sally's (Dorothy Collins) romantic longing in *Follies* (1971). © 1987 Martha Swope.

The exquisite costumes of Florence Klotz in the "Loveland" sequence from *Follies* (1971).

Desirée (Glynis Johns) *center* is joined by her daughter Fredrika (Judy Kahan) *left* and her mother (Hermione Gingold) *right* to bemoan the pleasures of "The Glamorous Life" in *A Little Night Music* (1973). © 1987 Martha Swope.

Desirée (Glynis Johns) welcomes her former lover Fredrik (Len Cariou) to her mother's country home at the opening of act 2 in *A Little Night Music* (1973). © 1987 Martha Swope.

Manjiro (Sab Shimono), dressed in American clothes, is joined by Kayama (Isao Sato) as they confront the fierce Lord Abe (Yuki Shimoda) in *Pacific Overtures* (1976). © 1987 Martha Swope.

The magnificent set of Boris Aronson in *Pacific Overtures* (1976). © 1987 Martha Swope.

Mrs. Lovett (Angela Lansbury) and Sweeney (Len Cariou) celebrate their unholy alliance in *Sweeney Todd, The Demon Barber of Fleet Street* (1979). © 1987 Martha Swope.

The vast brooding depths of Eugene Lee's set looms behind Sweeney (Len Cariou) as he prepares to slash a customer's throat in *Sweeney Todd, The Demon Barber of Fleet Street* (1979). © 1987 Martha Swope.

The youthful cast of *Merrily We Roll Along* (1981): Charley (Lonny Price), Mary (Ann Morrison), Franklin (Jim Walton) and Beth (Sally Klein). © 1987 Martha Swope.

The perfection of the final tableau at the conclusion of the first act of *Sunday in the Park with George* (1984). © 1987 Martha Swope.

Dot (Bernadette Peters) expresses her love to an oblivious George (Mandy Patinkin) in *Sunday in the Park with George* (1984). © 1987 Martha Swope.

Cinderella (Kim Crosby) rides off with her Prince Charming (Robert Westenberg) led by the Steward (Philip Hoffman) and watched by the spirit of her mother (Merle Louise) in *Into the Woods* (1987).

Rapunzel (Pamela Winslow) trapped in her tower by the Witch (Bernadette Peters) in *Into the Woods* 1987. © 1987 Martha Swope.

IS BEAUTY TRUTH, TRUTH BEAUTY?
Pacific Overtures

Pacific Overtures, first presented in New York on 11 January 1976, is even more remote from its creators' native idiom than the distant fantasy world of *A Little Night Music*. John Weidman, son of novelist Jerome Weidman, submitted a somewhat polemical straight play to Prince that focused on the American expedition of Commodore Matthew Perry to Japan in 1853. This bluntly one-sided condemnation of Western imperialism inspired Prince and Sondheim to create a Kabuki-style Broadway musical that synthesized the contrasting attitudes and techniques of popular American and Japanese musical theaters to a more artistic and thematically valid purpose.

Initially Sondheim was reluctant, insisting that he had little knowledge of, or enthusiasm for, Eastern theater and music. After careful consideration, some research, a crash course in oriental culture, and a brief visit to Japan, Sondheim became not merely convinced but excited. In order to bring the two disparate cultures together, he, Weidman, and Prince posited a hypothetical Japanese playwright who, they imagined, had visited America and then returned to his native country to write a "Broadway" musical. In an interview with Clive Hirschhorn, Sondheim explained that this fictitious playwright was the stylistic premise from which they worked, giving them "the tone and style of the show. And that's how we're preventing it from being *The King and I*. Because we're seeing it completely through oriental eyes."[1] It is this desire—a desire to see with oriental eyes and hear with oriental ears not only the events but also the theatrical form, structure, and sound—that informs the work.

The introduction of a completely foreign style of presentation was Sondheim's most adventurous academic experiment, and many critics hailed *Pacific Overtures* as Sondheim's finest achievement. There were, however, equally as many voices who demurred. *Pacific Overtures* is unquestionably innovative, complex, and theatrically exciting. Yet for all its intellectual audacity, many feel the dimension of emotional commitment, so poignant and powerful in *Company* and *Follies*, is absent. Sondheim created a fascinating conceptual divertissement, but the subliminal cry of outrage, which gave such resonance to the other works, is missing. Sondheim is a notorious inventor of intellectually challenging games, a master at anagrams, and creator of crossword puzzles. *Pacific Overtures* is his most elaborate puzzle, but not his most compelling theatrical composition.

Many critics charge that *Pacific Overtures* is an intricate game, which suggests that it lacks involvement and that an aloof creator is standing back impervious to his material. This accusation is curious, because *Pacific Overtures* is also condemned as being the most overtly didactic of the Sondheim-Prince collaborations. On a superficial viewing, *Pacific Overtures* can be criticized for its simplistic anti-American bias. This is clearly the response of many of its initial detractors, who claimed that the musical was merely a slick example of "trendy liberal" self-criticism, a fashionable manifestation of an easy moralism.[2] All these reviewers agree that the facile anti-American bias of the text is imposed rather than organic. The charge that the work is slickly packaged moralism reaches its apogee in the rather hysterical condemnation of Robb Baker of the *Soho Weekly News*, who attacks the work as "racist," "loathsome," and "disgusting" and the creators as "pseudo-liberal . . . uptown avant garde."[3]

Although there is some validity in these accusations, particularly with regard to Weidman's text, a careful examination makes clear that *Pacific Overtures* also criticizes both the solipsistic isolation and the corruption of feudal Japan. There is a conscious attempt to dramatize the positive and negative aspects of both cultures. In a taped conversation with Sondheim and Brendan Gill, made for the Performing Arts Research Center of the New York Public Library at Lincoln Center on 2 June 1975, Prince stresses that his intention was to avoid a one-sided didacticism. He maintains that although the work deals with Western imperialism, it reveals also the cost of isolation. The major theme, he contends, is the need for, as well as the price of, progress.

The attempt to balance the advantages and losses resulting from the occidental invasion of Japan is reflected in the development of the two central characters. Manjiro, the fisherman, and Kayama, the minor samurai, trace parallel paths through the tumultuous events of the era. They move in opposite directions, however. Manjiro shifts his belief in a Westernized modernity to a wish for a return to the traditions of ancient Japan, while Kayama slowly sheds his antique ways and accommodates himself to the gradual invasion of his country.

The intention is clearly to counterpoise the conflicting forces and reflect their opposition and reconciliation in a synthesis of Eastern and Western theatrical modes. The presentational form, the lyric style, and the aural impact of *Pacific Overtures* are neither in the conventional idiom of Broadway, nor are they authentic re-creations of Kabuki. Sondheim, Prince, and their collaborators combine various recognizable facets of both theatrical traditions in order to reinforce the meaning of the play.

The title itself is suggestive of the authors' intentions. A phrase used by Perry on contemplating his historic landing at Kanagawa, it alludes to the style of the work. The musical incorporates a series of negotiations; the content focuses on the opening of trade between Japan and the West, while the style, a subtle blend of both cultures, reinforces the narrative line and subject matter. The piece is clearly not authentic Kabuki, but its formal structure and aural quality are something more than the superficial gloss of an Eastern locale exploited by other Western works set in the East. Here style serves a functional, not merely a decorative, purpose.

In an interview (which Sondheim claims is distorted in order to suggest his arrogant assurance) Sondheim is reported to have claimed:

> The main thing about [*Pacific Overtures*] is that it is so *deeply* Japanese as opposed to, say *The King and I* or *Madame Butterfly* which are merely Western treatments of Eastern subjects. I mean, let's face it. *The King and I* might just as well be about a teacher coming to teach in Brooklyn, except that she comes to Siam. What we're attempting to create in *Pacific Overtures* is a genuinely Oriental musical.[4]

At a Dramatists Guild Special Projects session, however, Sondheim emphasized that he did not and could not write in an authentic oriental style. He instead maintained that his intention was to use Eastern techniques both in sound and lyric organization in order to give the audience the impression that it is listening to Japanese music. For example, he had to confront the problem of using harmony, which Japanese music does not use, without losing the oriental feeling. He explains how he achieves this:

> In the case of *Pacific Overtures* I kept a very limited harmonic language, with very little harmonic motion in the songs. *Pacific Overtures* had static songs, harmonically. They don't go anywhere. "Someone in a Tree" is an example of a song that's built almost entirely on two chords and an endless rhythmic vamp that bored the audience to death in some cases. But I found that since Japanese music is relentless, you've got to have some relentless songs. The score of *Pacific Overture* holds together because it all has the same harmonic texture and the same lack of variety within the songs, as opposed to a score like *Follies* which is *built* on variety.[5]

Sondheim does not merely write Western music with an Eastern flavor, but rather stresses the collision and fusion of the two cultures in his score. Just as he uses the techniques of Ziegfeld in *Follies* to make a point about an era and its zeitgeist, and just as he exploits the resonances of the waltz in *A Little Night Music* to suggest a fin-de-siècle decadence, so, in *Pacific Overtures*, he introduces the style, form, and structure of Eastern theater in order more intimately to reveal the patterns of thought and experience he intends to examine. His version of an Eastern sound is so intrinsic to the overall impact of the musical that it functions as a kind of "aural scenery."[6]

Yet despite all the best intentions of its creators, the preponderant impact of the drama is undoubtedly anti-imperialist and consequently anti-West. The primary reason for this overt didacticism is Weidman's book, which is heavy-handed in its satire and often resorts to simplistic caricature to make its points. Sondheim vehemently rejects the notion that one can divide a musical into its components. Emphasizing the collaborative nature of this kind of theater, he contends that Weidman is as responsible for what is successful in the lyrics and music of *Pacific Overtures* as he, Sondheim, is for what is deficient in the book. Sondheim further argues that as the show is intended to be specifically from a Japanese point of view, criticism of the overt satire is invalid. In spite of such arguments, the contrast in the tone and complexity between the book scenes and the musical sequences cannot be ignored.

Kabuki's popularity in Japan has diminished in the last fifty years or so, giving credence to the thesis of *Pacific Overtures* that with progress comes a loss of cultural tradition. Nevertheless, it is still the popular theater of Japan. Unlike the more religious orientation of the very formal, aristocratic

Noh, Kabuki is an eclectic theater of the common people. In its popularity, its emphasis on pure entertainment, its elaborate costumes, large stage, choreography, and music, it clearly has much in common with its American counterpart. Sondheim, Prince, Aronson (the set designer), Klotz (the costume designer), and Patricia Birch (the choreographer) used many facets of Kabuki theater but were never slavishly bound to creating an identical facsimile. In his melding of styles, his blending of East and West, Sondheim simply chose those forms he believed best conveyed the tone and spirit of his content. Authenticity, or lack of it, is not the point. *Pacific Overtures* is a theatrical creation.

Pacific Overtures opens to the distinctive sound of the *shamisen* (a three-stringed instrument used as an accompaniment in all Japanese theater), the plaintive wail of a voice, and the furious beating of wooden blocks. The sound, contributed by three musicians positioned in the Kabuki style on a low platform at the side of the stage, is distinctly oriental. These aural elements, combined with the *hanamichi* (flower walk), a pale wooden walkway running from the stage through the auditorium; the elaborately painted show curtain, designed by Aronson to suggest a collage of traditional Japanese symbols and calligraphy; and the formal presence of the Reciter, whose forehead is bowed to the floor in prayer, immediately set the tone for the performance. There is nothing Western in the ceremonial introduction. The audience is led into the remote isolated world of feudal Japan. In his opening address, the Reciter, a traditional Kabuki role used to comment on the action, establishes the mood. Employing a stylized delivery to echo, but not duplicate, the formal chant of the Kabuki actor, he informs his audience that for the last 250 years Japan has been a kingdom of "perfect peace" whose "changeless cycle of days"[7] has been untroubled by foreign interference.

It is this quality of static seclusion that Sondheim concentrates on in his opening number. The key verb, which recurs, is "to float," as Sondheim suggests that the tranquil isolation of the "floating kingdom" (p. 11) has both positive and negative aspects. The tight, hierarchical structure of the society brings order—but also exploitation. The suggestive beauty of its aesthetic results in an artistic delicacy, but also in a detachment from reality. There is serenity in this changelessness, but there is also stagnation.

Extending the formal quality of the opening, Sondheim implies ritual precision by manipulating the syntax of the first lines of the song:

In the middle of the world we float
In the middle of the sea.
The realities remain remote
In the middle of the sea.
(pp. 11–12)

The inversion of the first line, with its subject and verb at the end of the sentence, evokes a quality of unfamiliar formality and provides the line with a rhythmic impetus. This ceremonial tone is reinforced with the repeated phrases and with the alliterative effect of the third line.

The Reciter explains that Japan's withdrawal enables her to escape the upheavals that plague other lands:

Kings are burning somewhere,
Wheels are turning somewhere,
Trains are being run,
Wars are being won,
Things are being done
Somewhere out there, not here.
(p. 12)

By clinging to its aloofness, the culture implicitly lacks a certain dynamism. The verbs Sondheim uses to allude to the forces beyond the island may be harsh but they possess an active life that contrasts vividly with the static verb "to float."

In the next series of lines Sondheim suggests the aesthetic perception of the oriental world:

Here we paint screens.
Yes ... the arrangement of the screens:

We sit inside the screens
And contemplate the view
That's painted on the screens
More beautiful than true.
And no one presses in,
And no one glances out,
And kings are burning somewhere,

All

Not here!
(p. 12)

IS BEAUTY TRUTH, TRUTH BEAUTY?

The exclusion of reality is here more pointed, with the beauty and refinement of artistic contemplation not questioned. The emphasis on beauty rather than truth is distinctly noted, however.

The diction and syntax of *Pacific Overture*'s lines are interesting because Sondheim could not employ the witty, involuted complexities of his former work. It was the delicacy of haiku that served as his model as he created a lyric language for his Japanese characters. Consequently there is little of the urbane sophistication exemplified in *Company* and *Follies*. Yet despite the apparent simplicity of the lyrics, there is an oblique intricacy of thought suggested with an apparent guilelessness. With an unadorned vocabulary and straightforward sentence structure, the Reciter's first lines, for example, introduce the pictorial, aesthetic, and political significance of the characteristic Japanese screen.

The screen was an integral part of the musical's concept. For the initial production, Aronson painted huge panels that slid back to reveal both garish and delicate designs, while Patricia Birch and Harold Prince choreographed the actors in horizontal patterns to duplicate the screens' movements. Sondheim's lyrics, however, extend the pictorial function of the screen. His lines reveal that the pristine life of Japan, cut off as it is from outside intervention, constitutes a political and social screen. The result is an artificial life in a constructed reality that is as fragile as the airy rice paper of the screens. (The cloud motif Aronson used in the opening sequence of the original production supported the insubstantial quality of life mentioned in Sondheim's lyrics.) Yet the contemplative life of screen within screen possesses a hidden energy which Sondheim supplies with the impetus of the internal rhymes ("glide" / "aside," "scenes" / "screens").

In a subsequent stanza Sondheim's criticism of the life of detached aesthetic contemplation is more emphatic. If all life is objectified and distanced into the realm of art, then the vitality of living is denied:

> Life and death are but verses in a poem.
> Out there blood flows.
> Who knows?
> Here we paint screens.
>
> (p. 15)

The conditional adverb "but" in the first line indicates the reservations. The world beyond Japan is destructive and brutal though it possesses a vitality the controlled aesthetic and political seclusion lacks.

As the chorus—all of which are men, in accordance with Kabuki tradition—ceremonially depicts its world, Sondheim delineates feudal Japan's class structure:

> The farmer plants the rice.
> The priest exalts the rice.
> The Lord collects the rice.
> The merchant buys the rice.
> The craftsman makes the sword
> And sells it to the lord
> And buys at twice the former price
> What he counts on his lord to protect with his sword:
>
> *All*
>
> The rice!
> (p. 13)

This song is probably influenced by "The Song of Commodity" in Brecht's manifestly didactic play *The Measures Taken*, and in both songs not only order but also exploitation and rigid control are disclosed.

The lines that become increasingly important toward the conclusion of the song are "Arrange tomorrow to be like today, / To float" (p. 15). The rewards and the penalties of progress are set against the tranquil immobility of Japan. Using the spare, elliptical quality of haiku, Sondheim reflects the ephemeral, unreal life on the sequestered isle. The number concludes with a round that incorporates all the activities of the inhabitants of this bygone age, its repetitious form reflecting the nonprogressive, relentless stasis of their lives.

The action of the play is bracketed between this song, which delineates the quality of life in the floating kingdom of Nippon, and the final number, a harsh account of Japan's development. The movement from one state to the other provides the thematic spine of the play. But *Pacific Overtures* is not simply a sociopolitical treatise. The effects of Western imperialism and the opening of Japan are dramatically revealed through the development of its two central characters.

John Manjiro, a humble fisherman who six years previously was rescued from a storm at sea by an American vessel and taken to Massachusetts, returns to Japan to warn of the imminent arrival of an expeditionary force led by Commodore Matthew Calbraith Perry. Kayama Yesaemon, a samurai "of little consequence" (p. 19), is dragged from his faithful wife, Tamate, to face the corrupt and manipulative councillors of the Shogun. Having been judged sufficiently expendable, Kayama is promoted to the position of prefect of police for the city of Uraga and dispatched to repulse the unwelcome invasion. The changeless nature of feudal Japan, established in the opening number, is about to be drastically altered. The callous exploitation of the unimportant Kayama by the corrupt rulers indicates that the social system of preinvasion Japan is far from perfect, and the tone of the play is not unconditionally reverential.

In a brief, poignant scene, Kayama tells his wife of his promotion and its concomitant obligations. As he prepares for departure, his wife's fears, anxiety, and strong sense of duty are expressed in a lyrical song. In conformity with the dictates of Kabuki, Tamate was played by a man in the original production, but the performance was one of such quiet commitment that there was no sense of unease or humor in the Western audience's response. Within the parameters of the artificial theatrical form, Tamate was totally believable.

Tamate's emotions are stylized. She does not sing directly to her husband, for her feelings are expressed not by the actor playing the role but by two black-clad Observers. (Black is the color of invisibility in oriental theater, and the *Kurombo*—black-clad stagehand who moves props or adjusts costumes or makeup—was used frequently by Prince in his production.) These Observers are, alternately, the inner voice and the dispassionate observer. Sondheim distinguishes between the two voices by having the First Observer express Tamate's internal thoughts in verse, while the Second Observer recites her comments in a flat prose. The interior self is poetic and discovers truth in natural imagery:

> The word falls, the heart cries.
> The heart knows the word's disguise. . . .
>
> The bird sings, the wind sighs,
> The air stirs, the bird shies.
> A storm approaches.
> (p. 24)

The external self, the realist who accepts the inevitable, expresses the unemotional words of normality that the wife offers her husband: "I will have supper waiting," "I shall expect you then at evening" (p. 25).

As the Observers vocalize the conflict between her outer calm and her inner torment, Tamate expresses her pain in dance. Through this combination of movement and dual voices, Sondheim creates his own version of an oriental interior monologue. The lyric structure is spare, yet despite this apparent simplicity the song expresses a complexity of thought and conveys the emotional anguish of the character without losing its oriental restraint. The depth of Tamate's emotion is articulated with an appropriate sense of control and distance. (The song differs radically from Sondheim's usual interior monologue in that the audience *is* distanced from the character, with the emotions being suggested ambiguously in the muted tones of natural imagery. But its poetic purity and melodic beauty provide an excitement equal to the emotional charge traditionally expected of a song of confession and devotion.) Tamate's feelings are uttered in distinct units, aspects of her fragmented self, rather than in a more conventional form of expression. The character never says "I think" or "I feel," but facets of her experience are reported by the Observers:

> *First Observer*
>
> The eye sees, the thought flies.
> The eye tells, the thought denies.
>
> *Second Observer*
>
> I will prepare for your returning.
> (Is there no other way?)
> (p. 24)

In contrast to his previous urban American work, Sondheim feels free in *Pacific Overtures* to use the suggestive quality of natural imagery. For example, the metaphoric implications of the gentle disturbance in the natural world reflecting the turmoil in Tamate's life is used sparingly but to great effect:

> The leaf shakes, the wings rise.
> The song stops, the bird flies.
> The storm approaches.
> (pp. 24–25)

Tamate's determination to adhere to the dictates of duty, her acceptance of the rigid code of behavior, and her hopeless acquiescence in the inevitable tragedy of an unavoidable fate are convincingly conveyed as she slowly alters her pleading "Is there no other way?" to the bleak final statement: "There is no other way."

The haunting wind instrument the *shakuhachi* accompanies Tamate's song, reinforcing her controlled suffering. As the character's emotions intensify, the accompaniment is augmented by orchestral strings, which make the poignant musical connotations more accessible to the Western ear. The song is punctuated, furthermore, by the impatient clanging of a bell, reminding the characters and audience of the imminent arrival of the invaders. This suggestion of impending doom is intensified as Kayama slowly dons his ceremonial garb in preparation for his confrontation with the Americans.

The solemnity of Tamate's gloom is shattered as the clanging of the bell builds to a frenzy. The Americans have been sighted, and their arrival is described by a Fisherman and a Thief. In his treatment of Tamate's complex psychology, Sondheim reveals two aspects of one character's experience. He now inverts the situation and presents his audience with two interpretations of the same event. This kind of balance and deliberate patterning is characteristic of the premeditated formal structure of the work. The American fleet destroys the habitual tranquillity and order of the Japanese way of life, and the resultant panic and fear are succinctly conveyed in the dual accounts of the crisis.

The Fisherman's peaceful routine of spreading his nets to the morning sun is disturbed by the ship's appearance. A sense of serene monotony and vaguely encroaching unease is suggested in Sondheim's repeated use of the conjunction:

> It was early in July
> And the day was getting hot,
> And I stopped to wipe my eyes,
> And by accident I turned
> And looked out to sea ...
>
> And there came,
> Breaking through the mist,
> Roaring through the sea,
> Four black dragons,
> Spitting fire.
> (p. 27)

The disruption of the peace is conveyed in the active participles "breaking" and "roaring," which fracture the established rhythmic pattern of the verse and, by extension, convey the demolition of a culture. The ships are seen by the humble Fisherman as "four black dragons," their menace translated into something comprehensible within his frame of reference. The fearsome, stately advance of the vessels is suggested in the strong, persistent percussive rhythm that builds implacably through the number.

The stanzas of the song are separated by a brief comic interlude that shows the chaos resulting from the announcement of the invasion. For the second narrator, the Thief, the ships are like "four volcanoes" (p. 30), and he and the Fisherman sing together of their shared terror and awe. The rampant panic is communicated through a series of incomplete participial phrases suggesting the two characters' consternation and sense of impotence:

> *Fisherman*
>
> And I ran ...
>
> *Thief*
>
> Cursing down the halls ...
>
> *Fisherman*
>
> Cursing through the fields ...
>
> *Thief*
>
> Shouting to the priests ...
>
> *Fisherman*
>
> Shouting to the world ...
>
> *Both*
>
> "Notify the gods!"
>
> (p. 31)

Each man attempts to top the other's description in order to express his horror and fear.

As the dispassionate voice of the Reciter adds his description of the ensuing terror, his manner is controlled, his expression muted. He is a reporter from another time dimension, uninvolved in the actual event. Yet his very restraint contributes to the atmosphere of dread. The Reciter likens the general panic to the frightened screeching of the gulls, and his harsh birdlike cry contrasting with his otherwise detached observations intensifies the terror. The aural imagery of the number is as effective as the visual and verbal metaphors:

And the feet pattered
As the men came down to stare,
And the women started screaming
Like the gulls.
Hai!
Hai!
Like the gulls.
Hai!
(pp. 31–32)

For the people, the images become progressively more cataclysmic until finally they view the assault in hyperbolic, apocalyptic terms:

Group A	*Group B*
And the sun darkened And the sea bubbled And the earth trembled And the sky cracked, And I thought it was the end Of the world!	I had seen Dragons before, Never so many, Never like these, And I thought it was the end Of the world! (p. 33)

But it is the dry observation of the Reciter, who affirms "And it was" (p. 33), that gives the scene its ultimate sense of menace.

The actual arrival of the American fleet was handled in the Prince and Aronson production as a stylized, theatrical spectacle, visually the highlight of the show. A ship's prow, with two huge glaring eyes, loomed out of the darkness center stage. Then, slowly, a massive sailing vessel unfolded, accordionlike, toward the audience. Perched high on the bow was the dreaded Commodore Perry. Like the terrifying Kabuki lion, with floating white mane and exaggeratedly fierce makeup, he was lit by a ghostly blue spot. The sailors were depicted as figures from a fearful Kabuki nightmare. The uniforms were hyperbolized versions of those worn by nineteenth-century American sailors, yet with suggestions of an oriental line. The players, of course, were all oriental, and their speech and movement were also highly stylized. Perry did not speak at all, but communicated through the leonine roar of the trombone. The helpless inadequacy of the Japanese to deal with the aggressor was theatricalized as Kayama approached the huge, towering American craft in his tiny boat.

When the Americans refuse to deal with the lowly Kayama, he persuades the cowardly councillors to dress the fisherman, Manjiro, as a lord. Manjiro, with his knowledge of Western ways, will know how to deal with the aggressors. Despite Manjiro's insistence that no foreigner shall ever set foot on the sacred soil of Japan, Perry demands that either a meeting be arranged with the Shogun or the ship's guns will be turned on Uraga.

As the negotiations continue, the scene shifts to the Shogun's chamber. In the rear of the stage the huge eyes of the dragon-ships move about menacingly to a drum beat, reminding all of the ever-present threat of the invaders. The tone of the scene is humorous, however. The Shogun, played by the Reciter, lies bemused in an opium-induced stupor, and his faithful wife whines an irritating lament while his shrewd political mother seeks to find a way out of Japan's predicament. With each verse of her song, which indicates another passing day, the accompanying wail of the Shogun's wife grows more desperate and annoying. Sondheim does not resist the temptation of poking fun at the Eastern sound, so foreign to the audience's ear. Even the Shogun's mother is impelled repeatedly to silence the awful noise with a withering gesture.

The days pass with the advice of the soothsayers, priests, and samurai sought and rejected. As the Shogun's mother plies him with chrysanthemum tea, she reaches her inevitable, macabre decision. Unlike the simple Tamate, the Shogun's mother is a crafty, manipulative, comic character. Her devious mind is developed in the complexity of her thought patterns and the intricate sophistication of her rhyme scheme:

> As I started to say:
> From the first disturbing day,
> When I gave consideration
> To this letter they convey,
> I decided if there weren't
> Any Shogun to receive it,
> It would act as a deterrent
> Since they'd have no place to leave it,
> And they might go away, my lord ...
> (p. 53)

She has been poisoning the tea, and as the song ends the ineffectual Shogun finally succumbs.

The Americans will not be refused, and Manjiro devises the plan of constructing a treaty house in the small cove at Kanagawa and covering the ground with *tatami* mats, which can be burned after the Westerners depart. The letter can be delivered, but the sacred soil of Japan will not be desecrated.

Kayama, now promoted to governor of Uraga, and his ally, Manjiro, journey together to Uraga to tell Tamate of all that has occurred. Using the simulated walking movement of Kabuki, *michiyuki*, they travel back and forth across the stage. To pass the time and develop their friendship, the two men exchange poems. This is a gentle number in which Sondheim conveys, with the unadorned purity of haiku, the differing values and sensibilities of the two. Kayama focuses on his wife, while Manjiro is still entranced by his memories of the wonders of Boston.

The two men improvise upon each other's image patterns, exchanging ideas and metaphors in a gradually deepening camaraderie. Using the most delicate of images and symbols, Sondheim shows Kayama's devotion to his wife and Manjiro's appreciation of America:

> *Kayama*
>
> Moon,
> I love her like the moon,
> Making jewels of the grass
> Where my lady walks,
> My lady wife.
>
> *Manjiro*
>
> Moon,
> I love her like the moon,
> Washing yesterday away,
> As my lady does,
> America.
>
> (pp. 58–59)

With the rhythm of their journey reflected in the percussive accompaniment, their intimacy intensifies so that finally they sing together of their respective passions, which seem to spring from one source:

> Sun,
> I see her like the sun
> In the center of a pool,
> Sending ripples to the shore,
> Till my journey's end.
>
> (p. 60)

The imagery in this charming song typifies the kind of metaphoric language Sondheim consistently uses in *Pacific Overtures*. The poetry is rich in natural symbols and possesses an elegant simplicity. The only significant referent is the changing natural order. Yet Sondheim avoids any sense of ponderousness. As each man completes his haiku, he turns to his companion with a friendly challenge, "Your turn." This human touch relieves the song of any artiness it might otherwise possess. The melody, like the mood and image patterns, is sweet and unassertive—the musical equivalent of the evolving relationship.

On arriving home, the first tragic consequence of the invasion is made clear to the ebullient Kayama. His wife, fearing the worst, has committed ritual suicide. This scene is staged with poignance and restraint. The stricken Kayama cannot express his agony. It is the Reciter who gives voice to his wretched cries. Manjiro, unaware of his friend's grief, leads him away, extolling the virtues of America.

As the bereft Kayama and his loyal friend Manjiro make their way slowly up the *hanamachi*, they are passed by a garish middle-aged madam. A bawdy song follows in which the procuress attempts to instruct her unsophisticated recruits in the niceties of the geisha's art. This number provides an interesting focus for the conflicting critical responses to *Pacific Overtures*. Those writers who see the musical as one of Sondheim's best are generally offended by this song. Its humor, dependent on salacious innuendo and double entendre, displeases them. Martin Gottfried, for example, complains: "If the production includes one mistake, it is the unfortunately tasteless song turning the Orient's high erotic art into a kinky sex comedy song (one of the show's rare 'numbers') sung by a madam whose masculinity is emphasized as drag queenliness. The crude number only underlines a sag in the first act."[8] In contrast, those critics, like Douglas Watt of the *Daily News*,[9] who are less enthusiastic about the show, delight in the number. It was, for them, an oasis of entertaining humor in an evening of heavy-handed propaganda and didacticism.

Both responses are comprehensible, and both are guilty of simplistic overstatement. The song, which is similar in style to the Shogun's mother's deliciously cruel "Chrysanthemum Tea," does include snide innuendo. (The risqué quality was amplified in Prince's staging as the Madam titillated the audience with glimpses of her huge, pornographically explicit fan.) The humor is broad, but it is also very funny. The farm maidens, whom the Madam has recruited to service the arriving forces, each clutch an instructional fan, which the Madam points to as she instructs them in the techniques of the erotic arts:

> That you mustn't wash for,
> Not till you're done. . . .
> That you use a squash for—
> Or pumpkins are fun.
> (pp. 65–67)

Coarse belly laughs may seem out of place within the delicate suggestiveness of the other aspects of oriental culture, but the Madam is delightful and Sondheim heightens her appeal by giving her lyrics a tricky rhyme scheme that contrasts with the austerity of the other songs:

> You must neither be too wary
> Nor too bold,
> As there's no telling with barbarians,
> I'm told,
> Because not only are they hairy,
> But extremely uncontrolled.
> (p. 67)

Salacious humor makes the sequence not only very funny but theatrically necessary for Western audiences who need more than the elegance of haiku and ceremonial gestures to sustain their interest. Morever, Sondheim has an organic reason for introducing a more Western flavor to this number. "This is," he explains, "the first Western-influenced moment in the show. . . . The score grows more Western as the country does. Ditto the lyrics."[10]

Although the subsequent scene, involving the exchange of gifts between the two nations and the naïve attempts of the Japanese at self-defense, is another example of Weidman's satiric intentions, the Sousa-like march that Sondheim composes for the landing of the American forces possesses a delicately ironic overtone. The implied exposure of glorified aggression to ridicule is subtle. The music reveals the pomp and ceremony that are intended to disguise and dignify outright plunder.

The Japanese dignitaries and their American counterparts disappear into the newly constructed treaty house, and the Reciter regretfully informs the audience that there is unfortunately no authentic Japanese account of what took place at the secret meeting. He is interrupted by an elderly Japanese man, who tells him that there was, in fact, an observer. As a young boy the man had climbed a nearby tree and observed all that occurred. His account is the most complex number in the show.

In *Follies*, Sondheim experiments with the interaction of past and present; in other songs in *Pacific Overtures*, he gives various aspects of a personality different voices and shows different character responses to the same event. In "Someone in a Tree," he combines these splintering techniques. While the concentration on minute aspects of experience as a means to comprehending a larger truth has been characteristic of all Sondheim's work, in *Pacific Overtures* this epistemological premise is developed into a structural technique. History is viewed as random fragments of experience arranged in order to reveal a partial truth. Nothing can be known in its entirety. Nothing can be understood completely. All perception and all memory is of necessity limited and biased. All one can hope to achieve is a glimpse of some aspect of the past that will provide a clue to the meaning and significance of the totality of events. *Pacific Overtures* provides those hints, clues, and glimpses, and this number epitomizes the structural principle of the entire musical.

The old man cannot reconstruct everything. He certainly cannot clamber up the tree he once climbed as a youngster. So his younger self materializes to observe and comment for him. (Aronson contributed to this moment by transforming the dry, bare skeleton of the tree, seen by the old man, into the flowering beauty of youth as the boy climbs up into its branches. The large flowered fan Aronson used was consistent with his overall visual scheme, as the fan was an intrinsic design element throughout the production.) What the boy sees and relates is only a fragment of the event. Moreover, since he is young, he cannot comprehend the significance of what he does see:

Boy

Tell him what I see!

Old Man

I am in a tree.
I am ten.
I am in a tree.

Boy

I was younger then.

Old Man

In between the eaves I can see—

(To boy)
Tell me what I see.
(To Reciter)
I was only ten.
(p. 79)

The event is actualized, given reality by the character's perception and memory of it. But what he experiences and recalls is incomplete. Through the interaction of the old man and his younger self Sondheim articulates his epistemological position. Reality exists only in perception:

Boy

And there's someone in a tree—

Old Man

—or the day is incomplete.

Both

Without someone in a tree,
Nothing happened here.
(p. 80)

Every aspect of the event, every participant is an essential part of its reality. All that is known of the past is fragmentary and distorted. All knowledge is incomplete:

Boy

It's the fragment, not the day.

Old Man

It's the pebble, not the stream.

Both

It's the ripple, not the sea,
Not the building but the beam,
Not the garden but the stone,
Not the Treaty House,
Someone in a tree.
(p. 81)

Sondheim emphasizes that all significance is achieved through the interpretation of discrete units. By focusing on the scraps and tangible remnants of history, one can perhaps gain some comprehension of the fabric of the past. Understanding the meaning of life to the individual may lead to understanding the significance of political and social change. In dealing with the infinite complexity of East-West relations, Sondheim concentrates on the minute aspects of single events. History's contrasting effects on two men's lives reflects a greater political truth.

The Kabuki acting style is an ideal mode for expressing this philosophic position. It emphasizes the presentation of character in a series of detached, isolated units. Consequently the chronological structure of the text, the "and then" rather than the causal "and therefore" sequence of events is justified. Dramatic interest is sustained, for the audience comprehends that the real drama is to be found in the political upheaval discerned through the specific dramatized sequences. The discrete particulars indicate the pattern of the large events.

Various aspects of *Pacific Overtures* have been compared, both favorably and unfavorably, with the work of Brecht. Brecht, too, was inspired by and utilized oriental theater techniques. The objective observations of the Reciter, the overt didacticism, and the use of an Eastern setting and technique can be labeled "Brechtian." It is, however, in its chronicle-like structure—its epic theme and organization—that the work most resembles that of Brecht. Prince is obviously aware of this quality as he calls the musical a "documentary vaudeville," but explains that his production concept is closer to the work of Meyerhold than Brecht:

> We were a few weeks into rehearsal when I was leafing through an old issue of what used to be called the *Tulane Drama Review*. I came across a review by John Dos Passos of a production Meyerhold had done in 1924 of a play called *DE*. Dos Passos said it was "part American musical, part Kabuki, part Chinese opera, part French music hall, part agitprop." He went on to say, "If there is to be a future for the musical theater then this must be it." Those were precisely my comments to the cast on the opening day of rehearsals.[11]

Sondheim implements this production concept in his song for the old man and the boy. He extends the argument by introducing another character, a warrior who crawls out from beneath the treaty house. Placed under the floor in case of a surprise attack, he too is a "fragment" of the event. The boy can only see. The warrior can only hear. The partial quality of all experience is theatricalized:

> I hear floorboards groaning.
> Angry growls, much droning.

IS BEAUTY TRUTH, TRUTH BEAUTY?

Since I hear them, they are there!
(p. 84)

The old man, the boy, and the warrior share their perceptions and recollections. Their re-creation is necessarily fragmentary but their experience gives it veracity. All of life, they agree, is made up of small, apparently insignificant, details. It is, after all,

Only cups of tea
And history
And someone in a tree!
(p. 84)

The concise image, the concentration on the unique individual experience, and the reduction of grandiose events to minuscule units are techniques Sondheim has used throughout his work. He concentrates on the "little" things in the firm belief that the precise image, the particular emotion, the deftly chosen word and sound are our best means of penetrating the confusing complexity of existence.

The song ends and the Reciter gleefully informs the audience that Kayama's plan has been a success. The Americans depart. The mats are burned and the sanctity of Japan seems to have been preserved. But act 1 concludes with a spectacular lion-dance performed by the triumphant Perry. Synthesizing the music and choreography of East and West, Perry celebrates his Western exaltation in an Eastern form. (In the Kabuki, the lion-dance is an accepted expression of victory.) Again, East and West are contrapuntally intertwined. The long, swinging white mane and the percussion of the East are interrupted by a cakewalk to a Sousa-like march. The elaborately painted grimace and the bare stamping feet belong to oriental theater, but Perry wears the archetypal striped top hat of Uncle Sam. (In the original production,costumes were a humorous mixture of the two cultures, Perry's nineteenth-century navy uniform, with all its brass and gold stripes, having kimono sleeves.) It is clear that Japan's former isolation will never be regained.

The cultural transformation resulting from the opening of Japan is the subject matter of act 2. The act begins in the Imperial Court, where the nominal ruler of Nippon formally acknowledges the achievements of Kayama and Manjiro, naming them respectively governor of Uraga and samurai. The

Emperor's political impotence is emphasized by having the role played by a Bunraku stick-puppet, manipulated at will by his advisors. But the exhilaration of the rulers at the removal of the barbarian threat is short-lived. To the beat of a martial band, an American admiral strides down the *hanamachi*, and the real invasion of the island commences.

Sondheim encapsulates the subsequent rapid commercial penetration of Japan in a witty pastiche. Using his celebrated musical mimicry, he creates a vaudeville skit for five admirals (American, British, Dutch, Russian, and French), each of whom expresses his terms in the exaggerated style of his own country. Sondheim realizes precisely how much has to be included in the number: "When I did the admirals' number in *Pacific Overtures*, I wrote down on a separate piece of paper for each admiral what had to be accomplished with that admiral. I knew what the order had to be because I wanted to give a history lesson as well as write a funny number."[12]

In a condescending pidgin English, the American makes his requests to a rollicking military march. The garbled grammar, the simplistic vocabulary, and the excessively polite "Please, hello" of the refrain satirize the paternalism of the invaders. The American Admiral's diction is a subtle indictment of the offensive stereotype that Westerners continue to impose on the Japanese. His patronizing, oversimplified English phrases and superficial courtesy do not hide the threat implicit in his overtures. After listing the many recent inventions he has brought, he concludes his request with a menacing warning:

> —Also cannon to shoot
> Big loud salute,
> Like so:
> (*Explosion*)
>
> Say hello!

The British Admiral, using the polysyllabic intricacies of Gilbert and Sullivan, follows his demands with:

> Please,
> Hello, I come with letters from Her Majesty Victoria
> Who, learning how you're trading now, sang "Hallelujah, Gloria!"
> And sent me to convey to you her positive euphoria
> As well as little gifts from Britain's various emporia. . . .
>
> Her Majesty considers the arrangements to be tentative

Until we ship a proper diplomatic representative.
We don't foresee that you will be the least bit argumentative
So please ignore the man-of-war we brought as a preventative.
(pp. 96–97)

The Gilbert and Sullivan operetta style is emphasized as the Reciter drolly reiterates the British Admiral's final couplet.

The Dutch Admiral is a comic whom Sondheim describes as singing "Weber-and-Fields style, complete with Hans Brinker pockets and heavy clogs." The old American vaudeville team Sondheim refers to impersonated imbecilic immigrants with heavy Dutch accents. Sondheim's caricature is hardly subtle, but is funny:

Vait! Please hello!
Don't forget ze Dutch!
Like to keep in touch!
Zank you very much!
Tell zem to go,
Button up ze lips.
Vot do little Nips
Vant vit battleships?
(p. 98)

After the clamorous demands of the three negotiators are punctuated by the threatening explosions of their battleships, the lugubrious Russian arrives. To a plaintive, soulful sound, and with an all-consuming obsession that no one touch his magnificent fur coat, he makes his demands:

Please hello,
Is bringing Czar's request,
Braving snow
With letter to protest:
Since we know
You trading with the West,
You might at least
(Don't touch the coat!)
Start looking East—
(Thinking about it)
—Or closer West—
(Thinking again)
—Well, farther North—
(Looking around)
Are we the fourth?

I feel depressed.
(Don't touch the coat!)
(p. 101)

Finally an Offenbach-like Frenchman prances out his terms to a brief can-can. Using a catch word familiar to an audience of the Kissinger era, he demands:

It's détente! Oui, détente!
Zat's ze only thing we want!
Just détente! Ooh, détente!
No agreement could be more fair!
Signing pacts, passing acts,
Zere's no time for making warfare
When you're always busy making wiz ze
Mutual détente!
(p. 104)

The number concludes with a spirited can-can danced by all five dignitaries. By suggestive musical references and apposite, witty lyrics, Sondheim condenses and communicates the implacable rape of Japan and its culture. The invasion is dramatized with the introduction of each particular country's musical style.

After a messenger sent by the disgruntled Lords of the South relates the civil unrest provoked by the foreign intervention, the focus returns to the two friends, Kayama and Manjiro. The dichotomy of the musical is crystallized in the divergent paths of the two men. The choices, direction, and cultural priorities of the society are reflected in the contradictory development of these characters. Paralleling the split-screen technique of film, the scene begins with the two men on either side of the stage, kneeling behind delicately wrought Japanese tables. Both men are dressed in traditional Japanese kimonos. Manjiro is in white; Kayama in black. Manjiro is preparing for the tea ceremony and Kayama is writing on a scroll with a brush. As the scene progresses years pass. Kayama gradually sheds his oriental accoutrements and accommodates to the trappings of the West. Manjiro—the fisherman made samurai, who, at the beginning of the play so passionately declares, "It is not the Americans who are barbarians. It is us! If you could have seen what I have seen in America"—retreats further and further into the traditionalism of feudal Japan. His focus throughout the sequence centers on performing the ancient tea ceremony with precision and grace. His silence is as telling as Kayama's song.

Kayama, writing to Lord Abe, the Shogun, informs him of the progress of the relationship between the people of Uraga and the Westerners. Time is compressed. The black-clad stagehands (*kurombo*) subtly alter the makeup of each man between the stanzas of the songs to suggest the aging process. As extracts of Kayama's continuing correspondence are read by the Reciter, Japan's inability to deal with the foreign influx is made depressingly clear.

Each verse of Kayama's song focuses on some newly acquired Western object. The stanzas are composed of a series of apparent non sequiturs, but each fragment of thought gives the audience a key to the transitions in Kayama's mind. The verses are held together by their related image patterns rather than a well-defined rhyme scheme. The rapid and radical alterations apparent in this one individual's life-style and values serve as a microcosm of the changes occurring in the community.

Kayama's gradual transformation from an insecure minor official, intimidated by all things foreign, into a shrewd and appetitive manipulator is traced in each successive verse. For Manjiro, the lines of age are the only manifestation of change, but Kayama's life undergoes a major alteration. As the Reciter informs the audience of the unrestrained invasion by the West, the effects of this upheaval are reflected in Kayama's gradual rejection of the traditional patterns of his existence.

Each verse is carefully interconnected with the one that precedes it. Consequently Kayama's evolution from a humble man who venerates the Dutch Ambassador to one who bears grudges and has little tolerance is delineated:

> The Dutch Ambassador is no fool.
> I must remember that. . . .
>
> The Dutch Ambassador was most rude.
> I will remember that. . . .
>
> The Dutch Ambassador is a fool.
> He wears a bowler hat.
> (pp. 114–16)

As the bowler hat was Kayama's initial, tentatively acquired Western acquisition, the audience understands that he has grown arrogant, confident in the complexities of Western diplomatic maneuvering.

Kayama had been a sensitive man, whom the audience had seen in silent torment over the loss of his wife. Yet in the progression of this number he acquires and loses a wife without any apparent emotion. Sondheim suggests Japan's capitulation to Western consumerism in Kayama's acceptance of Western gifts, life-style, and values. He begins by declaring that his "house is far too grand" (p. 114). This is modified when he complains that "the house is far too small" (p. 115) and when, in the final verse, he boasts, "I have a house up in the hills / I've hired British architects to redesign" (p. 117). In accepting the foreigners' wine and pills, he becomes dependent on them. Scoffing at the quaint superstitions of his servants, he reads Spinoza and self-consciously sprinkles his language with foreign expressions such as "*Formidable*" (p. 116).

Yet Kayama is Japanese, and Sondheim suggests, through the use of natural imagery, his comprehension of all the changes in his life:

> The swallow flying through the sky
> Is not as swift as I
> Am, flying through my life. . . .
> No eagle flies against the sky
>
> As eagerly as I
> Have flown against my life. . . .
>
> No bird exploring in the sky
> Explores as well as I
> The corners of my life.
> (pp. 114–16)

The gentle swallow becomes the aggressive eagle, and the final image suggests the arrogance of a man who feels he knows and controls his own existence.

The song's gentle and unassertive melodic line and rippling rhythmic accompaniment suggest the inevitable passing of time and gradual and unobtrusive change. Kayama is barely aware of his drastic transformation. The isolated stasis he was a part of in the opening is modified in him to the shifting fluidity of the receptive host. The simple, loyal, honest man has evolved into an arrogant bureaucrat who belongs neither to the world of Eastern traditionalism nor to that of Western progress.

The gradual erosion of the traditional way of life depicted in "A Bowler Hat" is reinforced in the brief scene that follows. The exploitation of the Japanese underclass is dramatized as an American entrepreneur (the Reciter in yet another guise) joins with a Japanese merchant to introduce the rickshaw.

IS BEAUTY TRUTH, TRUTH BEAUTY?

The spirit of capitalism triumphs as a series of old men sink to the ground in their efforts to pull the American and his Japanese colleague in a rickshaw, "Invented, manufactured, marketed by Westerners . . . but pulled by Japanese" (p. 121).

In the subsequent scene Sondheim manages delicately to capture the poignancy of cross-cultural misunderstanding. While Manjiro and his older mentor practice the ancient swordsman's art of *kenjutsu*, demonstrating their unswerving adherence to tradition and incidentally revealing the impotence of their stand, the elderly man's daughter wanders through the garden. She is spotted by three visiting English sailors who, mistaking her for a prostitute, attempt to proposition her. Although the audience must be aware of the lust prompting their advances, Sondheim writes an achingly sweet melancholic song of seduction. The gentle lyricism of the melody and the repetition of the phrase "pretty lady" belie the violence that seethes beneath the surface.

Consequently, when the girl cries for help and her father cuts down one of the young men, there is a sense of horror, shock, and waste. The sailors mean no harm. They are bewitched by the girl's loveliness and bewildered by a code of behavior so different from their own. They are lonely and far from home, and she is "the cleanest thing [they've] seen all year" (p. 125). The tenderness of the melody and the lyric disguise but do not negate the harshness of their intentions. (Sondheim uses a similar technique in *Sweeney Todd*, when the homicidal Sweeney sings his most beautiful aria just as he is about to slit his loathed enemy's throat.) The contrast between the delicacy of the girl in the garden, the tenderness of the song, and the coarseness of the sailors' lust and the father's murderous rage provides the scene with its dramatic tension. The conflict, misunderstanding, and waste inevitable in the clash of two such different cultures are succinctly dramatized in this brief interlude. The fact that Sondheim introduced a cockney intonation into these lyrics, which in the original production were sung by oriental actors, and that the lovely lady is in fact a man, adds a further dimension of theatrical interest.

The final scene of the play takes place on the road from Edo to Kyoto. The collision course upon which the two major characters have been traveling reaches its inevitable climax. Kayama, with Lord Abe, the Shogun, represents those who have capitulated to the uncontrollable forces of Western influence, while Manjiro, who has joined the Lords of the South, longs to restore Japan to its pristine isolation. The two former friends meet. To dramatize the opposing direction of their lives, Prince had his actors express their changing values in their speech patterns and vocal style, Manjiro, the American-educated fisherman, gradually assuming the formal chantlike intonation of the traditionalists and Kayama adopting the rhythmic patterns of the West. Throughout the play, the aural effects of the players' voices serve as an additional aspect of the musical imagery. The ingenuous, outgoing young fisherman has become an austere figure. The shy, inhibited minor samurai has been transformed into a loquacious negotiator.

Manjiro confronts and kills his one-time friend and savior. He is hailed by the traditionalists, but their dream of a return to the past is hopeless. The emperor puppet finally breaks the manipulating sticks of those who control him. (The theatricality of this gesture as the puppet comes to life was another example of Prince's innovative use of Eastern stage techniques.) The Emperor gradually sheds his outer garments and immobile mask, and it is the Reciter who emerges. The authority figure of the theater-piece becomes the political power. Implicit control becomes explicit.

As the stagehands remove layer after layer of the imperial robes, the Emperor/Reciter symbolically rejects the ancient ways. Manjiro, in slaying his friend, has acted in accordance with the traditional moral code, but it is this ethic that the Emperor spurns. Manjiro is stripped of his faith and his dignity by a ruler who capitulates to the avaricious goals of the invaders. Finally, having shed the last vestment of his ceremonial garb, the Emperor stands proud in the "gold braid and buttons of a nineteenth-century Western general" and proclaims:

> In the name of progress we will turn our backs on ancient ways. We will cast aside our feudal forms, eliminate all obstacles which hinder our development.
>
> We will organize an army and a navy, equipped with the most modern weapons. And when the time is right, we will send forth expeditions to visit our less enlightened neighbors. We will open up Formosa, Korea, Manchuria and China. We will do for the rest of Asia what America has done for us! (p. 133)

In the final number Japan's precipitous assimilation of all the techniques and attitudes of the West and her ultimate domination of the world of materialism and power are dramatized. In contrast to the subtle control of the earlier pieces, the last song is loud and vibrant as Sondheim expresses both the positive and negative impact of rapid industrialization. The frantic rhythm, the short phrases, the active verbs, and the staccato shout "Next!" which punctuates the lyric, emphasize the feverish pace of the transition. In contrast with the tranquillity and stasis of the "floating" lyric that commenced the evening, the words and music of the final number pulse with an impatient frenzy. The pale, delicately etched screens are replaced by the harsh glare of foil, and the dancers (for the first time in the original production women were introduced) gyrate with an abandon that obliterates the restraint and order of the opening. (Patricia Birch, the choreographer, had the women fling their hair about in a seemingly unconscious caricature of the tossing lion's mane of Commodore Perry's triumphant dance.)

In the first song, the Reciter proudly declares, "Kings are burning somewhere, / Not here!" Now the upheavals of the outside world intrude:

> Kings are burning,
> Sift the ashes ...
> Next!
> (p. 134)

The rhythmic pattern, the use of only essential nouns and verbs, and the compact rhyme scheme emphasize the abruptness of the change. The convoluted, leisurely meandering of image patterns is replaced by a staccato, abbreviated shorthand:

> Tower crumbles,
> Man revises.
> Motor rumbles,
> Civilizes.
> More surprises
> Next!
> (pp. 134–35)

The negative and positive aspects of progress are synthesized. There is advance but there is also a concomitant loss and destruction:

> Streams are flying,
> Use the motion—
> Next!
> Streams are drying—
> Mix a potion.
> Streams are dying—
> Try the ocean.

Brilliant notion—
Next!
(p. 136)

The harsh, relentless march of progress is accentuated in the lyric and the emphatic urgency of the rhythm. The cumulative effect of this rhythmic insistence and the concentrated tightness of the rhyme make the forward thrust of the song and the culture impressive but frightening.

Dry statistical interjections, delineating the results and cost of progress, interrupt the song, giving added force to the satiric content of the lyrics: "There are 8 Toyota dealerships in the city of Detroit, and Seiko watch is the third best selling watch in Switzerland"; "Fifty-seven percent of the Bicentennial souvenirs sold in Washington, D.C., in 1975 were made in Japan"; "1975 Weather Bureau statistics report 162 days on which the air quality in Tokyo was acceptable" (pp. 136–37). Finally Kayama and Tamate, dressed in traditional costume, pass before the company. The contrast between past and present is strikingly theatricalized in the silent tableau.

The disparity between past and present is the true subject of *Pacific Overtures*. The effects of unfettered progress, its advantages and disadvantages, are what interests the authors. In a statement Sondheim made regarding the significance of the work, this concern is apparent (one can also see its relationship to his previous musicals, particularly *Follies*):

> I would like [the audience] to have a sense of exhilaration, but also of thoughtfulness. I want them to consider what's happened in the world, how time is catching us at the throat, how we are being rushed into careless and thoughtless decisions, as a government and as a people.
>
> We Americans have a special tendency to ignore history. We remember only what is pleasant. We must have a sense of the past. Without it the present is meaningless and stupid.[13]

This modification of the Santayana dictum that "those who cannot remember the past are condemned to repeat it" is clearly the thematic center of *Pacific Overtures*. It is not a simplistic, anti-American, anti-imperialist tract, but a serious attempt to examine the effects of a cultural collision. The almost total metamorphosis of a society in a mere 120 years provides the focus for their interest, but the significance of the events should not be restricted to a particular historical moment. The authors do not deny their didactic commitment. They are proud that *Pacific Overtures* is a "play of ideas." They do not, however, believe that their work is one-sided advocacy.

IS BEAUTY TRUTH, TRUTH BEAUTY?

Both the necessity for cultural exchange and progress, and the inevitable loss of identity and tranquility, are the subject matter of *Pacific Overtures.*

The significant question is, how persuasively are these concerns communicated to the audience? The show's overtly anti-American bias has already been mentioned. But there are other problems that may have impeded audience comprehension. Prince's production was spectacularly beautiful. The overwhelming impact of sets, costumes, and lights is commented upon in almost every review: "Visually breathtaking"; "The visual impact of *Pacific Overtures* is ravishingly beautiful"; "The visual is the only complete asset of the evening."[14] But, as Stanley Kauffmann, who begins his review by detailing his admiration for the work of Aronson and Klotz, points out, "obviously if a review begins with a comment on costumes and scenery, the show itself lacks something."[15]

Were the production's visual values so powerful that they overshadowed the characters and theme? There is one participant, at least, who believes that this was so. Mako, the actor/director who took the role of the Reciter and received unanimous critical acclaim for his performance, directed *Pacific Overtures* with his small company of semiprofessionals, The East/West Players, several years after its Broadway debut. In a tiny space in Los Angeles, with no proscenium, no elaborate costumes or sets, the musical was an artistic and commercial triumph. The impact of perceiving the history of cultural change through the life of two men, through an individual drama reflecting a universal political reality, was far more immediate. Kayama and Manjiro were lost as individuals within the huge framework of the Prince production. In the intimacy of the Mako production their personalities emerged and their centrality to the overall dramatic theme was clarified.

In the opening number the screens are described as "more beautiful than true" (p. 12). This is an apt epitaph for *Pacific Overtures.* The beauty in the original production was not only visual; it was also a beauty of the intellectual conceit. The incorporation of two distinct presentational modes as a means of expressing the antitheses and synthesis of contrasting cultures is theatrically brilliant. The work possesses a cerebral complexity seldom encountered in the theater, musical or dramatic. Yet despite this feast for the eye, ear, and intellect, its potential impact remained unrealized. Lacking any real sense of empathic concern, the audience was impressed but not moved. The conceptual daring of the creators inspired awe, but their deeper philosophic concerns failed to arouse their audiences.

Martin Gottfried attributes this sense of disappointment to the unusual and unexpected quality of the show:

> We have been conditioned to define a Broadway musical as an emotionally charged one. The tradition of our musical theater involves strong beats, soaring lines of melody and pulse-setting dance numbers. One way or another, through thrill or surprise, our spines chill.
>
> The primary colors of the stage experience have always been the joy of our musical theater. *Pacific Overtures* seeks the watercolors of the Orient, intellectually, emotionally, visually and theatrically. It goes against our expectations. It does not provide what we have been conditioned to anticipate from the musical theater.
>
> The initial disappointment was much like sitting down in a restaurant and not being served the dish one has always ordered. To be presented with its opposite was so disappointing that the surprise itself couldn't be appreciated.[16]

Pacific Overtures is radically different from the traditional Broadway musical. But the same can be said of all the previous Sondheim-Prince collaborations. Each, in its own way, is innovative, unexpected, and calculated to stimulate and disturb, rather than soothe and comfort. Gottfried concludes his article with a paean of praise to Prince, whom he hails as the "genius" whose overriding concept informs the work. No one would dispute Prince's tremendous creative ability, but had the production been a little less spectacular perhaps the personality of the drama and its thematic import might have been more clearly communicated.

The huge financial investment involved in mounting any Broadway musical made Sondheim and Prince's commitment to *Pacific Overtures* particularly important. While never pandering to the demands of the average theatergoer, this show took the two even further beyond conventional commercial ventures. Their economic risk and artistic audacity was acknowledged.[17] There were those, however, who believed that the creative team was being too intellectually smart, that its apparent erudition, social awareness, and uncompromising commitment to a concept hampered its creative effectiveness. Once again the argument that serious theater cannot be married to the musical's structure was reiterated.[18]

Even Gottfried, the show's most articulate defender, acknowledges that the conflict between commercialism and creative integrity needs to be resolved. On the day before the show closed, after a brief five-month run, having lost its entire investment, he wrote:

> *Pacific Overtures* closes tomorrow leaving in its wake financial failure, embittered creators and serious questions for the New York theater: Being privately financed, can Broadway be reasonably expected to present the best without regard to commercial appeal? . . .
>
> . . . It is possible that as a combination Sondheim and Prince do not have the common touch. . . . Their professional career has in a real way existed in a hot-house. There is something about their shows that does not generate sufficient audience enthusiasm and if they persist in a bull-headed way they will cost themselves and the theater their prodigious work.
>
> They cannot go on doing marvelous but money-losing shows in the commercial theater because nobody will foot the bills.[19]

Are Sondheim and Prince's aims for the commercial theater too ambitious? Is Ned Brinker, critic for *Opera News*,[20] correct when he gleefully chortles that the pair has left the musical behind and is up for adoption by the serious music lovers of the opera?

Sondheim and Prince did not capitulate. There was no compromise of artistic integrity. Far from being cowed by the commercial failure of *Pacific Overtures* and retreating into the lighthearted, unthreatening world of Broadway vulgarity or, conversely, seeking the shelter of a well-endowed opera company, their next collaboration was just as ambitious, as commercially risky, and, if anything, even more creatively innovative. With *Sweeney Todd*, Sondheim's ability as a composer and lyricist was not only more firmly established, but the artificial distinction between the American musical and serious musical theater was once again assailed.

7

GRANDER THAN GUIGNOL
Sweeney Todd

Ever since the prolific George Dibdin Pitt dramatized the harrowing tale of a murderous barber and his culinary accomplice for presentation at London's Britannia Theater in March 1847, *Sweeney Todd* has been a staple of the English dramatic repertoire. Although there is much speculation as to the origins of the barber's story, with attempts to trace Sweeney to real-life counterparts in England and France,[1] Pitt apparently based his play on the blood-chilling stories of Thomas Peckett Prest. Prest's serial, "A String of Pearls," had been published earlier in *The People's Periodical*, a Victorian penny dreadful that titillated and edified its readers with a combination of pious homilies and tales of gore.

Prior to Christopher Bond's adaptation of the legend in the early 1970s, there were at least six other versions of the grisly yarn. A theatrical tradition had evolved in which the piece was played as a jolly romp. By sending up all elements of romance and pathos, exaggerating villainy, scoffing at virtue, and playing in an extravagantly artificial and condescending style, the melodrama of Sweeney Todd exemplified the most obvious form of one-dimensional playwriting and crude presentation. Audiences were invited to laugh at the characters, and there was no attempt to make the macabre horrors enacted on the stage even remotely believable.

For the contemporary theatergoer, of course, the term *melodrama* has pejorative connotations and is associated with sentimental excess, violent action, and gratuitous villainy. It is primarily viewed as a form of theater in which a condescending audience is invited to scoff at the naïvete of its dramatic forebears. But this was not always so. The term derives from the Greek words for *song* and *drama*, because the use of sound and music to underscore and comment upon dramatic action is an essential characteristic of nineteenth-century melodrama. The form was popularized by Guilbert de Pixérécourt in France. His synthesis of scenic spectacle and amalgam of tragedy, comedy, and pantomime became the pattern for much subsequent work. The impresarios of melodrama pandered to their audiences with mechanical plots rich in violent conflicts, unmotivated twists, miraculous coincidences, deceptions, and conspiracies. The plays, never intended to be read, depended for their effectiveness on "coups de theatre" (seductions, kidnappings, grisly murders, sinister tombs, yawning graves, and last-minute escapes). Stock characters, a virginal heroine, a leering villain, and the ultimate triumph of virtue were mandatory in all the melodramas of the mid–nineteenth century. This type of theater originally appealed only to the uneducated: in contrast to the exclusive court theater, it was a theater of and for the common man. Gradually, however, melodrama was embraced by the bourgeoisie as a sensational, escapist diversion. "Entertain us or be gone" was the standard requirement of early Victorian audiences.

Yet most of the successful melodramas contain elements of sociopolitical comment. The broad plot treatment of noble heroine and sinister villain readily lends itself to the support of such disparate causes as the abolition of slavery, anticlericalism, and even tax and prison reform. With predominantly illiterate audiences, the theater was a source of information as well as entertainment. This is not to suggest that the typical melodrama is a profound work of social criticism. Nevertheless, in its glorification of the common man, its emphasis upon the ultimate triumph of justice, and its depiction of Gothic horror and murderous greed, Grand Guignol served an ultimately useful and moral purpose.

When Christopher Bond, a contemporary British playwright, decided to rework the Sweeney legend, he modified the extant versions of the melodrama in order to recapture some of the social implications inherent in the Victorian original—but without sacrificing its theatricality. By including a motive other than pure greed for Sweeney's murderous behavior, Bond creates a measure of sympathy for his protagonist. In order to appeal to contemporary sensibilities, he transforms the traditionally avaricious Sweeney, who murders only for plunder, into an ordinary working-class man whose life is invaded and destroyed by a powerful and malevolent social system. Sweeney becomes representative of those who, without money or influence, try vainly to exact justice from a corrupt and ruthless power structure. Only after he realizes his impotence is his mission transformed into monomaniacal carnage for its own sake.

The dichotomy between the Victorian theatrical exaggerations and the comprehensible (if unjustifiable) behavior of Bond's central character attracted Sondheim. Stimulated, he sought once more to create a form that would simultaneously explore and expose its underlying theatrical and sociopolitical assumptions. On one level Bond's, and subsequently Sondheim's, *Sweeney Todd* is a melodramatic thriller, filled with horror, blood, and sensationalism. But Bond injects into the play a chain of causality and an awareness of the social conditions that could give rise to such seemingly incomprehensible malignance. His work is an implicit critique of Victorian England's class structure and frequent perversions of justice. The rampant materialism of the industrial revolution and its demeaning impact on human dignity is also suggested, if not fully explored, in his text.

However, the thematic impact of Bond's play is not restricted to its exposure of Victorian England. Bond tries to create characters that are "large but real" and places them in "situations that, given a mad world not unlike our own, are believable."[2] The implication that Sweeney's excesses reflect a truth about contemporary society provides Sondheim with a key. Working from the Bond text, Sondheim re-creates the world of melodramatic excess, but in doing so holds up a distorting mirror to the horrors of modern life. In a world in which brutality has reached apocalyptic proportions, in which horror films and violence on television have become so commonplace that they no longer shock or thrill, Sweeney's theatrical extravagance is intended to reawaken an audience's awareness of its own insensitivity and inurement to aggression. In contrast to the writers of Victorian melodrama, whose purpose ultimately was to reassure an audience that good will always triumph over evil, thus offering a temporary escape from life's inequities, Sondheim intends to unsettle and disturb. The melodramatic form provides an ideal structure within which Sondheim can explore the pervasiveness of individual violence and societal culpability in contemporary life.

To reinforce the relevance of the piece, Sondheim incorporates modern musical connotations into his score. In contrast to nineteenth-century melodrama, which relied on musical overstatement, sobbing violins, and Victorian music-hall conventions, Sondheim invests his melodramatic structures with a distinctly modern sound. The nineteenth-century forms thus gain a contemporary resonance. Sondheim works within comfortingly popular musical and theatrical norms but infuses them with tension. Though the nineteenth-century ambience is acknowledged and established in the music, Sondheim is never confined by it. Pastiche and parody have their function within the score yet never dominate it.

Sondheim first saw Bond's *Sweeney Todd* performed by Joan Littlewood's company in 1973 at the Theater Royal, Stratford, in London's East End, and was very excited:

> This new version is a tiny play, still a melodrama, but also a legend, elegantly written, part in blank verse which I didn't even recognize till I read the script. It had a weight to it, and I couldn't figure out how the language was so rich and thick without being fruity; it was because he wrote certain characters in blank verse. He also infused into its plot elements from Jacobean tragedy and *The Count of Monte Cristo*. He was also to take all these disparate elements that had been in existence rather dully for a hundred and some-odd years and make them into a first-rate play. It's the other side of farce.[3]

Thus, from the very beginning Sondheim treated the project seriously, ignoring the disparaging connotations associated with melodrama. He initially envisaged adapting the material into an opera, but finding himself unable to reduce it to a manageable size he invited Hugh Wheeler to collaborate. The finished work, however, is all but entirely musical. Great sections of the action are conveyed and developed in sound and lyric, with spoken interjections reduced to the barest minimum. Text and score are fused into a perfect unity through Sondheim's seamless construction. The work's musical complexity, density, and weight are such that *Sweeney Todd* has been rapidly incorporated into the standard repertoires of American opera companies.

Despite Bond's addition of a psychological motivation, the basic plot of the play, like that of so many opera libretti, is essentially primitive. The story line is contrived, filled with convenient coincidences, arbitrary hindrances, and unwieldy theatrical devices. Fifteen years after being exiled to Australia on a trumped-up charge, a sometime barber, Benjamin Barker (alias Sweeney Todd), returns to London, intent on avenging himself upon a corrupt Judge (and his unctuous accomplice, the Beadle), who had framed him in order to seduce his young wife, Lucy. Joined in his enterprise by his former neighbor, Mrs. Lovett, a pie-shop owner looking for a way to bypass the exorbitant cost of meat, Sweeney is initially thwarted in his plans to kill the Judge and Beadle. Having fallen in love with Sweeney's daughter, Johanna, Anthony Hope, the young sailor who helped Sweeney return to London, attempts to free her from the Judge and further delays Sweeney's revenge. In frustration, Sweeney widens his vengeance to encompass all of humankind. He ultimately kills blindly. His victims include his own wife, who has gone mad as a result of being raped by the Judge shortly after Sweeney's exile began. Finally, after shoving Mrs. Lovett into the pie-shop oven, Sweeney has his own throat cut, leaving the stage in carnage.

Out of this relatively unsophisticated tale, rich in violent action and emotional extravagance, Sondheim fashions a serious musical drama that synthesizes the extremes of tragedy and comedy in order to reveal the universality of the revenge ethic and the corrosive effects of societal corruption and indifference.

Unlike previous collaborations between Sondheim and Prince, this project was Sondheim's, and Prince was initially reluctant to tackle it. He saw little in Bond's script beyond an elaborate Sherlock Holmes thriller. Once he realized, however, that the work could be made to reflect the dehumanizing effects of the industrial revolution and class structure and to comment upon "the incursion of the industrial age on souls, poetry and people,"[4] his interest was aroused. Although neither Sondheim nor Prince had any intention of using *Sweeney Todd* as a vehicle to preach, they saw that these deeper reverberations would give the work a resonance that could transform it from a superficial yarn of blood and vengeance into a dramatic piece with tragic overtones.

The play opens to the funereal sound of an organ. A cadaverous organist sits crouched over the keys under the ironic inscription "The Blood of Jesus Christ His Son Cleanseth Us from All Sins." The sententiousness of Victorian moralism is captured in sound and theatrical image. A huge drop, depicting the intricate social order of nineteenth-century England as an elaborate beehive with the all-powerful queen sitting at its pinnacle and workers descending in stages from there, hangs above the forestage. A couple of gravediggers enter and begin to shovel dirt as, to the piercing shriek of a factory whistle, two workers pull down the drop, suggesting the inevitable demolition of the exploitative social structure. The cavernous interior of a bleak Victorian factory is revealed.

The combination of eerie organ chords and the screaming blast of the whistle is significant. The organ suggests an ominous, "Gothic" atmosphere.

Its sonorous chords evoke the period's ponderous system of government, suffocating religiosity, and false gentility. But *Sweeney Todd* is not simply the re-creation of a Victorian thriller. The hard shrill of the factory whistle suggests unambiguously the unremitting oppression of economic power. This earsplitting sound will be used repeatedly to arrest the audience. It conveys a sense of sinister presentiment and is employed with horrifying effect to underscore each murder. The synthesis of eerie organ sounds and the blaring, abrasive factory whistle is used to disturb and unsettle the audience.

Prince set the work in a huge iron foundry, complete with rusty beams, enormous cogs, pipes, and rotting handrails. No light could penetrate the vaulted ceiling. Even when the corrugated-iron back wall was raised, the only vista in this Dickensian world—with no escape short of the unceremonious descent into a dirty grave—was a seemingly endless black-and-white vision of factories belching wastes along the Thames. In addition to the huge structure designer Eugene Lee reportedly reconstructed from an extant foundry, the original production featured various whirring, clanking machines. While these more obvious symbols of the industrial age were eliminated from the London and road-show productions, the chilly oppression of the vast factory space unmistakably signaled a society based on toil and exploitation. The overwhelming structure engulfed and dominated the cluttered confines of Mrs. Lovett's shop, a smaller structure rolled on and off the stage, where most of the action takes place. The characters are intentionally diminished by the towering scale of the workplace.

Some critics found the pervasive influence of the industrial revolution established by the set too blatantly didactic, but the impact of this stylistic choice permeates every aspect of the production: music, lyrics, acting style, costumes, and makeup. As Harold Prince quips, "Usually 'Less is More,' but for *Sweeney* 'Less is Bore!' We were going for More and More."[5] In another interview he adds:

> It amuses me the number of people who tell us the set for *Sweeney* is large, as though we hadn't noticed! . . . The emotions, the style of acting would have been considered embarrassingly large and Victorian twenty years ago. . . screaming like that and chewing scenery that way. Well, I maintain that it's thrilling because we are doing it within the confines of the period, the characters they are playing and the style of the piece. It becomes new—again.[6]

As a member of the ensemble steps forward and sings "Attend the tale of Sweeney Todd," the tone and thematic significance of the piece is established. This line, reminiscent of the Anglican liturgy, informs the audience that what they are about to see is a tale, a legend, a parable that will teach of corruption, oppression, and revenge. Though set within the specific confines of Victorian England, like all moral tales it will have universal implications. Although some critics (Erica Munk, James Fenton, and Stanley Kauffmann among them) found the social criticism of the class structure superficial and extraneous, it should be noted that these themes are introduced from the start and are consistently developed throughout the musical.

The score begins with a deep rumble, which seems to well up from the depth of the grave the two gravediggers are digging. Sondheim sets this introduction in the lowest possible register, as the singer dryly enunciates the cold, logical lyric; his low voice and soft threatening tone introduce the sense of menace that characterizes the musical. In this opening number, Sondheim lifts the audience by building to a slight crescendo but drops it again with an unresolved dissonance. The combination of the gaping grave and the musical treatment holds the audience in a state of mounting tension. They expect something to happen but nothing occurs in musical or lyric structure to release the strain.

The tight rhyme scheme and unadorned vocabulary remain faithful to the language of Sondheim's chosen period and milieu. The Victorian overtones are not forced but suggested in the slightly archaic words. This is a parable, relating the extraordinary career of the Demon Barber:

> He kept a shop in London Town,
> Of fancy clients and good renown.
> And what if none of their souls were saved?
> They went to their Maker impeccably shaved
> By Sweeney,
> By Sweeney Todd,
> The Demon Barber of Fleet Street.[7]

The irreverent black humor serves to lighten the tone, but the metaphysical reference here introduces an important musical and dramatic theme. After a bundled body is dumped unceremoniously into the grave on the forestage, the sacramental aspect of the drama is amplified as the chorus bursts into a modified Gregorian chant. The *Dies Irae*, high point of the Catholic funeral mass, provides a thematic musical clue to the significance of Sweeney's actions. Occurring in a barely disguised form in this opening chorus and reappearing intermittently in various guises throughout the work, this solemn medieval chant, with its widely recognized message of doom and its vision of the horrors, guilts, and irreversible decisions of the Day of Judgment, provides a key to the morbid complexity of Sweeney's character.

Images of corrupt and fearful lost souls finally confronted by the impartial judge are suggested in Sondheim's adaptation of the *Dies Irae*. The lyric, with its internal rhymes and binding alliteration and assonance, is equally significant:

> Swing your razor wide, Sweeney!
> Hold it to the skies!
> Freely flows the blood of those
> Who moralize!
> (p. 2)

Though Sondheim does not equate Sweeney with the Godhead come to sit in judgment on the evils of a corrupt world—he is, after all, a murderer, a "Demon Barber"—Sweeney *is* a towering figure whose passionate anger is an understandable response to the injustice to which he has been subjected. As a result of the intensity of his pain and all-consuming commitment to revenge, Sweeney transcends the merely mortal and becomes a distorted deity. This transformation is implicit in the grandeur of Sondheim's score and the connotative breadth of his lyrics.

Sweeney's suprahuman persona is further suggested in the prologue's lyric:

> Back of his smile, under his word,
> Sweeney heard music that nobody heard.
> Sweeney pondered and Sweeney planned,
> Like a perfect machine 'e planned.
> Sweeney was smooth, Sweeney was subtle,
> Sweeney would blink and rats would scuttle.
> (p. 3)

Sweeney might well be compared to the tragic protagonist of classical Greek drama. Sondheim has stated that he wanted his audience to be "moved" and "scared" by Sweeney's story, thus echoing the Aristotelian cathartic elements of "pity" and "fear." Like Philoctetes, Sweeney reeks of a kind of corruption, but he is equally heroic when contrasted with the evil of those who surround him. Nonetheless, Sweeney is very much a product of his society. The cold, mechanistic efficiency of his actions ("like a perfect machine") reveals that he is as much a result of the diabolical system as he is its victim.

A desperate and fearful cry for "Sweeney" builds to a shrill scream, reminiscent of the factory whistle that accents each climactic moment, as Sweeney is called forth from the grave. He rises from below, white-faced and staring, like a living corpse. He will enforce a kind of retribution, but the deity he serves is a "dark and a vengeful god" (p. 3). To an accompaniment that reflects the frantic turbulence of Sweeney's emotions and the inhuman clatter of the machine age, Sweeney demands that the audience attend his tale. The prologue then concludes with the reminder that all that will be enacted on stage is illusory, an allegory beyond the realm of reality. As the chorus spits out one last "Demon Barber of Fleet Street," the orchestra creates a frantic scuttling sound suggestive of the retreat of rats through London's maze of filthy streets. To this clamor, the ensemble vanishes into the murky darkness.

The prologue is entirely Sondheim's creation. There is nothing comparable in the Bond play. It sets the time, place, and major themes and establishes the story as a theatricalized fable. The action can now commence. The prologue broadens the horizon of the work by clarifying its social milieu and concerns while at the same time providing a justification for what will be an exaggerated presentational style.

After a brief blackout the early morning lights come up, to the call of the brass and the tolling of the morning bells. As this new day shines down on Sweeney and his companion, the sailor Anthony Hope, Sweeney's final journey begins. But the gentle melodic accompaniment, echoing the swell of the ocean, gives no hint of the horrors that lie ahead.

Bond's play opens with the cheery and naïve comments of the sailor: "I have sailed the world, beheld its fairest cities, seen the pyramids, the wonders of the east. Yet it is true—there *is* no place like home."[8] Sondheim converts these hearty clichés into a gentle lyric air that reflects the sailor's bluff optimism:

> I have sailed the world, beheld its wonders
> From the Dardanelles
> To the mountains of Peru,
> But there's no place like London!

I feel home again.
(p. 5)

The similarity to the Bond text is clear, but the melody transforms the simple phrases. The musical line rises to the phrase "But there's no place like London." The town is, for the jingoistic Anthony, the pinnacle of civilization.

As a good-natured, loyal sailor Anthony is a stock character, a recognizable type in British melodrama. In various guises the naïve and patriotic "Jolly Jack Tar" appears again and again in numerous plays from the late eighteenth century onward. Anthony Hope fits the stereotype to perfection. Even his name is appropriately symbolic. While Sweeney and Mrs. Lovett cannot be contained within the limitations of the melodramatic form, the minor characters all conform to the formula.

In *Sweeney Todd* Sondheim uses the leitmotif far more extensively and pointedly than he does in his previous work. Each character is identified with a particular musical theme; all their music evolves from that theme, and each song depends on the one prior to it. Anthony's ingenuous good humor as well as his nautical identity are conveyed in his theme, its lilting, upward inflection reflecting the essential optimism of his personality.

As Todd bids his companion farewell, they are approached by a bedraggled beggar woman, a figure straight out of Hogarth's *Gin Lane*. This character, who can be seen as a symbol of the effects of a corrupt society, initially pleads for alms in an aching soprano. But like the broken doll she clutches to her breast, her personality is shattered, a disintegration conveyed when the dulcet tone is replaced by a leering suggestiveness:

'Ow would you like a little squiff, dear,
A little jig jig,
A little bounce around the bush?
(p. 6)

The salaciousness is crude, yet pathetic. The pathos, furthermore, is heightened by Sondheim's providing a "musical clue" to the identity of the character: the raunchy tune she sings is in fact the minuet later played in the scene that flashes back to the rape of Sweeney's wife. This kind of intricate interweaving is characteristic of the complexity of the score.

After her pitiful attempts to sell herself have failed, the Beggar Woman looks up into Todd's face and mutters, "Hey, don't I know you, mister?" (p. 7). The elements of confused identity and complex plotting, so much a part of Victorian melodrama, help to sustain the period character of the play. Todd repulses the crazed woman's overture, excusing his excessive harshness with the curt explanation, "My mind is far from easy, for in these once-familiar streets I feel the chill of ghostly shadows everywhere" (p. 8). The irony of this observation is revealed only in the final moments of the play.

Anthony's persistent curiosity about Sweeney's identity provokes the older man into revealing his misanthropic vision of the city. Sweeney's cynicism counterbalances the sailor's enthusiasm:

> There's a hole in the world
> Like a great black pit
> And the vermin of the world
> Inhabit it
> And its morals aren't worth
> What a pig could spit
> And it goes by the name of London. . . .
>
> I too
> Have sailed the world and seen its wonders,
> For the cruelty of men
> Is as wondrous as Peru,
> But there's no place like London!
> (pp. 8–9)

Barely singing, Sweeney spits out his disgust.

Critics perceive in this black creed an echo of Brecht and Weill, both in tone and satiric content.[9] The comparison is valid, but Sondheim intensifies his social criticism by combining it with the apocalyptic reverberations of the *Dies Irae*. Sweeney's obsession with the horror of his world is unbalanced, but the reason for his excessive bitterness, his inversion of Anthony's optimism, is immediately provided:

> There was a barber and his wife.
> And she was beautiful.
> A foolish barber and his wife.
> She was his reason and his life,
> And she was beautiful.
> And she was virtuous.
> And he was—
> Naive.
> There was another man who saw
> That she was beautiful,

A pious vulture of the law
Who with a gesture of his claw
Removed the barber from his plate.
Then there was nothing but to wait
And she would fall,
So soft,
So young,
So lost,
And oh, so beautiful!
(pp. 9–10)

The gentle melody reflects Sweeney's aching longing for a peaceful existence that can never be regained. The simplicity of the tale and the quiet bliss of the past are emphasized in the repetition of the phrase "And she was beautiful," while the emotional intensity builds as Sweeney enumerates her qualities. The repeated words and simple phrases contribute to a sense of his total commitment to his lost marriage, but the melody and lyric lines break at the midpoint, re-creating the destruction of Sweeney's life and happiness. Just as his life was cruelly interrupted, so the music and lyrics halt as he painfully seeks to describe his former self. The word *naive* goes against the melodic expectation, is set to an unexpectedly low note, and reflects his descent into misery.

As the events in Sweeney's life took on a pace of their own, so he is driven to continue his story. His wife's seduction, described in a series of accelerating phrases, is climaxed with his reaffirmation of her beauty. But the song does not end here. The tale is incomplete and to Anthony's tentative inquiry whether the woman succumbed, Todd offers the inconclusive "Oh, that was many years ago ... / I doubt if anyone would know." The scene ends with Sweeney's reasserted and intensified vision of the unfathomable evil of the world:

There's a hole in the world
Like a great black pit
And it's filled with people
Who are filled with shit
And the vermin of the world
Inhabit it ...
(p. 10)

The bleakness of Todd's London is shattered by the ebullient entrance of Mrs. Lovett, as the rhythmic pattern alters from a somber monotony to a bright, vigorous lustiness. Although the opening numbers for the show are mostly heavy and grim, Sondheim has no intention of sustaining this unmitigated gloom: the relentless misanthropy of the title character is matched by the zany humor of his delightful future consort-in-crime. Her comic introduction is structured with split-second precision. She is a dynamic character whose every phrase is emphasized by a hearty gesture.

Sondheim captures this hyperkinetic energy by punctuating her song with specific business. The rhythms are broken and syncopated as she pounds her dough, flicks away dust, and pounces on the occasional crawling pest. Each beat, each pause in the incessant flow of chatter is utilized:

> Did you come here for a pie, sir?
> (*Todd nods. She flicks a bit of dust off a pie with her rag*)
> Do forgive me if me head's a little vague—
> Ugh!
> (*She plucks something off a pie, holds it up*)
> What is *that*?
> But you'd think we had the plague—
> (*She drops it on the floor and stamps on it*)
> From the way that people—
> (*She flicks something off a pie with her finger*)
> Keep avoiding—
> (*Spotting it moving*)
> No you don't!
> (*She smacks it with her hand*)
> (pp. 11–12)

Mrs. Lovett explains the reason for her shop's lack of success. Her pies, she confesses, are "the worst pies in London" (p. 12). She cannot make good pies owing to the exorbitant cost of meat, and unlike her inventive neighbor, Mrs. Mooney, she, as yet, has not found another source of filling. Her description of Mrs. Mooney's "enterprise" possesses its own comic potential and also hints at the inevitable direction of the plot:

> Mrs. Mooney has a pieshop,
> Does a business, but I notice something weird:
> Lately all her neighbors' cats have disappeared.
> Have to hand it to her—
> Wot I calls
> Enterprise,
> Popping pussies into pies.
> (p. 13)

Attention to detail, like the witty rhyme, alliteration, and the vaguely lewd suggestiveness in the key lines heighten the humor. Mrs. Lovett concludes her tale of woe with the lament "Times is hard" (p. 14), which has a deliberately Dickensian ring. Sondheim's comedic skill is given full reign in the relief provided by the horribly engaging Mrs. Lovett.

In the case of certain dramatic characters it is very difficult to separate the role from the actor who originated it. This is undeniably true of Angela Lansbury's acute realization of Mrs. Lovett. In this case, Sondheim knew in advance for whom he was writing: "*Sweeney Todd* was easy to write the minute we had cast Angela Lansbury—it wasn't a matter of writing for Angela Lansbury. It was a matter of writing for Angela Lansbury as Mrs. Lovett. . . . That's the best kind of collaboration."[10] Lansbury's bravura performance makes this murderous opportunist appealing and even lovable. Synthesizing the techniques of the British music hall comic—the rapid delivery, the broad asides—with an intimate domestic coziness that both repels and appeals, it is a dazzling achievement.

Some critics, however, maintain that Mrs. Lovett's extravagant comedy is at odds with the tragic intensity of the tortured Sweeney. Harold Clurman, for example, asserts that the humor "obviate[s]" and "negate[s]" the "brutality." John Simon bemoans the lack of consistency, labeling the show a "mélange des genres," and argues: "There are ways of treating profuse demises—either steady seriousness or black comedy—but *Sweeney Todd* is like a mad dinner party at which the dessert interrupts the hors d'oeuvre and the pousse-café is poured into the soup. What we have here is neither fish nor fowl but a clear case of what T. S. Eliot called the dissociation of sensibility."[11]

While, theoretically, *Sweeney Todd* may reflect a disintegration of any unified sensibility, as a theatrical experience it succeeds in blending the many facets of life and theater. It is a schizophrenic work, but the comic and tragic elements coexist and reinforce each other without losing their integrity. The title character dramatizes the dark implications of tragic revenge, but Mrs. Lovett's amoral exploitation of his murderous rage is couched in the comic tones of black comedy and burlesque. In this work, Sondheim is able to combine two of his favorite theatrical modes: melodrama and farce.

The tensions between the two forms serves an important aesthetic purpose. The overpowering immensity of Sweeney's pain and fury is relieved yet sustained through the respites offered by Mrs. Lovett's comically perverse practicality. The comedy is never simply "high jinks." It is designed to magnify the horror and the pathos of Sweeney's destructive impotence. The audience's response is not diffused by the comic interludes. On the contrary, the absurdity of these segments deepens the ultimate angst. Laughter and despondency go hand in hand and augment each other. As Gerald Rabkin of the *Soho Weekly News* points out, the interconnection of violence and humor is accepted in most absurdist theater.[12] The humor in *Sweeney Todd* distances the horror but does not trivialize it. Moreover, the dichotomies of style and character intention reflect the wide gulf between the moralism of Victorian ethical precepts and the immorality of Victorian behavior, between the complacency of contemporary audiences and the brutality of modern society.

The sharp Mrs. Lovett suspects the true identity of her customer, but in order to be sure she relates in graphic detail the tale of the barber and his wife who once occupied the rooms above her shop. One can appreciate the complexity, compactness, and narrative skill of Sondheim's lyric sequence if one compares it with the following Bond prose version:

> *Todd*
>
> Yes. (*After a pause*) Don't the family that live above pay you any rent?
>
> *Mrs. Lovett*
>
> No, there's no-one lives up there, sir. Been empty for years. There was a barber and his family that lived there once—ooh, a lovely man, he was, a *real* man, but he got transported across the seas. Mind you, he deserved it.
>
> *Todd*
>
> Deserved it! What was his crime?
>
> *Mrs. Lovett*
>
> Foolishness. Mind you his wife didn't help much. She was a brainless creature. Two proper gentlemen took a fancy to her, you see, but she wouldn't have none of it, and her husband, poor fool, instead of fetching her one round the mouth and leaving his bed for a couple of nights—he encouraged these fancy notions in her. Well—daft, weren't it? I would have had him down here for a couple of nights—and more if he'd wanted. But no, he had to make a song and dance of it. Well, stands to reason, they shipped him off.
>
> *Todd*
>
> What became of his wife? And were there no children?

Mrs. Lovett

There was a daughter, yes. Both cried themselves silly, they did, when he'd gone. (*During Mrs. Lovett's narration of the following events a dumb show is performed of them. It opens with Mrs. Todd and Johanna weeping. Beadle, Judge and Onlookers enter and join in as described*) Then one day Beadle came to call on her—to try his luck, you see—but she wasn't having any. Then he says as how the Judge had repented of himself and wanted to try and help get her husband back. And she, poor soul, believed him. Beadle said as how the Judge had taken to his bed in a terrible state and would she come to the Inns of Court that night to see what could be done for her poor husband. Well, she went, but when she got there they was having this fancy dress ball, you see, all in masks, they was, and she didn't know what to do, couldn't find the Judge anywhere. But he found her soon enough, and he were in a terrible state all right—but it weren't with repentance or nothing like that. She tried to fight him off, but the Beadle helped like, and what could she do on her own? All of them at the ball just looked on, you see. Watched, like. (*By this time Mrs. Todd, surrounded by Onlookers, is being raped by the Judge. Sweeney Todd can bear it no longer*)

Todd

Will no-one have mercy on her? (*The Onlookers laugh as the dumb show dissolves*) Then I will have no mercy either. None.

Mrs. Lovett

Here, you are in a state. You've hardly touched your pie.

Todd

(*Seizing Mrs. Lovett and forcing her to look at him*) I am that poor unfortunate woman's husband: that foolish barber so unjustly transported. Now tell me, woman, what became of my wife and daughter?[13]

Sondheim uses Bond's narrative detail and the idea of an enacted dumb-show, but his characters' motives and responses are more complex and serve not only to enlarge audience understanding of particular people and events but also to develop the major themes of the drama. Using the same melody that Sweeney uses in telling his story to Anthony, Mrs. Lovett begins her version of the events. (This *Rashomon*-like technique will be reemployed when the tale is retold a final time, once again using the same melody but revealing more accurately the reality of the crisis.) Mrs. Lovett, like Sweeney, begins with the words "There was a barber and his wife" (p. 14), but almost immediately her difference in perspective is disclosed. Whereas Sweeney sang with an aching longing "And *she* was beautiful" (p. 9), Mrs. Lovett leers "And *he* was beautiful" (p. 14). Mrs. Lovett not only wants to confirm her suspicions regarding Sweeney's identity, she wants the story to help her seduce him.

Following the Bond original, the action recounted by Mrs. Lovett is portrayed in dumbshow, an accepted mode of presentation in nineteenth-century melodrama. Mrs. Lovett, who characterizes the barber as "a proper artist with a knife" (p. 14), repeats Sweeney's story of the Beadle and Judge's attempted seduction, but her contempt for the soft and helpless wife is undisguised. She describes her as a "pretty little thing" and a "silly little nit" (p. 15). Here Sondheim gives his favored word *little* another gradation of meaning, suggesting vulnerability and weakness. It is in Mrs. Lovett's description of what occurred after Sweeney's deportation that the true horror of the family's fate is revealed. With increasing delight, Mrs. Lovett repeats the phrase "poor thing" (p. 15), heartlessly devaluing its meaning.

As Mrs. Lovett relates each gruesome detail, the chorus dons grotesque animal masks and dances an elegant minuet around the bewildered girl. The refined sound of the dance music and the measured precision of the choreography heighten the brutality of what is to occur. As Mrs. Lovett describes how the girl was raped as the callous guests stood around to watch, the brutal act is enacted behind the pair in a formal but violent dance sequence. As the music blares to a crescendo, Sweeney screams out in agony, "Would no one have mercy on her?" Mrs. Lovett acknowledges the success of her ploy with a cool "So it is you—Benjamin Barker" (p. 17). But Sweeney's torment is not yet complete. In unemotional prose Mrs. Lovett then informs him that his wife subsequently swallowed poison, and his daughter, Johanna, has been taken in by Judge Turpin as a ward. Thus, Sweeney is supplied with more than ample cause for his vengeful course of action.

Sweeney's anguish and desire for revenge are couched in the elevated tones of the tragic hero. Mrs. Lovett, on the other hand, is portrayed as a realist. Her response to Sweeney's pain is practical: "You got any money?" Her indispensability to Sweeney's very existence, however, is immediately revealed. She has saved Sweeney's razors during his long years of exile, and as she reverently hands these instruments of vengeance back to him—thus establishing his role as vengeful lawgiver—she is readily identified as his votary.

The ritualistic solemnity of the moment is reinforced by the score as Sweeney and his blades become one. The musical connotations of the *Dies Irae* are employed. Sondheim inverts the four opening notes of the medieval chorus for Sweeney's intense song of love to his instruments of death. Like

Sweeney rising from the grave, the razors are piously lifted from their case. There is a sense of ceremony and awe as he holds them aloft and quietly sings:

> These are my friends.
> See how they glisten.
> See this one shine,
> How he smiles in the light.
> My friend, my faithful friend. . . .
>
> Well, I've come home
> To find you waiting.
> Home,
> And we're together,
> And we'll do wonders,
> Won't we?
> (p. 20)

The unity of man and instrument is emphasized as Sweeney casts off his despondency and his role as avenger becomes explicit. His life lies in ruins. His hoped-for reunion with his wife and child is thwarted. Consequently he focuses all his passion on the blades. They become the loved ones, his union with them suggesting an almost sexual consummation. Sweeney's new-found sense of purpose, bringing with it a crazed kind of peace, is conveyed in the rich melody and upward sweep of the musical line.

As Sweeney continues his ardent serenade, Mrs. Lovett interjects her aspirations, the duet a perfect expression of two people who desire disparate things but are totally at one with each other. Sweeney's fixation is with the razors and the direction they indicate, whereas Mrs. Lovett reveals her amorous designs. Their complementary ambitions are revealed in the words they sing in unison, but the profound distinctions of their objectives are clarified as their words and worlds diverge:

Todd	*Mrs. Lovett*
You, there, my friend. Come, let me hold you. Now, with a sigh You grow warm In my hand, My friend, My clever friend.	I'm your friend too, Mr. Todd. If you only knew, Mr. Todd— Ooh, Mr. Todd You're warm You've come home. Always had a fondness for you, I did.

(pp. 20–21)

He is in love with vengeance and death. She eyes him lustfully and longs for a domestic liaison. He sees beauty in images of murder. Drops of blood are transformed into "precious rubies." Her interest is more material: "Silver's good enough for me."

The duet concludes as Sweeney shouts out in triumph, "My right arm is complete again!" (p. 21). The dehumanized Sweeney becomes a death machine, a negative deus ex machina at one with his instruments. His role as inhuman dispenser of punishment is reinforced as the ensemble intones its *Dies Irae* chant:

> Lift your razor high, Sweeney!
> Hear it singing, "Yes!"
> Sink it in the rosy skin
> Of righteousness!
> (p. 21)

As the chorus slowly exits, the notes of its ballad once more descend into the deepest rumble before a high chirping sound is heard. A dissonant flute and piccolo conclusion to the Sweeney theme is transformed into the twittering introduction to Johanna's bird song. Sweeney rises from the depths; his daughter descends from the heights, actually, emotionally, and musically. Appearing on the topmost level of the Judge's mansion and, tossing her profusion of golden curls, she sings in a high soprano.

Like Anthony Hope, the sailor, Johanna is portrayed within the confines of the melodramatic tradition. The threatened seduction of the pure young innocent and the maze of obstacles that keep her from her true love are mandatory to the basic plot structure of melodrama. But Sondheim pushes this stereotype to its ultimate limit of expression. Johanna's opening song is set in the upper reaches of a trilling soprano. Its predominant image, that of the bird in a cage, is a well-recognized cliché. Yet within these stylistic boundaries, Sondheim manages to infuse a sense of frustrated panic, a genuine pathos in the heroine through the beauty of her song. The sentimentality of the role is not denied, but heightened. Consequently there is a dual quality of theatrical excess and sincere poignancy.

Looking down on a bird seller, with his bizarre collection of birds in wicker cages, Johanna sings:

> Outside the sky waits,
> Beckoning, beckoning,

Just behind the bars.
How can you remain,
Staring at the rain,
Maddened by the stars?
How is it you sing anything?
How is it you sing?
(pp. 22–23)

The parallel between her life and that of the caged birds is obvious, her longing for freedom expressed not only in the lyrics but in the notes that soar constantly higher.

As the song progresses, Johanna reveals that the tension of confinement is becoming unbearable. She initially hears the bird's melody as "rejoicing" but ultimately hears it as "screaming" (p. 23). A materialistic theme is then introduced, for the girl feels that she, like the birds, is merely a pretty ornament, whose very existence depends on her decorative commercial value. Like a caged bird who sings when it is told to, Johanna remains safe but stifled in her cage. Her life is one of comfort but not delight. She is entombed in a dismal, deathlike existence:

My cage has many rooms,
Damask and dark.
Nothing there sings,
Not even my lark.
Larks never will, you know,
When they're captive.
Teach me to be more adaptive.
(p. 23)

As the young ingenue trills out a sad arpeggio, Anthony enters. In keeping with the tradition, he is immediately transfixed by her loveliness. His journey has found its destination. Repeating his earlier theme, he emphasizes this sense of discovery and arrival:

I have sailed the world,
Beheld its wonders,
From the pearls of Spain
To the rubies of Tibet,
But not even in London
Have I seen such a wonder ...
(p. 24)

Initially she is oblivious of his presence, but as they sing together she becomes aware of him. Therefore, rather than take the concluding top note, she and her song fade away in confusion.

Determined to gain Johanna's attention, Anthony buys one of the birds, and when the girl tentatively returns to her balcony he holds out his gift. She shyly descends, and as their fingers touch he croons a gentle love song. In a similar mode to her aria, the melodic line yearns upward, but the serenade has none of the frenzy of the girl's song. Their wooing is interrupted by the arrival of the Judge and Beadle, who react with fury at the boy's intrusion. They attempt to scare him off by graphically wringing the bird's neck and forcing the girl back into her "cage."

The sailor is undeterred, however, and gives full expression to his love and longing after Johanna has been hustled into the house. The melody, which expresses the adoration of the young man, builds as his sexual desire intensifies. Johanna and Anthony play the part of Victorian lovers, but Sondheim acknowledges a physical longing in their attraction with contemporary openness as the song concludes to an insistent, measured rhythm that reinforces the sailor's determination to free his love:

> I feel you, Johanna,
> And one day I'll steal you.
> Till I'm with you then,
> I'm with you there,
> Sweetly buried in your yellow hair ...
> (p. 29)

In Bond's text, by contrast, the meeting of the lovers is not dramatized and certainly there is no extended metaphor of the caged bird. Anthony simply relates the encounter:

> As I was walking along, deep in thought,something made me stop and look up— and there above, just in the casement of her window, I saw a lady of so pure and true a countenance I could not pass the place while she stood there. The sight of her seemed to—stop my breath. I stood and gazed in such rapturous admiration that the passers-by avoided me as if I was struck mad. Just as she seemed to leave her window, she glanced down, and her eyes met mine. What passions passed between us in that instant I cannot say, for I have never known the like before. Then modesty compelled her to avert her eyes, and she was gone; but not without a sigh that seemed to draw my soul out of my body.[14]

The dramatic superiority of Sondheim's active adaption in contrast with Bond's after-the-fact description is evident.

The focus returns to the barber. In order to advertise his newly opened establishment, Sweeney displays his tonsorial skill with a challenge. Sondheim encounters certain problems with this sequence, which he calls a "peasants on the green" kind of number. In order to infuse the group of bystanders with some degree of dramatic realism, he tries to find some motive for the choral singing, to create a valid reason for all these people to be singing the same thing at the same time. He achieves a tension and believability by dividing the ensemble into those who want to buy hair tonic from Sweeney's rival, Pirelli, and those who do not. He further sustains audience attention by introducing a series of inventive rhymes a la Cole Porter. Using as his key word *elixir*, he keeps his audience fascinated, wondering whether he will find yet another rhyme:

> 'Twas Pirelli's
> Miracle Elixir,
> That's wot did the trick, sir,
> True, sir, true.
> Was it quick, sir?
> Did it in a tick, sir,
> Just like an elixir
> Ought to do!
> (p. 32)

Yet despite Sondheim's inventiveness and the inclusion of a delightfully exaggerated pastiche of an Italian barber's song, the scene is not an unqualified success. Although necessary to the plot, it interrupts the action far too long and its comic effect is really not sufficient to justify its length.

Sweeney, knowing that he has aroused the Beadle's interest, is thrown into a state of impatient excitement. He can barely control his desire for revenge. His fervor, however, is restrained by Mrs. Lovett. She knows what he is plotting but responds as if she were handling a very ordinary domestic problem. It is this domesticity that makes her character so horribly funny.

The first word of Mrs. Lovett's entrance song, *wait*, now becomes the theme of her number. (Each character's musical and lyric development is patterned successively in this way.) As Sweeney paces his confined room, she flits about, diverting him with chat about redecorating:

I've been thinking, flowers—
Maybe daisies—
To brighten up the room.
Don't you think some flowers,
Pretty daisies,
Might relieve the gloom?

Ah, wait, love, wait.
(p. 52)

Her soothing little lullaby, filled with cozy homilies about anticipation increasing enjoyment, provides a perfect foil for Sweeney's all-consuming passion, and the song prefigures and explains his subsequent delay in killing the Judge. Mrs. Lovett's unquestioning acceptance of Sweeney's murderous intentions highlights her corruption. She is far more concerned about how to make the room look pleasing than about what is actually to take place there. Sondheim emphasizes the conversational quality of the character as her song dwindles into a series of indecisive questions:

Gillyflowers, maybe,
'Stead of daisies ...
I don't know, though ...
What do you think?
(p. 53)

The cozy tête-à-tête is interrupted by Anthony, who tells Sweeney of his love for Johanna and begs permission to leave her in the barber's shop while he hires a coach. Sweeney, prompted by Mrs. Lovett, reluctantly agrees, but after the sailor rushes off, he expresses his chagrin. He will find his daughter only to lose her again. Mrs. Lovett, in order to calm and delight the passionate Sweeney, replies:

> Oh, that sailor! Let him bring her here and then, since you're so hot for a little ... (*Makes a throat-cutting gesture*) ... that's the throat to slit, dear. Oh Mr. T., we'll make a lovely home for her. You and me. The poor thing! All those years and not a scrap of motherly affection! I'll soon change that, I will, for if ever there was a maternal heart, it's mine.
> (p. 56)

It is significant that the first actual mention of throat slitting is hers, and she has no better motive that the desire to please and manipulate him.

The two are interrupted again, this time by the Italian barber and his adolescent assistant, Tobias. While Mrs. Lovett entertains young Tobias in her parlor below, Pirelli reveals his true identity as one Daniel O'Higgins. He has recognized Sweeney and is determined to blackmail him. Believing that he has bested Sweeney, he breaks once again into his crowing, phony Italian-style tenor, but as he reaches his triumphant high note, Sweeney pounces and strangles him.

Although, in his review, Martin Gottfried complimented Sondheim on finally abandoning his musical jokes and mimicry, Sondheim has not altogether eliminated this kind of musical comment. Pirelli's song, Johanna's introduction, and Mrs. Lovett's escapist fantasy "By the Sea," all make their points through the distinctive connotation of their recognizable musical forms. A significant aspect of Sondheim's achievement is his ability to evoke periods or attitudes by re-creating musical structures without being constricted by the limitations of any particular form.

As Sweeney shoves the prostrate body into a chest, he is interrupted by young Tobias. There follows a brief scene of black comedy, based on the Bond original, in which Tobias sits on the chest unaware of the feeble gestures of his former boss's hand that has been left dangling. The boy is eventually sent off once again to the motherly ministrations of Mrs. Lovett, and Sweeney finishes off the bothersome barber. As the factory whistle shrieks its piercing accompaniment, he graphically slits the blackmailer's throat.

The chorus, in a modified Gregorian chant, then gives a kind of sanction to Sweeney's actions:

> See your razor gleam, Sweeney,
> Feel how well it fits
> As it floats across the throats
> Of hypocrites ...
> (p. 62)

Sweeney's self-styled justice is immediately contrasted with the official corruption of the courts. The Judge, cold and unfeeling, arbitrarily condemns a very young boy to death. This juxtaposition provides an ironic comment on the nature of justice and the law. Although both these scenes are to be found in the Bond version, they do not follow each other, so provocative comparison is lost.

As the Judge and Beadle stroll home together, the Judge confesses his intention to marry his young ward, despite her reluctance. Sondheim originally wrote a panting song of self-loathing and carnal desire for the Judge in which the contrast between his sanctimoniousness and lust is depicted in his self-flagellation. It was decided, however, that although the number gave greater depth to the character, it had to be cut for the sake of a comfortable playing length. The Judge's lechery and disingenuous solution are consequently reduced to a few lines of dialogue.

The focus shifts from the elderly prurient pair to the young lovers. Johanna expresses her dread of the Judge's intentions in brief, staccato phrases, where the intricate rhyme scheme and the agitated speed emphasize the girl's terror. A sense of period is sustained in words like *reticule* that function both in sound and meaning as clues to the milieu, without being so obtrusive as to deny the contemporary emotional veracity. When she confesses that the reticule is "the only thing / My mother gave me" (p. 72), a Dickensian ambience is reinforced.

As the lights fade on the embracing lovers, the audience's attention is refocused on the Judge and Beadle. In wheedling tones, the Beadle persuades the Judge that all he needs to win young Johanna's heart is the attentions of a good barber. The Uriah Heep humility of the man, broaching so delicate a subject as personal hygiene, is conveyed in the formality of his vocabulary and the repeated use of the salutation "my lord":

> Excuse me, my lord,
> May I request, my lord,
> Permission, my lord, to speak?
> Forgive me if I suggest, my lord,
> You're looking less than your best, my lord,
> There's powder upon your vest, my lord,
> And stubble upon your cheek,
> And ladies, my lord, are weak.
> (p. 68)

The tune and rhythm recapture the flavor of a refined Victorian ditty. The Beadle, played as an obese, ponderous individual, trips delicately on the phrases, verbal and musical, as he strives, without giving offense, to suggest that the Judge needs to be polished and shaved:

> Personal disorder cannot be ignored,
> Given their genteel proclivities.
> Meaning no offense, it
> Happens they resents it,
> Ladies, in their sensit-

> lvities, my lord.
> (p. 69)

The formality and grace of the song are placed in ironic contrast to the spiritual and physical grossness of the character and the unpleasant aspirations of the Judge. Little details, like the grammatical error ("they resents it"), emphasize the false gentility of the singer. It is, indeed, the conflict between the external decorum of Victorian manners and the ugliness they attempt to disguise that Sondheim relishes in this number.

Just as he is about to enter his house and find the lovers, the Judge decides to heed the Beadle's advice and visit the barber. The four characters, lovers and lechers, then join in a complex four-part harmony. The ardor of the youngsters blends with and contrasts to the fulsome ingratiation of the Beadle and the Judge's reluctant grumble. The identity of character is retained despite the combination of the voices. The characters are now all embarked on their destined paths, and as the lovers sink to the couch in a passionate embrace, a spot illuminates Sweeney, silently cleaning his razor. It is he who will be the pivot of all the action.

As Sweeney settles the Judge into his chair it seems that his desire for vengeance is finally to be satisfied. He appears to have learned Mrs. Lovett's lesson of patience and enjoys the anticipation. Rather than seek immediate gratification, he delays and relishes each moment that he has the Judge in his power. His bloody intentions are suppressed as judge and executioner share a strangely tender love duet in praise of women. Sweeney whistles, the Judge hums, and the scene appears to be one of jolly camaraderie. The vast gap between appearance and reality, between demeanor and inner desire, is exposed in the lilt of the murderer's song. The Judge relaxes. Sweeney rhythmically strops his gleaming weapon and sings quietly his inverted *Dies Irae*:

> Now then, my friend.
> Now to your purpose.
> Patience, enjoy it.
> Revenge can't be taken in haste.
> (p. 81)

Sweeney almost loses control and the accompaniment surges to a shrill crescendo when the Judge blithely confesses that his bride-to-be is none other than Sweeney's daughter, Johanna. But Sweeney controls himself by returning to his tribute to women, the two men eventually singing together:

> *Both*
>
> Pretty women!
> Blowing out their candles or
> Combing out their hair ...

Judge	*Todd*
Then they leave ...	
Even when they leave you	Even when they leave,
And vanish, they somehow	They still
Can still remain	Are
There with you,	There.
There with you.	They're there.

(p. 83)

Both men are obsessed and destroyed by their love of the same women. This identity is expressed in their exchange of lines. "Pretty," an adjective Sondheim uses almost as frequently as "little," contrasts with the dark, feverish passion of the two. The melody, one of Sondheim's loveliest, further distances the horror. The more evil the passion, the more lyrical the music.

Sweeney's repugnance intensifies as the song progresses, but just as he is about to sweep his razor across the Judge's exposed throat, Anthony bursts in, singing eagerly: "She says she'll marry me Sunday, / Everything's set, we'll leave tonight—!" (p. 84). Sweeney has lost his chance: the Judge, recognizing the sailor, rushes out and Anthony is unceremoniously forced from the shop.

Up to this point, Sweeney's motives have been clear, his intentions specific. But now his tolerance for pain and frustration finally cracks, and he slips over into a state of monumental madness. The shift is from the personal to the universal. He no longer seeks merely to find justice for his own cause but takes the role of a godlike judge, condemning all of humanity. The implications of the *Dies Irae* theme at last find expression in Sweeney's mighty wrath. He becomes a superhuman creature determined upon a course of indiscriminate bloody purgation. Sondheim titles the sequence "Epiphany" to emphasize the conjunction of divine and mortal.

Spurning Mrs. Lovett's tentative attempts to calm him, Sweeney spews forth his embittered diatribe. In his initial encounter with Anthony, he expresses his excremental vision of the world. Now, he repeats it, with even more venom. Then, as the rhythmic pounding of the lyric dramatizes his fury, he finds his release and his raison d'être:

> They all deserve to die!
> Tell you why, Mrs. Lovett,
> Tell you why:
> Because in all of the whole human race, Mrs. Lovett,
> There are two kinds of men and only two.
> There's the one staying put
> In his proper place
> And the one with his foot
> In the other one's face.
> (p. 87)

The neat British beehive that originally hung in front of the audience is interpreted by Sweeney as the ultimate form of exploitation. Capitalism, he reveals, depends on oppression and the only relief is death:

> Because the lives of the wicked should be—
> (*Slashes at the air*)
> Made brief.
> For the rest of us, death
> Will be a relief—
> We all deserve to die!
> (p. 87)

A memory of his personal grief is briefly allowed to penetrate as Sweeney keens a threnody for his lost wife and daughter, but his solution of taking men from "shave" to "grave" (p. 88) is paramount. The twin themes of life and death, vengeance and salvation, are emphasized as Sweeney sings out with awesome power: "I will have vengeance, / I will have salvation!" However, Sweeney can never appease his desires. There can never be peace:

> Not one man, no,
> Nor ten men,
> Nor a hundred
> Can assuage me.

Personal revenge is transformed into transcendental fury and the assertion of universal guilt. A life of bloody murder, the cleansing of a corrupt world, gives him a reason for existence. He lives now only to destroy:

And my Lucy lies in ashes
And I'll never see my girl again,
But the work waits,
I'm alive at last
And I'm full of joy!
(p. 88)

Under Sweeney's voice the engine theme pounds, emphasizing the destruction of the human spirit by the implacable forces of the industrial revolution. The splintering of Sweeney's personality is reflected in the abrupt changes in music and lyrics, as he alternates between lamentation and loathing. The musical pattern reflects his disintegration as sequences of staccato determination are juxtaposed with sustained yearning for lost happiness. The lie behind Sweeney's bravado is revealed in the unresolved final note of the solo. Although the lyric concludes on a note of triumph, the musical line denies it.

This shattering tour de force could easily have been chosen as the concluding moment of the first act. The audience has shared the transformation of an embittered individual into a sinister deity of death. The sequence's cathartic impact of pity and fear results in a synthesis both poignant and frightening. Yet this tragic breakdown does not conclude act 1. The musical was never intended to be a purely tragic vision, so Mrs. Lovett's black comic vision is given equal weight.

Mrs. Lovett has sat and patiently observed Sweeney's passionate outburst. When he finally drops to his chair emotionally and physically drained, she reminds him that his orgy of killing must wait till they have disposed of the body in his trunk. Sweeney is willing to drop the body anywhere, but the ingenious Mrs. Lovett has a better plan. As a high note sounds, suggesting in comic-book fashion the bright flash of an idea, she sings:

Seems an awful waste ...
Such a nice plump frame
Wot's-his-name
Has ...
Had ...
Has ...

With the practicality of a born entrepreneur, she cautiously suggests that Pirelli's corpse can be put to use. Unsure of Sweeney's response, she hints, not very subtly, at her plan:

I mean,
With the price of meat what it is,
When you get it,
If you get it—

Todd

(*Becoming aware*)
Ah!

Mrs. Lovett

Good, you got it.
(p. 90)

The humor of her changing tenses ("has," "had," "has"; "get," "got") and the incremental effect of rhymes in the subsequent lines ("lift," thrift," "gift," "drift") camouflage the macabre quality of her suggestion.

When Sweeney grasps her meaning he is titillated, his dour melancholy replaced for a time by a sardonic euphoria. Sondheim conveys this transformation in an exhilarating tempo:

Todd	*Mrs. Lovett*
Mrs. Lovett,	
How I lived without you	It's an idea ...
All these years I'll never know	Think about it ...
How delectable!	Lots of other gentlemen'll
Also undetectable!	Soon be coming for a shave,
	Won't they?
	Think of
How choice!	All them
How rare!	Pies!

(p. 91)

As Mrs. Lovett contributes her encouraging interjections, Sweeney's bizarre punning begins. The double entendre of "delectable," "choice," and "rare" introduces the manic wit of the number.

As the rhythm accelerates and Sweeney warms to the exciting possibilities of her suggestion, he inquires with derisive delight:

For what's the sound of the world out there? . . .
Those crunching noises pervading the air?
... It's man devouring man, my dear,
And who are we

To deny it in here?
(pp. 91–92)

The implicit corruption he has detected in all his experience has finally been given clear expression. The exploitation and abuse at the core of his society is given a concrete form in Mrs. Lovett's plan, the perversion of the social contract and the breakdown of all fellow feeling fittingly symbolized by the capitalistic cannibalism she proposes.

The two conspirators then launch into an uproarious routine. Imagining the different taste, flavor, and consistency of their prospective pie filling, they try gleefully to top each other's comic invention:

Mrs. Lovett

Have a little priest.

Todd

Is it really good?

Mrs. Lovett

Sir, it's too good,
At least.
Then again, they don't commit sins of the flesh,
So it's pretty fresh.

Todd

(*Looking at it*)
Awful lot of fat.

Mrs. Lovett

Only where it sat.

Todd

Haven't you got poet
Or something like that?

Mrs. Lovett

No, you see the trouble with poet
Is, how do you know it's
Deceased?
Try the priest.

Todd

(*Tasting it*)
Heavenly.
(pp. 92–93)

Sondheim structures the number like a typical British music hall turn. The plentiful puns and jingling rhythm suggest a lighthearted playfulness. Despite the gruesome premise underlying all the jokes, the song's lively beat seduces them into complicity, sweeping both characters and house effortlessly into mayhem.

In true music hall tradition, the lascivious Mrs. Lovett can't resist the risqué, and to a comic vamp skittishly teases:

> Since marine doesn't appeal to you, how about rear admiral?
>
> *Todd*
>
> Too salty. I prefer general.
>
> *Mrs. Lovett*
>
> With or without his privates? "With" is extra.
> (p. 98)

While Mrs. Lovett is quite carried away, Sweeney never forgets the plan's relevance:

> *Todd*
>
> The history of the world, my love—
>
> *Mrs. Lovett*
>
> Save a lot of graves,
> Do a lot of relatives favors ...
>
> *Todd*
>
> —Is those below serving those up above.
>
> *Mrs. Lovett*
>
> Everybody shaves,
> So there should be plenty of flavors ...
>
> *Todd*
>
> How gratifying for once to know—
>
> *Both*

—That those above will serve those down below!
(pp. 94–95)

Nor does he lose track of his original cause. His manic humor threatens to become uncontrollable when he mentions the Judge and the Beadle, but Mrs. Lovett manages to restore the balance with more outrageous culinary suggestions. In a raucous parody of Sweeney's former fury, the number concludes as he reasserts his intention to punish indiscriminately all who approach him:

Todd

We'll not discriminate great from small.
No, we'll serve anyone—
Meaning anyone—

Both

And to anyone
At all!
(p. 100)

The reverse love duet elicits a response of laughter and then an after-reaction of profound unease, similar to that achieved in *Company*. The flippancy, the wild tempo, and the characters' exultant vivacity undermine the ultimate horror of the plan and add a dimension of callousness that implicates the audience, which has been laughing along with the couple.

Act 2 opens with visual confirmation of the success of Mrs. Lovett's baking skills. Her pie store is filled with gluttonous customers enthusiastically guzzling pies and ale. Dressed in a new fancy gown, "a sign of her upward mobility" (p. 101), Mrs. Lovett presides. Tobias, using the same tune that he used to drum up customers for the unlamented Pirelli, now sells pies with equal commercial zeal. His sales pitch and delivery are overly elegant and artificially refined. This high style provides a satiric comment on deceptive advertising, particularly considering the true nature of his goods:

Ladies and gentlemen,
May I have your attention, perlease?
Are your nostrils aquiver and tingling as well
At that delicate, luscious ambrosial smell?
Yes they are, I can tell.
(p. 101)

Like the beginning of act 1, the beginning of act 2 is set entirely to music. Action is advanced, character motive and response are explored, without a word of spoken dialogue. The complex interaction between Mrs. Lovett, Tobias, Sweeney, and the crowd is organized into a mosaic of musical interjections. As Tobias concludes his paean to his pies, the crowd bellows their orders. But this is no "peasants on the green" number: though each member of the ensemble makes his or her request individually, the voices are woven together. The recurrent shout of insatiable delight, "God, that's good!" (p. 102) punctuates the cries throughout the sequence, emphasizing the crowd's voracious appetite and greedy consumption.

Mrs. Lovett's frenetic energy grows ever more pronounced. As she dashes about, controlling her unruly customers, making sure she gets paid, serving her seemingly endless supply of pies, issuing instructions, and chasing the Beggar Woman from the premises, her attention is sought by an agitated Sweeney. Oblivious to her booming business, he is anxiously awaiting the arrival of something. Though Sweeney's vision of the world's inhabitants' consuming each other is dramatically realized in the clamorous scene before him, he finds no satisfaction in the fulfillment of his prophecy and remains distracted by his obsessive desire to become the perfect instrument of vengeance.

Finally a huge crate appears, suspended from a crane, high above the "tonsorial parlor." It descends slowly, like a gift from some dark god. Sweeney manages to drag Mrs. Lovett away from her thriving business and opens the crate, which contains an elaborate barber's chair. As Mrs. Lovett clucks a delighted "It's gorgeous" (p. 110), Sweeney sings a love song to this new machine of death. Like the factory owners of the industrial revolution, who constantly strove to make their production more efficient through mechanization, so Sweeney, as a merchant of death, seeks to perfect his means of destruction. To highlight the union of man and instrument, Sweeney echoes the phrase he previously sang to his razors, "I have another friend" (p. 110). (Sweeney's passion is always directed toward instruments of death; he serenades no human with such tenderness.) As the blades made his arm complete, so the chair's ingenious construction, which will dispatch his customers by shooting them into the basement, perfects his system of mass murder.

The unity of purpose between the ambitious commercialism of Mrs. Lovett and her tenant's homicidal aspirations is underlined when Tobias, in the pie shop, picks up the melody Sweeney has sung to his chair and employs it to extol his wares. Mrs. Lovett interjects, with equal enthusiasm, "It's gorgeous" (p. 110). The customers' hungry yells and gratified moans, Mrs. Lovett and Tobias's sales pitch, and Sweeney's test of his elaborate executionary system are interwoven into a mélange of differing sounds and rhythms, ending with the code of knocks and bangs the meticulous Sweeney rehearses with the impatient Mrs. Lovett.

As the voracious crowd continues to shout for pies, the audience sees Sweeney's assembly-line mechanism of death in action for the first time. Mrs. Lovett descends into the bake house, a hellhole of flaming ovens and murky darkness. Sweeney pushes a lever on the chair, and a stack of books he has placed on the seat disappears through a trap and hurtles through a chute in the bake-house wall. The efficacy of the fully operational dispatch system is immediately illustrated when Mrs. Lovett, who is about to put up her "Sold Out" sign, sees a man approaching the barber's shop and jocularly sings out, "Bless my eyes—! / Fresh supplies!" (p. 115). The sequence concludes with the crowd singing one final tankard-pounding libation to Mrs. Lovett's pies.

In contrast to the clamor and noise, the lone figure of Anthony wanders the streets of London, searching for his missing beloved. The gentle haunting melody of his plaint reveals that tenderness and love are still possible in a nightmarish world. As if his poignant longing has floated up to the tormented barber, Sweeney joins Anthony in his serenade to the absent Johanna, and the characters share a dreamlike duet of love and longing. As Sweeney sings, he welcomes an unsuspecting customer, and, without pause, absently slits his throat. Sweeney has entered a state of benign detachment, killing not in heightened passion but as a necessary part of his existence.

While Anthony's love is filled with promise and hope, Sweeney sings of parting and farewell. He has achieved a kind of peace, but he realizes that he has of necessity abandoned human affection:

Todd

And if you're beautiful, what then,
With yellow hair, like wheat?
I think we shall not meet again—
(*He slashes the customer's throat*)
My little dove, my sweet
Johanna ...

Anthony

I'll steal you,
Johanna ...

Todd

Goodbye, Johanna.
You're gone, and yet you're mine.
I'm fine, Johanna,
I'm fine.
(*He pulls the lever and the customer disappears down the chute*)
(p. 117)

As the lights gradually fade, smoke fills the stage and the audience can see Mrs. Lovett tossing the remnants of her supplies into the furnace. The Beggar Woman, like the bedraggled conscience of the city, tries to alert passersby to the evil she knows exists in this hell on earth, but no one will heed her desperate pleas:

Smoke! Smoke!
Sign of the devil! Sign of the devil!
City on fire!
Witch! Witch!
Smell it, sir! An evil smell!
Every night at the vespers bell—
Smoke that comes from the mouth of Hell—
City on fire!
(p. 118)

Her warning cries add another theme to the symphony of sound. References to perverse religious practice ("devil," "witch," "hell," "evil," "unholy," "fiend") recur in her alarms, which are interspersed with Sweeney's lyric song of lost love, Anthony's patient search, and Johanna's sad cries of longing.

The melodic line is primarily Sweeney's, whose gentle acceptance that he has lost the ability to love is emphasized as he efficiently shoves various cutomers down the chute. His loss of particular motive and need for generalized revenge is expressed as a song of lost love and innocence, poignant and beautiful both in melody and lyric simplicity:

If angels could prevail,
We'd be the way we were,
Johanna ...

Wake up, Johanna!
Another bright red day!
We learn, Johanna,
To say
Goodbye ...
(pp. 121–22)

He accepts that only divine intervention can restore his humanity, and he has no faith. Through a complex blend of word and sound, each repetition and juxtaposition in this thematically and dramatically varied sequence enhances and enriches mood, motive, and melody.

As the composition draws to its tranquil conclusion, Anthony finally hears Johanna's plaintive voice and traces it to the barred door of Fogg's Asylum. He naïvely pleads with the Beadle for help; when he is refused, even the innocent Anthony begins to comprehend the corruption endemic in his beloved London. Meanwhile, in the cozy interior of Mrs. Lovett's parlor, signs of prosperity are everywhere. As if to prove her refined gentility, Mrs. Lovett sits at her newly acquired harmonium, a bargain obtained when the chapel burned down, and sings a nauseatingly sweet ditty, another example of Sondheim's facility as a mimic. Unlike the bulk of the score, which retains the flavor of its Victorian milieu but is designed primarily to reflect character needs and desires, this song is an almost exact replica of polite late-nineteenth-century parlor music. The sense of recognition is so strong that the song feels authentic. Later the Beadle will delicately warble the piece and the sense of a popular song familiar to all will be reinforced.

As the preoccupied Sweeney broods about ways to lure the Judge back into his grasp, Mrs. Lovett chatters on. Delighted by her commercial success, she tentatively broaches the more delicate subject of their personal relationship. As she flirts with, teases, and caresses a largely unresponsive Sweeney, she expresses her own dreams. Choosing a structure that will accord perfectly with the character's world view and experience, Sondheim has Mrs. Lovett reveal her desires in the form of a typical seaside fantasy. The urge to escape the grime of the city and live the life of one long holiday is found in many popular Victorian songs, so again the form is familiar, the lyric pattern almost recognizable. But here the structure reflects the mind-set of the character. This is her dream, expressed in her terms. The song and the personality are perfectly matched.

To a bright, jaunty rhythm (one can almost hear the brass band on the promenade), Mrs. Lovett prances about with coyly lifted skirts. Her dream is simple. She longs for domestic bliss, a little seaside cottage alone with her beloved "Mr. T." The lyric is filled with witty play on words. Patterns are made ("kippered," "kip," "kippers"; "straight," "Straits"; "slippin'," "slippers") that delight the ear as well as the intellect.

Mrs. Lovett's plan is not grandiose. She longs only for bourgeois gentility. Indeed, ironically, her amorality is linked with her desire to be respectable. She acknowledges that Sweeney needs to murder, but nonetheless she craves the legitimacy of marriage:

> By the sea, in our nest,
> We could share our kippers
> With the odd paying guest
> From the weekend trippers,
> Have a nice sunny suite
> For the guest to rest in—
> Now and then, you could do the guest in—
> By the sea.
> Married nice and proper,
> By the sea—
> Bring along your chopper
> To the seaside,
> Hoo! Hoo!
> By the beautiful sea!
> (p. 130)

The absurdity of her moral system is emphasized by Sondheim's rhyme of "proper" and "chopper." Mrs. Lovett never questions the ethics of her existence. She accepts Sweeney's murderous philosophy without qualms and, as the ultimate pragmatist, seizes any opportunity that will promote her personal comfort and security.

Mrs. Lovett's sexual innuendoes and coy advances climax as she plays "Here Comes the Bride" (p. 130), giggles, and kisses the indifferent Sweeney. But this would-be seduction is interrupted by the arrival of a dispirited Anthony, who announces Johanna has been confined to a madhouse. Sweeney is immediately revitalized as he conceives a plan to free her—because the wigmakers of London obtain their hair from Bedlam, Sweeney will disguise Anthony as a wigmaker and instruct him regarding the subtleties of their craft.

After discharging Anthony to rescue Johanna, however, Sweeney adds a new twist to the plot. He writes a letter to the Judge, telling him of Anthony's plan, and uses Johanna as a bait to lure the Judge back into his clutches. The mechanistic escalation of events is echoed in the machinelike repetition of the choral chant, for as Sweeney develops his plan, the ensemble observes and comments:

> Sweeney was sharp, Sweeney was burning,
> Sweeney began the engines turning.
> (p. 134)

The complexity and ambiguity of his motives are conveyed as they sing out his missive, distorting and repeating words and phrases to suggest the tortuous meandering of his mind.

While Sweeney waits, Mrs. Lovett and Tobias share a cozy interlude. Suspecting that there is something perverse in the relationship between his beloved employer and the lugubrious barber, the simpleton Tobias assures Mrs. Lovett that he would do anything to defend and protect her. Tobias casts the mercenary Mrs. Lovett as his damsel in distress, couching his tender declaration of love in the archaic terms of the chivalric code. His idealism is suggested in the high, aspiring notes of the melody. As he sings in long, ascending lines, Mrs. Lovett clucks out her interjections. While his affection is gentle and sweet, her concern is purely selfish:

> *Tobias*
>
> Demons are prowling
> Everywhere
> Nowadays.
>
> *Mrs. Lovett*
>
> And so they are, dear.
>
> *Tobias*
>
> I'll send 'em howling.
> I don't care—
> I got ways.
>
> *Mrs. Lovett*
>
> Of course you do ...
> What a sweet, affectionate child it is.
> (p. 139)

The demon Tobias fears is clearly the Demon Barber. The hint of supernatural evil is deliberate.

Paralleling Tobias's anxiety to convince Mrs. Lovett of his loyalty, the rhythm changes and the ascending notes are replaced by short staccato phrases:

> Not to worry, not to worry,
> I may not be smart but I ain't dumb.
> I can do it,
> Put me to it,
> Show me something I can overcome.
> Not to worry, mum.
> (p. 140)

In her attempt to divert him, Mrs. Lovett pulls out the purse she lifted from Pirelli's body. Tobias recognizes it, and his worst suspicions are confirmed. She tries to calm him by repeating his love song, but it now takes on a menacing tone. The ever-enterprising Mrs. Lovett finds a way to still the boy's fears, however. He has always wanted to assist in the baking of the pies, so she leads him down into the dungeon bakehouse and locks in the gullible Tobias.

The chorus that has, in a Brechtian manner, observed and commented upon Sweeney's deterioration, transforms itself into the inmates of Fogg's Asylum. The subsequent sequence in the madhouse, Dickensian in its revelation of exploitation and cruelty, balances and gives some modicum of legitimacy to Sweeney's towering rage. The sequence is played in silhouette, and the distorted shadows add a dimension of grotesque evil. This stylization, like the earlier sequence of Johanna's mother's rape, conforms with convention, in which climactic moments often are intensified with exaggerated theatrical devices. Anthony arrives at the Asylum and Sweeney's plan seems to be working. Fogg finally detects the deceit and tries to prevent Johanna's escape. There is a scuffle. The sailor is unable to bring himself to shoot Fogg, so Johanna grabs the gun and kills her captor. Followed by the chattering inmates, the pair flee into the streets of London.

As the escaping lunatics run madly about the stage, they sing in contrapuntal harmony:

> City on fire!
> Rats in the grass

And the lunatics yelling in the streets!
It's the end of the world! Yes!
(p. 155)

Their vision of doom echoes the Beggar Woman's prognostications. The idea that only the deranged see clearly is amplified as these pathetic creatures run about warning of the rampant spread of corruption.

This scene can be compared to Sondheim's earlier experiments in *Anyone Can Whistle*, but although the "Cookie" ballet of the earlier work is similar in theme, the style and intention of the two pieces are radically different. In the earlier show there is humor and delight in the inversion of madness and sanity. In *Sweeney Todd* the vision is far more pessimistic and filled with foreboding and dread. The ensemble's anxious phrases are punctuated by the shrill note of the police whistle, which echoes the factory whistle, the voice of ultimate destruction. The dispensers of the law and the capitalists are audibly united in their oppressive tactics.

As the lunatics chant out their vision of apocalyptic horror, they are interrupted by brief snatches of Johanna's feverish panic, Todd's and Mrs. Lovett's calls luring the terrified Tobias out of hiding, and the Beggar Woman's frantic cries for the Beadle. The pace accelerates, and the choral images become more and more horrific:

Hunchbacks kissing!
Stirrings in the graves
And the screaming of giant winds!
Watch out! Look!
(pp. 156–57)

The day of judgment has dawned. The connotations of the *Dies Irae* theme are now articulated and made plain.

This chilling sequence subsides as Anthony leads a terrified Johanna into Todd's shop. Disguised in a sailor's uniform, she is reluctant to be left alone, but the young man stills her fears, and the two lovers once more sing their duet. In his earlier work Sondheim avoids the use of reprises, for he maintained that as characters develop they should not repeat previous emotional states. In this work, however, he uses thematic reprises to clarify and develop characters and relationships. These thematic leitmotifs become more prominent and significant as the drama reaches its conclusion. The score, in fact, consists of a complex mosaic of developing themes and brief ephemeral melodic patterns, with even fewer traditional musical theater set pieces than in Sondheim's previous work. In the final twenty minutes of *Sweeney Todd*, all the different leitmotifs associated with the individual characters are combined as the multiplicity of plots draws to a unified conclusion.

After Anthony leaves Johanna in the barber's shop, she hides in Sweeney's large trunk. The Beggar Woman shuffles in, looks about her, opens a window, picks up an imaginary child, and croons a crazed but gentle lullaby. She seems strangely at home. Sweeney storms in, razor held high, and tries to force her from the room, but she clings desperately to him, trying to convince him of Mrs. Lovett's evil. Seeing the Judge approach, Sweeney yells in fury, "I have no time," slits the woman's throat, and shoves her body down the chute. Sweeney's vengeance/salvation theme sounds as he unknowingly executes his own wife.

The Judge enters, demanding his ward. Once again Sweeney calms him, and seduces him into his chair. The two men then reprise their song in praise of women just before the final recognition and coup de grace, after which Sweeney expresses his sense of release as he lays down his instruments of vengeance and tenderly sings:

> Rest now, my friend,
> Rest now, forever.
> Sleep now the untroubled
> Sleep of the angels ...
> (pp. 166–67)

It seems that the ultimate horror must occur as Sweeney grabs at the disguised Johanna, and the chorus chants its perverse *Dies Irae*, but at the last moment Sweeney is diverted by Mrs. Lovett screaming from the cellar and Johanna slips away.

The final moments of the musical are set in the dark dungeon and Sondheim's intricate musical patterning is apparent when Mrs. Lovett, forced to reveal the truth about Sweeney's wife, uses the now-familiar story melody to relate how Lucy took poison and did not die, but was sent to Bedlam. Mrs. Lovett tries to justify her deception by declaring her love for Sweeney and asserting, "I'd be twice the wife she was" (p. 171).

Throughout her tale, Sweeney keens in the background but gradually his lamentation ceases. He rises, smiles, and to the waltz that first cemented their macabre relationship, sings:

Mrs. Lovett,
You're a bloody wonder,
Eminently practical and yet
Appropriate as always.
As you've said repeatedly,
There's little point in dwelling on the past.
(p. 172)

She is taken in and relaxes into their familiar dance. As he swings her about, she delightedly babbles her song of seaside escape. But Sweeney dances her closer and closer to the oven and finally heaves her into its flaming depths.

All this destruction, however, brings no release. As Sweeney cradles the broken body of his wife in his arms, he croons the song he sang to Anthony early in the play. The words and music are unchanged, for Sweeney's life is still hopeless and without meaning. He is oblivious of Tobias, who timidly emerges from the shadows. The boy's hair has turned white from the terror of his experience, and he chants a crazed parody of a children's nursery rhyme. When Sweeney finally becomes aware of him and pushes him violently aside, Tobias grabs the razor. As the factory whistle's fearsome blast announces the final murder, Tobias draws the gleaming blade across Sweeney's throat.

It is in these final moments that Sweeney achieves the status of tragic hero. He does not resist death. He must die because he understands both what has been done to him and what he himself has wrought. His is not the arbitrary death of melodrama but the necessary death of tragedy. The question of Sweeney's moral regeneration remains moot. Unlike traditional melodrama, Sondheim's *Sweeney Todd* lacks the unambiguous idealistic certainty of the simplistic tract. Good and evil, right and wrong, are not clearly defined in the emotional torment of the protagonist. Yet as Robert Cushman of the *London Observer* notes, *Sweeney Todd* "ends up as a moral show, not by preaching, simply by the old approved method of showing passion spending itself."[15]

But the drama does not conclude with a macabre tableau. The reestablishment of the balladlike mythic quality must be achieved. Thus, the lights abruptly brighten and the actors step out of character to sing once again "The Ballad of Sweeney Todd." They emphasize that this has been a parable, not a series of real events. Gradually their tone alters from cautionary to accusatory. The pervasiveness of contemporary destruction is introduced:

The more he bleeds, the more he lives.
He never forgets and he never forgives.

Perhaps today you gave a nod
To Sweeney Todd,
The Demon Barber of Fleet Street.

The suggestion is that Sweeney, as the arbitrary force of destruction, is all about us:

Sweeney waits in the parlor hall,
Sweeney leans on the office wall.
No one can help, nothing can hide you—
Isn't that Sweeney there beside you?
(p. 176)

Echoing the technique employed by Laurents in *Anyone Can Whistle* and Peter Brook in his production of *Marat/Sade*, Sondheim has the company move downstage and confront the audience, implying that there are Sweeneys here, now and always. In a world full of Sweeneys, revenge generates revenge and violence proliferates.

The ensemble then turns from the audience and points to the grave as slowly a staring, bloody Sweeney and his grisly cohort rise from the pit. They join the company and sing one final stanza:

Todd and Company

Attend the tale of Sweeney Todd!
He served a dark and a hungry god!

Todd

To seek revenge may lead to hell,

Mrs. Lovett

But everyone does it, and seldom as well

Todd and Mrs. Lovett

As Sweeney,

Company

As Sweeney Todd,
The Demon Barber of Fleet Street ...
(p. 177)

The chorus exits. Mrs. Lovett and Sweeney give each other one last malevolent glance, part, and exit in opposite directions. The final moment is between the audience and the Demon Barber, who turns from his backstage exit to cast one final glare before slamming the iron door behind him.

The theatrical and philosophical statements implicit in this last Brechtian sequence provoke much conflicting critical debate. Despite the clear evidence throughout the work of a subtext of social satire and human concern, some reviewers condemned *Sweeney Todd* for its nihilistic misanthropy, its sympathy for a mass murderer, and its implied criticism of its audiences. Their position is best summarized in the response of T. E. Kalem:

> My objection basically is rather more moral than aesthetic. . . . *Sweeney Todd* starts out on the course of revenge, but then that revenge becomes simply a general mindless destruction of people and the knifing of them . . . or "razoring" of them. And if there is a kind of moral message—quite apart from the whole nineteenth-century bit which is used as a rational crutch and not as an intrinsic part of the story of *Sweeney Todd*—it's at the end when they're pointing at the audience. The general impression there is, "You're debased; I'm debased; you're degraded; I'm degraded; we all do the same thing. How can you point a finger at us?"
>
> But we don't all do the same thing, either within that *Sweeney Todd* framework, or in a Brechtian sense of always eating someone else or being eaten. Yes, there's an element of truth in that. But it's not the whole truth and I think this musical tries to present it as the whole truth.
>
> On a different realm. I think there is and has been sometimes in Sondheim and Prince . . . the idea: "Okay, you middle-class buzzards, with your phoney respectability, you take this and swallow it. You're shits, we're shits." I don't really buy that. I think it's an attempt to outrage the audience in a way that I, as a member of the audience . . . don't accept. I don't think that I've lived my life in that way; I haven't been eating or being eaten.[16]

These sentiments are echoed by James Fenton, of the *London Sunday Times*, who writes:

> At the climax of the evening, the chorus points wildly at the audience and accuses it of adopting, only rather less successfully, the same methods as Sweeney Todd. This accusation is, like a great deal else in the musical, pretentious and fatuous. Mass-murderers we may all be in some sense, and in other circumstances we would be prepared to listen to the charge.
>
> *Sweeney Todd* the musical is, if one can imagine such a thing, a tissue of bullshit from start to finish. . . . Mrs. Lovett couldn't give a damn about the barber's victims. Nor could Stephen Sondheim and nor could Hal Prince. If they didn't pretend to care one would leave the musical feeling,

> well, that was a massively tasteless exercise, but never mind. The pretentiousness has been introduced in an attempt to keep down the tastelessness, in rather the same way as people put goats into graveyards in order to keep down the weeds. The result is that one emerges with the sensation of having been dishonestly handled.
>
> Victorian melodrama was not dishonest in this way. Melodrama provided a crudely expressed, but substantially accurate, account of the seamy side of Victorian life. Those poisoners, those deportations, those repentances were real. By contrast, the psychology at Drury Lane is sham.[17]

Sondheim emphatically denies this kind of distorted criticism: "The pointing at the audience is about revenge, not murder. Critics all willfully ignore the lyric and take refuge in something the song doesn't say: namely, that I'm accusing the audience of being murderers."[18] But the responses of Erica Munk of *Village Voice*, Brendan Gill of the *New Yorker*, and Stanley Kauffmann of the *New Republic* are in a similar vein. These critics are repelled by what they see as a heartless, chic, exploitative cynicism. They condemn the work by asserting that its social satire is nothing more than a trendy artiness posturing as art. By drawing unfavorable comparisions with the work of Brecht and Weill they attempt to prove that *Sweeney Todd* is derivative and distasteful both in style and content.

Other critics are confused by the moral overtone, and, like Martin Gottfried, Richard Eder, and Walter Kerr, accuse the creators of obfuscation and lack of clear direction. Kerr, for example, argues: "We are without a perspective from which to view the mayhem. . . . We are plainly in the hands of intelligent and talented people possessed of a complex, macabre, assiduously offbeat vision. Unhappily, that vision remains a private and personal one. We haven't been lured into sharing it."[19] Close examination of *Sweeney Todd*, however, has revealed the implausibility and inaccuracy of these responses. Even if one ignores the sociopolitical satire, historical and contemporary, one cannot dismiss the complexity of musical form, the sophistication and depth of the lyrics and their appropriateness to character development, the innovative use of the melodramatic genre, and the inventive theatricality of the musical. *Sweeney Todd* is not only a consummate theatrical tour de force, it is also an intelligent, penetrating exploration of societal oppression and individual vengeance, impotence, and obsession. Sondheim deliberately chooses a theatrical structure that magnifies the horrific excesses of exploitation and carnage. But the Grand Guignol elements of murder, gore, and destruction are selected not simply for their sensationalistic impact. The work exposes—but does not espouse—misanthropy, nihilism, and chaos.

If the theatrical experience facilitates a cathartic release, penetrates the defenses of audience indifference, and provokes sympathetic compassion, then it has undeniable value. One must reject those critics who insist that for a musical to succeed it must be an unambiguous celebration of the positive joy of existence. Musical theater can be light, escapist, and blindly optimistic, but it need not be. For the theatrical experience to be exhilarating and meaningful the audience needs to be stimulated, engaged, and disturbed. The drama of *Sweeney Todd* does constitute a celebration of sorts—a celebration of shared compassion and humanity. The sense of unease the work generates can be compared to the impact of tragedy, rather than the delight of comedy or the titillation of melodrama. But this enhances rather than detracts from its value. Some argue that this intensity of emotion has no place on the Broadway musical stage, that Sondheim and Prince should eschew the world of popular theater and take their creations to the rarefied domain of serious music and opera. Certainly, if "operatic" simply means "the highest form of theater, a way of capturing all the energy, all the emotional rhythms of the drama in music," as Howard Kissel argues,[20] then *Sweeney Todd* is indeed operatic. If popular American theater cannot absorb such serious, provocative musical theater, then the development and evolution of the form are in jeopardy.

There is no simplistic moral to be extracted from the work. Sondheim and his collaborators could have chosen to ridicule the material and encouraged the audience to mock Sweeney's melodramatic excesses. They did not do so. They could have elevated their protagonist into a clear-cut champion of the underclass, killing only exploiters and oppressors. But Sweeney's visionary violence transcends the particular orientation of the social censor. The work serves as a warning against the kinds of conditions that provoke uncontrollable, impotent rage, but it is not merely social satire. As the epitome of failure, illuminated by a transcendent vision, Sweeney possesses an epic grandeur. His passionate outrage drives him outside a moral code, truly "beyond good and evil." He becomes greater than any individual, yet less than human, a god of wrath corrupted by his own righteousness. His suffering and fury are the consequence of horrendous social conditions, but transcend the particular time and place.

The accusation implicit in the final moments of the work stems from the conviction that oppressive social structures are still intact and from the awareness that contemporary audiences, glutted on their diet of entertainment heavy with sadism, are easily seduced by violence. The musical reminds us of the indiscriminate, terrifying, and motiveless violence that still lurks in our midst. The horror *Sweeney Todd* reinforces is our realization that no society is immune, no individual safe from becoming the victim or even the potential perpetrator of irrational savagery. Sondheim's score, which both elevates and dignifies the title character, lures the audience into sharing Sweeney's vindictive delight. The point is not that we are all Sweeneys, seeking any excuse to embark on a mad course of mayhem, but that we can at times find cruelty and destruction appealing. Contemporary indifference and ruthlessness have so brutalized our sensibilities that emotional and moral corruption can become epidemically infectious.

Murder is commonplace, exploitation rife. Yet the violence in *Sweeney Todd* is sufficiently stylized to distance the horror. Moreover, the amoral humor of Mrs. Lovett deflects the brutality, mitigates the pessimism, and exposes the perversity in the distorted mirror of her crazy pragmatism. Michael Feingold is correct when he points out that mass murder can hardly be regarded as legitimate social criticism and that the universal urge to violence is no excuse for damning all of humankind.[21] But *Sweeney Todd* is not primarily social criticism. In its operatic boldness, its schizophrenic synthesis of elemental comedy and tragedy, it approaches the greatness of total theater. It elicits both intellectual excitement and shattering emotional intensity. By crossing all the accepted boundaries of musical theater, Sondheim has redefined, regenerated, and dignified the genre.

A BUMPY RIDE: *Merrily We Roll Along*

The original production of *Merrily We Roll Along* opened on Broadway on 16 November 1981 and closed after only sixteen perfomances. Although Sondheim emerged relatively unscathed in terms of critical disparagement, the book by George Furth was savaged. Based on a fifty-year-old Kaufman and Hart play, the plot structure of *Merrily We Roll Along* is inverted. Time goes backwards as a disillusioned, middle-aged songwriter, Franklin Shepard, retraces his path through failed marriages, stormy friendships, professional compromises, and commercial corruption back to his idealistic youth as a talented composer. As Shepard, Charles Kringas (his lyricist), and Mary Flynn (his novelist friend), grow progressively younger, scenes move from the forty-three-year-old Shepard's 1980 commencement address at his former high school back to 1955 when he graduated.

Furth's writing does warrant some attention. The script is too arbitrarily episodic and, while some of the one-liners possess the characteristic brittle Furth wit, the dialogue of the central characters is too often emblematic and superficial, with pivotal motivation blurred when not ignored. Furth's dialogue reveals that the character's youthful idealism is frustrated, but not why. One has to rely almost entirely on the lyric and musical development to understand the inner emotional regression and evolving opportunism of Franklin Shepard and his friends' gradual disillusion with him.

In 1985 Sondheim and Furth decided that the musical was too valuable simply to be tossed onto the heap of forgotten Broadway failures. The reputation of these two artists, who were joined by director James Lapine, resulted in an invitation to remount the work at the La Jolla Playhouse in San Diego. In this production, which Furth refers to as the "grown-up" version, many of the script's problems were solved. It was decided that rather than cast the show with young, inexperienced actors, as had been done on Broadway, the work would be performed by more seasoned professionals. This choice did result in more convincing performances, but some of the charm of the earlier production was sacrificed. Moreover, one of the loveliest melodies, a youthful commencement hymn, was eliminated. Other changes included the replacement of "Rich and Happy," a song dealing with the superficiality of Hollywood fame, with "That Frank," as Sondheim felt that the former number portrayed "a kid's idea of success." In addition, Sondheim composed "Growing Up," which helped elucidate the fairly sketchily drawn character of Gussie (wife to Frank's agent and subsequently the second Mrs. Franklin Shepard).

Despite good reviews and capacity audiences this production did not return to Broadway, and yet another reinterpretation was successfully mounted in Seattle in 1988. The score is unquestionably worth cherishing. As befits its subject matter, the loss of innocence and human warmth, it is easily the most melodic and approachable of Sondheim's works. The songs, which Frank Rich of the *New York Times* describes as "crushing and beautiful . . . that soar and linger and hurt,"[1] exemplify the unique synthesis of intellectual depth and emotional passion that characterizes Sondheim's best scores.

Moreover, the retrogressive action provided Sondheim with exciting musical possibilities. As he explains:

> Since *Merrily We Roll Along* is about friendship, the score concentrates attention on the friendship of Mary, Frank and Charley by having all their songs interconnected through chunks of melody, rhythm and accompaniment. And since the story moves backwards in time, it presented an opportunity to invent verbal and musical motifs which could be modified over the course of the years, extended and developed, reprised, fragmented, and then presented to the audience in reverse: extensions first, reprises first, fragments first. For example, a release in one song would turn up later—in the show but earlier in time—as a refrain in another (e.g., "Rich and Happy"/"Our Time"), a melody would become an accompaniment ("Old Friends"/"Opening Doors"), a chorus would be reprised as an interlude ("Like It Was"/"Old Friends"), and so on, according to the relative importance of the characters' feelings at each point in their lives. Along with this would be the transformation of Frank's hit song from "The Hills of Tomorrow" through his development of it during "Opening Doors," which we actually witness, to its emergence as "Good Thing Going."
>
> In fact, if the score is listened to in reverse order—although it wasn't written that way—it develops traditionally.[2]

Just as the characters begin as mature, assertive adults and move slowly backward into their innocent, idealistic youth, so the musical structure traces the evolution of tunes and melodic variations, introduced first in their finished form and reaching back to their tentative beginnings.

The lyric development is equally complex. The permutation of time is a central motif in the musical. The thematic thrust of many of the songs is consequently focused on the nature of past, present, and future. These references are complicated and give further resonance by the inverted structure of the action, with the first words of the commencement song opening the show rich with a hope for the future:

> Behold the hills of tomorrow!
> Behold the limitless sky!
> Fling wide the gates
> To a world that waits!
> As our journey starts,
> Behold! Our hearts
> Are high![3]

While the reverse direction of time is traced in each of the musical sections—each of which functions as a connecting thread linking the segments of the protagonist's life—the score's impact is not solely dependent on its novel structure. The idiom is firmly within the tradition of the musical theater loved by both composer and audience. Although the score possesses Sondheim's characteristic ironic perspective, it is closer to the Rodgers and Hammerstein prototype than any of his previous work. The odd musical clue and subtle joke reinforces this provenance.

The work is an homage but not an imitation, something the critics tended to misunderstand. A familiar musical language is evoked in the songs of friendship and theatrical bonhomie, but this sound is used symbolically as well. It suggests an era, an attitude, and an innocence that has been lost. Numbers like "Old Friends" are enriched by an echo of the earlier musical theater they suggest. It has been argued that "Old Friends," for example, recaptures the flavor of Jule Styne's "Together Wherever We Go" from *Gypsy*,[4] for which Sondheim was the lyricist. This is not imitation, plagiarism, or parody, but a subtle use of musical connotation to extend the meaning of the immediate theatrical statement. Like "Side by Side by Side," in *Company*, or "Me and My Town," in *Anyone Can Whistle*, "Old Friends" uses the sound, form, and warmth of the musical "standard" to comment on the quality of the relationship it is conveying.

Some critics condemned the work as being derivative, not only of other composers' work but also of Sondheim's own sound.[5] It is true that the piece to some extent echoes the brittle world of *Company* and the nostalgic longing of *Follies*, but these are appropriate references. *Merrily We Roll Along*, like *Follies*, looks back on lost love, lost chances, and lost dreams; and the harsh, discordant clamoring of the smart set evoked in "Rich and Happy" and in the cocktail party introduction to "Good Thing Going" does remind us of the frenetic world of *Company*. But it is meant to. The fragmented world of "getting and spending," empty relationships, lack of privacy and security, is underscored in this very characteristic Sondheim sound. So too the aching lament of "Not a Day Goes By" expresses the sacrifice of love and hope that characterizes the blasted ideals of *Follies*. This is an aspect of the musical's strength.

The autobiographical aspects of the text cannot entirely be ignored. The schizoid demands made on Sondheim as a serious artist working in the mercantile arena of Broadway are dramatized as the idealist lyricist, Kringas, struggles against the commercial designs of his collaborating composer, Shepard. Those who have followed Sondheim's career cannot fail to smile ruefully at the self-parody contained in the satiric depiction of the young idealists' encounter with the crass Broadway producer who demands:

> There's not a tune you can hum.
> There's not a tune you go bum-bum-bum-di-dum.
> You need a tune you can bum-bum-bum-di-dum—
> Give me a melody! . . .
>
> Oh sure, I know,
> It's not that kind of show.
> But can't you have a score
> That's sort of in-between?
> Look, play a little more,
> I'll show you what I mean ...

The tune the producer hums incorrectly is Rodgers and Hammerstein's "Some Enchanted Evening."

Sondheim also incorporated a revue number into the show. Although he had written some revue material previously, he was not known for his use of this medium. Yet even in the revue format, the theme of lost innocence is not forgotten. In a Greenwich Village nightclub in the 1960s, the aspiring performers sing a gentle satire on the Kennedys. For an audience that knows only too well what is destined to happen to all that young enthusiasm and boisterous self-assurance, the skit is painfully apposite. Despite this prescience of doom, however, the number retains its humor.

Perhaps the most significant quality of the lyrics and music of *Merrily We Roll Along* is its expression of affection, love, idealism, and hope. Sondheim has long been superficially viewed as misanthropic, cynical, and acerbic. This score, however, reveals a tenderness and melodic richness only hinted at in his previous work. The ode to friendship in "Old Friends" is warm and unabashed:

> What do you say, old friend,
> Are we or are we unique?
> Time goes by,
> Everything else keeps changing.
> You and I,
> We get continued next week.

Some of the complexities of love are interestingly expressed in "Not a Day Goes By." This song is first poignantly sung by the disillusioned wife as she finally leaves her husband, who has destroyed their relationship with his driving ambition. But later in the show, earlier in their lives, it is sung by the young husband as a marriage tribute. It is a duet sung not with the bride but with his old friend Mary, whose unrequited love for him is never confessed. (In the La Jolla version the emotional ramifications of this number are further enhanced when Sondheim reveals the complex interweaving of the relationship by making the song a trio sung by bride, groom, and desolate friend.) The central thematic focus on time is developed in this love song, which ingenuously insists that love can endure through time, that it is in some way immutable and eternal.

This romantic assertion is slightly modified in the lyric ballad sung by young Frank and Charley, as they try to promote themselves at a society party. Using a song as a metaphor for love, the young composer and lyricist trace a love affair from its tentative beginnings, through its tender encounters, to its gradual disintegration. The melody and lyrics are simple but convey a wistful sincerity:

> And while it's going along,
> You take for granted some love

Will wear away.
We took for granted a lot,
But still I say:
It could have kept on growing,
Instead of just kept on.
We had a good thing going,
Going,
Gone.

What time can do to love and friendship is the subject of the number, which uses the language of music to suggest the withering away of love. Thus it functions as a microcosm of the musical. This kind of complex interweaving displays Sondheim at his best.

Perhaps the most poignant expression of the ravages of time is sung by the mature Mary, early in the show:

Charley,
Why can't it be like it was?
I liked it the way that it was,
Charley—
You and me, we were nicer then ...

Charley,
Nothing's the way that it was.
I want it the way that it was.
God knows, things were easier then.

Trouble is, Charley,
That's what everyone does:
Blames the way it is
On the way it was,
On the way it never ever was.

This requiem to lost innocence and to the wish for a better, simpler time characterizes the work's combination of melancholy and a world-weary wisdom. Although the three leads will travel back in time and briefly recover their naïvete and faith, the audience is aware that one can never go back. Life can never be "like the way it was" because "it never ever was" that way. This lyric clarifies the parallel between the gradual loss of innocence of the three friends and the disintegration and disillusion of American society. These larger reverberations are the intended effect of the creators,[6] but unlike *Follies*, in which the sociological implications are clearly conceptualized and theatricalized, *Merrily We Roll Along* does not lend itself so readily to this kind of extended reference.

Perhaps one of the reasons for the harsh critical reception of *Merrily We Roll Along* can be found in Sondheim's musical language. His score does refer to earlier sounds but these musical references deal almost exclusively with the world contained within the restrictions of musical theater. If the disintegration of one man's life and integrity is intended to reflect the gradual disillusionment and loss of ideals occurring in America between the naïve 1950s and the decadent 1980s, then the microcosm should reflect the macrocosm in sound. Certainly topical references are made in both dialogue and lyric that place each scene in a particular historic context (these verbal references are increased in the second version), but Sondheim makes little attempt to capture the popular sound idiom of each period. His musical language remains firmly grounded in the world of the theater. Yet this choice can be justified. The characters are all theater people. This is their milieu, and the idiom and sound of Broadway and Hollywood reflect their world.

Innocence and idealism, although they are revealed to be qualities that can almost never survive, are captured in Sondheim's haunting "Our Time," whose soaring melody is evocative of "Somewhere" from Bernstein's *West Side Story*, another Sondheim collaboration. At the end of the show, as the three very young leads wait on their apartment roof for the first sighting of Sputnik, they sing of hope, belief, and romantic vision:

> It's our time, breathe it in:
> Worlds to change and worlds to win.
> Our turn coming through,
> Me and you, pal,
> Me and you!

This optimism proved to be prophetic. After *Merrily We Roll Along* closed, Sondheim, unbowed by the critical assault, began work on perhaps his most adventurous and provoking work to date. The life of the artist Georges Seurat, explored through his work *A Sunday Afternoon on the Island of La Grande Jatte*, was the subject, and it was to earn Sondheim the ultimate critical accolade, the Pulitzer Prize.

9

THE MUSICAL STOPS SINGING AND FINDS ITS VOICE: *Sunday in the Park with George*

After the cavalier dismissal of *Merrily We Roll Along*, it would have been understandable if Sondheim had simply thrown up his hands and turned his back on unpredictable Broadway forever. He had written a melodic, accessible score whose emotional impact was undeniable, yet some critics dismissed the work as too "complex." Sondheim's reputation for cool intellectualism seemed to blind the New York reviewers to the musical's charm and warmth. This critical stereotyping, coupled with the successful incorporation of *Sweeney Todd* into the repertoire of the New York City Opera and several regional opera companies, might have served to force Sondheim away from the exigencies of musical theater into the rarefied atmosphere of subsidized opera. But Sondheim's reaction was predictably unpredictable.

Disenchanted with the do-or-die economics of the huge Broadway production, Sondheim decided to sever his fifteen-year partnership with Hal Prince and develop his new work through the more gradual evolutionary process of the off-Broadway workshop. Joining playwright/director James Lapine, whose previous writing had included *Twelve Dreams* (a Jungian fantasy) and *Table Settings* (an unconventional satire focused on family frictions), and who had directed William Finn's successful off-Broadway musical *March of the Falsettos*, Sondheim began the development of *Sunday in the Park with George* in this less stressful setting.

The source of their inspiration was the life and work of the painter Georges Seurat, primarily his huge masterpiece *A Sunday Afternoon on the Island of La Grande Jatte*. Little is known about Seurat. He was born in 1859 and died in 1891. A French neoimpressionist, he perfected his own unique painting technique, which became known as pointillism or divisionism. Seurat was an extremely private person. He kept no diary, and his few extant letters reveal little of the man. On the rare occasion that he painted a self-portrait, the artist is seen only from the rear. Some believe that not even his friends knew the woman with whom he lived. After dedicating his short life to the pursuit of an original mode of artistic expression, Seurat died of pneumonia at the age of thirty-one, having sold none of his major paintings.

Seurat shared the overriding concern of the impressionist painters for color and light. Artists such as Monet and Renoir, however, found his work too extreme and categorically rejected his canvases, in large part because Seurat adapted the emotional subjectivism of the impressionists to suit his more rigorously scientific inclination. Where the impressionists chose pigments that approximated the colors they found in nature, Seurat determined instead to analyze each color phenomenon into its primary components. He then applied minute dots of complementary pure color to his canvas, depending on the perceiver's eye to fuse the contiguous hues. Microscopic examination reveals that Seurat did not simply juxtapose his brush strokes but applied the primary and secondary colors in several layers. This optical process, which demanded the active participation of the viewer, resulted in a canvas that shimmered with startling vividness.

Seurat was not concerned solely with the application of color, however. Unlike the fleeting effects of most impressionist works, Seurat's compositions were rigidly, almost mathematically ordered. His paintings clearly reveal his preoccupation with form. He ascertained that certain shapes possess definite emotional and aesthetic connotations. The strong vertical accents of trees, for example, are always contrasted with horizontal shadows, which in turn balance the human figures in his landscapes.

For the creation of his monumental masterpiece—the canvas measures 81 by 120 inches—Seurat made numerous sketches outdoors. He then returned to his studio for the painstaking application of color, a relatively mechanical but extremely laborious process. Although La Grande Jatte, a sliver of land in the middle of the Seine, was primarily a meeting place for the working classes, Seurat included a few members of fashionable Paris in the finished work, thus depicting a cross section of Parisian society. In attempting to describe the painting's compositional complexity, Norbert Lynton writes:

> It is a painting full of monumentality that Impressionism lacked. The compositional left-right movements, stressing the picture's space, is counteracted by the figures which are grouped on clearly differentiated planes and most face to the left. Colors are contrasted; straight lines act against curves. There is a sufficient sense of space and bodily presence, but the picture as a whole has the simple strength of a mural.[1]

Imbued with a cool tranquility, the painting nonetheless teems with palpable life. From this remarkable yet cryptic work Sondheim and Lapine bravely began to fashion a musical.

The thematic focus of *Sunday in the Park with George* centers on the nature of artistic creativity: What does it mean to be an artist? How does one make art? And most significantly, how does being an artist affect relationships with the world and other people? Because such issues are central to understanding the lives of all artists, this work is the most clearly autobiographical of all Sondheim's works. Unlike the essentially unrewarding comparison of Sondheim with Robert in *Company*, a recognition of Sondheim's identification with George reveals both the individual and universal struggles of the artist. *Sunday in the Park with George* involves an artist's self-revelation, but in a highly sophisticated form. In examining that which concerns him most intimately—the nature of creativity and the conflicting demands of art and life—Sondheim is free to create, in this seemingly austere, nonnarrative study, his most personal musical.

Although Sondheim is reluctant to acknowledge Seurat's emotional turmoil as his own, he does recognize the similarity of their artistic techniques. To his world of theatrical composition, Sondheim brings the same assiduous concentration that Seurat brought to the pictorial realm. Seurat's demand for scientific precision is echoed in Sondheim's concern with the relationship between music and mathematics:

> Music is the organization of a certain finite number of variables. Language has an infinite number of possibilities; diatonic music does not. You're juggling a group of known forces. And what makes up the diatonic scale has a clear mathematical basis. The relationships of notes to each other, the needs of dissonances to resolve into consonance, have a mathematical principle. When you look at an octave, it's not just two C's; there's an eight there. It's almost subconscious, but if you study music, you must be aware of these things. It's a language. It's almost computerese.[2]

And like Seurat, Sondheim atomizes his work, breaking it up into its component parts and then recombining these units into a musical totality.

In answering the question, "How do you begin to write for a character?" Sondheim replies:

> I always start with motifs. Always. That's partly because of my training with Milton Babbitt, who taught me the long-line technique of musical development, whereby small musical ideas are expanded into large structural forms, and the point is to make the most out of the least and not vice-versa. I've always taken that to be the principle of art. Specifically, in terms of music, if you look at a Bach fugue you see this gigantic cathedral built out of these tiny little motifs. I've always composed that way, and I think that's why I'm attracted to the kind of musical I'm attracted to—the kind that offers opportunities to take characters and assign motifs to them which can grow with them.[3]

Notes, words, and rhythm patterns are Sondheim's primary units of expression. The choice of each is critical. Because creating a work of art involves a myriad of small-scale decisions, Sondheim rejects the notion that the artist is suddenly visited by inspiration, with the work pouring forth spontaneously from inner genius. Seurat's painstaking, almost ploddingly methodical approach to art is something to which Sondheim readily relates. As Sondheim explains:

> He put hundreds of thousands of dots on that canvas. And every one was a separate decision. Some people say there were five million individual decisions.
>
> And that is what art is. You spend four days working out the flower on the hat, then you spend 10 days working on the hat. Then you have 20 other hats to do. Then all the hats are part of a pattern. Then you start working on the face. It is just . . . hard . . . work.[4]

This is the side of creativity Sondheim wants to dramatize: the rigorous, unglamorous, often monotonous, dedication required of the artist.

Seurat's emphasis on form is echoed in the meticulous structure of a Sondheim musical: nothing is random; nothing is arbitrary; each detail is essential to the overall composition. But comparison between the techniques of the two artists can be extended even further. *Sunday in the Park with George* is, as Frank Rich points out in his *New York Times* review, a truly modernist musical.[5] It has no linear, casually connected plot. Its narrative structure is focused on evolving states of mind rather than a conventionally developed story. Events are less important than aesthetic decisions.

Indeed, the significance of narrative and the exploration of alternative structures were among the crucial issues that shaped the work's development. Initially, Sondheim had not conceived of any narrative at all, intending to structure the piece as a theatricalization of a musical theme and variation: "Every time I listen to Rachmaninoff's *Variations on a Theme of Paganini*, I'm stunned, and I thought it would be fun to try theatrically. When we'd fastened on the idea of using Seurat's painting and showing how it was made in the first act, I was all excited because I thought the second act could be a series of variations or comments on the painting."[6] This intriguing form was modified, however, when Lapine insisted that interest in form alone was insufficient to sustain audience attention, that a narrative continuity was necessary to make the piece dramatically viable.

Nonetheless, Sondheim fulfilled his aims to a significant degree by using music, lyrics, even characters, in associative patterns whose significance is fully appreciated only when refracted through the audience's perception. Each distinct note may be regarded as a sonic equivalent of an individual dot of color. This identity of technique is noted by Sondheim: "Seurat experimented with the color wheel the way one experiments with a scale. He used complementary color exactly the way one uses dominant and tonic harmony. When you start thinking about it, there are all kinds of analogies. It started from the painting and the more I found out about Seurat, the more I realized, 'My God, this is all about music.' "[7] Seen from a distance, Seurat's painting is a harmonious ideal, nature and humanity balanced in an ordered world. Yet on close examination the abstract rigor of the artist's technique becomes apparent. So with *Sunday in the Park with George*, careful analysis reveals a myriad of discrete units patterned into an incremental totality. Sound, meaning, feeling, and aesthetic beauty have autonomous significance, yet are combined into a unified work of art.

But perhaps the most important affinity between the nineteenth-century painter and the twentieth-century composer/lyricist lies in their individual commitment to artistic perfection. The emotional subtext of this musical probes the isolation implicit in this kind of fanaticism. *Sunday in the Park with George* not only mirrors Sondheim's need to shatter tired categorizations—it is a clear example of his ability to redefine the genre of musical theater—it also forces Sondheim's audiences to rediscover aesthetic truth through his art. Consequently, this musical not only dramatizes its subject matter, it is the thing itself.

Act 1 portrays the creation of Seurat's masterpiece. The audience is introduced to the various characters who inhabit the painter's world, but these introductions are fleeting and fragmented. Most of the people the artist encounters are seen by him strictly in terms of their utility, and the audience perceives them through his eyes. They are configurations of color and light that briefly inspire or interrupt George's artistic endeavors, their significance compositional rather than dramatic. Only the painter's lover and his mother truly impinge on the artist's awareness.

The curtain rises on a white stage—the blank page of a sketchbook vividly translated into a theatrical image. A bearded figure sits downstage and, as he begins to draw, the elements of his reality miraculously materialize on stage. To a series of ascending arpeggios (a musical motif that will recur again and again), the white world rolls away and George's world begins to emerge. The arpeggio is the musical objective correlative of the palette; the primary triad becomes Sondheim's harmonic analogue for Seurat's primary colors. Just as Seurat atomizes blocks of color into dots, Sondheim fragments his lyrics and musical themes. Both artists juxtapose their primary units in varying combinations to achieve both aesthetic and emotional shade and intensity. Sondheim finds his metaphor for Seurat's use of pure color in subtle impressionistic harmonies and diatonic chord clusters. For Sondheim: "The idea was to keep the music open and pure the way the painting is, and to give it a shimmer. I was also fiddling with chord clusters, because that seemed to me some kind of analogue to Seurat's close juxtaposition of different colored dots."[8]

The apparently disjointed words that open the musical are in fact George's aesthetic creed and serve as a thematic framework both for the artist's life and the musical's structure:

> White. A blank page or canvas.
> The challenge: bring order to the whole.
> Through design.
> Composition.
> Tension.
> Balance.
> Light.
> And harmony.[9]

With each word the initial motif in the accompaniment is embellished. The units of Sondheim's score and the elements of George's world are matched.

THE MUSICAL FINDS ITS VOICE

As George sketches and erases the components of his world (a tree will appear and disappear at his whim), Sondheim manipulates the score. The first arpeggio is clear and simple. As it is repeated, a certain controlled dissonance is introduced. The notes are gradually arranged into more complex patterns to coincide with George's demand for "design." The tension mounts on "composition." The final note is held on "balance" and "light," and the implicit dissonance is ultimately resolved and the music coalesces into a theme as the artist emphasizes "harmony."

In these few opening moments, the dramatic scheme of the score is set. We are propelled into the artist's universe. Anything is possible. Worlds can materialize and vanish. This reality is created both by the constantly changing picture on stage and by the impressionistic quality of Sondheim's score. Its idiom, reminiscent of Britten, certainly helps to evoke the period of the piece, but it also suggests both the magic of Seurat's universe and its flowing inconsistency. Sondheim's intention was to create an enchanted realm, a strange, unexpected, and wonderful place the audience would be reluctant to leave.[10]

Once the basic elements of his world are in place, George escorts his lover, Dot, into the park. In the opening scene the conflicting preoccupations as well as the affinities of the two characters are explored. Dot (her name is perhaps a bit too literally emblematic of George's obsession) is a bright, vivacious person. The lovers' bantering exchange makes clear that, while she may be the focus of his work, she is not the center of his life. She is interested in fashion; he is interested in the way the light reflects off the water and onto her. Arpeggios like those that punctuate the opening words of the score are used repeatedly in this scene to reflect George's feverish sketching. One sounds as he erases a tree on his pad and the tree disappears into the fly space, another as he calls for boats and the craft appear on the horizon, another as more trees track onto the stage (this arpeggio does not advance the melodic development of the score; it hangs suspended, complete in itself, a musical counterpart of the artist's drawing).

After the tranquility of the early morning is shattered by an elderly lady—later revealed to be George's mother—and her nurse, a new and distinctive musical idea is introduced as the focus returns to Dot. George is absorbed in his work as Dot attempts valiantly to get his attention. Although she enjoys being the apparent focus of his work, she finds the static boredom of modeling intolerable. To express her frustration Sondheim uses a staccato pointillist style that duplicates both George's painting technique and Dot's barely controlled irritability. Just as George atomizes her into dots of color, so she enunciates each element of her discomfort:

> A trickle of sweat.
> The back of the head.
> He always does this.
> Now the foot is dead.
> Sunday in the park with George.
> (pp. 9–10)

Dot's impatience is illustrated in these broken phrases and apparently disconnected notes but, as she warms to her subject, her jealousy finds more sustained expression. As units of sound and color are repeated, key phrases in the lyric are reiterated:

> Artists are bizarre. Fixed. Cold.
> That's you, George, you're bizarre. Fixed. Cold.
> I like that in a man. Fixed. Cold.
> (p. 11)

The emotive connotations are further emphasized by Sondheim's setting the words *bizarre* and *cold* on notes so low that they stand out prominently. The apparent aloofness of the artist is an important theme that will be further developed.

The contradictions of Dot's character are clearly visible when she complains about George's introversion and almost simultaneously recognizes that it is that quality that attracts her. George's icy detachment is also in clear juxtaposition with Dot's physical heat. He sits in the shade, she stands in the sun. He is cool and preoccupied; as the sweat trickles down her neck, she is aglow. Dot has all the warm tones of the musical and emotional palette, and the oppressiveness of posing is expressed in her long open vibrato: "God, it's hot out here" (p. 11).

Then, as George's hand flies over the paper, Sondheim launches Dot into an incredibly long and breathless vocal line that creates a remarkable fusion of the painter's style, the frustration of the character, and the visual impact of the scene:

> There are worse things
> Than staring at the water
> As you're posing for a picture

Being painted by your lover
In the middle of the summer
On an island in the river on a Sunday.
(p. 11)

The technique recalls the bride's explosive "I'm Not Getting Married Today" from *Company*. In both lyrics Sondheim conveys a frustration so great that the character transcends the mundane limits of controlled conversation and bursts out with a stream of vehement indignation.

As George rushes over to her, it appears that Dot has penetrated his creative barriers. But he comes only to adjust the fold on her dress and scarcely sees her. Her barely suppressed impatience is reflected in the solo cello line that now accompanies her.

Dot

The petticoat's wet,
Which adds to the weight.
The sun is blinding.
(Closing her eyes)
All right, concentrate ...

George

Eyes open, please.

Dot

Sunday in the park with George ...

George

Look out at the water. Not at me.
(pp. 11–12)

Sondheim's meticulous attention to detail is evident here. The characters' physical movements and reactions are written into the lyrics, while the music carries the emotional subtext, expressing the characters' repressed thoughts.

George demands concentration from his flighty model, and finally she understands. But as her thoughts and feelings float free, her state of physical quietude is depicted in a delightful theatrical gimmick. The front of her heavy, bustled gown springs open, allowing Dot to escape. The dress closes behind her and, as she flits about in her frilly underwear, George scribbles on, oblivious to his model's fantastical escape. Dot cavorts to a sprightly pizzicato that contrasts with the former more restrained rhythmic pattern. Her longing for immortality is captured with characteristic Sondheim wit:

> Well, if you want bread
> And respect
> And attention
> Not to say connection,
> Modelling's no profession.
> (p. 12)

But Dot does recognize and admire George's genius. It is the wellspring from which her passion flows. This is acknowledged in the change of rhythm as she sings out her yearning in elongated romantic phrases:

> All it has to be is good.
> And George, you're good,
> You're really good.
> (p. 13)

Dot edges closer to self-understanding, to comprehending her adoration of George's art; the harmonic accompaniment changes, introducing the undulating fluid chords that suggest the wondrous world of George's painting as she sings: "But most of all, / I love your painting . . ." (p. 13). The rippling undertone is beautiful, but it is also unsettling. It is the artist in George that Dot simultaneously loves and loathes.

In this opening number the audience has been drawn into an Elysian world, has learned of the artist's obsession and the model's frustration and fascination, with precision and economy. The empathic contract between stage and audience is established, and the audience is now ready to wander through the world of Seurat's, Sondheim's, and Lapine's creating.

As the park fragments into various pools of action, the music becomes more frenzied, suggesting the addition of more colors, textures, and shapes. The musical and visual turmoil mounts as a wagon bearing a *tableau vivant* of Seurat's first major work, *Bathing at Asnières*, is rolled onto the stage. The figures in this painting are noisy and vulgar until they are frozen into harmonic stasis with a gesture of the artist's arm. The park is thus miraculously transformed into an art gallery. Jules, a successful though mediocre artist, and his wife, Yvonne, stroll in and pause before the work.

To a steady ostinato accompaniment the pair comment about the painting in terms that are all too recognizable. The complacent laughter, the mocking aphorisms have all been leveled at Sondheim's own work:

> *Jules*
>
> It has no presence.
>
> *Yvonne*
>
> No passion.
>
> *Jules*
>
> No life. . . .
>
> *Yvonne*
>
> So drab, so cold.
>
> *Jules*
>
> And so controlled.
>
> *Both*
>
> No life.
>
> *Jules*
>
> His touch is too deliberate, somehow. . . .
> All mind, no heart.
> No life in his art.
>
> *Yvonne*
>
> No life in his *life*—
>
> *Both*
>
> No—
> Life.
>
> (pp. 19–22)

With this compendium of all the pat dismissals of his intellectualism and complexity, Sondheim adroitly satirizes his detractors and establishes his own aesthetic standards. The identity of creator and character is unmistakable. The carping concludes on a sour note that exemplifies the mean-mindedness of the characters, but the critics are not given the final word: as the tableau is rolled off, the boy in the picture gives them a loud Bronx cheer.

When he returns to his studio, George works feverishly behind a large scrim upon which portions of *A Sunday Afternoon on the Island of La Grande Jatte* are visible. Dot too is busy. George applies paint to canvas, and with the same rhythmic intensity Dot—posed to resemble Seurat's painting *La Poudreuse*—applies powder to herself. The pointillist technique of both is echoed in the pizzicato rhythms of Sondheim's accompaniment. The artist's fervor grows, and Sondheim's lyrics fragment, reflecting the artist's preoccupation with dabs of color. The brief mention of each color as it is applied to the canvas, interspersed with humming and the occasional sip of beer, leads George into a state of intense creative bliss. His passionate animation is balanced with an inner tranquility. He has entered his enchanted world of "color and light" (p. 30) where nothing else exists.

George anoints his canvas; Dot applies color to herself. The traditional dichotomy of mind and body is given vivid theatrical form in the two figures balanced on either side of the stage. George lives in a rarefied atmosphere of pure creativity; Dot embodies the rich sensuality of the flesh. Her own fecundity is briefly alluded to when she complains that her clothes no longer seem to fit her. Although George may be reluctant to acknowledge it, Dot's sensuality is the source of his inspiration. He paints her again and again, and his genius is kept alive not only on his canvas but in her womb. Sondheim may identify with George but he does not shortchange Dot.

The same accompaniment that earlier reflects George's daubing accompanies Dot as she examines herself attentively in her mirror. Each plucked eyebrow is set to a bell chime. George's demand for concentration should induce calm, but instead Dot bursts into an unrestrained fantasy. Her longing for energy and life is translated into a bouncy can-can, but this bubbly delight is ephemeral. Sondheim gently directs Dot toward a realization of her need for George as the upbeat tempo of the can-can gives way to a slower, more pensive rhythm, and Dot echoes George's words "color and light" (p. 30). On these words the focus returns to George, who addresses the figures on his canvas lovingly, while Dot's resentment returns.

As the staccato notes that mirror George's brush strokes resume, the painter is given an extraordinary soliloquy of sound. Like something out of James Joyce's *Ulysses*, the soliloquy possesses a free-form structure that barely contains a flood of words linked not grammatically or logically but emotionally. This song is structured around the pigments George applies to his canvas. Interspersed with these word colors, which are shaped and distorted at will, George's stream-of-consciousness is voiced:

> Blue blue blue blue
> Blue still sitting

Red that perfume
Blue all night
Blue-green the window shut
Dut dut dut
Dot Dot sitting
Dot Dot waiting
Dot Dot getting fat fat fat ...
(p. 31)

George knows Dot is there. He notices that she is gaining weight. He understands her needs but he cannot break away from the urge to paint. He has to "finish the hat." Acknowledging both the fevered activity of creation and the stifling temperature of the studio, George joyously utters the same formula of words and sounds that recurs throughout the piece: "It's hot in here ... / Sunday / Color and light!" (p. 32).

His concentration now absolute, George forgets Dot completely. He immerses himself in the world of the canvas, and again she tries to penetrate his insularity. His painting is expressed in song, her immediate concerns in prose. He sees a world of his own creation, a world of wondrous colors, of startling light and shade. His very perceptions are transmuted into color, "It's getting hot ... / It's getting orange ..." (p. 33). Dot comprehends the impenetrability of his gaze and begins to see herself only as a subject for his art—"studied like the light" (p. 33)—rather than a person in her own right. But she cannot resist George's hypnotic power for long. Gradually she recognizes her need and acknowledges her adoration of his genius. (Sondheim expresses the character's acceptance of love by altering the lyric structure; Dot begins her reverie in prose but describes her love in poetry.) George is equally obsessed by his model. He is baffled by her apparent narcissism but her beauty stops him both as an artist and a man. That she is a source of inspiration is revealed by the conjunction of her with the light: "But the way she catches light ..." (p. 34).

The two lovers finally reach a shared communion as the accompaniment returns to the shimmering sound of creation and the two harmonize:

George	*Dot*
And the color of her hair	
I could look at her	I could look at him
Forever ...	Forever ...
	(p. 34)

This blending of voices gives both the audience and the characters a momentary emotional release, but it cannot last. George almost immediately loses himself again in his world of dots, forgetting his promise to take Dot to the Follies. Their conflicting perspectives are highlighted by the lyrics. He wavers for a moment, then quickly finds solace in his work. Wondering "What should I do?" (p. 36), George's initial focus is on Dot and his guilt at disappointing her, but as he ponders and the music pauses, his attention is claimed by the truly paramount decision, his choice of color. The moment of indecision passes as he sighs, "Red."

After the stage is once more transformed into the island, the audience is introduced to some of the other characters who inhabit George's world. The aggressive one-eyed Boatman and his dog, the two giggling shopgirls (facetiously named Celeste I and II), and George's mother and her nurse are all titillated when Dot enters with her new lover, Louis the baker. Like the staccato patterns of the rhythmic figure that accompanies George's painting, certain patterns of sound identify these prominent components of his work. All the gossip and commentary is arranged into discrete units that coalesce to form the musical canvas. Thus, George is bombarded with sound, shape, color, and light. The recognizable musical identity of each group corresponds to the various hues of the painter's palette. These thematic patterns resemble the leitmotifs Sondheim used in *Sweeney Todd* but are more fragmented and impressionistic.

Dot sits down and attempts to study her grammar book. A symbol of Dot's striving to achieve George's intellectual level, this book will ultimately provide a key to the understanding of his complex genius. As George sketches, his voice fades in and out, sharing the expression of a particular character's thoughts or sitting back in amusement and capturing the various intrigues on paper. Eventually his focus settles on the Boatman's dog. In the same way that Dot examines herself in the mirror earlier, George examines the dog:

Dot	*George*
If my legs were longer.	If the head was smaller ...
If my bust was smaller.	If the tail were longer ...
If my hands were graceful.	If he faced the water ...
If my waist was thinner.	If the paws were hidden ...
If my hips were flatter.	If the neck was darker ...
If my voice was warm ...	If the back was curved ...
(p. 29)	(p. 48)

THE MUSICAL FINDS ITS VOICE

As George enters the world of his creation, becoming one with the dog and voicing the dog's thoughts, Sondheim transforms the artist's empathy into a show-stopping theatrical number. He has fun, using puns to suggest both the barking of the dog and the quality of his life:

> Ruff! Ruff!
> Thanks, the week has been
> *(Barks)*
> Rough!
>
> (p. 48)

The dog's world is also seen in terms of its component parts, adroitly chosen to reflect the dog's point of view:

> Bits of pastry ...
> *(Sniffs)*
> Piece of chicken ...
> *(Sniffs)*
> *Here's a handkerchief*
> *That somebody was sick in.*
> *There's a thistle.*
> *That's a shallot.*
> *That's a dripping*
> *From the loony with the palette.*
>
> *(pp. 49–50)*

When the Boatman's mutt is joined by a pampered pug, social-class distinction is satirized as the two dogs exchange pleasantries and complain about their contrasting life-styles. The two dogs introduce the primary melodic line as they pay tribute to Sunday. They are joined by other characters who explore the freedom of their day off in individual segments. This typifies Sondheim's characterization techniques for this musical. Each of the characters is incomplete, merely a fragment of George's perception. Their own concerns and preoccupations are mentioned and then abandoned. Eventually George's vision coalesces as the figures sing together of the pleasures of Sunday in the park: a Sunday in which they will endure forever in the perfection of Seurat's painting and Sondheim's musical.

The one-eyed Boatman, a social outcast himself, understands the artist, but rejects the validity of his painted reality. He cynically asserts that the artist can never see truth, for he sees only what he wants to see:

Who the hell you think you drawing?
Me?
You don't know me!
Go on drawing,
Since you drawing only what you want to see,
Anyway! . . .
Draw your conclusion,
All you artists do.
I see what is true.
(pp. 59–60)

This fragmented notion of perception coheres with George's painting technique, but also reflects a recurrent Sondheim theme. In many of his works, but most definitively in *Pacific Overture*'s "Someone in a Tree," Sondheim explores the idea of reality as the sum total of many different perspectives. This point of view, which underlies much of Sondheim's writing, here serves as yet another link between creator and protagonist.

Having completed his sketching, George exits and the focus returns to Dot. Sondheim contrasts her feelings for the two men in her life by using different rhythmic patterns. Her longing for George is expressed in protracted, slow lines, whereas her relationship with Louis is depicted in an upbeat tempo. Like so many of Sondheim's characters, Dot is trying to convince herself of the truth of what she sings. She wants to want the warm, uncomplicated baker:

Everybody loves Louis,
Louis' simple and kind.
Everybody loves Louis,
Louis' lovable.
(p. 61)

A bouncy rhythm suggests the uncomplicated quality of Dot's relationship with Louis, and Sondheim's repeated use of the liquid "l" sound gives Louis an almost palpable sensuality. Sly puns, furthermore, suggest the appetitive delight Dot derives from the lusty baker:

The bread, George.
I mean the bread, George.
And then in bed, George ...
I mean he kneads me—
I mean like dough, George.

(p. 62)

But Dot's doubts keep recurring. Through the song she voices these misgivings and confronts her reluctance until she can ultimately articulate the distinction between the two men:

> And there are Louis's
> And there are Georges—
> Well, Louis's
> And George.
> (p. 62)

Dot's choice betweeen the two men reflects a larger issue, the difference between popular and unpopular artists and art. George's esoteric and uncompromising fanaticism is contrasted with the sticky sentimentality of Louis's popular art. Dot knows George is unique and her pain is reflected in the accompaniment, but for her own self-preservation she finally takes an enormous bite of Louis's cream puff and leaves.

George is finally left alone in the park leafing through his sketches. As he glances at each page he assumes the individual personalities of each drawing. He tries to concentrate on his work but is eventually forced to confront his aching sense of loss:

> Yes, she looks for me—good.
> Let her look for me to tell me why she left me—
> As I always knew she would.
> (p. 70)

This troubled introspection introduces one of Sondheim's loveliest ballads and one of the most heartfelt explorations of the artist's temperament. All the musical suggestions implicit in the opening arpeggios of the show are synthesized in this song. The pain of Dot's departure is expressed in sustained notes, gentle and tremulous. As George confirms his belief that he could never retain her love, the liquid underscoring that has been used consistently to suggest the artist's imaginary world, is reprised. Even as he sings of his loss, he is drawn back into his inner world of obsessive creativity. He accepts that most people cannot understand the artist, but his longing for Dot's understanding is conveyed in the high clear notes to which he sings, "But if anybody could ..." (p. 70).

This longing and the chords that underlie it lead George to explore in song the wonder of creativity, the painful joy of the artist. He acknowledges the isolated loneliness of the painter who must "watch the rest of the world / From a window," but the godlike grandeur is also suggested in his passionately sung pleasure at "planning a sky." This is counterpointed by the detailed attention to minutiae emphasized in George's compulsive need to "finish the hat." George balances the conflicting demands of life:

> Mapping out a sky,
> What you feel like, planning a sky,
> What you feel when voices that come
> Through the window
> Go
> Until they distance and die,
> Until there's nothing but sky.
> (p. 70)

The minor intrusions of the outside world are conveyed in the tiptoe quality of the note on "window," which sinks to "go" and fades away on "distance and die" as the artist returns to the absolute tranquility of his created universe.

Here Sondheim finds an ideal fusion of musical suggestion and meaning. This is a moment of truth for the character. Torn apart by two worlds, he accepts that his attraction to the world of human emotion will always be subordinate to the absolute imperatives of his art. He ruefully admits that the only kind of woman who could pull him down from the dazzling "height" (p. 70) (the rhyme in "height" and "light" is not accidental) into the sensual world of darkness is not the kind of woman who will tolerate the emotional insularity of the artist.

George's pointillist technique is also examined. Through the small details, the daubs of color, the single words or notes, the artist reaches his totality:

> Studying the hat,
> Entering the world of the hat,
> Reaching through the world of the hat
> Like a window,
> Back to this one from that.
> (pp. 70–71)

The single unit of perception serves as a window to the inner world of creativity, but Sondheim carefully balances two worlds. The world that calls through the window of the studio is the world of human warmth and companionship. The world that calls through the other window (the perception of the hat as the opening through which the artist can reach into the enchanted world of imagination) is the world of subjective truth. This latter world is evoked for the audience in the accompaniment, with its suggestion of Debussy and Ravel, which may be seen as the objective correlative of George's art. The fluid repetition of the accompaniment's constantly modulating patterns expresses the evolution of the art work, which alters and modifies and cannot be bound by any structure.

The verbs Sondheim uses to suggest the artist's aspiration—"studying" (p. 71), "entering" (p. 70), and "reaching" (p. 71)—all invoke the never-ending search for perfection. Looking, even at his lover, leads him not into human commitment but into his world of art:

> Studying a face,
> Stepping back to look at a face
> Leaves a little space in the way like a window,
> But to see—
> It's the only way to see.
> (p. 71)

George tries to reconcile himself to his loss, recognizing that he can never give himself entirely to human relationships because his most urgent drive is toward a nonhuman world, and that urge can never be assuaged:

> And when the woman that you wanted goes,
> You can say to yourself, "Well, I give what I give."
> But the woman who won't wait for you knows
> That, however you live,
> There's a part of you always standing by,
> Mapping out the sky,
> Finishing a hat ...
> Starting on a hat ...
> Finishing a hat ...
> (p. 71)

As George reaches a state of contentment and release, he concludes, with almost childlike delight: "Look, I made a hat ... / Where there never was a hat ..." (p. 71). George is alone in the park, so he makes this assertion to his only companion, the subject of his art, the dog.

As a trumpet voluntary summons the other characters back to the park, one senses that time has passed, the painting is progressing, and the various relationships are growing more entangled. There is a sense of tension and animosity. Singing fragments of their themes, the characters are polarized between Dot and George, who circle each other warily. Finally, Dot defiantly confronts George, reversing her bustle to suggest that she is pregnant.

The scene then shifts back to the studio for the decisive altercation between the two lovers. Knowing that he has no right to demand her love but furious at her infidelity, George retaliates by refusing to give her a portrait he has promised her. He claims that the child in her belly should be sufficient memento.

Their argument is interrupted by the arrival of Jules and Yvonne. While the men discuss George's painting, Yvonne confesses her envy of Dot. She recognizes that Dot is the inspiration for George's work, but Dot tries to explain her need for someone to care for her, rather than immortalize her. George makes a passionate attempt to clarify the significance of his technique to an obdurate Jules, and the parallel between his approach and Sondheim's must again be emphasized. Jules complains at the lack of individuality in George's painting, "You can't even see their faces" (p. 79). Sondheim has himself adopted this style. The characters who inhabit both the canvas and the musical stage are not defined in the same way as they would be in a realist work of art. Although their essential qualities are suggested, their passions are ephemeral. This was not always the case with Sondheim's piece. In the workshop production of the show at Playwrights Horizons, the subjects of George's paintings all had fuller stories of their own. Lapine hoped to contrast the tranquility of their final pose with the reality of their own discordant existence. But the audience was not interested in these digressions, and focus was consequently returned to the central figures of George and Dot. These two characters do possess a psychological complexity, but the others must be viewed as components whose significance is realized only when they are blended into the unified canvas.

Although Sondheim repeatedly emphasizes the distinction between character and creator, and takes pains to point out that the scene between George and Jules was written by Lapine, nevertheless he acknowledges that many of his own frustrations and beliefs are expressed as George tries to justify his compulsion to create something unique. Sondheim's dominating compulsion has always been to discover his own voice and find for each musical its own individual form. This fundamental drive is shared by the protagonists in acts 1 and 2 and functions as a thematic link.

The couple finally leaves, but George has become so involved with his work that he quite forgets Dot. She angrily confronts him with her decision to go with Louis to America. His only response is to pick up his brushes and return to his painting, the friction between the two characters expressed in the agitated rhythms of the underscoring as Dot attacks George for his apparent heartlessness. George tries to explain that he is not hiding but living in his canvas, and the arpeggios associated with his art are reintroduced. Resentment mounts as accusations fly. George characteristically begins to withdraw until, with a long cry of pain, Dot's long suppressed desires are finally articulated in a rapid assault on George's emotional defenses:

> . . . Tell me not to go.
> Tell me that you're hurt,
> Tell me you're relieved,
> Tell me that you're bored—
> Anything, but don't assume I know.
> Tell me what you feel!
> (pp. 83–84)

In this confrontation between the voluble Dot and the taciturn George, Sondheim explores the pain caused by conflicting human needs. George cannot be what she wants, and Dot cannot survive on what he can give.

Sondheim then captures the identity of the artist in the line "I am what I do." The poetic exactness of this line is further enhanced as George's own anger and frustration are expressed in the subsequent lines:

> I am what I do—
> Which you knew,
> Which you always knew,
> Which I thought you were a part of!
> (p. 84)

This reply provokes Dot into a final retaliation and subsequent self-awareness. She realizes things about herself, George, and their relationship as she sings:

> You are complete, George,
> You all alone.
> I am unfinished,
> I am diminished
> With or without you.
> (p. 85)

As "We Do Not Belong Together" develops, the paradox of relationship, of individual need and separate identity, is poignantly dramatized. Dot recognizes the precious quality of their love but finally must accept its destructiveness. This painful realization is conveyed in an exquisite melody that suggests both the hurt and the romantic desire. She hungers for his love, but knows that what he can offer is not sufficiently nourishing. His obsessive creativity is what makes him special. It is the source of her passion, but it eventually drives her away. Dot progresses from an initial pleading for George's attention to a growing sense of self-worth. She acknowledges his right to insularity, but also asserts her own rights. Yet Sondheim avoids making George into a heartless monster. While the words he expresses are harsh, the music to which they are set undermines their cruelty and expresses his suffering. When, for example, he protests that he cannot speak the words she longs to hear, the word *need* lies on a tender high note that conveys the magnitude of his feelings. Dot finally draws upon an inner strength and leaves him with a quiet acceptance, singing "I have to move on" (p. 85). Her resolution is reminiscent of George's own need to move on to something that is uniquely his own. The artist is left alone with his canvas and paint.

This scene is searing, conveying as it does that passion is not exclusively the province of romance. The artist's commitment to his or her work can be equally intense. The achingly beautiful torment of "We Do Not Belong Together" exemplifies the distinction Sondheim draws between the shallowness of sentimentality and the complexity of true passion: "People mistake sentimentality for feeling. I believe in sentiment but not sentimentality. . . . I also think people don't understand the difference between passion and sentimentality. . . ."[11] But Sondheim does not condescend to his audiences. He challenges them to embrace the intricacies of his melodies and lyrics and share his commitment to adult emotion and intellect.

Like his character, Sondheim is an extremely passionate artist, but the intensity of his emotion seems to be invested chiefly in his art. This may explain the coldness some critics find in his work. But, as Frank Rich argues: "If the maintenance of that solitary emotional distance means that Seurat's art, (and, by implication, Mr. Sondheim's) is 'cold,' even arrogant, so be it. 'Sunday' argues that the esthetic passion in the cerebrally ordered classicism of modern artists is easily as potent as the sentimental passion of romantic paintings or conventional musicals."[12] The artist embraces the canvas (or music) rather than the sentimentally conventional partner, but Sondheim dramatizes the agony that making such a choice involves. The absolute demands of art take a huge emotional toll.

The departure of Dot, who has declared her intention to move on to a new land and a new life, is balanced by the next scene, in which George and his mother contrast their memories of the past. She longs for a past he denies ever existed, and the passion of the lovers is replaced by a gentle melancholy. The Old Lady's song is tinged with nostalgia and regret, as the undulating chords under the voice emphasize the passage of time and change. She resents change, but George tries to convince her that all perception is beautiful. He contrasts the beauty of nature, the trees, with the beauty of humankind's technology, exemplified by the Eiffel Tower, which is being constructed in the distance. To George the two verticals are complementary, not antagonistic. Sondheim converts the aphorism "Beauty is in the eye of the beholder" into an aesthetic dictum:

> Pretty isn't beautiful, Mother,
> Pretty is what changes.
> What the eye arranges
> Is what is beautiful.
> (p. 88)

Following George's gentle persuasion, his mother almost accepts her son's vision. She shares his wonder that the artist can capture an ephemeral reality and keep it forever. The polarities of progress and stagnation, life and art, transience and permanence are balanced in the apparent simplicity of the lyric. The world can be what the artist creates: "You watch / While I revise the world" (p. 88). Yet in a poignant coda the Old Lady returns to the conservatism of age, muttering "Oh, Georgie, how I long for the old view" (p. 89).

The park again becomes a setting for dalliance and confrontation. Dot tries once more to force George to acknowledge his child. None of the other characters are with their legal mates, but all are trying to hide their clandestine assignations. The apparent tranquility of the sylvan setting erupts into acrimonious conflict. Sexual jealousy is the key to the antagonisms, and Sondheim and Lapine tease the audience with brief hints about the lascivious activities of the strollers. But tantalizing glimpses are all the audience gets: these characters are George's models and their utility is limited. Once they have been frozen into their perfect static form, their narratives will simply cease. They have no further dramatic relevance.

As confusion mounts, George is tempted to flee the noise and anger. He prepares to leave but his artist's soul cannot tolerate the unstructured chaos. He turns on the squabbling mass and as an arpeggio sounds and his mother makes her final plea, "Remember, George" (p. 101), he takes a long look at the raw material of his art. Muttering his aesthetic creed, he begins to revise his world.

To the same series of chords that opened the show, George arranges the characters into their final tableau. He takes the chaos of sound, motion, and emotion and recomposes it into a balanced composition. Once again, the chords mount to an almost agonizing tension before being resolved at the word *harmony*. The music possesses an almost sacramental character, for this is the first time the ensemble combines into full-voiced harmony. Each voice reflects a different hue of the visual, emotional, and musical canvas. As the artist omnipotently moves his characters and objects about the park, there is a sense of peace and inevitability. His control over the animate and inanimate world is complete, and through his delight we share the miracle of creation. The clarion call of the horn, which has sounded intermittently throughout the act, now calls the characters and objects to their final positions. The petty concerns of the individual characters are transformed and subsumed into the artistic totality. This is the moment of release both George and the audience have been working toward. Finally, too, George is able to acknowledge his love for Dot. The work becomes dedicated to her as he reverently leads her to the foreground of his masterpiece.

Sondheim fuses all the colors and shapes of George's art into the complex design of his lyric, while the haunting melody synthesizes the disparate units of the score into a satisfying harmony. Words like *triangular, elliptical, verticals*, and *mass* (p. 102) suggest the artist's formal concerns, but the song, like Seurat's art, is vibrant and alive with emotion. Slowly, inexorably, the living characters are transmuted into figures on a canvas. Art and reality merge. The audience recognizes the reality of the actors, but at the same time can perceive the perfection of Seurat's masterpiece. As the cast becomes the artwork, the moment is magical. This is not simply a clever example of *tableau vivant*. When at last a frame descends around the figures and George steps back to survey his work, the audience shares with him a sense of liberation and achievement. The audience is moved "not because a plot has been resolved but because a harmonic work of art has been born."[13]

Sondheim and Lapine realized that after so perfect a conclusion to act 1 there could be no satisfactory return to the enchanted world of La Grande

Jatte. They chose instead to follow Dot to the New World. Act 2 opens in an art gallery, with the trials and tribulations of being an objet d'art amusingly expressed by the disgruntled figures in the painting. Echoing her complaint from the opening of act 1, Dot grouses about the heat. This kind of repetition and patterning of word, idea, and musical phrase echoes Seurat's pointillism and helps to unite the two acts. The technique serves not only to link the content and emotion of acts 1 and 2 but reinforces the textual consistency of the work. As Sondheim explains:

> In its use of motifs, it's actually halfway between *Sweeney* and *Merrily*, in that it's partly developed and partly modular blocks. I made parallels between the two acts: like the whole "Day Off" sequence, which is in the middle of the first act, parallels the sequence in the art museum in the second act, which becomes the theme in "Putting It Together." The theme in "Putting It Together" is the same tune as "Finishing the Hat." So the attempt is to re-use sections of songs to tie both the two centuries and their relationship together."[14]

Dot's irritable remarks are amplified as the other characters, in turn, grumble about their discomfort:

> *Dot*
>
> It's hot up here.
>
> *Yvonne*
>
> It's hot and it's monotonous.
>
> *Louise*
>
> I want my glasses.
>
> *Franz*
>
> This is not my good profile.
>
> *Nurse*
>
> Nobody can even *see* my profile. (p. 107)

Such a juxtaposition of petty bickering with the formal serenity of the canvas itself provides a comic comment on the discrepancy between subject and effect in art. The staccato quality of the lyric, with its short sounds, single syllables, simple rhymes, and long pauses between each comment again serves to suggest the painter's divisionist technique. Also, because the harmonic structure is so tight and contained, it conveys the essence of being transfixed in time. There can be no change, no development in this hot, static world. The characters, however, no longer think as people, but as paintings; as Sondheim craftily points out, "They'll argue till they *fade*" (p. 111).

Contrasting with the curt complaints of the other characters, Dot's resentment is sustained and plaintive. She does not enjoy the eternal company of these argumentative strangers, although she relishes her focal position. Even in the longer line of Dot's lament, however, the pointillist quality is maintained through her constant repetition of George's name. The elegance, control, and the clearly articulated syllables reveal the repressed tension beneath the veneer of complete control.

After the final complaint about the heat, as the stage dissolves into whiteness, one by one the characters break their poses, come downstage and relate their feelings about George and the news of his untimely death. Their remarks have a dispassionate quality, the predominant attitude perhaps best conveyed in the cynical comments of the Boatman: "They all wanted him and hated him at the same time. They wanted to be painted—splashed on some fancy salon wall. But they hated him, too. Hated him because he only spoke when he absolutely had to. Most of all they hated him because they knew he would always be around" (p. 118). The figures depart and the stage is left bare, once again a pristine white.

Then, to the blare of electronic music, the contemporary world bursts on the scene. The same ostinato figuration that accompanied Seurat's artistic endeavors is now played very rapidly on a synthesizer, a variation immediately evoking the mechanistic excitement of contemporary art. George, great-grandson to Dot and Seurat, wheels in his grandmother, Marie; they are played by the same actors who in act 1 played George and Dot. The scene is an art museum where young George is about to unveil and activate his latest work, an electronic creation of light and sound entitled Chromolume #7. Although the young artist is unconvinced of his ancestry, the connection to the nineteenth-century George is immediately established, for they share more than a name. Seurat called his work chromo-luminarism, so George's work is linked to the artistic style and direction of his great-grandfather's. The two artists have been drawn to explore the same phenomena, color and light.

To bridge the hundred-year gap between acts 1 and 2, Lapine introduces a slide show in which George and his grandmother explain to the museum audience the connections between the two artists. George then introduces his latest creation, but before it can be fully activated there is an explosion. The circuits were overloaded. The problem of the contemporary artist's dependence on technology is humorously theatricalized in the frantic efforts of George and his collaborator to make their contraption function. Allusions to the set-heavy shows of Broadway are certainly deliberate. The technical wizardry of the laser show that follows the initial fiasco is thus placed in ironic relief.

While George attempts to concentrate on his art piece, Marie tries to convince him and the audience of the validity of the relationship between the two artists, citing as proof Dot's little red grammar book, which she clutches. George's light show, which on Broadway was an extravaganza of projectors and lasers, serves to introduce the smart set of the contemporary art cognoscenti. Their remarks, paralleling the envious disapproval voiced by the Parisians in act 1, annihilate the twentieth-century George with the same lofty superciliousness. The contemporary comments may be different, but their malicious intent is not. The two periods are united as both groups express their disapproval with a trite "I'm not surprised" (pp. 39, 128). Whereas the nineteenth-century gossips concentrated on George's unconventional life-style, however, the twentieth-century critics express their disapproval in trite aphorisms:

> *Harriet*
>
> You can't divide art today
> Into categories neatly—
>
> *Billy*
>
> Oh.
>
> *Harriet*
>
> What matters is the means, not the ends.
>
> *Billy*
>
> I'm not surprised.
>
> *Both*
>
> That is the state of the art, my dear,
> That is the state of the art.
> (p. 129)

Sondheim's ear for the buzz words of popular speech is effectively employed in this satiric number. The emptiness of the chatter, the cruelty of the superficial judgment, and the thoughtless inanity of these critical vultures is suggested in this accumulation of contemporary clichés. Words like *trends* (p. 128), *categories* (p. 129), *nouveau* (p. 129), *passé* (p. 130), along with the double-edged phrase "state of the art" sharpen the thrust of Sondheim's lyrics. There is no love or understanding of art in these people for whom art is a commodity, a status symbol. Their vicious prattle reflects no clearer an appreciation of art than the snide remarks of the silly shopgirls in La Grande Jatte. Art today involves big business, and the business of art—grantsmanship, fund drives, dinners, and the sale of air rights above the museum—is effectively pilloried here. (The disillusioned bitterness of the subtext relates this song to "Franklin Shepard, Inc." from *Merrily We Roll Along.*)

The same horn voluntary that calls the subjects of Seurat's painting in act 1 summons George, who is greeted by polite applause by the museum guests. To a modified version of the melody sung by Dot when she informs George about Louis, contemporary George fortifies himself, hones his communicative skills, and begins to mingle. He works the room, trying to say what each little knot of people wants to hear. His disgust and boredom with these necessary social niceties is conveyed by a clever theatrical device. As the patrons jabber on, George raises cutouts of himself and leaves these cardboard replicas to listen politely while he expresses his cynical acceptance of the charade.

> Art isn't easy—
> Even when you're hot. . . .
> Advancing art is easy— . . .
> Financing it is not. . . .
> A vision's just a vision
> If it's only in your head. . . .
> If no one gets to see it,
> It's as good as dead. . . .
> It has to come to light!
> (pp. 136–37)

In the final line, Sondheim modifies the expected phrase: the work of a Seurat must come to "light" rather than "life."

George then goes on to explain the fate of the artist today. On one level he could be describing the painstaking technique of the artist, more specifically the pointillist technique of his ancestor:

Bit by bit,
Putting it together. . . .
Piece by piece—
Only way to make a work of art.
Every moment makes a contribution,
Every little detail plays a part.
Having just the vision's no solution,
Everything depends on execution:
Putting it together—
That's what counts.
(pp. 137–38)

The rapid accompaniment suggests the style and fervor of nineteenth-century George, but as the song proceeds the audience realizes that George is describing not the creative process, but the necessary financial machinations the artist must now endure in order to be recognized.

With each double entendre Sondheim reveals his character's cynical detachment. Moving among the chic gallery patrons George seeks to make "connections" (p. 139). The "foundation" he strives to build is financial rather than aesthetic, and his "preparation" and "execution" allude to his social urbanity, which has little to do with rigorous artistic endeavor. The "dots" George uses build up his "image," for only through "cocktail conversation" (p. 138) will he gain "recognition" (pp. 141, 138, 142). He is on display. Each cynical observation in this lyric possesses this kind of double reference: "perfecting the design"; "a dab of politician"; "knowing where to draw the line"; "minor details"; "major decisions"; "keep things in scale"; "hold to your vision" (pp. 139, 140), all clearly illustrate the complexity of both Sondheim's ideology and his lyrics.

George understands, acknowledges, and plays all the necessary games, but as a result he despises himself, his art, and his patrons.[15] The modern artist acknowledges the need for "hype" but mourns the inevitable loss of privacy. The confusion of the artist with the art and the problems of being a cult figure are succinctly conveyed when George observes "So that you can go on exhibition," which he hastily modifies to "So that your work can go on exhibition" (p. 145).

"Putting It Together" traces George's frustration as he listens to snide critical comments and professional jealousies, learns that his partner wants to dissolve their collaboration, and is assaulted by the demand for constant innovation. His controlled irritation is dramatized when the cutouts start to totter and he dashes about the stage trying to keep his polite social facade intact. The number builds to a contrapuntal climax as each character adds his or her tidbit of artistic observation. George is permitted to reveal his disillusion, but Sondheim makes clear that the exigencies of contemporary creativity will not be denied. George concludes by accepting irascibly:

> The art of making art
> Is putting it together—
> Bit by bit—
> Link by link—
> Drink by drink—
> Mink by mink—
> And that
> Is the state
> Of the
> Art!
> (pp. 151–52)

During this crescendo, George has rushed about supporting his shaky cardboard images. On the final beat, he stands back and frames the successfully completed picture, just as Seurat did at the end of act 1. Contemporary George has fashioned and sustained his creation, his social image, but as he exits, the cutouts collapse and disappear. There is no immortality to be found in the ephemeral world of the beau monde. Fame is as fleeting as fashion.

During all this commotion, Marie has quietly drifted off to sleep. The company saunter off to dine, while George tries unsuccessfully to communicate with his former wife and Marie is left gazing at the painting. The song Marie then sings to the painted image of her mother and her confused grandson has the apparent simplicity of a nursery rhyme and the tinkling quality of a nineteenth-century music box, a gentle soothing sound wholly appropriate for Marie. She quietly affirms that there are only two things of worth one can give the world, "children and art."

This song possesses none of the characteristic Sondheim complexity. It is a straightforward expression of faith, without doubt or dissonance. Marie is sleepy and the lullaby is an appropriate form. Unlike the phony smart set, she readily admits she does not understand George's work, but she retains an uncomplicated acceptance:

> You should have seen it,
> It was a sight!

Mama, I mean it—
All color and light—!
I don't understand what it was,
But, Mama, the things that he does—
They twinkle and shimmer and buzz—
You would have liked them ...
It ...
Him ...
(p. 156)

Pointing to figure after figure in the painting, Marie claims that they were all inspired by her mother, Dot. In the painting she finds confirmation of Seurat's love for Dot. This heritage, the source of her pride and sense of self, she longs to share with her grandson.

Marie's song gives the audience a sense of the wandering mind of the aging character but again reveals a consistency with Seurat's technique. In attempting to convey Dot's magic and sensuality, Marie tries to convince George to accept his emotional self:

Mama said, "Darling,
Don't make such a drama,
A little less thinking,
A little more feeling—" . . .
I'm just quoting Mama ...
(p. 158)

Marie recognizes Dot's appeal, and emphasizes an emotional warmth that she feels emanates from the canvas:

Mama enjoyed things.
Mama was smart.
See how she shimmers—
I mean from the heart.
(p. 158)

Marie concludes her song with a gentle "Good-bye, Mama." Child and parent, youth and age are confused and fixed in the sweet poignancy of this farewell. Having delivered her message of family, love, and the identity of children and art, Marie falls asleep and is quietly rolled offstage.

In *Sunday in the Park with George*, more than in any previous Sondheim work, the division of passion and intellect seems to be made clearly in terms of gender. Curiously in this, his most experimental musical, Sondheim adopts a conventional stereotypical posture. Dot and Marie are far more warm, sensual, compassionate, and instinctive than the two Georges, who are seen as fanatical, intellectual, and creative. The women are the passive source, the men the active shapers. Marie has given George all she can. She has tried to teach him to love and to connect to his heritage, his "family tree" (p. 158).

As he gazes at the painting, George murmurs intensely, "Connect, George, Connect ..." (p. 159). The painting flies out and he is on the Island of La Grande Jatte. The twentieth-century artist is seeking to rediscover his faith in himself and his talent. The theme of connection, initially explored in act 1 as Seurat sought to find the connection between the primary colors, now becomes the principal dramatic action. George has lost his sense of self and artistic integrity. He cannot find his aesthetic voice. He consequently decides to return to the site of his ancestor's inspiration. In this musical the past serves, not as a reflection of former innocence, as in *Follies* and *Merrily We Roll Along*, but as a source of redemption. In order to rekindle his artistic fervor, George needs to discover his heritage and relate once more to the world beyond self. In contrast to Seurat, who, although he was unable to sustain any human relationship, never expressed any doubt about the significance of his aesthetic vision, George profoundly mistrusts his own artistic instincts.

The island on which George finds himself bears little resemblance to the tranquil park of the painting. He is surrounded by high-rise buildings, and the only vaguely recognizable element is the tree under which the Old Lady and her nurse once sat. George and his collaborator, Dennis, are setting up a chromolume. Through their conversation the audience learns that Marie has died before she could make the trip. All George has left of the family is Dot's grammar book. He is tense and unhappy. The mood is exacerbated when he persuades Dennis to confess that he is quitting their partnership because he, too, feels that George's work is repetitive and not progressing.

Dennis leaves and George sits alone, leafing through the grammar book. He smiles at Dot's naïve marginal notes, but as he reads the simple phrases that refer to someone named Marie, he finally makes the connection between his grandmother and Dot. It is this realization that convinces him of the truth of Marie's stories. His reverie gives way to despondency as he recognizes how much he misses his grandmother and how abandoned he feels. He has been deserted by his family, his inspiration, and his ability. The accompaniment resumes the impressionist ripples but without bringing tranquillity or creativity. George is disturbed, lost and directionless. This aimless drifting is suggested in the flowing notes of the melody, while his sense of dislocation is conveyed as he sings:

> George looks around.
> He sees the park.
> It is depressing.
> George looks ahead.
> He sees the dark.
> George is afraid.
> Where are the people
> Out strolling on Sunday?
> (pp. 163–64)

George had sought to embrace the beauty, harmony, and tranquillity that he had found in Seurat's painting by returning to the place itself. But instead this pilgrimage and the transformation of the place have forced him to confront the barren sterility of his life and art. Where he had hoped to discover light and inspiration, he finds darkness and confusion both in his surroundings and within himself. With simple economy Sondheim evokes the artist's sense of doubt and anguish. George had hoped to propel himself into the future but can only wish longingly for the past. Using the style of the pronoun lesson contained in the language primer, George repeatedly uses the third person to refer to himself. Sondheim thus suggests the character's alienation in the detached tone of the song, without allowing the character to become self-pitying. This is not a song of gut-wrenching torment such as *Sweeney Todd*'s "Epiphany," but one that reveals the isolation and helplessness of the artist who has lost focus and direction.

George tries to recall the wonder of creativity, and with deliberate ambiguity Sondheim fuses the two Georges:

> See George remember how George used to be,
> Stretching his vision in every direction.
> See George attempting to see a connection
> When all he can see
> Is maybe a tree—
> The family tree—
> Sorry, Marie.
> (p. 164)

The two artists shared the joy of creation, but now George feels separated from the source. He wants desperately to connect. Yet George (or Sondheim) cannot resist the irony implicit in fusing the one actual remaining tree with the idea of a family tree.

The self-obsession of the artist is suggested in Sondheim's repeated use of the name "George," a repetition that also helps sustain the style of the grammar book and the pointillist technique used throughout the musical. During the course of this song the audience follows George's journey into self. He begins by seeking his solace and inspiration in the external world of the park and gradually grows more contemplative. Though George can find no peace either beyond or within self, the introspection is effective. As George sits in brooding silence, Dot appears behind him. Whether the authors intend this figure to represent the spirit of creativity, the ghost of lost innocence, or the representative of inspiration is not significant. She is a theatricalization of life and art, hope and light. Sondheim explains: "Dot appears because George summons her—it's a personification of his finally making a connection with his heritage and the picture's legacy, both personally and in a continuum of art."[16]

Dot mistakes George for his great-grandfather and gently prods him into confession. Using many of the melodic elements employed when she decides to leave George in act 1, and an accompaniment based on the opening arpeggio, Dot now compels George to see the beauty about and within him. This song is the culmination of a musical development that can be traced through the show. The evolution of the score is, Sondheim explains, based on the relationship of the two central characters:

> Theirs is a continuous and continuing love song that isn't completed until the end of the show. In the song "Sunday in the Park with George," Dot, in one section, begins a lyrical theme, which is her affection and her love for George. This is picked up later in "Color and Light," and it develops and starts to reach a climax, and just at that point, they break off and they speak. Then in "We Do Not Belong Together" it's picked up and further developed as if it's almost where they left off, and ends with an unrhymed line where she sings, "I have to move on." And when their love is finally consummated, which is the end of the second act, it all comes together and becomes a completed song in "Move On." "Move On" is a combination of all the themes involving their relationship, including every harmony and every accompaniment; it's where everything culminates. Only it's over a period of four major scenes covering a hundred years. It's one way of threading the theme through time.[17]

Consequently, although the score can be viewed as a series of distinct numbers, it is in fact a totality, connected like Seurat's dots, to form a complex, increasingly resonant composition reflecting the complete resolution of the focal relationship.

Just as, earlier, Dot moves on, leaving the oppressive frustrations of the relationship but retaining the vision George shares with her, so contemporary George must now break the bonds of his own sense of impotence and sterility. Knowing the need to choose life, Dot convinces him that it is commitment and choice that matter:

> Stop worrying where you're going—
> Move on.
> If you can know where you're going,
> You've gone.
> Just keep moving on.
>
> I chose, and my world was shaken—
> So what?
> The choice may have been mistaken,
> The choosing was not.
> You have to move on.
> (p. 167)

Dot's parting from George in act 1 is painful, her gentle prodding in act 2 is tender and compassionate. This serenity is something she learns from the first George, and consequently the cycle of art and humanity is continued.

Dot's sense of urgency shatters George's insular depression, forcing him to begin again to look about him, to see with her eyes. Her joy and wonder impel him to rediscover his own sense of urgency and excitement. Their shared excitement is conveyed in the contrapuntal structure of the lines:

> *Dot*
>
> Look at what you want,
> Not at where you are,
> Not at what you'll be.
> Look at all the things you've done for me:
>
> Opened up my eyes,
> Taught me how to see,
> Notice every tree—
>
> *George*
>
> ... Notice every tree ...
>
> *Dot*

Understand the light—

George

... Understand the light ...

Dot

Concentrate on now—

George

I want to move on.
I want to explore the light.
I want to know how to get through,
Through to something new,
Something of my own ...
(pp. 167–68)

The excitement is highlighted in the soaring notes Sondheim gives Dot on "opened up my eyes" and George on "something of my own." Their shared feeling and sense of communion is suggested in the harmonized "move on."

As Dot gently encourages George, he begins to see the world anew:

Dot	*George*
Look at all the things	
You gave to me.	Things I hadn't looked at
Let me give to you	Till now:
Something in return.	Flower in your hat.
I would be so pleased ...	And your smile.
	And the color of your hair.
	(pp. 168–69)

George finally achieves a state of peace and tranquillity. His appreciation of her beauty is conveyed in the gentle rhythms and melody that build to an irresistible climax as he sings:

And the color of your hair.
And the way you catch the light.
And the care.
And the feeling.
And the life
Moving on.
(p. 169)

His belief in his own creativity is reawakened as the same revolving accompaniment found in "Finishing the Hat" is played under the word *care*.

The culminating unity of the contrasting rhythm patterns in this climactic number is not accidental. Sondheim justifies his use of rhythmic ideas:

> It seemed effective to use rhythm to reflect putting dots on the canvas, to show his distraction as well as his concentration. But that, of course, becomes motivic, that rhythmic idea. There are two basic rhythms, actually: there's the arpeggiated rolling rhythm that is set up right in the opening arpeggios and eventually becomes "Finishing the Hat" and the kind of rolling vamp in "Sunday in the Park with George"; then there's the painter's theme, which is sharp and staccato and jabbed. That, combined with the rolling vamp, becomes "Move On."[18]

The emotional climax is built musically, so that the tension is almost unbearable as George sings "And the feeling." But as George breaks through and makes a real connection with his tradition, Sondheim achieves a release through a traditional dominant. The characters and the audience experience renewed connection and resolution as George sings "And the life / Moving on." If one contrasts the tranquillity of the harmony with the conflicting meters and melodic lines that conclude the unholy alliance of Sweeney and Mrs. Lovett, one can appreciate how perfectly Sondheim evokes the unity of George and Dot's love.

The two figures are now simultaneously artist and inspiration, Seurat and Dot, George and art. Their poignant duet concludes as a traditional love song. They are two elemental forces which must of necessity be together. The antithetical poles of reason and emotion, art and life, subject and object have been the fundamental structures of dramatic conflict since the earliest expressions of Greek drama. Sondheim finds his own version of this classic opposition. Yet the musical does not conclude on this swelling duet. George needs a final nudge from Dot, who sings her last plea for honesty and integrity:

> Anything you do,
> Let it come from you.
> Then it will be new.
> Give us more to see ...
>
> (p. 169)

The disclosure of a new facet of reality, the revelation of a new truth—this is the sacred mandate of the artist.

At last George is ready to understand the message contained in Dot's grammar book. He realizes that it is the artistic litany written in the back of the book that is significant. Dot explains that these are the words Seurat muttered while he was working. As George begins to read the artistic manifesto by now so familiar to the audience, the two worlds, past and present, begin to fuse. The present gradually fades and slowly the characters and objects of the past appear. George struggles to make out illegible ciphers, but when Dot supplies the word *harmony*, all the figures of the nineteenth-century world begin to sing a reprise of "Sunday." The sense of tranquillity, of emotional and musical harmony, is reestablished in the stately promenade of the figures singing their splendid hymn. In a nerve-tingling theatrical moment, Dot takes George by the hand and turns him to face the otherworldly figures who bow to him. Art acknowledges artist; the connection between inspiration and creative energy is reestablished. In this moment comes the recognition that the artist takes the ordinary and transforms it into the extraordinary, rendering the mortal world immortal.

All torment dissolves. The characters slowly disappear. Only Dot remains in silhouette as the picture frame descends. Once more the artist is left alone with a blank canvas. This final image synthesizes tension and release. The unlimited world of the artist opens up again as George mutters: "White. A blank page or canvas. His favorite. / So many possibilities ..." (p. 173). Thus, the musical achieves a perfect unity of design. Opening and closing are linked, but not in a static circularity. Rather there is a sense of an ever-ascending spiral as each artist strives to contribute a unique vision to the many-faceted nature of artistic truth.

This formal finale did not develop easily. Sondheim was late in finishing act 2, and two important songs, "Children and Art" and "Lesson #8," were completed only three days before the scheduled opening, which was postponed from April 23 to May 2. A concluding tableau had been rejected as too similar to the ending of act 1, and an attempt to dramatize contemporary George's version of La Grande Jatte was discarded as too literal and didactic. The collaborators wanted a conclusion that would satisfy the audience emotionally but also open up imaginative possibilities. Their solution achieved both these seemingly disparate goals. The return to white opened up the future for both artists and audience.

THE MUSICAL FINDS ITS VOICE

The formal structure of *Sunday in the Park With George* is ideally suited both to Seurat's exact stylistic objectives and Sondheim's own aesthetic philosophy. Confronted with a question regarding the apparent contradiction between the innovative form of the musical and its content, which emphasizes the conservative values of order and harmony, Sondheim declares:

> That's something I believe. All good art has that, whether it's contemporary or not. I think *Sunday in the Park*, though it might strike you or others as radical, is meticulously formed—as formed as the picture. Yet its surface is a little . . . heady. . . .
>
> In philosophy of art, generally, I'm a conservative. My beliefs are conservative, but my work is not. That's the kind of art I like.[19]

The critical response to *Sunday in the Park with George* was varied. Predictably, some of the New York reviewers did not like the show. Clive Barnes of the *New York Post*, Douglas Watt of the *Daily News*, and Howard Kissel of *Women's Wear Daily* resorted to familiar complaints that Sondheim's music did not "sing," that the lyrics were superior to the score, and that the characters were "lifeless." But Frank Rich, who, as a student at Harvard had written one of the most perspicacious analyses of *Follies*, used his influential position on the *New York Times* to laud the work. This review, together with the highly complimentary critiques in the popular weekly magazines and—perhaps more significantly—Sondheim's now-indisputable reputation, negated the less favorable notices, and the musical enjoyed a successful run. It went on to win the New York Drama Critics Award, eight Drama Desk Awards, and three Tony Awards before receiving the Pulitzer Prize for Drama.

10

SONDHEIM ISN'T GRIM

Into the Woods

Sondheim's prolific output continues unabated. While the wellspring of creative talent on Broadway seems to have run dry, Sondheim continues to develop the form of the musical theater. Although there are a number of smaller shows evolving in regional theater, Sondheim is the only American composer or lyricist to both consistently have his shows produced and never cease in his exploration of the endless possibilities of the genre. His latest collaboration with James Lapine confirms his apparently limitless creativity.

As a very young man Sondheim attempted, unsuccessfully, to musicalize *Mary Poppins*. Almost forty years later he and Lapine discovered fertile ground for their imaginations by creating an original tale of their own in which the characters' quests propel them into the more familiar world of such classic fairy tales as Cinderella, Jack and the Beanstalk, Rapunzel, and Little Red Ridinghood. Influenced by the theories of Carl Jung and by the insights of Bruno Bettelheim, whose work on the significance of fairy tales, *The Uses of Enchantment*, explores the darker Freudian ramifications of these stories, Sondheim and Lapine evolved a musical that manages to be delightful, melodic, and entertaining as well as intellectually astute and psychologically complex.

The themes that unite these disparate stories concern the difficulties of achieving maturity, the complex relationship between parent and child, and ultimately the necessity of recognizing human interdependence. Like a contemporary brothers Grimm, Sondheim and Lapine weave a magical fabric of witches, giants, and spells but never allow the audience to forget the serious thematic underpinnings of the work.

Into the Woods enjoyed a gradual evolutionary birth. Beginning as a reading at Playwrights Horizons, the work went through three workshop readings in New York, and a tryout in San Diego, before opening on Broadway to generally favorable reviews and garnering for Sondheim yet another Tony Award for best music and lyrics. As with all of Sondheim's work, neither critics nor public were unanimous in their response, but judging from the general tenor of the reviews and the enthusiastic approbation at the Tony Awards ceremony, Sondheim has finally gained the respect of all. He is universally acknowledged to be the foremost American exponent of his chosen art form and is accorded a kind of awe not generally associated with either the musical or with other living artists. Some critics may not like his work, but all recognize his innovative genius. This respect is clearly evident in an article in *Time* magazine dedicated to America's best: "Sondheim has steadily pushed toward—or beyond—the limits of what the score, the narrative, the very premise of a musical can be. More than anyone else writing today, perhaps more than anyone who came before, he merges a consummate mastery of what musicals have been with a vision of what they should become."[1] While lacking the daring innovation and heartrending emotional revelation of *Sunday in the Park with George*, *Into the Woods* has a charm of its own.

Into the Woods opens with Cinderella, Jack and his Mother, and the original characters the Baker and his Wife in front of their fairy tale abodes bewailing their fate. With typical Sondheim style and finesse the characters' distinct desires are blended into a complex contrapuntal composition. The central motif is established in the opening words as Cinderella sings out plaintively, "I wish." This refrain is echoed by each of the characters and as the action progresses the consequences of these apparently innocent wishes are explored. These desires and the obstacles that will need to be overcome serve as the structure for the primary action of act 1.

The naïve wishes of the youthful protagonists—contrasted with the weary cynicism of Jack's Mother—are further enhanced as a young Little Red Ridinghood adds her demands. This character, perhaps the most humorous in a Sondheim musical since the zany excesses of *A Funny Thing Happened on the Way to the Forum*, has a voracious appetite, which will lead to her problematic encounter with the Wolf. Their adventure exemplifies the best combination of sagacity and wit in the show. Little Red Ridinghood's singing of the refrain of the title song sets the tone of the entire musical. She is carefree. The jaunty rhythm and simple melody reflect her optimism. The lyrics appear almost naïve, but they possess the simplicity of fairytales and a cautionary note is repeatedly sounded:

> Into the woods,
> It's time to go,
> I hate to leave,
> I have to, though.
> Into the woods—
> It's time, and so
> I must begin my journey. . . .
>
> Into the woods
> To bring some bread
> To Granny who
> Is sick in bed.
> Never can tell
> What lies ahead.
> For all that I know.
> She's already dead.[2]

It is this combination of delightful humor and suggestive bleakness that permeates all the songs in the score.

Each of the major characters needs to enter the dark entangled wood of their inner desires and journey through an elemental rite of passage; Little Red Ridinghood, who skips blithely into the woods, blissfully stuffing buns into her mouth, must learn the thrills and terrors of indulgence. Sondheim and Lapine combine an innocence and innuendo in each encounter between the Wolf and his plump young prey that is both extremely funny and unexpectedly poignant. There is a wonderfully lascivious song for the leering Wolf as he entreats the succulent young girl:

> Hello, little girl,
> What's your rush?
> You're missing all the flowers.
> The sun won't set for hours,
> Take your time.

Here the comedy is perfectly tailored to character and action.

This synthesis of humor and insight is taken one step further when Little

Red Ridinghood sings after she has been freed from the dark confines of the Wolf's belly. The conflict between parental advice and temptation is captured in her opening lines:

> Mother said,
> "Straight ahead,"
> Not to delay
> Or be misled.
> I should have heeded
> Her advice ...
> But he seemed so nice.

The loss of innocence is suggested but Sondheim is not didactic:

> And take extra care with strangers,
> Even flowers have their dangers.
> And though scary is exciting,
> Nice is different than good.

His characters learn, but even with experience do not lose their ambivalence: "Isn't it nice to know a lot! / And a little bit not . . ."

Jack must be taught a similar lesson. Perhaps because he is intended to be a simple lad, he lacks Little Red Ridinghood's energetic appeal and obvious comic potential. Yet in this character, too, Sondheim synthesizes humor and pain. He composes a melancholy, melodic song of farewell for Jack to croon sadly to his beloved cow but undercuts the sentimentality with the black humor of the concluding lines:

> I'll see you soon again.
> I hope that when I do,
> It won't be on a plate.

Jack, like Little Red Ridinghood, has an experience both stimulating and terrifying, and he too has to compromise his moral code to achieve his goals. The significance of his adventure is also revealed in song; his attitude is equally ambivalent:

> When you're way up high
> And you look below
> At the world you've left
> And the things you know,
> Little more than a glance

Is enough to show
You just how small you are.

Cinderella's journey is also fraught with danger and fulfillment. Her tale of family rejection and ultimate success is humanized in Sondheim's lyrics as she describes her experience at the ball to the enraptured Baker's Wife.

Cinderella

He's a very nice Prince.

Baker's Wife

And—?

Cinderella

And—
It's a very nice Ball.

Baker's Wife

And—?

Cinderella

And—
When I entered, they trumpeted.

Baker's Wife

And—?
The Prince—?

Cinderella

Oh, the Prince ...

Baker's Wife

Yes, the Prince!

Cinderella

Well, he's tall.

The Baker and his wife have a simple wish. They want a child. They have been cursed with infertility, however, by the vengeful "witch next door." In order to break her spell they must seek out:

One: the cow as white as milk,
Two: the cape as red as blood,
Three: the hair as yellow as corn,
Four: the slipper as pure as gold.

These items, clearly, can only be found in the lives of the other more well-known characters.

In their struggle to wrest these articles from their rightful owners, the Baker and his wife must confront certain painful choices. Initially the Baker discovers that he must shed his false male independence and recognize his need for love, understanding, and cooperation. Sondheim conveys his character's struggle to accept this in a tender duet:

Baker

It takes two.
I thought one was enough,
It's not true:
It takes two of us.
You came through
When the journey was rough.
It took you.
It took two of us.

In the couple's overwhelming desire to obtain their wish they lie and cheat, the consequences of which they must ultimately confront.

Sondheim intentionally modifies the intellectual complexity and sophistication of his previous work in the score of *Into the Woods*. Both lyrics and music express the stylistic purity of the fairy tale libretto and much of the score has a lively nursery rhyme quality. As Sondheim reveals:

> What I'm trying to do with the score is to sprinkle it with ditties; I'm trying to do little sixteen-, thirty-two-, and eight-bar tunes, almost cartoonish except in a sort of contemporary style. Morals, and travelling songs. And these little tunes start to go strange in the second act. You see, the first act is fast and funny and light and the second act is less goofy and a bit darker, so I would like the score to reflect that.[3]

But Sondheim's simplicity is never trite, as musical director Paul Gemignani points out:

> There is a kind of Disney thought-pattern to much of the show and I mean that in the best sense. For instance, when someone dies, you hear a little sad music. The witch has specific chords. The underscoring points out certain things. The subject matter lends itself to all of this. But it's deceptively simple. There are all kinds of colors in the score, and a complex rhythmic intensity. It's written as a chamber music piece, and the challenge is to make the sound crystalline.[4]

Sondheim originally intended identifying each of the major characters with an individual style and musical motif. Although this proved to be too schematic a limitation, many of the characters are in fact defined by their stylistic motifs. Cinderella sings her romance in a light operatic soprano, while Jack and his mother express themselves in simple folk tunes and childlike rhymes. The Wolf's lechery is translated into a soft-shoe shuffle while the Witch uses a unique rap style. This use of recurring motifs is similar to the technique used in *Merrily We Roll Along*, in which motifs are used, repeated, and transformed throughout the piece. As Sondheim explains: "The structure of the score is in a sense like *Merrily* in that it's modular again. . . . The whole prologue is a series of sixteen vignettes, each of which has a musical structure. And then there's one tune that keeps popping up, which becomes the major theme of the evening."[5]

Not all the score and lyrics depend on the spare emblematic charm of a child's tale. The music is richly melodic and Sondheim substitutes a warmth for his usual erudition. The emotional turmoil of the characters, particularly of the Baker and his wife, is perfectly conveyed in the melodic and harmonic development of the score. These two characters simultaneously inhabit the worlds of humanity and fairy tale. In their essentially middle-class aspirations and failures they most clearly exemplify the desires and limitations of the audience. Sondheim cements this fusion of audience and character by having these two express themselves in the language and rhythms of a typical urban couple. It is their moral and emotional journey that the audience must share.

The interrelationships of the characters are marvelously convoluted. The Witch, whose spell has caused the Baker's Wife's infertility, reveals that her garden was raped by the Baker's father and that she has consequently claimed his sister, Rapunzel, whom she keeps locked in a tower. Rapunzel in turn is loved by Cinderella's Prince's brother. As the various characters stumble through the woods seeking to fulfill their wishes, they encounter each other, interact, and then send the plot off in another direction. There are no revolving bedroom doors, but in its intricate design the plot more closely resembles French farce than the clear linear didacticism of the traditional fairy tale.

Yet the darker underside of these children's stories is the real subject of *Into the Woods*. This does not mean that the musical is overtly symbolic or that its psychological substructure intrudes. Rather, its central themes of the pain of growing up and the difficulty of parent/child relationships are carried almost subliminally in the music and lyrics, while Lapine's labyrinth of a plot keeps characters and audience constantly tumbling forward into the tangled briars. Sondheim suggests the inner struggles and personal growth of the characters with a delicate hand. His songs lightly express their essential pain and then release the characters to the forward demands of the action. (Sondheim acknowledges that in many ways he found this score the most difficult to compose since writing *Forum*, because with highly plotted shows the songs are respites from the frantic action that, nevertheless, must not slow the pace.)

The titular theme song binds the various plots and musical motifs together, as the characters march innocently into the original world of their unconscious. They begin act 1 blithely asserting "The woods are just trees, / The trees are just wood" but have to learn the inevitable consequences of pursuing their desires and compromising their integrity. This metaphysical journey is a familiar one for Sondheim characters, as Frank Rich points out in his review:

> Like the middle-aged showbiz cynics who return to their haunted youth in *Follies* and *Merrily We Roll Along* or the contemporary descendant who revisits Georges Seurat in *Sunday in the Park with George* or the lovers who court in a nocturnal Scandinavian birch forest in *A Little Night Music*, Cinderella and company travel into a dark, enchanted wilderness to discover who they are and how they might grow up and overcome the eternal, terrifying plight of being alone.[6]

But the conclusions drawn from the lesson of this journey differ markedly from the impact of Sondheim's earlier work. The cynicism, isolation, and alienation implicit in other works is tempered with an unfamiliar plea for commitment and communal awareness. The naïvete of youth is transformed into a sober acceptance of reality. Neither Sondheim nor Lapine finds this painful process of maturation daunting. As Sondheim discloses:

> I think the final step in maturity is feeling responsible for everybody. If I could have written "no man is an island," I would have. But that's what "No One Is Alone" is about. What I like about the title is it says two things. It says: no one is lonely, you're not alone—I'm on your side and I love you. And the other thing is: no one is alone—you have to be careful what you do to other people. You can't just go stealing gold and selling cows for more than they are worth, because it affects everybody else.[7]

And in describing the difference between the characters in acts 1 and 2, Lapine adds, "When you are young, you envision happiness in such an idealized way. As you get older you realize happiness involves a lot of problems. To me, that's not an unhappy kind of ending—it's just a more informed sense of happy, a happiness that's been earned."[8] The characters in *Into the Woods* do not mourn their loss of innocence but embrace it as a necessary ingredient to growing up. Their simplistic, unambiguous desires are relinquished as they understand the complexities of adult responsibility.

The impetus for character growth is implicit in the concluding moments of act 1. Each of the characters has apparently achieved his or her goal, but each has had to compromise integrity to do so. Consequently, although they all jubilantly sing "Happy now and happy hence / And happy ever after," there is a sense of unease. This happy-ever-after has none of the tranquillity of perfection achieved in the final moments of act 1 of *Sunday in the Park with George*. This sense of disquiet is suggested in the very superficiality of the rollicking optimism of the song. Through their excessive zeal, Sondheim hints at the ephemeral quality of the characters' joy:

> Into the woods to lift the spell,
> Into the woods to lose the longing,
> Into the woods to have the child,
> To wed the Prince,
> To get the money,
> To save the house,
> To kill the Wolf,
> To find the father,
> To conquer the kingdom,
> To have, to wed,
> To get, to save,
> To kill, to keep,
> To go to the Festival!
>
> Into the woods,
> Into the woods,

Into the woods,
Then out of the woods
And happy ever after!

This ability to clothe a serious theme in a lively rhythm and convey significance in a comic mode is one of Sondheim's achievements. Despite its serious and emotional numbers, *Into the Woods* contains some of the funniest of Sondheim's material. "Agony," for example, is a lament by the two princely brothers about the frustrations of unrequieted passion:

Both

Agony!

Cinderella's Prince

Misery!

Rapunzel's Prince

Woe!

Both

Though it's different for each.

Cinderella's Prince

Always ten steps behind—

Rapunzel's Prince

Always ten feet below—

Both

And she's just out of reach.
Agony
That can cut like a knife!
I must have her to wife.

Like "Lovely" in *Forum*, this song is given greater comic resonance when in act 2 it is reprised. The princes have now grown bored with their wives and long for new, unattainable maidens:

Cinderella's Prince

High in a tower—
Like yours was, but higher—
A beauty asleep.
All 'round the tower

A thicket of briar
A hundred feet deep ...

Rapunzel's Prince

I found a casket
Entirely of glass—
(*As Cinderella's Prince starts to shrug*)
No, it's unbreakable.
Inside—don't ask it—
A maiden, alas,
Just as unwakeable ...

Act 2 journeys into apparently recognizable Sondheim territory. All the characters are ready to discover what follows "happily ever after." Rather than concentrate on the characters' individual problems—although it is clear that Cinderella's marriage is far from perfect, that wealth has not solved Jack's problem, that a screaming infant does not bring endless joy, and that the Witch having regained her former beauty has lost both her daughter and her power— Sondheim and Lapine chose instead to sublimate the individual problems by confronting the characters with a new danger. The wife of the giant killed by Jack returns to seek revenge. This communal threat, which has been interpreted by various critics to represent forces of evil as diverse as nuclear proliferation, AIDS, and the deranged individualism of Reaganomics, is a handy device that serves to reunite the characters. In the face of almost certain annihilation they learn to accept that only through cooperation can they hope to survive. The intricacies of this new plot development are less interesting, however, than the brief insights into the personal conflicts provided in the score. Two of the finest examples of this contemporary yet timeless angst occur in the evolving relationship of the Baker and his wife.

While wandering in the woods in search of the giant, the Baker's Wife encounters Cinderella's Prince. After their brief liaison the conflicts of fantasy and reality, romantic escapism and practicality are dramatized.

Baker's Wife

What was that?

Was that me?
Was that him?

SONDHEIM ISN'T GRIM

Did a prince really kiss me?
And kiss me?
And kiss me?
And did I kiss him back? . . .

Back to life, back to sense,
Back to child, back to husband,
You can't live in the woods.
There are vows, there are ties,
There are needs, there are standards,
There are shouldn'ts and shoulds.

Why not both instead?
There's the answer, if you're clever;
Have a child for warmth,
And a baker for bread,
And a prince for whatever—
Never!
It's these woods.

The Baker's Wife longs to combine the wondrous ardor of the Prince with the domesticity of a husband and child. During the course of the song she grows to accept that life demands an either/or. She decides romance is ephemeral and feels compelled to return to the world of reality. She dies, however, before she can rejoin her husband. Despite certain accusations to the contrary, I do not think that this death is intended to be in retribution for her adultery.

It is the Baker who must finally confront reality and the truths of being alone. His desire to escape responsibility is expressed in one of the most impassioned sequences of the show. Sondheim's ability to translate anguish into music and expose all the ambiguity of emotional conflict is exemplified in the Baker's cry:

No more riddles.
No more jests.
No more curses you can't undo,
Left by fathers you never knew.
No more quests.

Although he is dealing with perennial human problems, Sondheim does not lose the archaic world of fairy tale in the language of his lyrics. This ability to go to the center of contemporary urban grief and yet never let go of the particular created milieu is quintessentially Sondheim.

Sondheim and Lapine experimented extensively and made a number of alterations in the plot after the tryout in San Diego; they eventually decided, however, to keep the structure of the piece virtually unchanged. The most extensive revisions and additions to the score involved the role of the Witch. This part was played by a number of different actresses during the musical's evolution, but it was Bernadette Peters who finally opened on Broadway. Whether it was the choice of this actress or the intrinsic demands of the musical that prompted modifications, Sondheim decided to write new and significant material for this character, whose transformations are charted in song. As an ugly old crone she describes her ravishment in a bitter but humorous rap song:

> He was robbing me,
> Raping me,
> Rooting through my rutabaga,
> Raiding my arugula and
> Ripping up the rampion
> (My champion! My favorite!)—

The justification of her expressive dedication to her daughter, Rapunzel, is set to a tender lament:

> Why could you not obey?
> Children should listen.
> What have I been to you?
> What would you have me be?
> Handsome like a prince?
>
> Ah, but I am old.
> I am ugly.
> I embarrass you. . . .
>
> You are ashamed.
> You don't understand.

Finally she is transformed into a beautiful but powerless woman who mourns the loss of her child and the uncontrolled violence that now pervades her world:

> This is the world I meant.
> Couldn't you listen?
> Couldn't you stay content,
> Safe behind walls,
> As I
> Could not?

SONDHEIM ISN'T GRIM

In a poignant threnody the Witch describes a world destroyed and points out the havoc wrought by selfishness:

> It's the last midnight,
> It's the boom—
> Splat!
> Nothing but a vast midnight,
> Everybody smashed flat!

Her frantic attempts to shield her child by walling her up in a tower are clearly symbolic and she must learn:

> No matter what you say,
> Children won't listen.
> No matter what you know,
> Children refuse
> To learn.
>
> Guide them along the way,
> Still they won't listen.
> Children can only grow
> From something you love
> To something you lose ...

This message is eventually modified in the final moments of the musical. Having clashed in a passionate orgy of accusation ("Your Fault"), the characters finally band together and conquer the giant. A quieter, more mature but tentatively optimistic group sings:

> Careful the wish you make,
> Wishes are children.
> Careful the path they take—
> Wishes come true,
> Not free. . . .
>
> *Witch*
>
> Careful the tale you tell.
> That is the spell.
> Children will listen ...

This mood of tranquillity may surprise audiences accustomed to Sondheim's dryer, more acerbic tone. But Sondheim's work can never be confined to rigid categorizations. With each new musical he not only reshapes the genre but redefines his own talent. Perhaps the glow of mature well-being that emanates from the stage in the final moments of *Into the Woods* may entice a larger share of the Broadway audience into the theater. But Sondheim's achievement must not be measured in box-office receipts.

Undeniably the public is gradually learning to appreciate Sondheim's genius. Perhaps one of the greatest ironies of Broadway history is that while British imports dominated the New York stage, the revised version of *Follies* played to sold-out houses in London. It took sixteen years for this masterpiece to find a producer, but finally the theatergoing public is beginning to catch up with Sondheim. Despite the decision to soften the cynicism and add a more upbeat conclusion, the message of *Follies* remains unchanged. It is the key to understanding all of Sondheim's work. This farewell to the naïvete and simplistic innocence of the past is Sondheim's tribute to all that came before him. There is nostalgia but no contempt. In its iconoclastic brilliance, *Follies* is also a clear monument to Sondheim's own creativity. Sondheim knows that the old forms must die to reveal the new art form that can evolve.

Although *Into the Woods* is gentler than his earlier musicals, this does not mean that Sondheim has deviated from his path of innovative individuality. The majority of his musicals do not express the unambiguous cheer and superficial gloss of the traditional musical, but Sondheim has discovered a more profound emotional and aesthetic truth. His audiences may be disturbed, but the dramatic catharsis engendered by his work is far more valuable than the soothing platitudes of escapist entertainment. *Into the Woods* has proven to be extremely popular and is performed extensively by regional and summer theater companies. Unlike most of Sondheim's earlier work, it was almost immediately transferred to London. The British, who for so long scorned the American musical, have finally embraced Sondheim. *Follies, Pacific Overtures, Sunday in the Park with George* and *Into the Woods* have been presented to great critical acclaim on the West End stage. Sondheim was also awarded the honor of being the first visiting professor of contemporary theater at Oxford University, an endowed chair established by the British producer Cameron Mackintosh. Sondheim's admission to these hallowed halls of academe conclusively establishes his legitimacy and that of his chosen art form.

Only two of Sondheim's musicals, *A Funny Thing Happened on the Way to the Forum* and *A Little Night Music,* have been adapted to the screen. Neither film really captured the charm of the theatrical original. Sondheim is, however, currently busy on two promising movie projects. He is collaborating with the Jim Henson Company on an adaptation of *Into the Woods* and working with director Rob Reiner and screenwriter William Goldman on an original movie musical. But most of his work remains unknown to the general movie-going public. This ignorance is diminishing. Sondheim has scored a number of films, including Warren Beatty's *Reds*. It is, however, his contribution to Beatty's *Dick Tracy* that has finally introduced the wit, charm, and music of Stephen Sondheim to a wider audience. His songs for the pop icon Madonna were immediately successful and won an Academy Award for Sondheim.

11

FROM MADONNA AND MUPPETS TO MAYHEM

Assassins

With all this popular acclaim and apparent acceptance into the mainstream, it may seem that Sondheim's work has finally become safe and accessible to Middle America. On December 18, 1990, Stephen Sondheim once again displayed courage and artistic daring and surprised his audience. At Playwrights Horizons, the tiny off-Broadway space where *Sunday in the Park with George* had been workshopped, Sondheim and his collaborator John Weidman began previews on a show that shocked almost as many people as it thrilled.

America was in a frenzy of patriotic fervor. War was brewing in the Persian Gulf and yellow ribbons were sprouting up all over the continent. The jingoistic ultimatums of George Bush touched a responsive chord in the American public and there was a groundswell of chauvinistic pride and clamor for war. This seemed an inappropriate time for a piece of theater which not only dramatized the lethal power of guns but more significantly examined the lies implicit in the American Dream. Although *Assassins* was not written in response to the conditions in the Gulf (for Sondheim's and Weidman's work long predated the conflict), the composer and playwright chose to create a polemical piece that questioned the very assumptions upon which the edifice of American idealism is based. Sondheim acknowledged that the subject would alienate people:

> There are always people who think that certain subjects are not right for musicals.... I remember that there was a letter of protest when Rodgers and

> Hammerstein's "South Pacific" opened that said, "How dare they write a musical about miscegenation?" "South Pacific" hardly seems like a shocker today, but it was in 1949. There were people who were horrified that such a serious and upsetting subject as interracial marriage should be dealt with by the most popular musical writers of the day.
>
> We're not going to apologize for dealing with such a volatile subject.... Nowadays, virtually everything goes.[1]

Gone was the comforting humanism of *Into the Woods*. *Assassins* dramatizes the unpopular thesis that the most notorious killers in our culture are as much a product of that culture as the famous leaders they attempted to kill. No concession was made to the flood of public support for the Gulf war and the satiric piece opened to a sold-out run. The audiences, small as they were—for the theater seats only 139 people and the run was extremely limited—were excited by the work. Many of the critics were less enthusiastic. The musical attracted a substantial amount of negative criticism, not because of its lack of artistic merit, but because of its political content. M. G. Lord of *Newsday* was more vociferous than most, but her response was typical:

> In the present political environment, "Assassins," which might otherwise be dismissed as an innocuous piece of failed art, is sinister and dangerous.[2]

Even critics like Julius Novick, who appreciated *Assassins'* complexity, was uncomfortable with the piece, and wrote:

> But what's the point of the whole thing, anyhow? That assassins are lonely people who suffer from feelings of powerlessness and worthlessness? Who doesn't already know that?
>
> Yet there are various kinds of knowing. I was grateful to Booth—with Oswald, with the rest of that gang of villains and lunatics and fools—to be reminded feelingly of how deep alienation can cut, how desperate is the human need for self-respect and how twisted are the ways in which that need can express itself. I think this show, for all its weaknesses, can help us understand Saddam Hussein (and perhaps, paradoxically, George Bush, on the theory that given the vicissitudes of human life, even the world's ultimate insider must experience himself on some basic level as lost, lonely and worthless).[3]

There seemed to be a concern that the musical satire "trivialized tragedy."[4] Even Frank Rich, the most powerful critic in America, equivocated. Rich, who, since his days as a college reporter, has championed Sondheim, understood the courage it took to present the work. He comprehended that the work expressed Sondheim's conviction that the underprivileged peoples of America have to be acknowledged by the prosperous majority if the cycle of violence represented by assassination is to cease. He argues:

> This is not a message that audiences necessarily want to hear at any time, and during the relatively jingoistic time of war in which this production happens to find itself, some may regard such sentiments as incendiary. But Mr. Sondheim has real guts. He isn't ashamed to identify with his assassins to the extreme point where he will wave a gun in a crowded theater, artistically speaking, if that's what is needed to hit the target of American complacency.[5]

But Sondheim did not intend to write a political thesis. His interest has always been on the theatrical event. Consequently, he maintains, it was not what the assassinations reflected but the characters of the assassins themselves that intrigued him:

> And what attracted us to the topic? In Europe, assassinations are considered political acts for the most part. In this country, it's always the work of a loner, a conspiracy, the Mafia. I could go on and on, but it would only make *Assassins* sound more academic than it should. The fact is it's just a fascinating subject. It has many ramifications and it is extremely theatrical. When we started to look into the lives of the assassins, we found they were fascinating people, so it had character, too. Had it just been a political tract, I wouldn't have wanted to do it, either. One of my objections to Brecht is that he always put the politics at the forefront and the character to the rear. What I hope we've done with *Assassins* is put the character at the forefront, with all the political and social implications around them.[6]

What Sondheim and the company achieved was a riveting, hallucinatory evening of theater which posed some tough questions in a dramatically innovative way. Yet, extraordinary as it may seem, despite Sondheim's reputation, the musical did not transfer to a larger house. It was only after the passions of war had cooled, and with the release of the compact disc and cassette, that the significance of the musical began to be appreciated. The three-piece band of the original was expanded into a full orchestration by Michael Starobin. This did contribute to the score's impact but orchestral richness alone cannot account for the shifting critical attitudes. Time has passed and perspectives have altered. Stephen Holden's assessment of the recording is characteristic of the glowing reviews: "What emerges on disc is a cohesive song cycle on a theme that is as unpleasant as it is American."[7]

The idea for *Assassins* first occurred to Sondheim when he was on a panel at producer Stuart Ostrow's Musical Theater Lab. There he read a script about a fictional presidential assassin by a young playwright, Charles Gilbert. Although Sondheim felt that Gilbert's play was weighed down by its narrative structure, he was intrigued by some of the ideas contained in the peripheral material, letters, and anecdotes from actual assassins. Some years later John Weidman, who had collaborated with Sondheim on *Pacific Overtures*, came to him with a desire to create a musical about Woodrow Wilson and the League of Nations. Sondheim was not excited by this idea, but recalled Gilbert's script. Weidman was interested and the two artists located Gilbert and asked him to permit them to use his idea. Gilbert generously acquiesced and work began.

Initially, the plan was to examine assassins throughout history, beginning with Julius Caesar. But Sondheim and Weidman soon discovered that the subject was huge. They decided to confine their work to a study of people who had tried, with varying degrees of success, to kill the President of the United States. They investigated the lives of the assassins and the social matrix that resulted in the violence. This provided them with a vast amount of information, as Weidman explains:

> They [the assassins] really are fascinating. . . . Not just because of the dramatic and horrifying way in which they put punctuation marks at the end of their own lives and the lives of others, but because it turned out that the journey they had followed on the way to that moment was in each case extraordinary. When you put them together and looked at them as a group, they formed a kind of mosaic that had meaning and suggested that we really had something to write about.
>
> One of the things we found out as we looked at them is that we were not writing about shooting at the President of the United States. . . . What's provocative and upsetting and disturbing is the lives they led up to that point and what those lives reveal. So in a sense the appalling and horrifying acts with which they ended their journeys were like tickets of admission into the show, rather than what the show was about.[8]

After two workshop readings, the piece which resulted was a relatively brief, ninety-minute revue that encompassed a kaleidoscopic examination of both the notorious individuals of the title and the historical reality that gave birth to the murderous deeds.

The musical opens under the tawdry lights of a carnival as the calliope plays out the central theme. This musical motif, which is repeated throughout the piece, is in fact a variation of "Hail to the Chief." The pomp and ceremony surrounding the President of the United States is thus immediately, but subtly, placed in comic relief. The dark comedic tone is established as the Proprietor of a shooting gallery importunes a motley crowd to "C'mere and kill a President." This iconoclastic sales pitch sets the satiric tone. The red, white, and blue bunting and lights surround a revolving wheel on which various Presidents are depicted. Without regard to their chronological order in history, the would-be assassins stroll in. The personality of each malcontent is immediately defined by the lyrics and musical connotation of their interaction with the barker. Czolgosz, the angry leftist who murdered President McKinley, is welcomed with:

> No job? Cupboard bare?
> One room, no one there?
> Hey pal, don't despair—
> You wanna shoot a President?[9]

Whereas John Hinckley, the inept would-be assassin of President Reagan, who acted in order to attract the attention of film star Jodie Foster, is lured to the stall with the promise:

> You can get the prize
> With the big blue eyes
> *(Indicates a sexy doll)*
> Skinny little thighs
> And those big blue eyes...
> (p. 1-2)

Guiteau, the ever-optimistic killer of President Garfield, is greeted:

> Hey fella
> Feel like you're a failure?
> Bailiff on your tail? Your
> Wife run off for good?
> Hey, fella,
> Feel misunderstood?
> C'mere and kill a President...
> (p. 1-4)

The wit in the run-on rhyme is characteristically Sondheim, but is achieved without destroying the dramatic content. Zangara, the Italian immigrant who attempted to take the life of Franklin D. Roosevelt, is hailed in a mocking Italian accent:

> What's-a-wrong, boy?
> Boss-a treat you crummy?

Trouble with you tummy?
This-a bring you some relief.
(*Holds out gun*)
Here, give some
Hail-a to da chief—
(p. 1-4)

Sondheim and Weidman exploit the frustrated man's stomach problems as the ostensible reason for his murderous endeavors. This may appear a facile and humorous explanation for violence, but it is based on an accurate historical fact. Much of the black comedy results not from the creators' fancy, but from their use of actual details and responses to the events. The constant juxtaposition of intensely dramatic sequences with scenes of broad comedy gives the musical a nightmare quality that is intentional. The absurdity of some of the characters caused the critics to accuse the writers of going beyond the excesses of the satiric skits in television programs like *Saturday Night Live*. This accusation is not inaccurate, but wrong-minded. The satiric absurdity is directed not at the characters, but at the society that helped create them. The two women, Squeaky Fromme and Sarah Jane Moore, are drawn broadly, but this does not lessen the disturbing quality of their distorted psyches. The comedy sequences serve to highlight the horror, and these two characters serve a similar purpose to Mrs. Lovett in *Sweeney Todd*. Their humorous excesses reflect and intensify the ultimate confusion that gives rise to murder.

In the barker's lilting refrain, Sondheim composes an apparent paean in praise of the American Dream:

Everybody's
Got the right
To be happy,
Don't stay mad,
Life's not as bad
As it seems.

If you keep your
goal in sight,
You can climb
To any height
Everybody's
Got the right
To their dreams...
(p. 1-3)

This deliberately banal song provides the audience with the key to understanding *Assassins*. It is a gentle and melodic, lyrically optimistic show tune. It expresses both in the straightforward lyric and the unassertive melodic line the basic tenet of the American System. Each individual can and should aspire to happiness and success. It is this incontestable truism that lies at the heart of the great American musicals of the 1940's and 1950's. It is consequently fitting that Sondheim, who has redefined the form and scope of the musical theater, once again uses the musical theater as his touchstone to examine and assess American society. Just as in *Follies* Sondheim analyzed the *Zeitgeist* of the disillusioned 1970's through the distorted prism of musical theater history, so in *Assassins* he uses the music of America to explore the changing aspirations of the American Dream. Beginning with the unambiguous optimism of the opening refrain, Sondheim's music ranges through the past two hundred years of American music. By remaining true to these musical antecedents, Sondheim has composed a score that is immediately appealing, readily available, and melodic. It is a compendium of American musical history from Civil War ballads and the tender nostalgia of Stephen Foster, to John Philip Sousa marches, soft rock sentimentality, barbershop quartets, and the lilting waltzes of turn-of-the-century America—juxtaposed with gospel, Western hoedown, and Copland-like cadences. Each musical style suggests a different era and set of values, but at the heart of each song is the belief that "Everybody's got the right to be happy." It is this fiction lurking behind the glossy facade of American success stories that *Assassins* exposes. One can't help but see the analogy to the longing that Sondheim explored in *Gypsy* so many years ago. Everybody wants to be a star. The show business metaphor has been amplified to include all of society. *Assassins* dissects the thwarted hopes and the effect that those blasted dreams can have on a society that continues, despite all evidence to the contrary, to be lulled by the myths. This dream trip through America's past exposes its hypocrisy, pain, and destruction with both poignancy and mordant humor.

Sondheim's and Weidman's exploration of the various individuals who have committed the ultimate crime in attempting to destroy the representative of the system which in some way has repressed them combines historical fact with wild flights of fancy. Characters from different periods meet and interact with little regard to historical accuracy, but at the core of the piece is the indisputable truth that each of these men and women did exist and each did try to kill. With the arrival of John Wilkes Booth, the satiric edge becomes a little more keen. Booth is in many ways the most interesting character in the work, and if the ensemble show has a central character at all, then it must be Booth. He is suave, debonair, and passionately committed to the justness of his actions. Urbane and elegant, he cannot be dismissed as a deranged social misfit. Picking up the Proprietor's refrain, Booth takes command. The shabby group become his acolytes and he proclaims:

Don't be scared
You won't prevail,
Everybody's
Free to fail.
No one can be put in jail
For his dreams.
(p. 1-7)

In a jaunty contrapuntal duet the barker and Booth spell out all the advantages of a "free country." The irony of these apparent truisms is confirmed as the perverse chorus line of killers stretch out across the stage and glare down at the audience with Brechtian contempt. They sing out their demands:

Rich man, poor man,
Black or white,
Pick your apple,
Take a bite,
Everybody
Just hold tight
To your dreams
Everybody's
Got the right

To their dreams...
(p. 1-8)

It is in chilling moments like this, when music and dramatic image are placed in stark juxtaposition, that *Assassins* achieves brilliance. Singing their jaunty theme tune, they slowly raise their weapons and take aim at their targets. The easy lyrical tune with its pop sentiment expressed in a popular form contrasts vividly with the disturbing undercurrents and imminent violence expressed in the action.

As the group takes aim, "Hail to the Chief" is played by a military band. Booth excuses himself. A shot rings out and the assassin's history of America commences. Our guide through this panoramic survey is a twentieth-century folk singer, who, with his accordion and harmonica, sits on the sidelines, observing and commenting. His observations reflect the average man's view of the events. To him, these misfits are aberrant individuals who may interrupt the flow of history, but do not really alter it. With folksy wisdom he proclaims:

> Every now and then
> A madman's
> Bound to come along.
> Doesn't stop the story—
> Story's pretty strong.
> Doesn't change the song...
> (p. 2-9)

His description of Booth is of an actor who was never quite the success he hoped to be. Jealousy of his brother and his own drinking problem could have caused Booth's angst, or as Sondheim has the Balladeer snidely suggest, perhaps it was "bad reviews." This apparently glib and humorous explanation of Booth's action offended many critics. What they failed to understand was that Sondheim was basing his lyric on historical data. People at the time of Lincoln's assassination did in fact attribute Booth's deed to professional jealousy. Many of the most bizarre motives and events in the script are not inventions, but are based on research of the period. Sondheim prefers the term "received wisdom" to refer to the factual foundation upon which he built his creation. The recurrent reference to Booth's "bad reviews" is not an example of egregious poor taste. Booth was an actor whose act expressed his theatricality and was even staged in a theater. More significantly, Sondheim uses the theatrical metaphor throughout the piece as a means of exploring the distorted values of American society.

Booth lies helpless in a barn awaiting capture. His leg has been broken during his escape and he begs his accomplice to assist him set down his justification for posterity. He is desperate that his actions be understood. Sondheim gives the dying Booth dignity and passion. He sings with the melodic intensity of a tragic hero. The most apt comparison is the aggrieved fury and despair of Sondheim's Sweeney Todd. Booth's reasons for his act are idealistic, if politically suspect. In a beautiful aria he expresses his indignation:

> Hunt me down, smear my name,
> Say I did it for the fame,
> What I did was kill the man who killed my country.
> Now the southland will mend,
> Now this bloody war can end,
> Because someone slew the tyrant
> Just as Brutus slew the tyrant—
> (p. 2-13)

But Sondheim does not allow Booth's ideology to be unquestioningly accepted. The melodic grandeur suggests to the audience the character's honest dedication to the Confederate cause, but the song ends and Booth's hatred and bigotry emerge in the ascending line of the climax:

> How the union can never recover
> From that vulgar
> High and mighty
> Niggerlover
> Never—!
> (p. 2-14)

But this loathing is modified in the gentle coda as Booth sadly sings:

> ...Damn my soul if you must,
> Let my body turn to dust
> Let it mingle with the ashes of the country.
> Let them curse me to hell,
> Leave it to history to tell:
> What I did, I did well,
> And I did it for my country.
> (p. 2-14)

and puts a gun to his head.

The mounting pathos of the melody and the passion of the lyrics result in an inevitable audience empathy but this bond is broken by the Balladeer who has the final word. This character does not serve as the authors' mouthpiece but rather provides an historical perspective. It is he who voices the point of view of the nation at the time of the murder. He dismisses Booth's act as madness and, extending the theatrical metaphor, sings out his homily:

But traitors just get jeers and boos
Not visits to their graves
While Lincoln, who got mixed reviews,
Because of you, John, now gets only raves.
(p. 2-15)

Clutching Booth's diary, the folk singer strolls off. Booth's actions have become the stuff of folk legend and his legacy is enshrined in song.

As "Hail to the Chief" is banged out on a honky-tonk piano, the scene shifts to a bar, its period indeterminate, its guests a diverse assortment of malcontents. There is nothing heroic about these men, as they share their sense of impotence and despair. Like Sondheim, Weidman does not adopt a single attitude or style in depicting his characters. Some are ludicrous figures of fun, while others assume a dignity and pathos. Byck, who hijacked a plane and attempted to kill Nixon by crashing into the White House; Guiteau, the ever-cheerful killer of Garfield; the inept Hinckley; and the immigrant Zangara with his stomach cramps, never have the power of Booth. But the passionate Czolgosz represents oppressed workers with great intensity.

Prompted by Booth, Zangara strides out, determined to cure his aching belly by killing the man who represents the oppressive system which is the source of his agony. As a band plays Sousa's march "El Capitan," the scene shifts to Miami and the dulcet tones of an announcer are interrupted by a shout. Zangara has made good his threat, but missed. The eager eyewitnesses crowd the radio microphone to give their account of the historic event. Sondheim sets his lyrics to the Sousa march and again this is a perfect juxtaposition. Sousa suggests everything that is upbeat, patriotic and essentially American. The vanity of the crowd is set in ironic contrast to this music. Each bystander claims to be a hero and to have saved Roosevelt. Again the satire is pointed. It is not simply the deluded assassin but the self-important throng who are being skewered. The focus of the scene is divided. On one side of the stage the onlookers trumpet their bravery to the Sousa march. On the other, Zangara, strapped to an electric chair, sings out his plaint to an Italian tarantella. The bouncy folk-song contrasts with Zangara's angry rejection of capitalist exploitation. Sondheim evokes his fury and broken English in the structure of the lyric. It is in the interjections of the crowd, however, that Sondheim's genius at dramatizing the inanities of media-struck American society is evident:

> *Bystander #1 (man)*
> *(Suddenly coming to life and seizing the microphone)*
> We're crowded up close,
> And I see this guy,
> He's squeezing by,
> I catch his eye,
> I say to him, "Where do you
> Think you're trying to go, boy?
> Whoa, boy!"
> I say, "Listen, you runt,
> You're not pulling that stunt—
> No gentleman pushes their way to the front."
> I say, "Move to the back!", which he does with a grunt—
> Which is how I saved Roosevelt!
> (p.4-21)

They jostle each other in a desperate attempt to get the attention of the media. Sondheim is not cruel. There is no Swiftian violence but his ear is so acute that the audience cannot fail to get his point. As the song reaches its conclusion, the self-important, shallow bystanders sing out with righteous zeal:

> Lucky I was there
> I'm on the front page ... is that bizarre?
> And all of those pictures, like a star!
> (p. 4-25)

and Zangara is electrocuted in a flash of electricity. Again, this bizarre juxtaposition has the force of black comedy.

The scene that follows is based on fact. The socialist revolutionary Emma Goldman did meet presidential assassin Czolgosz. The content of the meeting is Weidman's imaginative construct but it provides another perspective on the plight of the working man. Although Zangara declares passionately that his act is neither "left nor right" but "only American," his accent and the emphasis on his stomach rob his act of any dignity. Czolgosz is different. He has none of Booth's flair, but possesses a quiet dignity. His infatuation with Goldman is not satirized. The scene between the intense demagogue and ignorant worker is the gentlest and most poignant in the play.

The mood is immediately shattered in the comedic sequence which follows. This disjunction of tones gives the piece its nightmare energy. The exchanges between Charles Manson groupie Squeaky Fromme and the confused middle-class housewife Sarah Jane Moore, both of whom tried unsuccessfully to kill Gerald Ford, are certainly the funniest in the musical. Their girlish confidences, the satiric pillorying of contemporary pop culture, and their ineptitude provide Weidman with hilarious comic material. Some critics mentioned that the authors are drawing a parallel between the quality of the President and his assassin: the more inept the President, the more blundering his killer.

The focus returns to Czolgosz who stands caressing his gun and contemplating the pain in the lives of the many men who were exploited to manufacture it. This song ennobles the unhappy assassin, and as he is joined by some of the other members of the company, the essence of each character is exemplified in Sondheim's musical language. Booth is the Mephistophelean tempter, insidiously urging the simple Czolgosz that:

> *(Softly)*
> And all you have to do
> Is
> Move your little finger,
> Move your little finger and—
> (*Czolgosz clicks the trigger*)
> You can change the world.
> (p. 7-36)

His melody and lyric is insinuating and contrasts both with the workman's simple plaint and the ebullient Guiteau who sings his paean of praise to a sprightly rhythm. Sondheim's careful contrast of the dramatic impact of his work is clear as he stops lyric and music for Guiteau to make his point:

> What a wonder is a gun!
> What a versatile invention!
> First of all, when you've a gun—
> (*He points it out front, slowly panning over the audience; music stops*)
> Everybody pays attention.
> (*Music resumes*)
> (p. 7-36)

The power of the gun pointed straight at the audience is undeniably effective. When Sarah Jane Moore joins the men, the musical line is altered. Reminiscent of Mrs. Lovett's opening number, Moore is a frenetic creature whose disorganized character and life Sondheim joyously depicts in the starts and pauses of her solo:

I got this really great gun—
(*Fishing*)
Shit, where is it?
And you can make a state—
—ment—
(*Pulls out a shoe*)
Wrong—
With a gun—
Even if you fail.
It tells 'em who you are,
Where you stand,
This one was on sale. It—
No, not the shoe—
Well, actually the shoe was, too.
(pp. 7-37-38)

The explosion of chaotic energy is hilarious and Sondheim perfectly duplicates the tone of Weidman's earlier scene. The four assassins join in a tightly harmonized barbershop quartet. Again, the sound and image are at odds and make a humorous but pointed comment. The turn-of-the-century American quality of the sound and the unanimity of purpose suggest that the extraordinary foursome are perfect representations of their culture, but they brandish guns, not flags, and the terrifying violence at the core of cozy America is reaffirmed.

John Hinckley's disarmingly simple statement, "Guns are neat things aren't they? You can kill extraordinary people with very little effort,"[10] seems to be the inspiration for this disturbing number. Guns are the force of equality. The leader of the most powerful nation in the world can be blown away by a gun in the hands of a nonentity. Czolgosz concludes the song by repeating the opening verse, but the lyric is significantly altered. At the start he sings, "It takes a lot of men to make a gun," but with resolute determination he concludes, "A gun kills many men before it's done." The men he enumerates are the workers who toiled to make the gun.

Just as the Balladeer breaks the emphatic bond between the audience and Booth, so he again appears to comment on Czolgosz's murder of McKinley. He sets the scene for the assassination which occurred at the Pan-American Exposition in Buffalo. Sondheim uses two devices to inform this song. The first is the simple technique of adding a detail each time the refrain is repeated, which gives the number the feel of a folk song.

Consequently, the initial refrain:

> To the Pan-American Exposition
> In Buffalo . . .
> (p. 8-40)

is modified in the final refrain to:

> In the temple of music
> By the Tower of light
> Between the fountain of abundance
> And the court of lilies
> At the great Pan-American Exposition
> In Buffalo . . .
> (p. 8-42)

Sondheim augments this form by structuring the scene and song around the notion of waiting in line. This is utilized in the staging and the lyric. The fair goers wait in line to greet the President and Czolgosz joins them. He is waiting in line to kill—but the idea that all men can metaphorically work their way to the head of the line and be successful is articulated by the Balladeer:

> In the U.S.A.
> You can have your say,
> You can set your goals
> And seize the day,
> You've been given the freedom
> To work your way
> To the head of the line—
> (*Czolgosz at last reaches McKinley—and shoots—Bang!*)
> To the head of the line!
> (p. 8-42)

It is this lie that Czolgosz attacks and the blithe optimism of the folk singer is punctuated by the blast of the workman's gun.

Samuel Byck, decked out in a Santa Claus suit, sends a rambling message to Leonard Bernstein. A tape was actually sent by Byck to Bernstein. The contents were never divulged, but Weidman creates a funny, poignant monologue in which Byck bemoans the lack of real love songs. This wanna-be hero is both pathetic and funny. There is comedy in his grandiose impotence but his frustration will have a tragic outcome. Byck's monologue is suspended in time and space, as the lights come up on a fanatic Squeaky Fromme and a melancholy John Hinckley. Sondheim has written a perfect duet for this desolate pair. It drips with the treacly sentimentality of seventies pop music. If one doesn't know the characters, nor pay too much attention to the lyrics, one could easily mistake this for a Karen Carpenter hit. Again Sondheim's musical mimicry works with devastating precision. This is the sound of the characters' generation and the excessive devotion promised in the lyric is typical of sentimental pop tunes. It is only when these emotions are placed in context and the dedication to Charles Manson and Jodie Foster is clarified, that the sickness behind the passion emerges. Even the diminutives inherent in the names "Charlie" and "Jodie" add a horrible cloying quality to the unrequited love of the intense acolyte and the deranged fan. Their feelings of lack of self-worth, "I am nothing" (again a recognizable phrase from this genre of music), become ominous when the audience realizes that the only way for these two to show their devotion is to kill. The gallant lover of the traditional love song is in fact a pathetic loser with his shirt hanging out of his pants. He can only assert his identity with a gun. Their shared passion is expressed in this macabre duet. As he shouts repeatedly at an ever-brightening picture of Reagan, she taunts him by repeating Reagan's wisecracks.

Perhaps the most bizarre pairing that Weidman comes up with occurs in the next scene in which Guiteau attempts to instruct Moore in the niceties of shooting. The debonair entrepeneur attempts simultaneously to seduce the frumpy woman. Guiteau is finally given his moment of glory by Sondheim in a gospel-like song whose buoyant rhythms push him up the stairs to the gallows. Sondheim has composed a perverse dance of death as he cakewalks his way to eternity. The first line of the song is based on an actual poem that Guiteau wrote on the morning of his execution. His unfailing faith and optimism last as he struts up and down the scaffold and finally stands on top of the trap door waiting to be hanged. As his body falls his moment of triumph is commented on with gusto by the Balladeer, who gives the assassin a cheerful send-off:

Just wait until tomorrow,
Tomorrow they'll all climb aboard!
What if you never
Got to be President?
You'll be remembered—
(Guiteau dances briefly)

Look on the bright side—
(*Again*)
Trust in tomorrow—
(*Once more*)
Guiteau, Balladeer
And the Lord!
(p. 12-56)

Moore's problems are far from over. In the best tradition of slapstick comedy she, Fromme, and a bemused Gerald Ford struggle ineptly to be assassins and victim. They struggle with dogs, children, and falling bullets. Their zany farce is succeeded by a poignant monologue by Byck. His anger at the political mess in America becomes entangled in his own lack of self-worth and longing for parental approval. In Weidman's work, the anguish behind the comedy is always present. The musical does not have an extended narrative line. The characters are revealed to the audience in brief, bright flashes. This is an episodic kaleidoscope, not an in-depth analysis.

It is, however, in the final twenty minutes of *Assassins* that this survey is pulled into focus. Over a wordless lamentation, the assassins file forward and justify their acts. As this ghostly chorus importunes the audience, Byck harangues them with a repeated demand, "Where's my prize?" The significance of the opening scene in the shooting gallery is consequently recalled without repeating the dramatic metaphor. As the tempo accelerates, the demands grow more strident and the others join Byck in laying claim to their promised reward. They are silenced by the Balladeer who wistfully sums up their achievements:

And it didn't mean a nickel,
You just shed a little blood,
And a lot of people shed a lot of tears.
(p. 15-67)

All the assassins are made to confront the meaninglessness of their acts as the Balladeer proves that their grandiose gesture didn't achieve what they had hoped for. At first the assassins appear to accept his negative assessment:

No, it
Doesn't make a bit of difference,
Does it?

Others
(*Variously*)
Didn't.
Ever.
Byck
Fuck it!
(p. 15-67)

It seems that the sensible common man's view will prevail as the Balladeer reasserts, to an easy folk rhythm, the verities of the American Dream. He attempts to convince the belligerent killers that they can achieve their goals if only they will believe in the system. Here Sondheim permits his scepticism to become more blatant as the Balladeer's promises are clearly disingenuous:

I just heard
On the news
Where the mailman won the lottery.
Goes to show:
When you lose, what you do is try again.
(p. 15-68)

He promotes the fantasies and cynically suggests that the killers wait for chance or fate to grant them their inevitable reward. The Balladeer becomes an apologist for the promises of the capitalist ideal. In his world anyone can grow up to be President, but the deception inherent in these expectations stands before the audience. The despondent and frustrated group of assassins emerges as a testament to the failure of this fool's paradise. They are the nightmarish underside of the dream and for them Sondheim composes "Another National Anthem." This song is the most powerful in the musical and perhaps the most overtly political piece of music Sondheim has ever written. Yet it is not simply didactic but functions within the dramatic context as a plea for this group of individuals who have failed so completely to come to terms with and function within the system. The musical language no longer harkens back to the traditions of Broadway but is rather "closer to one of Tom Waits's lurching quasi-Salvation Army Band marches."[11] The group of assassins is not grotesque but pathetic as they sing to a militaristic beat:

It's the other National Anthem, saying—
If you want to hear—
It says, "Bullshit!" ...

Czolgosz
It says, "Never!"—
Guiteau
It says, "Sorry!"—
Loud and clear—
(p. 15-69)

They are the failures, the outsiders, "the ones," as Sondheim expresses it, "that can't get in to the ball park." This baseball imagery is quintessentially American and serves as a perfect indictment of the society and its mores.

The song is structured like a debate. The assassins present their negative views of the world and the Balladeer counters their arguments with his breezy optimism. He offers them a bandaid philosophy:

There are those who keep forgetting
That the Country's built on dreams—
(p. 15-70)

But the assassins march to a different drum and their confidence grows as they gradually realize their own power. They can make people pay attention as they express their anger to a martial beat:

They may not want to hear it,
But they listen,
Once they think it's gonna stop the game...
(p. 15-70)

The "music" they hear becomes "screams" as the song builds in intensity into a powerful refain:

Like the other National Anthem
Says to each and every fan:
If you can't do what you want to,
Then you do the things you can.
You've got to try again!
(p. 15-71)

The Balladeer attempts to counter their growing fervor with promises:

And you forgot
That it's a place
Where you can make the lies come true—
(p. 15-71)

But the assassins drive him from the stage. Yet despite the pounding impetus of this other "National Anthem," Sondheim ends the song with

Byck's cynical comment, "Sure, the mailman won the lottery." It is this pessimistic disbelief in anything with which Sondheim leaves his audience as the scene changes one final time, and we are transported to the Texas School Book Depository, November 22, 1963.

Contemporary audiences have not had sufficient time to distance themselves from the Kennedy assassination. In treading on this still very painful ground, the authors opened themselves to all kinds of accusations of irreverence and tastelessness. Yet it is the immediacy of the event that gives the sequence such power. The audience knows the inevitable consequences, but the tension lies in the self-deceptive hope that perhaps this time the outcome will be different. Sondheim and Weidman exploit this quality and do not make the assassination a foregone conclusion. Oswald has to be persuaded to kill. His conspirators, however, are not the Mafia or the F.B.I., but the other assassins, those who came before and those who will follow him. Lincoln's assassination began the chain of events that led, the piece argues, inevitably to the death of Kennedy. There is no humor in this scene. The horror is too immediate.

The distraught Oswald sits alone, preparing to take his own life. Booth becomes his Mephistopheles, transforming Oswald into an agent of vengeance. It is he who will validate all their acts and give them a place in history. His action, Booth argues, will establish the legitimacy of their deeds. For the contemporary audience the implications are clear. Kennedy's death is a watershed event—the crucial test against which all other acts of political violence are measured. The progressive horror of the scene is intense as the impotent audience watches Oswald move towards the inevitable conclusion. The wily Booth dismisses Oswald's doubts. He argues convincingly that the only path to immortality for the impotent loser is through violence. Alone he is not sufficiently persuasive, but the other assassins materialize and add their pleas to his. They become a force of history as their chant builds to a fortissimo:

> We admire you...
> We're your family...
> You are the future...
> We're depending on you...
> Make us proud...
> All you have to do is squeeze your little finger.

> Squeeze your little finger...
> You can change the wor—
> (*Oswald fires.*)
> (p. 16-89)

But this is not the final image. The assassins return and sing with sadness:

> Everybody's
> Got the right
> To be happy.
> Don't be mad,
> Life's not as bad
> As it seems.
> (p. 7-90)

The shallow promises of the American Dream are reestablished. The macabre chorus line reforms and glares out at the audience. As they sing the superficially optimistic tune, they longingly caress their weapons, slowly raise them and point them at the audience. *Assassins* ends with the echo of their shots.

This is not theater for the weak of stomach. It is brave, innovative, and controversial. As *New York Times* critic David Richards remarks:

> Mr. Sondheim and Mr. Weidman have produced a morality play about the forces of good and bad, and then boldly exiled goodness to the wings.
> No musical in the last decade has dared this much.[12]

Sondheim has again crossed the boundaries that he himself has drawn and has taken the musical into uncharted territory. He examines assassins not because of some sick fascination with violence and death, but in order better to understand and perhaps alter the mores of our society. He confronts pain in order to cauterize the decay and heal the sickness which lurk at the core of our society. This kind of catharsis is what makes theater significant, and Sondheim has proved yet again that the musical form does not trivialize, but enhances the dramtic event.

Sondheim is not easy, but art is not easy. His talent is defined by the challenges he sets himself and his audiences. Like his protagonist in *Sunday in the Park with George*, Sondheim is impelled to keep "moving on." His work is a never-ending source of theatrical exhilaration and intellectual challenge, and the prospect of his ongoing creative output guarantees the continuing growth in stature of the American musical.

Notes

1. The Musical Comes of Age

1. George Jean Nathan, "A View of Musical Comedy," *American Mercury* 64 (Feb. 1947): 196–97.

2. Clive Barnes and Walter Kerr are the most obvious examples.

3. See, for example, Gerald M. Bordman, *American Musical Theater: A Chronicle* (New York: Oxford Univ. Press, 1978); Jack Burton, *The Blue Book of Broadway Musicals* (New York: Century House, 1976); Lehman Engel, *The American Musical Theater* (New York: Macmillan, 1975); Martin Gottfried, *Broadway Musicals* (New York: Abrams, 1979).

4. John Lahr, "Sondheim's Little Deaths," *Harper's*, Apr. 1979, p. 71.

5. Sheldon Harnick, in "Symposium: The Anatomy of a Theater Song," mod. Richard Lewine, *Dramatists Guild Quarterly*, Spring 1977, p. 19.

6. Harold Prince, *Contradictions: Notes on Twenty-six Years in the Theater* (New York: Dodd, Mead, 1974).

7. Stephen Sondheim and Harold Prince, "On Collaboration Between Authors and Directors," *Dramatists Guild Quarterly* 16 (Summer 1979): 14.

8. Harold Prince quoted in Hubert Saal, "How to Play Hal Prince," *Newsweek*, 26 July 1971, p. 70.

9. Sondheim quoted in Craig Zadan, "A Funny Thing Happened on the Way to the Follies," *After Dark*, June 1971, p. 26.

10. Sondheim quoted in Guy Flatley, "When Stephen Sondheim Writes Words and Music, Some Critics Don't Leave the Theater Humming," *People*, 5 Apr. 1976, pp. 69–70.

11. See Prince, *Contradictions*, pp. 73, 128.

12. Sondheim quoted in Tom Burke, "Steve Has Stopped Collaborating," *ASCAP Today*, Aug. 1970, p. 17.

13. Sondheim quoted in Zadan, "A Funny Thing Happened on the Way to the Follies," p. 24.

14. Gottfried, *Broadway Musicals*, p. 322.

15. Lehman Engel, *Words with Music* (New York: Macmillan, 1972), p. 16.

16. Sondheim quoted in Charles Michener, "Words And Music—By Sondheim," *Newsweek*, 23 Apr. 1973, p. 55.

17. Sondheim quoted in John S. Wilson, "Everything's Coming Up Sondheim," *Theatre Arts*, June 1962, p. 64.

18. Stephen Sondheim, "Theater Lyrics," in *Playwrights, Lyricists, Composers on Theater*, ed. Otis Guernsey (New York: Dodd, Mead, 1974), p. 87.

19. Lahr, "Sondheim's Little Deaths," pp. 76–78.

20. Robert Marx, "Drama and the Opera Libretto," *Yale Theater* 4, no. 3 (1973): 125.

21. Sondheim, "Theater Lyrics," p. 61.

22. Arthur Laurents quoted in Michener, "Words And Music—By Sondheim," p. 55.

23. Sondheim, "Theater Lyrics," p. 64.

24. Ibid.

25. Ibid., p. 65.

26. Ibid., p. 66.

27. Ibid., p. 70.

28. Ibid., p. 71.

29. Ibid., pp. 75–76.

30. Ibid., pp. 84–85.

31. Gottfried, *Broadway Musicals*, p. 71.

32. Lahr, "Sondheim's Little Deaths," pp. 72–74.

33. Ibid., p. 76.

34. Ibid., p. 78.

35. Ibid.

36. Ibid.

37. Julius Novick, "In Search of a New Consensus," *Saturday Review*, 3 Apr. 1976, p. 39.

38. Alan J. Lerner in Arthur Laurents and others, "The Librettist: Indispensable Stylist, Sometimes Forgotten," *Dramatists Guild Quarterly*, Winter 1980, p. 17.

39. Novick, "In Search of a New Consensus," pp. 39–42.

2. *A Funny Thing Happened on the Way to the Forum* and *Anyone Can Whistle*

1. Gottfried, *Broadway Musicals*, p. 29; John Simon, *Theatre Arts*, July 1962, p. 66.

2. Robert Brustein, "Vox Populi, Vox Box," *New Republic*, 28 May 1962, p. 29.

3. Burt Shevelove quoted in "The Musical Theater: A Talk by Stephen Sondheim," *Dramatists Guild Quarterly* 15 (Autumn 1978): 12.

4. Sondheim quoted in Wilson, "Everything's Coming Up Sondheim," p. 65.

5. Burt Shevelove quoted in Craig Zadan, *Sondheim and Co.* (New York: Avon Books, 1976), p. 77. All subsequent citations will be from this edition unless otherwise noted.

6. Sondheim quoted in Dan Sullivan, "Stephen Sondheim Now Sleepy Giant of Lyricism," *Los Angeles Times*, 10 Oct. 1971, Calendar, p. 28.

7. Sondheim, "The Musical Theater," p. 12.

8. Sondheim, "Theater Lyrics," p. 66.

9. Stephen Sondheim, *A Funny Thing Happened on the Way to the Forum* (New York: Music Theater International, 1962), p. 6. All subsequent quotations will be from this edition, with page numbers cited parenthetically within the text. Authorial elisions have been indicated throughout my study by the conventional spaced ellipsis points; Sondheim's own use of points has been indicated throughout by three closed points.

10. Sondheim quoted in Zadan, *Sondheim and Co.*, p. 79.

11. Sondheim, "The Musical Theater," p. 11.

12. Engel, Words with Music, p. 106.

13. Henry Hewes, "Mostellaria Zero-Zero," *Saturday Review of Literature*, 26 May 1962, p. 22; Simon, *Theatre Arts*, p. 67; John McCarter, "Cheerful Chaos," *New Yorker*, 19 May 1962, p. 103; John McClain, "Zero Mostel Guarantees a Merry Time," *Journal American*, 9 May 1962, reprint, *New York Theatre Critics' Reviews* (hereafter cited as *NYTCR*), May 1962, p. 290; Norman Nadel, "*A Funny Thing*—at Alvin," *New York World-Telegram and the Sun*, 9 May 1962, reprint, *NYTCR*, May 1962, p. 292.

14. T. E. Kalem, "Laugh Potion," *Time*, 17 Apr. 1972, reprint, *NYTCR*, April 1972, p. 350; Douglas Watt, "Silvers Stars in *Forum* Revival," *New York Daily News*, 31 Mar. 1972, reprint, *NYTCR*, Mar. 1972, p. 349; Martin Gottfried, "A Funny Thing Happened on the Way to the Forum," *Women's Wear Daily*, 3 Apr. 1972, reprint, *NYTCR*, Apr. 1972, p. 349.

15. Sondheim quoted in Zadan, *Sondheim and Co.*, p. 93.

16. Ibid.

17. Stephen Sondheim, *Anyone Can Whistle* (New York: Random House, 1965), p. 6. All subsequent quotations will be from this edition, with page numbers cited parenthetically within the text.

18. Paul Sheren and Tom Sutcliffe, "Stephen Sondheim and the American Musical," in *Theater '74*, ed. Sheridan Morley (London: Hutchinson, 1974), pp. 203–4.

19. Norman Nadel, "Something to *Whistle* About," *New York World-Telegram and the Sun*, 6 Apr. 1964, reprint, *NYTCR*, Apr. 1964, p. 303.

20. Michener, "Words And Music—By Sondheim," p. 64.

21. Letter to the author, August 18, 1988.

22. Al Carmines in Jeff Sweet and others, "On Theater Music," in *Playwrights, Lyricists, Composers*, ed. Guernsey, p. 155.

23. Whitney Bolton quoted in Zadan, *Sondheim and Co.*, p. 105; Michael Charles Adams, "The Lyrics of Stephen Sondheim: Form and Function" (Ph.D. diss., Northwestern Univ., 1980), pp. 71–72.

3. *Company*

1. Sondheim, "The Musical Theater," pp. 15–16.

2. Ibid., pp. 13–15.

3. Leonard Harris, "Company," *WCBS TV2*, 26 Apr. 1970, reprint, *NYTCR*, Apr. 1970, p. 264.

4. *Time*, 11 May 1970, p. 62.

5. Sondheim quoted in Zadan, *Sondheim and Co.*, p. 131.

6. Stanley Kauffmann, "Company, *New Republic*, 23 May 1970, p. 20.

7. Prince, *Contradictions*, p. 150.

8. Ibid., pp. 149–50.

9. Sondheim, "The Musical Theater," p. 20.

10. Sondheim quoted in Zadan, *Sondheim and Co.*, pp. 139–40.

11. Prince, *Contradictions*, p. 149.

12. Sondheim, "The Musical Theater," p. 17.

13. Stephen Sondheim, *Company* (New York: Random House, 1970), pp. 9–10. All subsequent quotations will be from this edition, with page numbers cited parenthetically within the text.

14. Sondheim, "Theater Lyrics," p. 74.

15. Walter Kerr, "*Company* Original and Uncompromising," *Sunday Times* (New York), 3 May 1970, reprint, *NYTCR*, May 1970, p. 263; Clive Barnes, "*Company* Offers a Guide to New York's Marital Jungle," *New York Times*, 27 Apr. 1970, reprint, *NYTCR*, Apr. 1970, p. 262.

16. Sondheim quoted in Burke, "Steve Has Stopped Collaborating," p. 16.

17. Sondheim quoted in Zadan, *Sondheim and Co.*, p. 140.

18. Prince, *Contradictions*, p. 149.

19. John Simon, "Futile Fugue," *New York*, 11 May 1970, p. 56.

20. Sondheim, "The Musical Theater," p. 8.

21. Anthony Perkins quoted in Zadan, *Sondheim and Co.*, pp. 144–45.

22. Sondheim quoted in Zadan, *Sondheim and Co.*, p. 129.

23. Sondheim interview by Paul Kresh in *Stereo Review*, July 1971, p. 74.

24. Adams, "The Lyrics of Stephen Sondheim," p. 140.

25. Martin Gottfried, "*Company* Is Quite Simply in a League by Itself," *Women's Wear Daily*, 27 Apr. 1970, reprint, *NYTCR*, Apr. 1970, p. 261; Gottfried, *Broadway Musicals*, p. 322.

26. Michael Bennett quoted in Zadan, *Sondheim and Co.*, pp. 137–39.

27. Sondheim, "Theater Lyrics," p. 87.

28. Ibid.

29. Adams, "The Lyrics of Stephen Sondheim," p. 176.

30. *Marry Me a Little*, RCA Records ABL 1–4159.

31. Sondheim and Prince quoted in Zadan, *Sondheim and Co.*, pp. 140–41.

32. Gottfried, "*Company* in a League by Itself," p. 261; John J. O'Connor, "Company," *Wall Street Journal*, 28 Apr. 1970, reprint, *NYTCR*, Apr. 1970, p. 262; Henry Hewes, "Inside Fun City," *Saturday Review of Literature*, 9 May 1970, p. 4; Brendan Gill, "New Country," *New Yorker*, 2 May 1970, p. 83.

33. John Lahr, "Sondheim's Little Deaths," Apr. 1979, p. 78.

34. Kerr, "*Company* Original and Uncompromising," p. 263.

35. Jack Kroll, "City of Strangers," *Newsweek*, 11 May 1970, p. 79.

36. Sondheim quoted in Zadan, *Sondheim and Co.*, p. 131.

4. *Follies*

1. Martin Gottfried, "Flipping Over *Follies*," New York *Times*, 25 Apr. 1971, sec. 2, p. 1; Gottfried, "*Follies*," p. 310.

2. Prince, *Contradictions*, p. 158.

3. Sondheim interview by Brendan Gill, Lincoln Center Library, New York, 2 June 1975.

4. Jack Kroll, "Backstage in Arcadia," *Newsweek*, 12 Apr. 1971, reprint, NYTCR, p. 311.

5. Gerald Clarke, "The Meaning of Nostalgia," *Time*, 3 May 1971, p. 77.

6. Stanley Kauffmann, "Follies," *New Republic*, 8 May 1971, pp. 24, 37.

7. David Brudnoy, "Follies in Loveland," *National Review*, 8 Oct. 1971, pp. 1129–130.

8. Sondheim quoted in Zadan, "A Funny Thing Happened on the Way to the Follies," p. 26.

9. Prince quoted in Joyce Haber, "Hal Prince: The Brat About Town Makes Good," *Los Angeles Times*, 30 May 1971, Calendar, p. 11.

10. John Lahr, "Sondheim's Little Deaths," p. 76.

11. James Goldman and Stephen Sondheim, *Follies* (New York: Random House, 1971),

p. 3. All subsequent quotations will be from this edition, with page numbers cited parenthetically within the text.

12. Prince, *Contradictions*, pp. 159–60.
13. Sondheim quoted in Zadan, "A Funny Thing Happened on the Way to the Follies," p. 26.
14. T. S. Eliot, *Four Quartets* (London: Faber and Faber, 1963), p. 189.
15. Ibid.
16. Sondheim quoted in Zadan, "A Funny Thing Happened on the Way to the Follies," p. 24.
17. Michael Bennett quoted in Zadan, *Sondheim and Co.*, p. 155.
18. Prince and Bennett quoted in Zadan, *Sondheim and Co.*, p. 159.
19. Prince, *Contradictions*, p. 159.
20. Gottfried, "Follies," p. 310.
21. Ethan Mordden, *Better Foot Forward* (New York: Grossman, 1976), pp. 335–36.
22. Sondheim, "The Musical Theater," pp. 8–9.
23. Sondheim quoted in Zadan, *Sondheim and Co.*, p. 166.
24. James Goldman quoted in Zadan, *Sondheim and Co.*, p. 159.
25. Sondheim, "Theater Lyrics," p. 71.
26. Ibid.
27. Prince, *Contradictions*, p. 161.
28. James Goldman quoted in Prince, *Contradictions*, p. 158.
29. Gottfried, "Flipping Over *Follies*," p. 14.
30. James Harvey, "Original Follies," *Commonweal*, 14 May 1971, p. 240.
31. "The Once and Future Follies," *Time*, 3 May 1971, pp. 66–71.
32. Kroll, "Backstage in Arcadia," p. 311.
33. Sondheim quoted in "The Once and Future Follies," p. 73.
34. Leonard Bernstein, *The Joy of Music* (New York: Simon and Schuster, 1959), p. 267.
35. Goldman quoted in Zadan, *Sondheim and Co.*, p. 170.
36. Frank Rich quoted in Prince, *Contradictions*, pp. 169–70.

5. *A Little Night Music*

1. Sondheim quoted in Zadan, *Sondheim and Co.*, p. 202.
2. Sondheim, "The Musical Theater," p. 13.
3. Ibid., pp. 21–22.
4. Prince, *Contradictions*, p. 176.
5. Arthur Jackson, *The Best Musicals from* Showboat *to* A Chorus Line (New York: Crown, 1977), p. 89.
6. Prince, *Contradictions*, pp. 174–75.
7. Goldman quoted in Zadan, *Sondheim and Co.*, p. 212.
8. Stephen Sondheim, *A Little Night Music* (New York: Dodd, Mead 1973), pp. 16–17. All subsequent quotations will be from this edition, with page numbers cited parenthetically within the text.
9. Prince, *Contradictions*, p. 179.
10. Leighton Kerner, "Stephen Sondheim: Composer," *Musical Newsletter*, June 1975, p.6.
11. Sondheim in "Symposium," p. 18.

12. A good example of this kind of criticism is given by Leonard Bernstein in Zadan, *Sondheim and Co.*, pp. 241–42.

13. Sondheim quoted in "Princely Odds," *Time*, 5 Mar. 1973, p. 78.

14. "Here we are presented literally with six individuals whose relationships must be more satisfactorily arranged—for them as well as for us. We *will* it to happen and it happens. That is all we need. We do not care or need to care about the messy if all-important details that realistically must be taken into account of so drastic a rearrangement" (Engel, *The American Musical Theater*, p. 49).

15. See, for example, Martin Gottfried, "A Little Night Music," *Women's Wear Daily*, 26 Feb. 1973, reprint, *NYTCR*, Feb. 1973, p. 349.

16. Prince, *Contradictions*, p. 183.

17. Goldman quoted in Zadan, *Sondheim and Co.*, p. 211.

18. Stephen Sondheim quoted in "A Precious Fancy," *Time*, 19 Mar. 1973, p. 58.

19. Ingmar Bergman quoted in Prince, *Contradictions*, p. 178.

20. Ingmar Bergman, *Smiles of a Summer Night*, in *Four Screenplays of Ingmar Bergman* (New York: Simon and Schuster, 1960), pp. 59–60.

21. Sondheim quoted in Zadan, *Sondheim and Co.*, p. 202.

6. *Pacific Overtures*

1. Stephen Sondheim quoted in Clive Hirschhorn, "Will Sondheim Succeed in Being Genuinely Japanese?" *New York Times*, 4 Jan. 1976, sec. 2, p. 1.

2. See, for example, John Beaufort, "East Meets West—Results: 'Stunning,' " *Christian Science Monitor*, 16 Jan. 1976, reprint, *NYTCR*, Apr. 1976, p. 392; T. E. Kalem, "Floating World," *Time*, 26 Jan. 1976, reprint, *NYTCR*, Jan. 1976, p. 393; Brendan Gill, "The Case of the Missing Pinkerton," *New Yorker*, 19 Jan. 1976, p. 44.

3. Robb Baker, *Soho Weekly News*, 15 Jan. 1976.

4. Sondheim quoted in Hirschhorn, "Will Sondheim Succeed in Being Genuinely Japanese?" p. 1.

5. Sondheim, "The Musical Theater," p. 13.

6. Gottfried, *Broadway Musicals*, p. 327.

7. Stephen Sondheim, *Pacific Overtures* (New York: Dodd, Mead, 1977), p. 11. All subsequent quotations will be from this edition, with page numbers cited parenthetically within the text.

8. Sondheim quoted in Hirschhorn, "Will Sondheim Succeed in Being Genuinely Japanese?" p. 5.

9. Gottfried, "*Overtures*—A Remarkable Work of Theater Art," *New York Post*, 12 Jan. 1976, reprint, *NYTCR*, Jan. 1976, p. 390.

10. Douglas Watt, "*Pacific Overtures* Is a Pretty Bore," *New York Daily News*, 12 Jan. 1976, reprint, *NYTCR*, Jan. 1976, p. 388.

11. Prince quoted in Howard Kissell, "Hal Prince on the Theater: 'A Place to be Passionate,' " *Women's Wear Daily*, 6 Feb. 1976, p. 9.

12. Sondheim, "The Musical Theater," p. 24.

13. Stephen Sondheim quoted in Guy Flatley, "When Stephen Sondheim Writes Words and Music, Some Critics Don't Leave the Theater Humming," p. 70.

14. Beaufort, "East Meets West—Results: 'Stunning,' " p. 392; Kalem, "Floating World" p. 393; Harold Clurman, "Pacific Overtures," *Nation*, 31 Jan. 1976, pp. 124–25.

15. Stanley Kauffmann, "1976, 1915," *New Republic*, 7 Feb. 1976, p. 20.

16. Gottfried, "The Watercolors of the Orient," *New York Post*, 17 Jan. 1976, p. 16.

17. Alan Rich, "How the East Was Won," *New York*, 26 Jan. 1976, p. 54.

18. Kauffmann, "1976, 1915," p. 20.

19. Martin Gottfried, "Will Failure Spoil Harold Prince?" *New York Post*, 26 June 1976, pp. 14, 40.

20. Ned Brinker, "Pacific Overtures," *Opera News*, 28 Feb. 1976, p. 46.

7. *Sweeney Todd*

1. See Peter Haining, *The Mystery and Horrible Murders of Sweeney Todd, The Demon Barber of Fleet Street* (London: Muller, 1979).

2. Christopher Bond, *Sweeney Todd* (London: Samuel French, 1974), p. v.

3. Sondheim, "The Musical Theater," p. 16.

4. Prince quoted in Mel Gussow, "*Sweeney Todd:* A Little Nightmare Music," *New York Times*, 1 Feb. 1979, sec. C, p. 15.

5. Prince in "Scenes from the Making of a Musical," South Bank Show, London Weekend Television, produced and directed by Alan Benson, 11 July 1980.

6. Sondheim and Prince, "On Collaboration," pp. 46, 62.

7. Stephen Sondheim, *Sweeney Todd, The Demon Barber of Fleet Street* (New York: Dodd, Mead, 1979), pp. 1–2. All subsequent quotations will be from this edition, with page numbers cited parenthetically within the text.

8. Bond, *Sweeney Todd*, p. 1.

9. Critics who have compared Sondheim's *Sweeney Todd* to the work of Brecht and Weill include Bill Zakariasen, "*Sweeney* Returns Opera to Its Roots," *Daily News*, 4 June 1979, p. 25; Clive Barnes, "Sondheim's *Sweeney Todd* Is a Bloody Good Musical," *New York Post*, 2 Mar. 1979, reprint, *NYTCR*, Mar. 1979, p. 351; Stanley Kauffmann, "Slay It with Music," *New Republic*, 24 Mar. 1979, p. 24; and Gerald Weales, "Dinner Music Trapped by Sweeney Todd," *Commonweal*, 8 June 1979, p. 339.

10. Sondheim and Prince, "On Collaboration," p. 29.

11. Harold Clurman, "Sweeney Todd," *Nation*, 24 Mar. 1979, p. 315; John Simon, "A Little Knife Music," *New York*, 19 Mar. 1979, p. 74.

12. Gerald Rabkin in T. E. Kalem and others, "Critics' Roundtable Discuss *Sweeney Todd*," *New York Theater Review*, Apr. 1979, p. 13.

13. Bond, *Sweeney Todd*, pp. 3–4.

14. Ibid., pp. 9–10.

15. Robert Cushman, "The Demon Barber Strikes Again," *London Observer*, 6 July 1980.

16. T. E. Kalem in T. E. Kalem and others, "Critics' Roundtable," pp. 13–14.

17. James Fenton, "The Barberous Crimes of Sondheim and Prince," *Sunday Times* (London), 6 July 1980, p. 40.

18. Letter to the author, 18 Aug. 1988.

19. Walter Kerr, "Is *Sweeney* on Target?" *New York Times*, 11 Mar. 1979, sec. C, p. 6.

20. Howard Kissel, "Sweeney Todd," *Women's Wear Daily*, 2 Mar. 1979, reprint, *NYTCR*, Mar. 1979, p. 353.

21. Michael Feingold and others, "Sondheim, Bloody Sondheim," *Village Voice*, 12 Mar. 1979, p. 85.

8. *Merrily We Roll Along*

1. Frank Rich, "Stage: A New Sondheim, *Merrily We Roll Along*," *New York Times*, 17 Nov. 1981, reprint, Nov. 1981, *NYTCR*, p. 104.

2. Stephen Sondheim, data in recording of *Merrily We Roll Along*, RCA Victor, CBL 1–4197, n.p.

3. Stephen Sondheim, *Merrily We Roll Along*, libretto enclosed with recording, RCA Victor, CBL 1–4197. All subsequent quotations are from this libretto, which is unpaginated.

4. Robert Sacheli, "Sondheim's *Merrily* Rolls from Broadway," *Theatre News*, Summer 1982, p. 6.

5. Howard Kissel, "Merrily We Roll Along," *Women's Wear Daily*, 17 Nov. 1981, reprint, *NYTCR*, Nov. 1981, p. 106; John Beaufort, "That Sondheim Touch—Again," *Christian Science Monitor*, 17 Nov. 1981, reprint, *NYTCR*, Nov. 1981, p. 107; T. E. Kalem, "Rue Tristesse," *Time*, 30 Nov. 1981, p. 90.

6. Sondheim, unpaginated *Merrily We Roll Along* libretto.

9. *Sunday in the Park with George*

1. Norbert Lynton, *The Modern World* (London: Hamlyn, 1965), p. 46.

2. Sondheim quoted in Samuel G. Freedman, "The Words and Music of Stephen Sondheim," *New York Times Magazine*, 1 Apr. 1984, p. 30.

3. Sondheim, interview in *Book-of-the-Month Club Records* (Camphill, Penn.: Book-of-the-Month Club, 1985), p. 3.

4. Sondheim in Linda Winer, "Sondheim in His Own Words," *American Theatre* 2, no. 2 (May 1985): 14.

5. Frank Rich, "Stage: *Sunday in the Park with George*," *New York Times*, 3 May 1984, reprint, *NYTCR*, May 1984, p. 282.

6. Sondheim quoted in Michiko Kakutani, "How Two Artists Shaped an Innovative Musical," *New York Times*, 10 June 1984, Sec. 2, p. 27.

7. Sondheim quoted in Freedman, "Words and Music of Stephen Sondheim," p. 60.

8. Sondheim quoted in Kakutani, "How Two Artists," p. 27.

9. Stephen Sondheim, *Sunday in the Park with George* (New York: Dodd, Mead, 1986), pp. 3–4. All subsequent quotations will be to this edition, with page numbers cited parenthetically within the text.

10. Sondheim in Winer, "Sondheim in His Own Words," p. 13.

11. Ibid.

12. Frank Rich, "Stage: *Sunday in the Park with George*," p. 282.

13. Ibid., p. 283.

14. Sondheim quoted in Zadan, *Sondheim and Co.*, 2d ed. (New York: Harper and Row, 1986), pp. 302–3.

15. This sense of exploitation, compromise, and corruption is endemic in the contemporary art world. Its universal prevalence was substantiated when Barbra Streisand chose a modified version of this number to open her *Broadway* album, using Sondheim's lyrics and abrasive rhythmic patterns to reveal her sense of entrapment by the powerful forces of commercialism.

16. Letter to author, 14 Apr. 1987.

17. Sondheim quoted in Zadan, *Sondheim and Co.*, 2d ed., pp. 301–2.

18. Ibid., p. 303.

19. Sondheim in Winer, "Sondheim in His Own Words," p. 14.

NOTES TO PAGES 302–338

10 *Into the Woods*

1. William A. Henry, III, "More Than Song and Dance," *Time*, 16 June 1986, p. 90.

2. Stephen Sondheim, *Into the Woods*, libretto enclosed with recording, RCA Victor, 6796-1-RC-A. All subsequent quotations are from this libretto, which is unpaginated.

3. Zadan, *Sondheim and Co.*, 2d ed., p. 356.

4. Paul Gemignani quoted in Sheryl Flatow, "Sing a Song of Sondheim," *Playbill*, Jan. 1988, p. 20.

5. Zadan, *Sondheim and Co.*, 2d ed., p. 356.

6. Frank Rich, "*Into the Woods*, from Sondheim," *New York Times*, 6 Nov. 1987, p. 17.

7. Sondheim quoted in Michiko Kakutani, "Beyond Happily Ever After," p. 76.

8. James Lapine quoted in Kakutani, "Beyond Happily Ever After," p. 76.

9. Sondheim, "Theatre Lyrics," p. 66.

11. *Assassins*

1. Mervyn Rothstein, "Sondheim's 'Assassins': Insane Realities of History," *New York Times*, 27 Jan. 1991, p. 5.

2. M. G. Lord, "An Offing Broadway Musical," *Newsday*, 20 Jan. 1991, p. 58.

3. Julius Novick, "Grave Matters, Tones Less Grave: Sondheim's Nine Singing *Assassins*," *New York Observer*, 4 Feb. 1991, p. 18.

4. John Beaufort, "Fantasy Dodges History in 'Assassins,'" *Christian Science Monitor*, 8 Feb. 1991, reprint *NYTCR*, Feb. 1991, p. 365.

5. Frank Rich, "Sondheim and Those Who Would Kill," *New York Times*, 28 Jan. 1991, pp. C19-20.

6. Wayman Wong, "Sondheim Takes Careful Aim With Assassins," *Theater Week*, 4-10 Feb. 1991, pp. 28-29

7. Stephen Holden, " 'Assassins': Now Dead Right," *New York Times*, 1 Sept. 1991, sec. 3, p. 18.

8. Rothstein, "Sondheim's 'Assassins,'" p. 34.

9. Stephen Sondheim, unpublished script of *Assassins*, Aug. 22, 1991, p. 1-2. Courtesy of Stephen Sondheim. All subsequent quotations will be from this script, with page numbers cited parenthetically within the text.

10. Robert Jay Lifton, "Assassination: The Ultimate Public Theater," *New York Times*, 9 Sept. 1990, sec. 2, p. 9.

11. Holden, " 'Assassins,'" sec. 2, p. 18.

12. David Richards, "They Shoot Presidents, Don't They?" *New York Times*, 3 Feb. 1991, sec. 2, p. 28.

Bibliography

Works by Stephen Sondheim

A Funny Thing Happened on the Way to the Forum. Book by Burt Shevelove and Larry Gelbart. New York: Music Theater International, 1962.

Anyone Can Whistle. Book by Arthur Laurents. New York: Random House, 1965.

Company. Book by George Furth. New York: Random House, 1970.

Follies. Book by James Goldman. New York: Random House, 1971.

A Little Night Music. Book by Hugh Wheeler. New York: Dodd, Mead, 1973.

Pacific Overtures. Book by John Weidman. Additional material by Hugh Wheeler. New York: Dodd, Mead, 1977.

Sweeney Todd: The Demon Barber of Fleet Street. Book by Hugh Wheeler. New York: Dodd, Mead, 1979.

Merrily We Roll Along. Book by George Furth. New York: Music Theater International, 1982.

Sunday in the Park with George. Book by James Lapine. New York: Dodd, Mead, 1986.

Into the Woods. Book by James Lapine. New York: Crown, 1988

Assassins. Book by John Weidman. Unpublished script, August 22, 1991.

Recordings of Works by Stephen Sondheim

Anyone Can Whistle. Original Broadway cast recording. Columbia Records. KOS 2480.

A Collector's Sondheim. RCA Records. CRL 4-5359.

Company. Original Broadway cast recording. Columbia Records. OS 3550.

Do I Hear a Waltz? Music by Richard Rodgers. Original Broadway cast recording. Columbia Records. AKOS 2770.

Follies. Original Broadway cast recording. Capitol Records. SO-761.

Follies in Concert. RCA Records. MBC2-7128.

A Funny Thing Happened on the Way to the Forum. Original Broadway cast recording. Capitol Records. SWAO 1717.

Gypsy. Music by Jule Styne. Original Broadway cast recording. Columbia Records. OS 2017.

Into the Woods. RCA Victor Records. 6796-1-RC-4.

BIBLIOGRAPHY

A Little Night Music. Original Broadway cast recording. Columbia Records. KS 32265.

Marry Me a Little. RCA Records. ABL 1-4159.

Merrily We Roll Along. Original Broadway cast recording. RCA Victor Records. CBL 1-4197.

Pacific Overtures. Original Broadway cast recording. RCA Victor Records. ARL 1-1367.

Side by Side by Sondheim. Original London cast recording. RCA Victor Records. CBL 2-1851.

Sondheim. Book-of-the-Month Club Records. 81-7515.

Sondheim: A Musical Tribute. Original Broadway cast recording. Warner Bros. Records. 2WS-2705.

A Stephen Sondheim Evening. RCA Records. CBL 2-4745.

Sunday in the Park with George. RCA Records. MBC 1-5041.

Sweeney Todd: The Demon Barber of Fleet Street. Original Broadway cast recording. RCA Victor Records. CBL 2-3379.

West Side Story. Music by Leonard Bernstein. Original Broadway cast recording. Columbia Records. OS 2001.

Secondary Works Cited in the Text

For the sake of brevity (that is, to avoid the repeated form "Review of . . .") untitled reviews of works by Stephen Sondheim appear with the name of the work under review in roman type and in quotation marks.

Adams, Michael Charles. "The Lyrics of Stephen Sondheim: Form and Function." Ph.D. diss., Northwestern University, 1980.

Baker, Robb. *Soho Weekly News*, 15 January 1976.

Barnes, Clive. "*Company* Offers a Guide to New York's Marital Jungle." *New York Times*, 27 April 1970. Reprinted in *New York Theatre Critics' Reviews*, April 1970, p. 262.

———. "Sondheim's *Sweeney Todd* Is a Bloody Good Musical." *New York Post*, 2 March 1979. Reprinted in *New York Theatre Critics' Review*, March 1979, p. 351.

Beaufort, John. "East Meets West—Results: 'Stunning.' " *Christian Science Monitor*, 16 January 1976. Reprinted in *New York Theatre Critics' Reviews*, January 1976, p. 392.

———. "That Sondheim Touch—Again." *Christian Science Monitor*, 17 November 1981. Reprinted in *New York Theatre Critics' Reviews*, November 1981, p. 107.

Bergman, Ingmar. *Four Screenplays of Ingmar Bergman.* New York: Simon and Schuster, 1960.

Bernstein, Leonard. *The Joy of Music.* New York: Simon and Schuster, 1959.

Bond, Christopher G. *Sweeney Todd.* London: Samuel French, 1974.

Bordman, Gerald M. *American Musical Theater: A Chronicle.* New York: Oxford University Press, 1978.

Brinker, Ned. "Pacific Overtures." *Opera News*, 28 February 1976, pp. 45–46.

Brudnoy, David. "Follies in Loveland." *National Review*, 8 October 1971, pp. 1129–30.

Brustein, Robert. "Vox Populi, Vox Box." *New Republic*, 28 May 1962, pp. 28–29.

Burke, Tom. "Steve Has Stopped Collaborating." *ASCAP Today*, August 1970, pp. 15–17.

Burton, Jack. *The Blue Book of Broadway Musicals.* New York: Century House, 1976.

Clarke, Gerald. "The Meaning of Nostalgia." *Time*, 3 May 1971, p. 77.

Clurman, Harold. "Pacific Overtures." *Nation*, 31 January 1976, pp. 124–25.

———. Sweeney Todd." *Nation*, 24 March 1979, pp. 315–16.

BIBLIOGRAPHY

Cushman, Robert. "The Demon Barber Strikes Again." *London Observer*, 6 July 1980.

Eliot, T. S. *Four Quartets*. London: Faber and Faber, 1963.

Engel, Lehman. *The American Musical Theater*. New York: Macmillan, 1975.

———. *Words with Music*. New York: Macmillan, 1972.

Feingold, Michael; Munk, Erika; and Novick, Julius. "Sondheim, Bloody Sondheim." *Village Voice*, 12 March 1979, pp. 85–86.

Fenton, James. "The Barberous Crimes of Sondheim and Prince." *Sunday Times* (London), 6 July 1980, p. 40.

Flatley, Guy. "When Stephen Sondheim Writes Words and Music, Some Critics Don't Leave the Theater Humming." *People*, 5 April 1976, pp. 69–70.

Flatow, Sheryl. "Sing a Song of Sondheim." *Playbill*, January 1988, pp. 14–23.

Freedman, Samuel G. "The Words and Music of Stephen Sondheim." *New York Times Magazine*, 1 April 1984, pp. 22–37, 60.

Gill, Brendan. "The Case of the Missing Pinkerton." *New Yorker*, 19 January 1976, p. 44.

———. "Interview with Stephen Sondheim and Harold Prince." Lincoln Center Library, New York, 2 June 1975.

———. "New Country." *New Yorker*, 2 May 1970, p. 83.

Gottfried, Martin. *Broadway Musicals*. New York: Harry N. Abrams, 1979.

———. "*Company* Is Quite Simply in a League by Itself." *Women's Wear Daily*, 27 April 1970. Reprinted in *New York Theatre Critics' Reviews*, April 1970, p. 261.

———. "Flipping Over *Follies*." *New York Times*, 25 April 1971, sec. 2, pp. 1, 14.

———. "*Follies*." *Women's Wear Daily*, 5 April 1971. Reprinted in *New York Theatre Critics' Reviews*, April 1971, pp. 310–11.

———. "A Funny Thing Happened on the Way to the Forum." *Women's Wear Daily*, 3 April 1972. Reprinted in *New York Theatre Critics' Reviews*, April 1972, p. 349.

———. "A Little Night Music." *Women's Wear Daily*, 26 February 1973. Reprinted in *New York Theatre Critics' Reviews*, February 1973, p. 349.

———. "*Overtures*—A Remarkable Work of Theater Art." *New York Post*, 12 January 1976. Reprinted in *New York Theatre Critics' Reviews*, January 1976, pp. 389–90.

———. "The Watercolors of the Orient." *New York Post*, 17 January 1974, pp. 16, 42.

———. "Why Is Broadway Music So Bad?" *Musical Newsletter*, January 1971, pp. 3–8.

———. "Will Failure Spoil Harold Prince?" *New York Post*, 26 June 1976, pp. 14, 40.

Guernsey, Otis L., ed. *Playwrights, Lyricists, Composers on Theater*. New York: Dodd, Mead, 1974.

Gussow, Mel. "*Sweeney Todd*: A Little Nightmare Music." *New York Times*, 1 February 1979, sec. C, p. 15.

Haber, Joyce. "Hal Prince: The Brat About Town Makes Good." *Los Angeles Times*, 30 May 1971, Calendar, p. 11.

Haining, Peter. *The Mystery and Horrible Murders of Sweeney Todd, The Demon Barber of Fleet Street*. London: Muller, 1979.

Harris, Leonard. "Company." *WCBS TV 2*, 26 April 1970. Reprinted in *New York Theatre Critics' Reviews*, April 1970, p. 264.

Harvey, James. "Original Follies." *Commonweal* 94. 14 May 1971, 239–40.

Henry, William A., III. "More Than Song and Dance." *Time*, 16 June 1986, p. 90.

Hewes, Henry. "Inside Fun City." *Saturday Review of Literature*, 9 May 1970, pp. 4–5.

———. "Mostellaria Zero-Zero." *Saturday Review of Literature*, 26 May 1962, p. 22.

Hirschhorn, Clive. "Will Sondheim Succeed in Being Genuinely Japanese?" *New York Times*, 4 January 1976, sec. 2, pp. 1, 5.

Jackson, A. *The Best Musicals from* Showboat *to* A Chorus Line. New York: Crown, 1977.

BIBLIOGRAPHY

Kakutoni, Michiko. "Beyond Happily Ever After." *New York Times Magazine*, 30 August 1987, pp. 30, 76.

———. "How Two Artists Shaped an Innovative Musical." *New York Times*, 10 June 1984, sec. 2, pp. 1, 27.

Kalem, T. E. "Floating World." *Time*, 26 January 1976. Reprinted in *New York Theatre Critics' Reviews*, January 1976, p. 393.

———. "Laugh Potion." *Time*, 17 April 1972. Reprinted in *New York Theatre Critics' Reviews*, April 1972, p. 350.

———. "Rue Tristesse." *Time*, 30 November 1981, p. 90.

Kalem, T. E.; Rabkin, Gerald; and Wolf, William. "Critics' Roundtable Discuss *Sweeney Todd*." *New York Theater Review*, April 1979, pp. 13–20.

Kauffmann, Stanley. "Company." *New Republic*, 23 May 1970, pp. 20, 32.

———. "Follies." *New Republic*, 8 May 1971, pp. 24, 37.

———. "1976, 1915." *New Republic*, 7 February 1976, p. 20.

———. "Slay It with Music." *New Republic*, 24 March 1979, pp. 24–25.

Kerner, N. Leighton, "Stephen Sondheim: Composer." *Musical Newsletter*, June, 1975, p.6.

Kerr, Walter. "*Company* Original and Uncompromising." *Sunday Times* (New York), 3 May 1970. Reprinted in *New York Theatre Critics' Reviews*, May 1970, pp. 263–64.

———. "Is *Sweeney* on Target?" *New York Times*, 11 March 1979, sec. C, pp. 1, 6-7, 22–23.

Kissel, Howard. "Hal Prince on the Theater: 'A Place to be Passionate.' " *Women's Wear Daily*, 6 February 1976, p. 9.

———. "Merrily We Roll Along." *Women's Wear Daily*, 17 November 1981. Reprinted in *New York Theatre Critics' Reviews*, November 1981, p. 106.

———. "Sweeney Todd." *Women's Wear Daily*, 2 March 1979. Reprinted in *New York Theatre Critics' Reviews*, March 1979, pp. 352–53.

Kresh, Paul. "Stephen Sondheim." *Stereo Review*, July 1971, pp. 73–74.

Kroll, Jack. "Backstage in Arcadia." *Newsweek*, 12 April 1971. Reprinted in *New York Theatre Critics' Reviews*, April 1971, pp. 311–12.

———. "City of Strangers." *Newsweek*, 11 May 1970, p. 79.

Lahr, John. "Sondheim's Little Deaths." *Harper's*, April 1979, pp. 71–78.

Laurents, Arthur; Stewart, Michael; Lerner, Alan Jay; Stein, Joseph; and Kirkwood, James. "The Librettist: Indispensable, Stylish, Sometimes Forgotten." Symposium. Gretchen Cryer, Chairman. Maggie Grove, Director. *Dramatists Guild Quarterly*, Winter 1980, pp. 10–23.

Lynton, Norbert. *The Modern World*. London: Hamlyn, 1965.

McCarter, John. "Cheerful Chaos." *New Yorker*, 19 May 1962, p. 103.

McClain, John. "Zero Mostel Guarantees a Merry Time." *Journal American*, 9 May 1962. Reprinted in *New York Theatre Critics' Reviews*, May 1962, p. 290.

Marx, Robert. "Drama and the Opera Libretto." *Yale Theater* 4, no. 3 (1973): 123–33.

Michener, Charles. "Words And Music—By Sondheim." *Newsweek*, 23 April 1973, pp. 54–64.

Mordden, Ethan. *Better Foot Forward: The History of American Musical Theater*. New York: Grossman, 1976.

Nadel, Norman. "*A Funny Thing*—at Alvin." *New York World-Telegram and The Sun*, 9 May 1962. Reprinted in *New York Theatre Critics' Reviews*, May 1962, p. 292.

———. "Something to *Whistle* About." *New York World-Telegram and The Sun*, 6 April 1964. Reprinted in *New York Theatre Critics' Reviews*, April 1964, p. 303.

Nathan, George Jean. "The Theater: A View of Musical Comedy." *American Mercury* 64 (February 1947): 194–98.

Novick, Julius. "In Search of a New Consensus." *Saturday Review*, 3 April 1976, pp. 39–42.

O'Connor, John J. "Company." *Wall Street Journal*, 28 April 1970. Reprinted in *New York Theatre Critics' Reviews*, April 1970, p. 262.

"The Once and Future Follies." *Time*, 3 May 1971, pp. 66–74.

"A Precious Fancy." *Time*, 19 March 1973, pp. 58–59.

Prince, Harold. *Contradictions: Notes on Twenty-six Years in the Theater*. New York: Dodd, Mead, 1974.

"Princely Odds." *Time*, 5 March 1973, pp. 78–80.

Rich, Alan. "How the East Was Won." *New York*, 26 January 1976, p. 54.

Rich, Frank. "*Into the Woods*, from Sondheim." *New York Times*, 6 November 1987, p. 17.

———. "Stage: A New Sondheim, *Merrily We Roll Along*." *New York Times*, 17 November. 1981. Reprinted in *New York Theatre Critics' Reviews*, November. 1981, p. 104.

———. "Stage: *Sunday in the Park with George*." *New York Times*, 3 May 1984. Reprinted in *New York Theatre Critics' Reviews*, May 1984, p. 282.

Saal, Hubert. "How to Play Hal Prince." *Newsweek*, 26 July 1971, pp. 68–70.

Sacheli, Robert. "Sondheim's *Merrily* Rolls from Broadway to Campus." *Theatre News*, Summer 1982, pp. 5–6.

"Scenes from the Making of a Musical." South Bank Show, London Weekend Television. Produced and directed by Alan Benson. 11 July 1980.

Sheren, Paul, and Sutcliffe, Tom. "Stephen Sondheim and the American Musical." In *Theater '74*, edited by Sheridan Morley, pp. 187-213. London: Hutchinson, 1974.

Simon, John. "Futile Fugue." *New York*, 11 May 1970, p. 56.

———. "A Little Knife Music." *New York*, 19 March 1979, p. 74.

———. *Theatre Arts*, July 1962, pp. 66–68.

Sondheim, Stephen. Interview. *Book-of-the-Month Club Records*. Camp Hill, Penn.: Book-of-the-Month Club, 1985.

———. "The Musical Theater: A Talk by Stephen Sondheim." *Dramatists Guild Quarterly* 15 (Autumn, 1978): 6–29.

———. "Theater Lyrics." In *Playwrights, Lyricists, Composers on Theater*, edited by Otis L. Guernsey, pp. 61–102. New York: Dodd, Mead, 1974.

Sondheim, Stephen, and Prince, Harold. "On Collaboration Between Authors and Directors." Moderated by Gretchen Cryer. *Dramatists Guild Quarterly* 16 (Summer 1979): 14–35.

Sullivan, Dan. "Stephen Sondheim Now Sleeping Giant of Lyricism." *Los Angeles Times*, 10 October 1971, Calendar, pp. 1, 28.

"Symposium: The Anatomy of a Theater Song." Moderated by Richard Lewine, *Dramatists Guild Quarterly*, Spring 1977, pp. 8–19.

Sweet, Jeff; Carmines, Al; and Ford, Nancy. "On Theater Music: A Discussion." In *Playwrights, Lyricists, Composers on Theater*, edited by Otis L. Guernsey, pp. 149–64. New York: Dodd, Mead, 1974.

Time, 11 May 1970, p. 62.

Watt, Douglas. "*Pacific Overtures* Is a Pretty Bore." *New York Daily News*, 12 January 1976. Reprinted in *New York Theatre Critics' Reviews*, January 1976, p. 388.

———. "Silvers Stars in *Forum* Revival." *New York Daily News*, 31 March 1972. Reprinted in *New York Theatre Critics' Reviews*, March 1972, p. 349.

Weales, Gerald. "Dinner Music Trapped by Sweeney Todd." *Commonweal*, 8 June 1979, pp. 338–39.

Wilson, John S. "Everthing's Coming Up Sondheim." *Theatre Arts*, June 1962, pp. 64–65.

Winer, Linda. "Sondheim in His Own Words." *American Theatre* 2, no. 2 (May 1985): 11–14, 42.

Zadan, Craig. "A Funny Thing Happened on the Way to the Follies." *After Dark*, June 1971, pp. 21–27.

———. *Sondheim and Co.* New York: Avon Books, 1976.

———. *Sondheim and Co.* 2d Edition. New York: Harper and Row, 1986.

Zakariasen, Bill. "*Sweeney* Returns Opera to Its Roots." *New York Daily News*, 4 June 1979, p. 25.

Addendum

Beaufort, John. "Fantasy Dodges History in 'Assassins'." *Christian Science Monitor*, 8 February 1991. Reprinted in *New York Theatre Critics' Reviews*. February 1991, p. 365.

Holden, Stephen. " 'Assassins': Now Dead Right." *New York Times*, 1 September 1991, sec. 2, p. 18.

Lifton, Robert Jay. "Assassination: The Ultimate Public Theater." *New York Times*, 9 September 1990, sec. 2, pp. 9, 44.

Lord, M. G. "An Offing Broadway Musical." *Newsday*, 20 January 1991, p. 58.

Novick, Julius. "Grave Matters, Tones Less Grave: Sondheim's Nine Singing *Assassins*." *New York Observer*, 4 February 1991, p. 18.

Rich, Frank. "Sondheim and Those Who Would Kill." *New York Times*, 28 January 1991, pp. C19-20.

Richards, David. "They Shoot Presidents, Don't They?" *NewYork Times*, 3 February 1991, sec. 2, pp. 1, 28.

Rothstein, Mervyn. "Sondheim's 'Assassins': Insane Realities of History." *New York Times*, 27 January 1991, pp. 5, 34.

Sondheim, Stephen. Unpublished script of *Assassins*, August 22, 1991.

Wong, Wayman. "Sondheim Takes Careful Aim With Assassins." *Theater Week*, February 4-10, 1991, pp. 28-29.

Index*

Abbot, George, 21
Abe, Lord (*Pacific Overtures*), 198, 200
Adams, Michael, 53, 69
Admirals (*Pacific Overtures*), 195–97
Ado Annie (*Oklahoma!*), 12
"Agony," 310
Allegro, 2, 6
Amy (*Company*), 39, 60–62, 64–65, 71, 73
Anderson, Maxwell, 1
Anne (*A Little Night Music*), 123, 129, 132–33, 136, 137–38, 142, 143, 147, 149; soliloquy of, 132–33
Anne (*Smiles of a Summer Night*), 154, 155
"Another Hundred People," 39, 58–59, 69, 150
Anouilh, Jean, 123
Anyone Can Whistle, 9, 14, 28–37, 54, 247, 250; accomplishments of, 36. *See also* Cora; Nurse Fay Apple
"Anyone Can Whistle" (song), 35–36
April (*Company*), 39, 54, 59, 64–67
Armfeldts (*A Little Night Music*). *See* Desirée; Fredrika; Madame Armfeldt
Aronson, Boris, 40–41, 43, 79, 108, 109, 125–26, 178, 180, 191, 204
Art: as big business, 289; Sondheim on, 265, 300
Astaire, Fred, 109
Atkinson, Brooks, 107
Audience, as Sondheim "collaborator," 8
Babbitt, Milton, 265
Bach, Johann Sebastian, 265
Baker (*Into the Woods*), 302, 305–6, 307, 311–12
Baker, Robb, 175
Baker's Wife, 302, 305–6, 307, 311–12
Balanchine, George, 127
"Ballad of Sweeney Todd, The," 249–50
Barker, Benjamin. *See* Todd, Sweeney
Barnes, Clive, 47, 74, 300
Bathing at Asnières (Seurat), 271
Beadle (*Sweeney Todd*), 210–11, 222, 223, 227, 228, 230–32, 243
"Beautiful Girls," 85–86, 88, 107
Beckett, Samuel, 36
Beggar Woman (*Sweeney Todd*), 216–17, 240, 242, 247, 248. *See also* Lucy
"Being Alive," 48, 72, 73
Ben (*Follies*), 35, 81–82, 84, 92, 93–103, 105–7, 110, 111, 114, 117–21; solo of, 117–20
Bennett, Michael, 44, 63, 64, 76, 82, 83, 90, 107, 114
Bergman, Ingmar, 123, 128, 154, 155
Berlin, Irving, 1, 84–85, 88
Bernstein, Leonard, 112, 261
Bettelheim, Bruno, 301
Birch, Patricia, 143, 178, 180, 202
Blitzstein, Marc, 1
Boatman (*Sunday in the Park with George*), 275, 276–77, 287

*Names and titles from Chapter 11 have not been included in this index.

INDEX

Bond, Christopher, 207, 208–11, 215, 221–23, 227–28
"Bowler Hat, A," 198, 199
Brecht, Bertolt, 56, 252; and influence on Sondheim, 181, 193, 217, 325 n.9
Brinker, Ned, 206
Britten, Benjamin, 268
"Broadway Baby," 88, 89
Brook, Peter, 34, 250
"Brother, Can You Spare a Dime?" 2
Buddy (*Follies*), 81–82, 84, 94, 98, 103–5, 107, 110, 111–12, 113–14, 120; comic solo of, 113–14
"By the Sea," 230, 244

Cabaret, 6, 153
Campion, Carlotta (*Follies*), 87, 91
Carl-Magnus (*A Little Night Music*), 123, 140–42, 146, 151; soliloquy of, 140–42, 146
Carl-Magnus (*Smiles of a Summer Night*), 154
Carmines, Al, 36
Carousel, 2
Celeste I and II (*Sunday in the Park with George*), 275
Chaplin, Charles, 114
Charlotte (*A Little Night Music*), 123, 140, 142, 143, 151, 155
Charlotte (*Smiles of a Summer Night*), 155
"Children and Art," 299
Chomsky, Noam, 77
"Chrysanthemum Tea," 189
Cinderella, 301
Cinderella (*Into the Woods*), 302, 305, 307, 311
Clurman, Harold, 220
Collins, Dorothy, 85
"Color and Light," 295
Colt, Ethel Barrymore, 85
"Comedy Tonight," 21–22
"Come Play Wiz Me," 32
Company, 8, 9, 12, 16, 17, 21, 35, 36, 129, 153, 175, 180, 239, 264; as comedy of manners, 10, 47; criticism of, 40–41, 47–48, 49, 55, 69, 73–74; homosexual undertones in, 55; *Merrily We Roll Along* and, 258; opening number of, 22; plotlessness of, 42; popularity of, 152; set of, 40–41, 43, 44. *See also* Amy; April; David; Harry; Jenny; Joanne; Kathy; Larry; Marta; Paul; Peter; Robert; Sarah; Susan
"Company" (song), 45, 46, 49
Concept, 7
"Cookie," 247
"Cookie Chase," 32
Cora (*Anyone Can Whistle*), 28–32, 34–35, 54
"Could I Leave You?" 16, 105–7
Count of Monte Cristo, The (Dumas), 210
"Country House, A," 121
Coups de theatre, 208
Coward, Noel, 116
Cradle Will Rock, The (Blitzstein), 1–2
Crime, as musical theme, 3
Cushman, Robert, 249

David (*Company*), 39, 53, 54, 56, 66
"Day Off," 286
DE (play), 193
Debussy, Claude, 280
De Carlo, Yvonne, 85, 87
Deems, Stella (*Follies*), 90
Dennis (*Sunday in the Park with George*), 293
Desirée (*A Little Night Music*), 35, 123, 124, 129, 134–38, 140, 143, 144, 146, 147–49, 151
Desirée (*Smiles of a Summer Night*), 154
DeSylva, Brown, and Henderson, 81, 88
Dialogue of Self and Soul, A (Yeats), 81
Didacticism, 4
Dies Irae, *Sweeney Todd* and, 213–14, 217, 223, 225, 232, 247, 248
Dissolves, 83
Divisionism. *See* Pointillism
Do I Hear a Waltz?, 14
Domina (*A Funny Thing Happened on the Way to the Forum*), 25
D'Orsay, Fifi, 85, 89
Dos Passos, John, 193
Dot (*Sunday in the Park with George*), 268–71, 272–75, 277–78, 281–83, 284, 285, 286–87, 292, 293, 295–99

Drama, drawing-room, 10
Drama Desk Awards, 300
Dumbshow, 223

East/West Players, The, 204
"Echo Song," 114
Eder, Richard, 252
Egermans (*A Little Night Music*). *See* Anne; Fredrik; Henrik
8½, 79
Eliot, T. S., 59, 69, 80, 81, 220
Engel, Lehman, 11
"Epiphany," 233–39, 294
Eternal Road, The, 1
"Everybody Ought to Have a Maid," 20, 21, 26
"Everyday a Little Death," 155
"Everything's Coming Up Roses," 315

Fairy tales, 10, 301, 308. See also *Into the Woods*
Farce, 10
Feingold, Michael, 254
Fellini, Federico, 79
Fenton, James, 213, 251
Feydeau, Georges, 25
Field, Dorothy, 88
Fields, Weber and, 196
Finian's Rainbow, 2
"Finishing the Hat," 286, 298
Finn, William, 262
Fisherman (*Pacific Overtures*), 184–85. *See also* Kayama Yesaemon
Flynn, Mary (*Merrily We Roll Along*), 255, 256, 259, 260
Fogg (*Sweeney Todd*), 246
Follies, 9, 12, 16, 35, 38, 54, 135, 153, 175, 177, 180, 191; *A Funny Thing Happened on the Way to the Forum* and, 21; criticism of, 78–79, 81, 108–9, 122; inner monologue in, 129; in London, 121, 315; *Merrily We Roll Along* and, 258, 260–61; *Pacific Overtures* and, 203; popularity of, 152; revised version of, 121, 315; set of, 79, 80, 108, 122; and Ziegfeld revue, 10. *See also* Ben; Buddy; Phyllis; Sally
Forbush, Nellie (*South Pacific*), 12
Four Quartets (Eliot), 81
Frankel, Aaron, 41
"Franklin Shepard, Inc.," 289
Fredrik (*A Little Night Music*), 16, 123, 124, 129–31, 132–33, 135–38, 140, 143, 145–46, 147, 151; soliloquy of, 129–31, 133, 145–46
Fredrik (*Smiles of a Summer Night*), 154
Fredrika (*A Little Night Music*), 123, 128, 133, 147, 149, 152
"Free," 20, 22–23
Frid (*A Little Night Music*), 124, 147, 149
Friml, Rudolph, 88, 125
Funny Thing Happened on the Way to the Forum, A, 9, 14; criticism of, 28; opening number of, 21–22; out-of-town troubles of, 21–22; praise for, 27–28; revival of, 27, 28; and Roman farce, 10. *See also* Domina; Hero; Hysterium; Miles Gloriosus; Philia; Pseudolus; Senex
Furth, George, 38, 39, 42, 48, 49, 66, 255

Gambling, as musical theme, 2
Gelbart, Larry, 14, 19, 25, 28
Gemignani, Paul, 306
George (*Sunday in the Park with George*), 35, 264, 267–71, 272–77, 278–85, 287, 293, 298, 299; mother of, 268, 275, 284–85. *See also* Seurat, Georges; *and next entry*
George (grandson of above [*Sunday in the Park with George*]), 287–91, 293–99
Gershwin, George, 2, 81, 114
Gershwin, Ira, 88
"Getting Married Today," 61
Giant's wife (*Into the Woods*), 311
Gill, Brendan, 81, 175, 252
Girls Upstairs, The, 38. See also *Follies*
Goldman, James, 38, 76, 80, 81, 82, 88, 90, 100, 107, 108, 119, 120–21, 128, 153
"Good Thing Going," 256, 258, 259–60
Gottfried, Martin, 10, 16, 55, 76, 85, 189, 205, 230, 252
Green, Paul, 1
Grimm brothers, 301

INDEX

Group Theatre, 1
"Growing Up," 256
Gussie (*Merrily We Roll Along*), 256
Gypsy, 6, 9, 14, 20, 83, 257, 315; Hammerstein influence on, 20

Hammerstein, Oscar, 2, 3, 5, 8, 12; influence of, 5–6; on opening numbers, 21; as Sondheim influence, 13–14, 20
Hanamichi, 178
Hapgood (*Anyone Can Whistle*), 33
"Happily Ever After," 72
Harburg, E. Y. ("Yip"), 2, 88
Harnick, Sheldon, 3, 6, 15–16
Harris, Leonard, 40
Harry (*Company*), 39, 46, 49, 50, 51, 52–53, 66
"Have I Got a Girl for You," 56–57
Held, Anna, 88
Henrik (*A Little Night Music*), 123, 124, 128–29, 131–33, 143, 144, 147, 149; soliloquy of, 131–32, 133
Henrik (*Smiles of a Summer Night*), 154
Herbert, Victor, 125
Hering, Doris, 81
Hero (*A Funny Thing Happened on the Way to the Forum*), 24
Heyward, DuBose, 13
"Hills of Tomorrow, The," 256, 257
Hirschhorn, Clive, 174
Hope, Anthony (*Sweeney Todd*), 211, 215–19, 225, 226–27, 229, 231–32, 233, 241–48
Hostage, The, 8
How to Succeed in Business Without Really Trying, 2
Hysterium (*A Funny Thing Happened on the Way to the Forum*), 27

"I Feel Pretty," 15, 104
"I'm Not Getting Married Today," 270
Impressionism, 263–64
"I'm Still Here," 91–92
"In Buddy's Eyes," 98–99
Infidelity, as musical theme, 2
International Ladies' Garment Workers' Union, 1
Into the Woods, 10; criticism of, 302, 308; post-tryout alterations to, 312–13
"Into the Woods" (song), 303, 308
"Invocation," 21

Jack (*Into the Woods*), 302, 304–5, 307, 311; mother of, 302, 307
Jack and the Beanstalk, 301
Jackson, Arthur, 126
Jenny (*Company*), 39, 54, 56, 65, 66
Joanne (*Company*), 16, 39, 50–52, 64–65, 67–71
Johnny Johnson, 1
Johns, Glynis, 148
Johnston, Justine, 85
Jones, Dean, 49, 55, 74
Joyce, James, 273
Judge (*Sweeney Todd*), 210–11, 222, 223, 227, 229, 230–33, 245, 248
Jules (*Sunday in the Park with George*), 271–72, 281
Jung, Carl, 301

Kabuki, 177–78, 181, 182, 193, 194; *Pacific Overtures* and, 10, 174, 176, 178, 186, 188
Kalem, T. E., 81, 251
Kathy (*Company*), 39, 54, 55–56, 59–60, 65–66
Kauffmann, Stanley, 40, 204, 213, 252
Kayama Yesaemon (*Pacific Overtures*), 176, 181–82, 184, 186–87, 188–89, 194, 197–99, 200–201, 203, 204
Kenjutsu, 200
Kennedys, *Merrily We Roll Along* and, 259
Kern, Jerome, 1, 2, 5, 31, 88
Kerr, Walter, 47, 74, 78, 252
King and I, The, 8, 174, 176
King of Siam (*The King and I*), 12
Kissel, Howard, 253, 300
Klotz, Florence, 108, 109, 126, 178, 204
Knickerbocker Holiday, 1
Kringas, Charles (*Merrily We Roll Along*), 255, 256, 258, 259–60
Kroll, Jack, 74, 78, 81
Kurombo, 182, 198

INDEX

"Ladies Who Lunch, The," 16, 68–69, 105
Lady in the Dark, 65
La Fitte, Solange (*Follies*), 88, 89
Lahr, John, 11, 16–18, 74, 78–79, 107
Lansbury, Angela, 9, 28, 220
Lapine, James, 255, 262, 264, 266, 281, 284, 285, 287, 301, 303, 308, 309, 311, 312
Larry (*Company*), 39, 53, 57
Laurents, Arthur, 12, 28, 33, 34, 96, 250; as Sondheim influence, 13, 14
Lee, Eugene, 212
Lehár, Franz, 125
Leonowens, Anna (*The King and I*), 12
Lerner, Alan J., 5, 6, 18
"Lesson #8," 299
Lévi-Strauss, Claude, 77
Liebeslieder group (*A Little Night Music*), 126–27, 128, 134–35, 136–37, 144, 146, 151, 154
Liebeslieder Walzer, 127
"Like It Was," 256, 260
Lindquist (*A Little Night Music*), 127, 152
Little Night Music, A, 16, 33, 35; conceptualization of, 123–24; criticism of, 152–53; as operetta, 10, 124–26, 144; popularity of, 152, 153; set of, 125–26. *See also* Anne; Carl-Magnus; Charlotte; Desirée; Fredrik; Fredrika; Henrik; *Liebeslieder* group; Madame Armfeldt; Petra
Little Red Ridinghood, 301
Little Red Ridinghood (*Into the Woods*), 302–4
"Little Things You Do Together, The," 50–52
Littlewood, Joan, 8, 58, 210
Loesser, Frank, 5, 6
Loewe, Frederick, 5, 6
"Losing My Mind," 88, 101
Louis (*Sunday in the Park with George*), 275, 277–78, 282
"Love I Hear," 23–24
"Love Is in the Air," 21
"Loveland," 88, 107, 108, 109–10
"Lovely," 310
Loves of Sunya, The, 80
Lovett, Mrs. (*Sweeney Todd*), 210, 211, 216, 218–25, 228–30, 233, 235–50, 251, 254, 298
"Love Will See Us Through," 88
Lucy (*Sweeney Todd*), 210, 222, 223, 248. *See also* Beggar Woman
Lynton, Norbert, 263
Lyrics, Sondheim on, 12–13

McCarty, Mary, 85
Madam (*Pacific Overtures*), 189–90
Madame Armfeldt (*A Little Night Music*), 123, 124, 128, 134, 138–40, 147, 152; death of, 152
Madame Butterfly, 176
Magritte, René, 126
Mahler, Gustav, 31
Mako, 204
Manhattan, *Company* and, 39–41. *See also* "Another Hundred People"
Manjiro, John (*Pacific Overtures*), 176, 181, 187–89, 194, 197–98, 200–201, 203, 204
Marat/Sade (Weiss), 34, 250
March of the Falsettos (Finn), 262
Margie (*Follies*), 104–5, 113–14
Maria (*West Side Story*), 16
Marie (*Sunday in the Park with George*), 287–88, 291–92, 293
Marriage, Sondheim on (see *Company*)
"Marry Me a Little," 71
Marta (*Company*), 39, 54, 58, 60, 67
Martin, Hugh, 29
Marx, Groucho, 113
Mary Poppins, 301
"Me and My Town," 257
Measures Taken, The (Brecht), 181
Melodrama, 207–8; Victorian, 10, 209–10, 252
Merrily We Roll Along, 21, 35, 255–61, 307; criticism of, 255, 256, 258, 261, 262; failure of, 255; La Jolla Playhouse version of, 255–56, 259; Seattle version of, 256
Meyerhold, Vsevolod, 41, 193
Michener, Charles, 36
Michiyuki, 188
Miles Gloriosus (*A Funny Thing Happened on the Way to the Forum*), 23

INDEX

"Miller's Son, The," 149–51
Miscegenation, as musical theme, 2
Mizner, Wilson, 11
Monet, Claude, 263
Mooney, Mrs. (*Sweeney Todd*), 219
Mordden, Ethan, 85
Morgan, Helen, 114
Most Happy Fella, The, 2
"Move On," 295, 296–97, 298
Mozart, Wolfgang, 31, 125, 153
Munk, Erica, 213, 252
Musicals, 1–18; escapist, 2–3, 10, 18, 109–10; and plot, 7; socially relevant, 1–2. *See also* Revue
Musser, Tharon, 109
My Fair Lady, 18
"My Man's Gone Now," 13

Nathan, George Jean, 2, 17, 107
Nelson, Gene, 85
New York City Opera, *Sweeney Todd* and, 262
New York Drama Critics Award, 300
Noh, 178
"No One Is Alone," 309
Nostalgia, and *Follies*, 77, 78, 109, 121
"Not a Day Goes By," 258, 259
Novick, Julius, 18
"Now / Later / Soon," 16, 129–33
Nurse Fay Apple (*Anyone Can Whistle*), 32, 33, 35

Observers (*Pacific Overtures*), 182–83
O'Higgins, Daniel. *See* Pirelli (*Sweeney Todd*)
Oh, What a Lovely War!, 8
Oklahoma!, 2, 5, 8, 65; as landmark musical, 6, 7
"Old Friends," 256, 257, 259
"One More Kiss," 88
On the Town, 40
"Opening Doors," 256
Opening numbers, 21–22
Opera, *Sweeney Todd* as, 253, 262
Operetta, 5, 125, 151, 195–96; *A Little Night Music* and, 10; escapist nature of, 148
"Our Time," 256, 261

Pacific Overtures, 8, 12, 174–206, 277; bawdiness of, 189–90; criticism of, 175, 189, 204, 205–6; failure of, 206; and Kabuki, 10, 174, 176, 178, 186, 188; Mako version of, 204; and operetta, 195–96; set of, 178, 180, 186, 187, 191, 204. *See also* Kayama Yesaemon; Manjiro, John; Reciter
Parody, 31–32
Paul (*Company*), 39, 61–62
Perkins, Anthony, 49
Perry, Matthew, 174, 176
Perry, Matthew (*Pacific Overtures*), 181, 186, 187, 194, 202
Peter (*Company*), 39, 54, 57, 67, 73
Peters, Bernadette, 313
Petra (*A Little Night Music*), 124, 131, 144, 147, 149–51
Philia (*A Funny Thing Happened on the Way to the Forum*), 27
Philoctetes, 214
Phyllis (*Follies*), 16, 35, 81–82, 84, 87, 90, 92, 94–95, 99–100, 105–7, 110, 111, 115–16, 120–21; solo of, 115–16
Pins and Needles, 1
Pirelli (*Sweeney Todd*), 228, 230
Pitt, George Dibdin, 207
Pixérécourt, Guilbert de, 208
Plautus, 19
Playwrights Horizons, 281, 302
Plummers (*Follies*). *See* Buddy; Sally
Pointillism, 263, 273, 279, 286, 289–90; Sondheim use of, 10, 268, 273
"Poor Baby," 64, 65
Porgy and Bess, 2, 13
Porter, Cole, 1, 31, 88, 115
Poudreuse, La (Seurat), 273
Prest, Thomas Peckett, 207
"Pretty Girl Is Like a Melody, A," 84
"Pretty Little Picture," 20, 21
Prince, Harold, 6, 8, 36, 251, 253; and *A Little Night Music*, 123, 125–26, 127, 143, 148, 153, 155; and breakup with Sondheim, 262; and *Company*, 38–42, 45, 47, 58, 71–72; and *Follies*, 76–80, 83–85, 107, 114, 119; and *Pacific Overtures*, 174–76, 178, 180, 182, 189, 193, 201, 204, 205, 206;

and *Sweeney Todd*, 211, 212; on theater, 4, 5
Princes (*Into the Woods*), 305, 307, 310–12
Pseudolus (*A Funny Thing Happened on the Way to the Forum*), 22–23, 25, 27
Pulitzer Prize, 16, 261, 300
Purcell, Henry, 31
"Putting It Together," 16, 286, 290–91

Rabkin, Gerald, 221
Race, as musical theme, 2
Rachmaninoff, Sergei, 266
Rapunzel, 301
Rapunzel (*Into the Woods*), 307, 313
Rashomon, *Sweeney Todd* and, 222
Ravel, Maurice, 125, 280
Reciter (*Pacific Overtures*), 178, 179, 180, 185, 186, 189, 190, 193, 194, 196, 198, 199, 201, 202; as Shogun (*see* Shogun)
Reinhardt, Max, 1
"Remember?" 136–37
Renoir, Pierre, 263
Reprises, 2, 7; *Company* and, 42; in *Into the Woods*, 310; in *Merrily We Roll Along*, 256; in *Sweeney Todd*, 247–48
Revue, 10, 258
Rhyme, Sondheim on, 15–16. *See also* Sondheim, Stephen, rhyming genius of
Rich, Frank, 122, 256, 265, 283, 300, 308
"Rich and Happy," 256, 258
Ring 'Round the Moon (Anouilh), 123
"Road You Didn't Take, The," 97
Robbins, Jerome, 21
Robert (*Company*), 35, 38–39, 41–60, 62–68, 70–73; Sondheim as, 264
Rodgers, Richard, 2, 3, 5, 8, 12, 31; influence of, 5–6
Romberg, Sigmund, 88, 125
Rome, Harold, 1
Roscoe (*Follies*), 85, 86
Ross, Herbert, 33
Roxy Theater, 80
Russell, Bertrand, 9

Saal, Hubert, 5
Sally (*Follies*), 81–82, 83–84, 86–87, 90, 93–96, 97–103, 107, 110, 111–12, 114–15, 120; torch song of, 114–15
Santayana, George, 203
Sarah (*Company*), 38, 46, 49, 50, 51, 52, 65, 66
Satire, Sondheim and, 10
Scandals, George White's, 81
Scat, 55
Schiller, Heidi (*Follies*), 87, 92
"Send in the Clowns," 6, 147–49, 151
Senex (*A Funny Thing Happened on the Way to the Forum*), 24, 26
Seurat, Georges, 261, 262–67, 285, 286, 287, 292, 300; Sondheim identification with, 264–66, 272, 273, 281. *See also* George (*Sunday in the Park with George*); Pointillism; *Sunday in the Park with George*
Sex, 19, 26; in *A Little Night Music*, 126–27, 129–33, 136–40, 144, 146, 149, 153; in *Company*, 64–67
Shakuhachi, 184
Shamisen, 178
Shepard, Franklin (*Merrily We Roll Along*), 35, 255, 256, 258, 259–60
Shevelove, Burt, 19, 20, 25, 28, 36; as Sondheim influence, 13, 14
Shogun (*Pacific Overtures*), 182, 187; mother of, 187, 189. *See also* Abe, Lord
Showboat, 2, 5
Shutta, Ethel, 85, 89
"Side by Side by Side," 9, 39, 62–63, 257
Simon, John, 49, 220
"Simple," 33
Smiles of a Summer Night, 123, 154–55
Smith, Alexis, 85
"Some Enchanted Evening," 258
"Someone in a Tree," 177, 191–94, 277
"Someone Is Waiting," 48, 57–58, 66, 72

INDEX

"Somewhere," 261
Sondheim, Stephen: accolades earned by, 16, 36, 261, 300, 302; on art, 265, 300; and Bennett, 107; and breakup with Prince, 262; Brecht influence on, 181, 193, 217, 325 n.9; character of, 36; characters of, 11–13, 24, 28, 35–36 (*see also individual characters by name*); and "concept," 7; criticisms of, 3, 6, 10, 11–12, 16–18, 28, 302 (*see also individual plays by title, criticism of*); "desolateness" of, 16–17; and eroticism, 137; and Furth, 255; and Gelbart, 19, 25; genius of, 314–15 (*see also* Sondheim, Stephen, rhyming genius of); and Goldman, 81, 88, 107; Hammerstein influence on, 13–14, 20; as Hammerstein protégé, 6; as "hit" tunesmith, 6; and "hummability," 6, 21, 52; humor of, 11, 22–23, 310; on humor, 65; influences on, 13–14; as innovator, 3–11; and Lapine, 255, 262, 264, 266, 284–86, 301, 303, 308, 311, 312; and Laurents, 13, 14, 33, 96; Littlewood influence on, 8; lyrics of, 12–17, 116 (*see also* Sondheim, Stephen, rhyming genius of; *and individual songs by title*); on lyrics, 12–13; on Manhattan (see *Company*); music of, 6–7, 9, 11, 15 (*see also individual plays and songs by title*); musicality of, 264–65; parody of, 31–32; and Prince (*see* Prince, Harold); productivity of, 301; on rhyme, 15–16, 22; rhyming genius of, 51, 86, 116, 139, 149–50, 195–97, 228; and Ross, 33; and second-order (musical) language, 9–10, 31; and Shevelove, 13, 14, 19, 25, 36; and subtext, 14, 96–97, 98. *See also individual plays and songs by title*
"Song of Commodity, The," 181
Songs: "integrated," 9. *See also* Opening numbers; Sondheim, Stephen, lyrics of; Sondheim, Stephen, music of; *and individual Sondheim songs by title*
"Sorry-Grateful," 52–53, 145
South Pacific, 2
Stanley, Kim, 38
Stones (*Follies*). *See* Ben; Phyllis
"Story of Lucy and Jessie, The," 88
Strauss, Johann, 125
Strauss, Richard, 125
Streisand, Barbra, 326 n.15
"String of Pearls, A," 207
Stritch, Elaine, 50, 65, 67
Styne, Jule, 83, 257
Subtext, 14, 96–97, 98
"Summertime," 13
Sunday Afternoon on the Island of La Grande Jatte (Seurat), 261, 262–64, 266, 272
Sunday in the Park with George, 16, 35, 262–300, 302, 309; criticism of, 265, 283, 300; and pointillism, 10, 268, 273; workshop production of, 281. *See also* Dot; George; Marie; Pointillism; Seurat, Georges
"Sunday in the Park with George" (song), 295, 298, 299
Susan (*Company*), 39, 54, 65, 67
Swanson, Gloria, 80
Sweeney Todd (Bond), 207–11, 215, 221–23, 227
Sweeney Todd (Pitt), 207
Sweeney Todd (Sondheim), 4, 21, 33, 200, 206, 207–54, 275; and Brecht/Weill influence, 325 n.9; criticism of, 212, 213, 217, 220, 230, 249, 251–53, 254; *Dies Irae* subtheme of, 213–14, 217, 223, 225, 232, 247, 248; hero of (*see* Todd, Sweeney); opening number of, 22; and opera, 10; set of, 211–12. *See also* Beadle; Beggar Woman; Hope, Anthony; Judge; Lovett, Mrs.; Lucy; Tobias; Todd, Johanna; Todd, Sweeney

Table Settings (Lapine), 262
Tamate (*Pacific Overtures*), 181, 182–84, 188, 189
Tatlin, Vladimir, 41
"That Frank," 256
Theater: absurdist, 221; environmental, 8. *See also* Drama; Farce; Kabuki; Melodrama; Musicals
Thief (*Pacific Overtures*), 185

Thompson, Kay, 29
"Tick-Tock," 66
Tobias (*Sweeney Todd*), 230, 239–41, 245–47, 249
Todd, Johanna (*Sweeney Todd*), 211, 222, 223, 225–27, 231–32, 233, 241–48
Todd, Sweeney (*Sweeney Todd*), 200, 208–25, 228–53, 298
"Together Wherever We Go," 257
Tony Awards, 16, 27, 28, 300, 302
"Too Many Mornings," 100, 102–3
Tunick, Jonathan, 84, 98, 125
Turpin, Judge. *See* Judge (*Sweeney Todd*)
Twelve Dreams (Lapine), 262
"Twilight," 147

Ulysses (Joyce), 273
Unionism, musical-theater celebration of, 1
Uses of Enchantment, The (Bettelheim), 301

Vanessa (*Follies*), 87
Variations on a Theme of Paganini, 266
Vincent (*Follies*), 87

Waiting for Godot (Beckett), 36
"Waiting for the Girls," 94–95
Walker, Hattie (*Follies*), 88, 89
War, and musical theater, 1
Waste Land, The (Eliot), 69
Watt, Douglas, 189, 300
Weber and Fields, 196
"We Do Not Belong Together," 283, 295
Weidman, Jerome, 174
Weidman, John, 174, 175, 177, 190
Weill, Kurt, 1, 217, 252; Sondheim and, 325 n.9
Weismann, Dimitri (*Follies*), 81, 84, 86
Werfel, Franz, 1
West Side Story, 14, 15, 20, 261; as breakthrough, 6; Hammerstein influence on, 20
"What Would We Do Without You?" 63
Wheeler, Hugh, 123, 124, 128, 135, 143, 153–55, 210
White, George, 81
Whitman, Emily (*Follies*), 88
Whitman, Theodore (*Follies*), 88
"Who's That Woman?" 90
Witch (*Into the Woods*), 305, 307, 311, 313–14
Wolf (*Into the Woods*), 302, 303–4, 307
Wonderful Town, 40
W.P.A. Federal Theater, 2

Yeats, William B., 81
"You Could Drive a Person Crazy," 9, 54–56, 63, 67
"You're Gonna Love Tomorrow," 88, 111
"Your Fault," 314
Yvonne (*Sunday in the Park with George*), 271–72, 281, 286

Zadan, Craig, 47
Ziegfeld, Flo, 2, 10, 77, 79, 110, 177; Dimitri Weismann as, 81
Ziegfeld's Follies, 76, 89
Zorba, 6

A native South African, Joanne Gordon received degrees from the University of Witwatersrand before immigrating to the United States and receiving her doctorate in Theatre Arts from the University of California at Los Angeles. As head of the Acting Program at California State University at Los Angeles, she directed, among many other productions, *Sweeney Todd* and *Sunday in the Park with George*. She is now head of the Directing Program at California State University at Long Beach.

LaVergne, TN USA
12 November 2009

163821LV00003B/70/A